Homage to Horace

Homage to Horace

·o◍o·

A Bimillenary Celebration

Edited by S. J. Harrison

CLARENDON PRESS · OXFORD
1995

Oxford University Press, Walton Street, Oxford OX2 6DP
Oxford New York
Athens Auckland Bangkok Bombay
Calcutta Cape Town Dar es Salaam Delhi
Florence Hong Kong Istanbul Karachi
Kuala Lumpur Madras Madrid Melbourne
Mexico City Nairobi Paris Singapore
Taipei Tokyo Toronto
and associated companies in
Berlin Ibadan

Oxford is a trade mark of Oxford University Press

Published in the United States
by Oxford University Press Inc., New York

British Library Cataloguing in Publication Data
Data available

Library of Congress Cataloging in Publication Data
Homage to Horace : a bimillenary celebration
edited by S. J. Harrison.
Papers presented at a conference held at
Corpus Christi College, Oxford, England, in September 1992.
Includes bibliographical references and indexes.
1. Horace—Criticism and interpretation—Congresses.
2. Latin poetry—History and criticism—Congresses.
3. Rome—In literature—Congresses. I. Harrison, S. J.
PA6411.H57 1995   874'.01—dc20   94-43828
ISBN 0-19-814954-9

I 3 5 7 9 10 8 6 4 2

Typeset by Regent Typesetting, London
Printed in Great Britain on acid-free paper by
Biddles Ltd., Guildford and King's Lynn

Preface

THIS volume is the consequence of a conference held at Corpus Christi College, Oxford, in September 1992 to mark both the bimillenary of Horace's death (a little proleptically) and the retirement of Professor R. G. M. Nisbet as Corpus Christi Professor of Latin at Oxford. Thanks are due to the President and Scholars of Corpus for their hospitality and for their generous subsidy which made the conference possible, and to the Jowett Trustees of Balliol College, Oxford, and to the Craven Committee of the University of Oxford for further vital financial support. I would also like to thank the Oxford University Press for accepting this volume, and the copy-editor, John Waś, for improving it in both form and substance.

The distinguished gathering of Latinists at the conference showed the esteem and affection in which Robin Nisbet is held by his friends and colleagues, and the eminence attained by his pupils and by those many other scholars whom he has helped and influenced. This book, a tribute to the poet to whose interpretation he himself has so substantially contributed, is appropriately dedicated to him, and its appearance marks his seventieth birthday.

S.J.H.

Contents

Notes on Contributors

C. O. Brink† was Kennedy Professor Emeritus of Latin at the University of Cambridge and Fellow of Gonville and Caius College. He was author of *Horace on Poetry* (3 vols.; 1963–82).

Francis Cairns is Professor of Latin at the University of Leeds, and author of *Generic Composition in Greek and Roman Poetry* (1972), *Tibullus: A Hellenistic Poet at Rome* (1979), and *Virgil's Augustan Epic* (1989).

I. M. Le M. Du Quesnay is Fellow and Director of Studies in Classics at Jesus College, Cambridge, and University Lecturer in Classics; he is the author of a number of studies of Republican and Augustan poetry.

D. P. Fowler is Fellow and Tutor in Classics at Jesus College, Oxford, and University Lecturer in Greek and Latin Language and Literature. He has written a number of articles on Latin poetry and literary theory, and is preparing a book on Lucretius.

S. J. Harrison is Fellow and Tutor in Classics at Corpus Christi College, Oxford, and University Lecturer in Greek and Latin Language and Literature. He has written a commentary on Virgil, *Aeneid* 10 (1991), and edited *Oxford Readings in Vergil's Aeneid* (1990).

Margaret Hubbard is former Fellow and Tutor of St Anne's College, Oxford, and University Lecturer in Greek and Latin Language and Literature. She is co-author with R. G. M. Nisbet of commentaries on Horace, *Odes* 1 (1970) and 2 (1978), and author of *Propertius* (1974).

H. D. Jocelyn is Professor of Latin at the University of Manchester. He has edited the tragic fragments of Ennius (1965) and is author of many articles on Latin literature.

Antonio La Penna has taught at the University of Florence and at the Scuola Normale Superiore at Pisa. His books include *Orazio e l'ideologia del principato* (1963), *Orazio e la morale mondana europea* (1969), and *Saggi e studi su Orazio* (1993).

M. J. McGann is former Professor of Latin at The Queen's University of Belfast. He is author of *Studies in Horace's First Book of* Epistles (1969), and of a number of articles on Latin and neo-Latin poetry.

R. G. Mayer is Senior Lecturer in Classics at King's College, London, and the author of commentaries on Lucan, book 8 (1981), Seneca's *Phaedra* (with M. Coffey, 1990), and Horace, *Epistles* 1 (1994).

Frances Muecke is Senior Lecturer in Classics at the University of Sydney. She has edited Horace, *Satires* 2, with translation and commentary (1993), and is author of a number of articles on Latin poetry.

M. C. J. Putnam is Macmillan Professor of Classics at Brown University. Among his books on Latin poetry are *The Poetry of the Aeneid* (1965) and *Artifices of Eternity: A Commentary on Horace's Fourth Book of* Odes (1986).

H. P. Syndikus is former Studiendirektor at the Gymnasium, Weilheim, Bavaria, and author of *Lucans Gedicht vom Bürgerkrieg* (1958), *Die Lyrik des Horaz: Eine Interpretation der Oden* (2 vols.; 1972–3), and *Catull: Eine Interpretation* (3 vols.; 1984–7).

R. J. Tarrant is Pope Professor of the Latin Language and Literature at Harvard University, and author of editions with commentary of Seneca's *Agamemnon* (1976) and *Thyestes* (1985).

L. C. Watson is Senior Lecturer in Classics at the University of Sydney. He is author of *Arae: The Curse Poetry of Antiquity* (1991), and is completing a commentary on Horace's *Epodes*.

David West is former Professor of Latin at the University of Newcastle, and author of *Reading Horace* (1967), *The Imagery and Poetry of Lucretius* (1969), and a prose translation of the *Aeneid* (1992).

Gordon Williams is Thacher Professor of Latin at Yale University. He has edited Horace, *Odes* 3 (1969), and is author of *Tradition and Originality in Roman Poetry* (1968), *Horace* (1912), *Change and Decline: Roman Literature in the Early Empire* (1978), *Figures of Thought in Roman Poetry* (1980), and *Technique and Ideas in the* Aeneid (1983).

1

Some Twentieth-century Views of Horace

S. J. HARRISON

EVEN to list all the scholarly work that has been published on Horace since 1900 would consume a whole volume. This survey will therefore be limited to a brief sketch of some of the main lines of Horatian criticism in the present century, providing a context in which the studies which follow may be set. For the same reason, it will be largely confined to material published in book form; those seeking articles on particular subjects are directed towards the useful bibliographical collections of Kissel (1981) and Doblhofer (1992).[1]

I. TEXTS AND COMMENTARIES

For Horace, as for most other classical authors, the nineteenth century had seen much fundamental work on textual transmission. The text of Keller and Holder (1899 and 1925) still gives the most elaborate apparatus criticus and most extensive reports of manuscript readings. These were incorporated into the naturally much more selective apparatus of the Oxford Classical Text of E. C. Wickham (1900), with its second edition by H. W. Garrod (1912), still much used today, largely for the want of a successor in the same convenient series. F. Vollmer followed Keller and Holder in seeing three groups amongst the variety of Horatian manuscripts in his Teubner edition (second edition 1912); this was reduced to two by F. Klingner in his (third edition 1959). However, because of contamination such classification can be misleading (see Brink

[1] I am most grateful to Robin Nisbet for his extensive comments and suggestions on this piece, given with the helpfulness and generosity which have always characterized his support for the writer.

1971: 12–27); and when Klingner posits a third group (Q) which he regards as a conflation of his two main classes (Ξ and Ψ), his procedure has proved vulnerable to criticism (see Tarrant 1983).

Many modern editions have consequently preferred to treat manuscripts individually in the apparatus criticus even if formally recognizing groupings, e.g. the Budé edition by Villeneuve (1927–34), those for the Corpus Paravianum by De Gubernatis (1945) and Bo (1957–9), and the Leipzig Teubner of Borzsák (1984); Shackleton Bailey's Stuttgart Teubner (1985a) presents the evidence clearly by splitting up Klingner's Ξ group into its components but retaining the symbol Ψ for the more homogeneous second group. It is difficult for an editor of Horace to decide when to emend— cf. Tränkle (1993); vulgate readings are usually those of ancient editions and seldom incomprehensible, but sometimes seem infelicitous to sensitive critics. Many modern editors have been too conservative, especially Borzsák; the approach of A. Y. Campbell on the *Odes* (1945; 1953) is clearly too radical and is better at seeing problems than solving them. Shackleton Bailey (1985a) is sometimes too bold but is always stimulating—see Delz (1988) and Nisbet (1986). Future research on the manuscripts of Horace is unlikely to influence our choice of reading; but there is still room for an edition which presents generous reports of manuscript readings and conjectures and which follows Shackleton Bailey in grappling closely and sceptically with the many difficulties of the vulgate text.

In terms of commentaries, the nineteenth century also left a substantial legacy. Particularly notable were the scholarly commentaries on the complete works by Orelli and his successors (1886; 1892), Wickham (1874–91), Kiessling (1884–9), and L. Müller (1891–1900), and (in Britain) the school commentaries on the *Odes* by Gow (1896) and T. E. Page (1896). The twentieth century has built on these foundations; the commentary by Kiessling became the scholarly standard until the 1970s through its complete and justly influential revision by Heinze (1914–30), whose notes, sometimes compressed and terse, are still very valuable, acute on detail, and wide-ranging in literary knowledge, if a little conservative on textual matters, and which also formed the basis for the shorter Italian commentary on the *Odes* by Tescari (1936; 3rd edn. 1948). Important too was the commentary on the *Satires* by Lejay (1911), still the most important on that work, particularly notable for its analytical introductions to each poem and for its full use of the tradition of Greek popular philosophy. A mention should also be given here to Dilke (1961; revision of 1954 edn.), still useful on *Epistles* 1 despite its brevity.

In 1969 appeared the short but stimulating commentary on the third book of the *Odes* by Gordon Williams (1969), and in the next year the massive commentary on book 1 of the *Odes* by Nisbet and Hubbard (1970), with book 2 following in 1978. This editing of separate books broke new ground for the *Odes*, reflecting both an approach to ancient poems as individual literary artefacts open to judgement and the scholarly concern of Pasquali and Fraenkel with the Greek (and other) sources of Horace's poetry in the *Odes*, which required greater length of explanation than was permitted in the standard complete editions. Nisbet and Hubbard's concern with literary genre and category, seen also more schematically in the contemporary work by Cairns (1972), and their lengthy collections of relevant parallels, revealing how the literary tradition is moulded and reshaped in the *Odes*, have set a scholarly standard for all subsequent commentaries on Latin poets, while their forthright literary views have provided stimulating points of departure for literary discussion (for their critical position see 3 (*a*) below). The kind of detail which this depth of exegesis allows is further exemplified by Brink's vast edition of the *Ars Poetica* and *Epistles* 2 (1963*b*; 1971; 1982), which explores the language, meanings, and structure of these poems to a degree previously unparalleled in classical scholarship. His deep knowledge of Greek rhetoric and philosophy, his lexicographical thoroughness, and his determination to leave no stone unturned in interpretation make this an indispensable if somewhat ponderous work.

But the short commentary has not been neglected either, supplying the need for convenient school and university editions; thus Quinn (1980) has produced a lively if uneven commentary on the *Odes* for students, Rudd (1989) has capably summarized and varied Brink on *Epistles* 2 and the *Ars Poetica*, and Brown (1993) and Muecke (1993) have produced editions of *Satires* 1 and 2 respectively which are of considerable help in interpretation. The short notes in Macleod (1986) are a useful supplement to Dilke (1961), and another commentary on *Epistles* 1 is forthcoming from R. G. Mayer. The *Epodes*, in many ways Horace's most difficult poems, have been poorly served, but a full commentary is forthcoming from L. C. Watson. More interpretative running commentaries have also been produced; the most important of these is without doubt Syndikus (1972–3) on the *Odes*—succinct but pointed short essays on each poem which repeatedly identify the central points and problems and judiciously weigh up solutions. Particular strengths are a strong awareness of structure and of literary sources and allusions. Like the volumes of Nisbet and Hubbard, those of Syndikus are now indispensable for detailed work on the *Odes*. Most recent in this genre is Putnam (1986) on *Odes* 4, where the stress is always on the artistically crafted verbal icon and on close reading of imagery and emotional colour; there is still room for a conventional commentary on *Odes* 4.

2. GENERAL ACCOUNTS OF HORACE

Accounts of this kind were particularly favoured in the first half of the twentieth century, where the biographical view of ancient literature encouraged the chronological consideration of a Roman poet's whole output and its development in juxtaposition with his life and career. Again the nineteenth century had paved the way, in Britain at least, with Sellar (1892), where a quarter of the two hundred pages on Horace are devoted to biographical discussion. Of this type are a number of books published in English in this period, e.g. D'Alton (1917) and Sedgwick (1947). Their insistence on biographical criticism has made them date rapidly; such an approach does seem natural in considering the work of Horace, where the self-presentation of the poet is fuller than in many other Latin writers, but many of the statements made in the first person by Horace in his poems are misleading, and it is better to think of a manufactured literary self-image based on tradition and other elements rather than unmediated autobiography. Horace's poetry cannot be understood merely by teasing out his supposed biographical hints, or by establishing the likely site of his Sabine estate. Similarly biographical in tone is Wili (1948), showing that such a view was not restricted to the Anglophone world. Less biographical and more lively and literary (and controversial in its day) is Campbell (1924), particularly interested in Horace's ideas about poetry; some of its individual analyses are still valuable (e.g. p. 226 on the ending of *Odes* 3. 5), but the author's views, often highly moralistic and presented with great rhetorical flourish, sometimes verge on the eccentricity later shown in his editions of the *Odes* and *Epodes* (Campbell 1945; 1953).

The most important general book on Horace in the twentieth century is clearly Eduard Fraenkel's *Horace* (1957); it has now been formally marked as epoch-making by Doblhofer (1992). The biographical approach is not absent here; the book begins with the life of Horace and then goes through his works in chronological order, reflecting Fraenkel's general view that Horace's later work marks the heights of his development as a poet, especially in *Odes* 4, regarded by Fraenkel as a triumphant climax. This approach recalls the books of Wilamowitz on Pindar and Plato, and the chapter on Horace in Wilamowitz's *Sappho und Simonides* (1913) with its crisp and often perverse literary judgements is also a clear influence on Fraenkel. The great strength of the book lies in its close analysis of individual poems, bringing out their sources, structures, and other important elements; perhaps the most outstanding of these is the famous treatment of *Odes* 3. 4 as an imitation of Pindar's first *Pythian*. Such detailed treatment necessitates selection, but Fraenkel manages to deal with a high proportion of Horace's poems. His omissions are instructive: on the one hand most of the lighter erotic odes, on the other the *Ars Poetica* and *Epistles* 2. 2. The former are left out since they do not fit Fraenkel's picture of the dignified and serious poet, the latter because their fluid dating does not allow a neat placing in the development of Horace's career which forms the frame of the book. Apart from the concern with literary sources, which with the work of Pasquali leads directly to the achievement of Nisbet and Hubbard (see Section 1 above), a central theme of the book is Horace's relationship with Augustus, one of developing admiration and respect according to Fraenkel, who sees *Odes* 4. 5 (his favourite Horatian poem) as the final and most exquisite expression of the poet's loyal affection. Overall, the book is distinguished by humanity, enthusiasm, and an evidently professional approach to scholarship.

Other general books on Horace of this period were naturally overshadowed by Fraenkel's achievement, e.g. Grimal (1958) and Perret (1959), both of which gave capable summaries of Horace's career with some interesting literary judgements; the latter also has some interest in *Nachleben*, not part of Fraenkel's project. Becker (1963) likewise provided a different emphasis in an examination of the dating and coherence of all Horace's work after 23 BC, which despite some eccentricities still needs to be consulted on the late poems. Büchner's collection of interpretations (1962b) contains a number of papers, strong on technical and linguistic analysis; the collected Horatian papers of Klingner (1953; 1964) treat both transmission and literary interpretation, and show a depth and sympathy of interpretation which influenced both Nisbet and Hubbard and Syndikus. Fraenkel's book seems to have deterred others from large-scale general treatments; since 1957 there have been only short books of this kind, e.g. La Penna (1969), David West (1967), and Williams (1972). La Penna directly opposes Fraenkel, invoking the shade of Croce rather than Wilamowitz to argue that the 'real' Horace is the ethical private poet rather than the public bard; a revised version of this and other Horatian essays by La Penna, an important body of work which shows the development of Pasquali's influence in Italy, is to be found in La Penna (1993). West explores in some depth the imagery and thought-sequence of select passages of Horace, offering a model of practical criticism which is sometimes over-ingenious but always intelligent and thought-provoking. Williams, following the format of his series, provides a survey of issues and problems in Horace which usefully reacts against a number of Fraenkel's more extreme views (though it provides itself an unorthodox late dating of *Odes* 4). More recently, short treatments have been popular again: Shackleton Bailey (1982) is a mixed collection of studies, with a stress on interpretative difficulties appropriate to an editor of Horace, while Armstrong (1989) provides a lively personal view.

Collections of essays on Horace by different hands are a recent phenomenon. Still useful are Oppermann (1972) and Costa (1973), the latter containing stimulating pieces by Hubbard and West. Most recently, of course, the bimillenary of the poet's death (in 1992 or 1993 depending on one's arithmetic) has been an occasion for the generation of further collections, such as the present one: examples already out are Rudd (1993), a slim volume with several pieces of interest, Ludwig (1993), a weightier tome with several fundamental treatments, and Martindale and Hopkins (1993), an important collection of essays on the *Nachleben* of Horace in British literature which has a thematic coherence unusual in such celebratory productions.

3. SPECIALIST STUDIES

Specialist studies on Horace have burgeoned in the twentieth century, following the general trend in classical scholarship. Here only the most prominent will be discussed, largely under the headings of Horace's individual works.

(a) Odes

As in almost all periods of Horatian reception and scholarship, the *Odes* have bulked largest; a useful guide to the literature is Babcock (1981). A major landmark in the twentieth century was undoubtedly Pasquali's *Orazio lirico* (1920). Its main contribution was to stress that Hellenistic poetry, especially epigram, lay behind many of the most characteristic features and motifs of the *Odes*, and that it was at least as important as archaic Greek lyric in forming the character of Horace's lyric poetry. This thesis had been adumbrated by Reitzenstein, but after Pasquali's lengthy demonstration it was difficult to deny what had before then been a minority view. Fraenkel, who knew Pasquali well, acknowledged his work in his book and occasionally discussed Hellenistic sources there, but preferred to stress Horace's classicizing imitation of Alcaeus and other Greek lyric poets; again it is the detailed researches of Nisbet and Hubbard which have revealed most points of contact with the Hellenistic tradition, prose as well as poetry.

Another significant treatment of the *Odes* was Wilkinson (1945), which, like the author's later work on Ovid, set out to present Horace for a literate but non-expert reader. Its presentation is thematic rather than biographical or attached to individual poems, which sometimes makes it frustrating to use. It stresses the coherence of the poet's self-presentation in the *Odes*, expressing reservations (later taken up by La Penna) on Horace's commitment in the political odes, and making many useful observations on characteristic motifs and poetic techniques. This was the standard introduction to the *Odes* for a generation of English readers, though it perhaps viewed Horace as too much like an English gentleman. Collinge (1961) is an interesting formal analysis of the design of the *Odes*, stressing word-order and sequence of thought as the two central and complementary techniques, with a considerable interest in imagery. His emphasis on patterning derives at least partly from linguistic theory, and many will find it too mechanical and dogmatic; however, it does rightly point to the importance of internal dynamics in the *Odes* and the complex formal principles of their construction.

Commager's influential book (1962) concentrated on the poetic imagination of Horace as displayed in the *Odes*, regarding the significance of the poems as lying primarily in their imagery and emotional colouring. Like Collinge, he is interested in structural principles on both a small and a large scale, especially elements of contrast and tension in both word and thought; he also argues for the presence of parody and allegory, and provides salutary arguments against the biographical approach which show the influence of New Criticism. He also follows Wilkinson in his interest in Horace's views on poetry, but his primary contribution is the stress on the *Odes* as complex aesthetic artefacts worthy of admiration. Some of this is shared with La Penna (1963), who (as in La Penna 1969—see Section 2 above) prefers the aesthetic to the political in his analysis of the *Odes*; the real Horace is the thoughtful and urbane individual of the private odes, not the public *vates* of the political poetry, where La Penna finds a lack of 'authenticity of sentiment'. A good contrast with La Penna is Doblhofer (1966), who followed Pöschl (1956) in stressing the importance of the literary tradition of panegyric in Horace's political odes, but combined this with Fraenkel's belief that Horace was fully sincere in his praises of the great man Augustus.

Notable contributions on the *Odes* in the 1970s were the collection of articles by Pöschl (1970) and the commentaries of Syndikus and Nisbet and Hubbard (see Section 1). Pöschl provided a useful series of analyses of particular odes, stressing their symbolic and linguistic richness and giving a good instance of dense reading; Syndikus, in his introduction, gives a careful outline of the nature of the Horatian ode, beginning from Heinze's famous treatment (1923). But it is Nisbet and Hubbard who have set the agenda for most subsequent studies of the *Odes*, and it is their contribution which needs particular evaluation.

Nisbet and Hubbard provide in their introduction to book 1 a compressed but extremely useful general account of the *Odes*. Good material is presented on chronology and metre, but the most important part is the section on the literary form of the *Odes*, which continues the work of Pasquali and Fraenkel in the search for Greek models in Hellenistic poetry and archaic lyric, but considerably enlarges the purview by the application of formal generic categories, by the stress on Horatian poses and personae as well as genuine Horatian characteristics, and in particular by the important observation that prose literature is also an influential source. Like La Penna, they reacted against Fraenkel's view that the political odes showed Horace at his best, pointing out under the influence of Syme that Horace had no choice but to praise the regime, and that this detracted from the quality of the poetry: 'the virtues of irony and sense . . . desert him in the political odes' (p. xviii). Like Wilkinson, they identified various recurring motifs and topics which served to give the *Odes* their particular character (the dignity of poetry, the countryside, friendship, self-depreciation), and they provided some fundamental observations about style and poetic technique (some prosaic vocabulary, internal structure of poems, possibilities of arrangment within the book, use of rhetorical devices). Many of these themes have been taken up in later treatments, whether in agreement or disagreement (many might think that they had underestimated the possibilities of imagery and symbolism, perhaps as a reaction to Commager), and this critical introduction has been as important as the commentary itself in the study of Horace. The introduction to book 2, much shorter, discusses that book only, but stresses more fully the centrally important point of the relevance of Horace's addressees to the contents of the poems addressed to them; book 2 is also more liberal in recognizing features such as ambiguity, symbolism, and imagery stressed by writers such as Pöschl and Klingner.

The late 1970s and early 1980s were thin in general books on the *Odes*, understandably after the work of Nisbet and Hubbard and Syndikus. A further commentary was Quinn (1980): see Section 1 above. Lyne (1980) provided an analysis of the erotic odes, supplying a notable omission in Fraenkel and full of good points, though not all will believe that Horace could not envisage a permanent relationship (what of *Odes* 1. 13 and 3. 9?). Cremona (1982) reacted against La Penna (1963) in arguing that there was little tension between poetical and political purposes and values in Horace's political odes, and that the poet had a genuine social and political vision which included the praise of Augustus and imperialism (cf. also Cremona's recent summary (1993) of his own and others' arguments). Gall (1981) provided a useful (if mechanical) catalogue of Horatian imagery in the *Odes*. But in the late 1980s and early 1990s there has been something of a welcome revival. Apart from Putnam's running commentary on *Odes* 4 (see Section 1 above) and Connor's treatment of humour in the *Odes*, stressing an important aspect often underrated by critics—through in fact the book is more general than its title suggests (Connor 1987)—there have been three books on the *Odes* by American scholars: Santirocco (1986), Porter (1987), and Davis (1991). Both Santirocco and Porter are primarily concerned with the structure of the first collection of *Odes*; both argue that the order of the *Odes* is a complex design of the poet, with each poem carefully placed to relate to preceding and succeeding poems. Many might find it difficult to accept this claim in its strong form; Santirocco at least allows some flexibility in his structural scheme and has many interesting points of individual interpretation, but Porter is rather more rigid and mechanical and therefore has less to offer, often using somewhat forced interpretations to fit his ideas on arrangement.

Davis, however, provides perhaps the most stimulating recent treatment of the *Odes*. He uses a framework of 'modes'—modes of assimilation, treating the ways in which the *Odes* define themselves as lyric through encounters with other literary genres, modes of authentication, by which the poet defines and establishes his own poetic status and identity as a lyric poet, modes of 'consolation', i.e. the sympotic poetry, which stresses the brevity of human existence and the consequent message of *carpe diem*, and modes of praise and dispraise. Davis's interests lie partly in the rhetorical analysis of lyric (he is a pupil of E. L. Bundy), and he is skilled in eliciting the argument of an ode; but there are sometimes rhetorical issues which he does not address. One might wish for some discussion of the relevance of particular addressees to the rhetoric of particular poems, and indeed for discussion of the political odes, which are largely excluded from his treatment: political rhetoric is just as significant as other types of rhetoric for Horace. A particular emphasis of his is metapoetry in the *Odes*, where poems seem to talk about themselves and their own stylistic level: his analyses of 1. 38 (pp. 118–26) and 4. 2 (pp. 142–3) from this angle have some attractions.

Davis's approach is partly theoretical, but does not use literary theory as such. An instance of the application of the latter to Horace is Edmunds (1992), who uses his own version of the reception theory of Jauss to produce an exhaustive set of readings of the Soracte ode (1. 9). This book, though not wholly successful, is pioneering, and it is to be hoped that other elements of literary theory can be applied effectively to the *Odes* and indeed to Horace in general.

(b) Epodes

The *Epodes* have been less well served than most other Horatian poetry-books, especially in the absence of a scholarly commentary (see Section 1 above). However, Grassmann (1966) goes a fair way towards supplying a commentary on the poems that he deals with (8, 11, 12, 14, 15) in a useful treatment of the less popular erotic poems; similarly, the magical elements of *Epodes* 5 and 17 have been examined in some detail by Ingallina (1974). The perennially popular Actium *Epodes* 1 and 9 were discussed in detail by Fraenkel and subsequently by Wistrand (1958) and Kraggerud (1984); Kraggerud also deals with 7 and 16, treated previously by Ableitinger-Grünberger (1971) and often central to treatments of the *Epodes* which set them in their historical context (cf. especially Nisbet, 1984); there now seems little doubt among scholars that *Epode* 16 postdates and uses Virgil's fourth *Eclogue*, a matter which was the subject of a long-running dispute before Fraenkel's book. More generally, the influence of Callimachus' *Iambi* has been well considered by Clayman (1980), adding usefully to the account of the influence of archaic Greek ἴαμβος in Fraenkel, and stressing that these poems, like the *Odes*, have some Hellenistic colouring, while the arrangement of the collection has been somewhat speculatively discussed by Carrubba (1969). An annotated survey of literature on the *Epodes* from 1937 to 1978 is to be found in Setaioli (1981).

(c) Satires

Horace's *Satires* are usually mentioned in handbooks on Roman satire, and book 1 at least was treated in some detail by Fraenkel; but since the work of Fiske (1920), which, in a treatment which is still useful for the material collected, placed Horace against the background of Lucilius, the only major study until recently has been Rudd (1966). This provides not only a basic introduction to, cultural and historical setting of, and running commentary on all the *Satires*, particularly useful in these poems where the sequence of thought is often difficult to follow, but also has an important chapter on the names found in the poems; with Lejay's massive commentary (see Section 1 above), this provides the fullest guide to the *Satires* for the modern reader, and deservedly achieved a second edition in 1982. More recently, there is useful practical help from the smaller-scale commentaries with English translations of Brown (1993) on book 1 and Muecke (1993) on book 2 (see Section 1 above).

For further critical analysis, the work of W. S. Anderson on the persona of the satirist has been influential in disengaging scholars from the view that the *Satires* are simply autobiographical; this is now conveniently collected in Anderson (1982); Zetzel (1982) is also a noteworthy treatment of the structure of book 1 and its development of the persona of the speaker. Freudenberg (1993) is the first large-scale treatment of the *Satires* since Rudd. As its title suggests, it concentrates on the literary affinities and theoretical position of satire as used by Horace, making instructive links with the tradition of Roman popular drama, and exploring further the links with Hellenistic popular moralizing stressed by Horace himself. It also locates the *Satires* firmly in the middle of contemporary debates on style and Callimachean aesthetics. While it may be too emphatic about the importance of ancient literary criticism for the *Satires* (was Horace really so concerned with these particular issues?), it certainly provides a new angle and much food for thought. Food is the subject of another recent treatment of the *Satires*; Gowers (1993) explores Horace's use of food in these poems, stressing its role as a metaphor for moral and poetical attitudes. This is intriguing and intelligent, though not all will be convinced by every example adduced.

(*d*) Epistles *and* Ars Poetica

The first book of *Epistles* has been popular with critics. Most notable earlier in the century was Courbaud (1914), a substantial treatment of a rather biographical nature which held the field for many years; Heinze's influential essay (1919) should also be mentioned.

Two central issues have been how far this first book can be treated as a collection of 'real' letters, and what if anything can be said about the type of philosophy it promotes. On the first issue, Fraenkel (1957) thought that the epistles of book 1 could be legitimately treated both as real letters and as poems in an artistic poem-book; Williams (1968) opposed this in his first chapter, and his view that these are poems counterfeiting the form of letters for literary reasons (see also Williams 1972) remains the standard one (see the useful discussion in the last chapter of McGann 1969). On the second issue, McGann (1969) argued that Horace's explicit eclecticism was in fact a specific following of the tolerant Stoicism of Athenodorus and Panaetius; this strong thesis has not convinced all, but McGann remains an essential guide to the philosophical background of the book, and contains much useful analysis of its poems. Also notable on the ethics of the *Epistles* are the two papers in Macleod (1983), which perhaps present Horace as too relentlessly earnest. Much of the recent criticism of the first book of *Epistles* has been absorbed in Kilpatrick (1986), which is now the best guide, with its stress on the context of friendship and the dramatic situation and thought-sequence of each poem. The commentary by Dilke (see Section 1 above), though still useful, is showing its age and will soon be superseded by the work of R. G. Mayer (currently in proof); a recent contribution is the separate commentary on *Ep.* 1.7 by Horsfall (1993), which sheds new light on many of that poem's problems. Dilke (1981) is a useful survey of major issues in *Epistles* 1 and gives a bibliography for the years 1950–79.

The second book of *Epistles* has been less of a critical favourite, though it has been included with the *Ars Poetica* in the massive project of Brink's *Horace on Poetry*, producing Brink (1982), a full and learned edition and commentary. Brink's general view of the literary *Epistles* has been criticized as too earnest and too involved with Greek literary theory (on the particular controversy on the *Ars Poetica* see below), and readers of his work may agree with this (there is surely more humour and wit in these poems than he allows, and Horace's interest in Greek literary theory may have been limited); but Brink's scholarly virtues are very real (see Section 1 above). The monumental nature of Brink's work has allowed space for shorter and more convenient treatments which pursue some of the issues he highlights; apart from the commentary by Rudd (1989) (see Section 1), the brief account of all three literary *Epistles* by Kilpatrick (1990) usefully discusses the relation of the three to each other, the role of the addressees, and the perennial issue of the unity of the *Ars Poetica*. This last poem has always been popular among scholars for its many problems; the numerous treatments before Brink (1963*b*; 1971) are conveniently listed and discussed by Sbordone (1981), and many are taken up by Brink in his introductory essays and detailed edition. Brink famously sought to argue by detailed analysis that Horace's poem reproduced many elements of traditional literary theory, and indicated affinities with the Peripatetic tradition of Aristotle and (more closely) Neoptolemus of Parium, mentioned as Horace's source by an ancient commentator. These views have been found controversial, notably by Williams (1964; 1974), but provide a considerable collection of material and arguments in a continuing debate.

(*e*) *Miscellaneous*

(i) *Technical aids*   Numerous technical aids to the study of Horace have been produced, and with the advent of new technology this is likely to be a growth area in Horatian studies. Two lexica, Staedler and Müller (1962) and Bo (1965-6), have appeared, and a new concordance (Iso Echegoyen 1990), all based on different editions of the text; the last is unfortunately unsatisfactory (cf. Nisbet 1992). Cooper (1916) was based on yet another edition. Kissel (1981) provides a massive bibliography on all aspects of Horace for the years 1936-75, with a list of bibliographies back to 1873; Doblhofer (1992) gives a select and annotated bibliography of the years 1957-87. A considerable bimillenary enterprise is the *Enciclopedia oraziana* (1993), with some useful articles by leading Horatians.

(ii) *Diction*   There is still no authoritative overall treatment of Horace's diction, and the main contributions have been on the *Odes*; for the other works commentaries must be consulted, though Grassmann (1966) is useful on the language of the *Epodes*. The treatment by Axelson (1945) was influential in arguing for prosaisms as a central element of Horatian lyric vocabulary, though some of its conclusions were importantly modified by Williams

(1968). The introduction to Nisbet and Hubbard (1970) contains some important pointers on the *Odes*, as do the treatments in Wilkinson (1945; 1959; 1963), and the piece by Waszink (1972).

(iii) *Metre* Here again most work has been on the *Odes*, though Nilsson's work (1952) on the hexameters of the *Satires*, usefully linking metrical variation to literary context, is an exception, as is the exhaustive metrical analysis of the *Ars Poetica* by Ott (1970). There has been a wide range of articles on individual issues (collected by Kissel 1981: 1465–7). Work on the *Odes*, taking off from Heinze (1918), has been concerned (among many other topics) with the *Lex Meinekiana*, the view that all Horatian lyric metres can be divided into four-line stanzas (they can, most think): Büchner's well-known treatment of 1939 is reprinted in Büchner (1962b), and this was taken further by Bohnenkamp (1972). As ever, Nisbet and Hubbard (1970) provide a useful point of departure for metrical issues in their introduction.

(iv) *Historical and cultural background* As suggested in Section 2 above, the twentieth century has gradually moved from using Horace's tenuous biography to explain his poems to a more general understanding of the cultural circumstances of their composition. Griffin (1985), reacting against Nisbet and Hubbard (1970) and Williams (1968), has persuasively argued that much of the Graecizing world depicted in Horace's poetry is more realistic than has often been thought, though not all will agree with his views on the close relation between poetical motifs and real events (see Nisbet 1987). Syme (1939) provided a famously realistic analysis of Augustan politics, perhaps too influenced by European events of his own period, which remains important in considering Horace as a political poet; Syme (1986) has provided a good deal of information about the dating and addressees of Horace's later poetry; this is particularly illuminating for the fourth book of *Odes*, though Syme is also concerned with the *Ars Poetica*. On a broader front, the social conditions for the composition and patronage of poetry in late first-century Rome have received particular attention in the essays collected in Gold (1982) and in White (1993), while the coherence between poetry, the plastic arts, and architecture as expressions of Augustan ideology has been stressed in the important work of Zanker (1987); for other work on Horace and Augustus cf. Pöschl (1956), La Penna (1963), and Doblhofer (1966), all discussed in Section 3 (*a*) above.

(v) *Influence*   Investigations of the *Nachleben* of classical authors have been frequent in twentieth-century scholarship, and Horace is no exception. The collections of Stemplinger (1906; 1921) and Showerman (1922) formed a foundation for later work; a collection of surveys was published to mark the bimillenary of Horace's birth in 1936 (*Orazio* 1936), and since then a large number of studies have been produced, largely in article form (listed in Kissel 1981: 1528–41); the last chapters of Wilkinson (1945) and Perret (1959) give brief narratives of Horace's influence in Europe. The bimillenary of Horace's death looks set to produce further work of this kind; one important work which has already appeared is Martindale and Hopkins (1993), on the influence of Horace in English literature, and the medieval and Renaissance receptions of Horace in Europe form two of the major topics in Ludwig (1993).

2

Some Structures in Horace's *Odes*

H. P. SYNDIKUS

IN this paper I try to extend somewhat an idea which Friedrich Klingner introduced in interpreting some of Horace's poems.[1] In examining the shape and structure of the *Odes* of Horace people generally restrict themselves to the subdivision of a poem into two, three, or more parts.[2] In contrast to such a static principle of arrangement, Klingner traced dynamic developments, shifts, and alterations in content, emotional expression, and stylistic level.[3] In the poems of Horace he traced the shifts which take place within a poem as in pieces of music. In this respect he perceived an important difference from modern European lyric (especially since the time of the Romantics), which strives above all for unity of mood in an individual poem.

I

I shall begin with an observation which Klingner made about the endings of Horace's poems: poems on a high stylistic level with serious content often close with a very personal and apparently light-weight change of direction.[4] Here are a few examples.

I would like to thank Kathleen Coleman for the translation of my German text.

[1] Klingner (1964) 325-33; (1953), 395-418; Klingner's interpretations were first printed in 1935, 1938, and 1952. The change of mood in *Odes* 1. 27 and 3. 9 was also observed by Reincke (1929) 14-19.

[2] For instance, Daniels (1940), Collinge (1961), and Cupaiuolo (1976) 55-62 explain the structure of most of Horace's *Odes* in this way.

[3] Klingner (1953) 346: 'Ein römisches Dichtwerk ist von vornherein . . . ein in Worten gestalteter Bewegungsvorgang.' Cf. Brink (1971) 448: 'What strikes me about his thought is its unique flexibility', 450: 'It is here [sc. in the structure of a poem] that the shifting antitheses of thought and emotion meet.'

[4] Klingner (1964) 351, 447. The frequency and importance of such quiet

In *Odes* 1. 6 *Scriberis Vario*, in the first four strophes the epic themes which Horace is rejecting are represented by names and concepts from epic poetry in an elevated tone. In contrast to this, the manner in which he refers to his own poetry in the last strophe makes it appear to be nothing more than a light-hearted game, to which the poet himself does not mean to attach any importance.

In *Odes* 1. 19 *Mater saeva Cupidinum*, a reawakened love is first felt as something painful and violent. Venus is the wild mother of human passions: the repeated *urit* strengthens the impression of torment; and in the expression 'in me tota ruens Venus' the goddess of love seems almost like a demon falling upon its victim. Then in the closing strophe the preparations for a sacrifice to Venus arouse the expectation that the poet has yielded to pressure from the deity and only wants to implore her to guarantee that his love will be fulfilled: that is certainly how the goddess of love is generally entreated. One is all the more surprised by the last line: Horace hopes that the sacrifice will soften Venus and that she will treat him more gently, that is to say, no longer shake him to the core. By this unexpected closing twist the poet is distancing himself from being overcome by passion. As Nisbet and Hubbard say, the 'pomposity of the opening stanza and the high tragic tone of the ninth line dissolve, as so often, in a display of charm and humour'.[5]

The last strophe of *Odes* 2. 1 *Motum ex Metello* breaks decisively with the emotional depiction of the horrors of civil war: with the image of the poet composing cheerful melodies in the grotto of the love-goddess, a peaceful counterpart develops to the former dark and heavy vision,[6] and this leads us back to the fundamental tone of Horatian lyric.

In *Odes* 2. 4 *Ne sit ancillae* Horace urges a friend not to feel ashamed of his love for a beautiful slave-girl. When eventually, in the last strophe, Horace's praise of the girl's noble qualities dwells on her physical attractions, the poet is clearly afraid that his words have become too heated and his friend could suppose him to be a

---

endings of Horace's *Odes* is observed by many interpreters: cf. Wilkinson (1945) 40; Heinimann (1952) 202–3; Fraenkel (1957) 200; Schrijvers (1973) 140 ff.; Cupaiuolo (1976) 23–4; Esser (1976), esp. 3–4, 9–28; Nisbet and Hubbard (1978) 29. Schrijvers and Esser also describe other kinds of closure in Horace's *Odes*.

[5] Nisbet and Hubbard (1970) 238.   [6] Cf. Fraenkel (1957) 239.

rival. So, with a shift towards self-irony, he dispels such thoughts, should they arise: at his age there is nothing more to fear from him in this regard.

The first Roman ode, which begins in a lofty tone, ends in the last strophe with a very personal change of direction: the poet asks quite plainly why, instead of his simple life in the Sabine valley, he should aim for riches which can only bring trouble and arouse envy.[7]

After the heroic speech by Regulus, the fifth Roman ode also closes very quietly: the old-style Roman facing death leaves the city exactly as if he were withdrawing to his quiet estate after spending demanding days in court.

In the closing lines of *Odes* 3. 10 *Extremum Tanain* the tone unexpectedly changes: at first, in the conventional manner of a *paraklausithyron*, the lover's complaints are piled up in an exaggerated crescendo. Then in the last two lines Horace breaks off in sudden sobriety: he cannot endure this unpleasant situation for ever.

The close of *Odes* 3. 20 *Non vides* is similarly disillusioned. In the first strophes the bitter struggle between a man and a woman for the favours of a pretty boy was depicted with comic exaggeration: the man is cautioned against fighting a Gaetulian lioness. Then in the last lines of the poem we get a glimpse of the boy, watching the quarrel completely unmoved and, far from holding the prize of victory in his hands, stamping it underfoot as something entirely worthless. In view of this indifference, the earlier quarrel appears utterly pointless.

Odes 3. 26 *Vixi puellis* begins as a farewell to love and love poetry. When the third strophe then turns into a prayer to the goddess of love, one immediately expects thanks for her help up to this point. But in the last two lines, as a complete surprise, the poet asks Venus to soften the heart of a standoffish girl just once more. In the light of this closing change of direction, the farewell to love appears as a futile attempt to escape from the control of the love-goddess.

In *Odes* 3. 29 *Tyrrhena regum* the poet closes a long sequence of general considerations with a shift to the personal. While a rich merchant in a sinking ship panics about his wealth, Horace light-heartedly wants to climb into a lifeboat. As often, in this closing

---

[7] Cf. David. West (1973) 32, who detects similar contrasting endings in *Odes* 2. 16 and 2. 17.

change of direction towards what is apparently light-weight and trivial, there is contained what is for Horace a central idea.

Odes 4. 6 *Dive quem proles*, written in the manner of Greek choral lyric as far as form and content are concerned, ends with a quiet personal strophe in which Horace addresses the girls of the chorus at the Ludi Saeculares, and reflects that one day, when they have been married for a long time, they will still remember that they sang his celebratory song at the great festival.

One should also note that Horace closes the first book of the *Odes*, as a unit, in the same way. The entire poem 1. 38 *Persicos odi* has as its theme the plain simplicity which Horace loves in his personal life, and he also tries to express this simplicity in the plainness of his language.

II

Klingner and Pöschl outlined another characteristic mode of composition and structure in Horace's odes.[8] In a whole sequence of odes a movement away from the poem's point of departure or initial mood leads to more or less the opposite, usually moving from a distressed or strongly emotional mood to something light and cheerful.

A good example of this type of poetic structure is *Odes* 1. 2 *Iam satis*.[9] A flood of the Tiber is interpreted as a bad omen. At first Horace thinks of the end of the world, then, in a more concrete manner, he imagines the outbreak of a devastating new civil war. After six strophes have been filled with this despairing mood, a quiet hope emerges in the tentative questions in the next lines— which god can save Rome in this situation?—because now a certain confidence can develop, through the names of the deities in whom Rome has always believed. Then in the eleventh strophe comes the decisive naming of the ruler who is already operating on earth as a saviour-god. This leads in the last two strophes to the certainty that rescue is still possible, if only the ruler is preserved for the people.

Odes 1. 9 *Vides ut alta* effects a change from an uncomfortable situation to pleasant prospects in the private realm. In the

---

[8] Klingner (1964) 325–33; (1965) 395–418; Pöschl (1991) 44–5, 112–13.

[9] Fraenkel (1957) 247 explains the progression of thought with admirable succinctness.

opening lines of the first strophe the difficulties of a winter's day are described. But Alcaeus' advice helps in this respect: a warming fire on the hearth and a robust *vin ordinaire* make one forget about the bad weather. In what follows, 'permitte divis cetera' shows that of course one's worries cannot all be removed from the world like this; but the new image of the passing storm permits the hope that one's remaining troubles may also disappear. Through the changing course of imagery, Horace has freed himself from the concrete point of departure and can now proceed in more general terms. As frequently elsewhere, he recommends that one should not look fearfully into the future, but take the good which the present day offers. He encourages the friend who is present to take advantage of his youth before old age arrives. In the process the word 'love' is mentioned, and from here onwards this motif is formed into a concrete image: so long as his friend is young, he ought to spend his evenings in the squares of Rome meeting the girl who is going to become his lover. The poem draws on such subjects of semi-serious discussion as are well suited to a Horatian dinner-party, but it transforms these motifs poetically, creating its own artistic momentum.

In *Odes* I. 13 *Cum tu Lydia Telephi* the point of departure is a violent outbreak of jealousy, depicted in the manner of Sappho and Catullus. Then in the two closing strophes the poet frees himself from this crushing emotional assault. First, just like a concerned friend, he tries to persuade the girl to leave the unsuitable lover. Then in the last strophe, becoming clearer with regard to his own wishes, he praises a quiet and lasting happiness in love, which presents the exact opposite not only of the rival's reckless passion but also of Horace's own wild outburst of passion at the beginning of the poem.

In *Odes* I. 24 *Quis desiderio*, the poem mourning his friend Quintilius, the movement of the poem leads from the agitation at the beginning to a calmer state. At first the poet yields passionately to the universal distress, but then he comes to the quieter realization that death is an irrevocable destiny, and he thereby finds the strength to remind the grieving Virgil that pain becomes less when one accepts the inevitable.

Odes I. 27 *Natis in usum* aims to achieve a soothing effect in a different way.[10] The first two strophes take us to a noisy banquet

---

[10] The change of mood in the poem is well illustrated by Fraenkel (1957) 180-1.

in which the poet wants to stifle the noise and tumult which are developing. He suggests another theme: a participant is to tell the secret of his love. This is a theme cut out for a banquet attended by young people. In addition, the *risqué* tone in which the poet tries to wrest the secret from his hesitant companion suits the new theme. Finally, in the last lines, in the feigned dismay with which the poet comments on the secret which has finally been communicated to him, the mood changes to a comical one. One no longer has to fear a return to the confused tumult at the beginning.[11]

In *Odes* I. 31 *Quid dedicatum*, the poem to Palatine Apollo begins with the question, 'What should the poet ask the god for?' But then Horace paints a contrasting picture, turning to things which are of no importance for the poet: he does not beg for property and riches. In a further group of verses he airily concedes the most valuable possessions to those people who struggle to attain them. Once it has become clear in this way that his heart is not fixed on what the whole world is striving after he starts talking about himself. He is quite content with the simplest standard of living. Thus prepared, it is only in the last strophe that he utters his prayer to the god: he wants to be happy with what he has and, remaining in good health right into old age, not to have to give up the god's gift, the gift of poetry. The poem's direction moves in this way from what the world treasures to quiet inner values.

Odes 2. 6 *Septimi Gadis* also pursues a path away from the world's bustle. The first strophe talks about the promise of Horace's friend Septimius, who is ready to accompany him to the furthest and most dangerous parts of the world. This is a pathetic topos belonging to pledges of friendship, envisaging an active life in the world at large. In contrast to this, Horace displays what appears to be weary resignation: he is tired of travelling and fighting; he wants quiet Tibur as his place of retirement. For a metropolitan Roman this is an understandable desire. Many Romans had a villa there where they could recover from the stresses of the capital. But Horace does not stop here: he is ready to renounce this desire as well, and go to out-of-the-way, rarely visited Tarentum. But what would hold few attractions for others has its own allure for the poet: the beauty of nature and the seclusion itself would be the

---

[11] Porphyrio (commentary on I. 27. I) understands the point of the poem in this way too: 'Protreptice ode est haec ad hilaritatem.'

right setting for his poetry, and his friend Septimius would also be welcome there.

Odes 2. 11 *Quid bellicosus* purports to divert a friend from a depressed mood. At the beginning the friend's political and private worries are described. The poet replies with words which put this in perspective and focus upon how quickly life passes. In the second half the poet shows how the fleeting moment can be transformed into a fulfilled one: the friends should enjoy the beauty of nature, place wreaths upon their greying hair, fetch wine and a girl, and forget their cares in a party. Opening in a troubled tone, the poem finishes cheerfully with the image of the girl and her pretty hairstyle.

The *recusatio*-poem *Odes* 2. 12 *Nolis longa ferae* effects the transfer, both in subject and in tone, from the epic themes which are being rejected to the love poetry which lies closer to Horace's heart. After three strophes, full of words and names which make one think of fierce battles, Horace sketches the charming picture of Maecenas' beloved wife, and in the two concluding strophes he varies this contrast between external splendour and human qualities.

In *Odes* 2. 13 *Ille et nefasto* the course of the poem leads from a blind riot of fear to inner joy over the beauty of poetry.[12] The first three strophes are full of angry excitement. In an emotional tone Horace curses the farmer—he does not know his identity, of course —who once planted the tree which nearly fell on him and killed him. In the fourth and fifth strophes the excitement dies down to peaceful reflection. The poet is aware that the fate which nearly overtook him is the general lot of mankind which will overtake everyone sooner or later. Feeling already calmer, he imagines that he has almost entered Proserpina's dark domain. But this fantastic notion quickly yields to brighter thoughts. Horace thinks of his favourite poets, Sappho and Alcaeus, whose poetry he and the other shades could have listened to. Just as the sinners of the underworld forget their torment in listening to this poetry, Horace too, through the enchantment of art, seems to have freed himself from his human fears.

Thoughts of death and images of the underworld become less bright in *Odes* 2. 14 *Eheu fugaces*, but here too the direction of the poem moves from an emotional horror, via sober recognition of the

[12] Cf. Davis (1991) 82–8.

inevitable, to cheerful images which are supposed to tempt one to make the most of one's allotted span.

The first strophes of *Odes* 2. 17 *Cur me querelis* also convey a strong emotional outburst. Horace is horrified at the premonitions and fears of death experienced by his friend Maecenas. First, instead of trying to talk him out of it, he assures him that he wants to die with him. That is what fate has decided. But with this awareness of the equality of fate, Horace finds a direction leading away from the fears expressed at the beginning of the poem. Just as Maecenas has recently recovered from a serious illness, so Horace himself has been rescued from mortal danger. Thus, the same fate indicates not death but life, and for this they both owe a thank-offering. With the prospect of this thanksgiving celebration, the fears at the beginning of the poem have vanished and thoughts turn again to life and its pleasures.[13]

In *Odes* 3. 14 *Herculis ritu* there has appeared to some scholars to be a contradiction between the instructions for a public festival at the beginning of the poem and the preparations for a private celebration in the second half. But, as Klingner has demonstrated, both parts correspond to one another in detail and are connected in a common movement.[14] The first strophe begins in an elevated tone: the deeds of the Princeps in Spain are compared with those of Herakles, and the depiction of a procession, with the emperor's wife and sister marching at its the head, is in itself festive enough. But the tone is already starting to relax when the subject changes to the joy experienced by Livia and the Roman mothers whose sons and sons-in-law have come home from the war, and when, at the end, we catch a glimpse of the happiness of the reunited young couples, only the warning not to give vent to one's joy so audibly as to disturb the silence required on holy occasions reminds us that Horace is still thinking of the state procession. In the middle strophe of the poem he mentions his personal happiness. Like the Romans who have previously been enumerated, he too has been relieved of all anxiety by Augustus' safe return: so long as the emperor rules the world, he is assured a peaceful life. Then, in the last three strophes, when the poet turns to his slave and gives him instructions for a private celebration of this feast-day, the lively tone seems to be intended to anticipate the cheerfulness of the

[13] Cf. Arnaldi (1963) 139.
[14] Klingner (1965) 394–400; cf. Brink (1971) 461.

festival. But, just as the theme of personal joy was cautiously introduced and developed in the first half of the poem, so the public
theme is echoed in the closing strophe, even though this strophe is
apparently concerned only with private matters. When Horace
hopes that a cask of vintage wine from the time of the Social War
has escaped Spartacus' raids, and when he alludes to his own
stormy youth by mentioning the consuls for the year of the battle
of Philippi, in which he actually took part himself, all this is a
distinct recollection of the horrors of the civil war which Augustus
had brought to an end. And when, in the last lines, the poet
remembers with a smile that he is no longer as wild and violent as
he used to be, the change in himself matches the change in the
times.

Odes 3. 17 *Aeli vetusto* has a high-flown beginning in a consciously affected style; it leads to a concrete situation and the
advantage to be made of it. In the genealogical fantasies of the first
two strophes Horace smiles a little about his friend's aristocratic
pride. Then in the middle of the poem the shift to the present
moment occurs: Horace notices a weather-omen which promises
storms and rain. Since the approaching storm will not allow any
outdoor work the following day, his friend ought to arrange a
little celebration with the country people on his estate. So Horace
moves from conceitedness to true values: simple humanity and
good cheer.

Just as in *Odes* 1. 27, in 3. 19 *Quantum distet ab Inacho* Horace
tries to show a party of revellers the right road to merriment. He
speaks in the role of the so-called 'banquet-king', and gives his
instructions. In the first strophe he opposes topics which do not
fit in with the cheerful occasion: a participant obviously bored
the assembly with learned never-ending expositions. The place and
date of the next party seem to Horace a far more appropriate
theme. But then, as if he wants to infect everyone with gaiety, from
the third strophe onwards the poet increases the pace and the tone.
Toasts follow in quick succession, along with various instructions
to the cup-bearer, the musicians, and a slave who is to scatter
roses. As though to distance himself from the pedantic tone conveyed at the beginning, Horace pushes his friends into a Dionysiac
ecstasy in a manner that is usually foreign to his poems about
wine. This invitation to a boisterous carousal is in deliberate contrast to the beginning of the poem.

The movement of a poem in the opposite direction, from a noisy beginning to a very quiet ending, is demonstrated by *Odes* 4. 11 *Est mihi nonum*. The invitation to a girl is expressed in the first strophes with cheerful urgency. The minuteness of detail with which the busy preparations are described is unusual. Then the festive occasion is named—the celebration of Maecenas' birthday— and the invitation to what is for Horace such an important occasion suggests an intimate friendship. But then in line 21 a shadow falls across what at first appeared to be such a happy mood. We discover that the girl has her eye on a handsome man, obviously much younger than Horace. All of a sudden one notices that the vivacity of the first strophes was meant to conceal some- thing, namely the anxiety which is now coming into the open. He fears that the girl may not accept the invitation at all. Horace then tries to put the girl off his rival by depicting him as out of her reach. This desperate courtship strategy betrays a lack of con- fidence in his own intrinsic merit. In the repetition of the invitation in the closing lines the whole tone has changed: there is no more talk of pleasure and a festive spirit. The ageing poet accepts with resignation that the girl he has invited, if she comes at all, is his last love. But he still hopes for something from the songs which the girl is supposed to sing. By this means, both of them could forget their troubles a little.

Again in *Odes* 4. 13 *Audivere Lyce* the decisive shift is conditioned by the consciousness of ageing. Once, when a girl called Lyce was unfaithful to him, Horace wished she would pay for her faithless- ness by growing ugly in old age. Now, many years later, he sees that his wish has been fulfilled—the woman who has grown old and ugly still wants to sing at a dinner-party and arouse erotic feelings like a young girl, but she is scorned by everyone—and Horace's first reaction is a satisfied feeling of revenge. In a more objective tone he reminds Lyce that despite her purple dress and expensive jewellery she cannot bring back her long-departed youth. But this reminder of long ago leads in the fifth strophe to a sudden shock. Horace remembers that in those days, now long past, he was himself carried away by the girl's charm and attractiveness. So his own youth appears before his mind's eye: another girl whom he loved has long been dead and Lyce has become a mockery of youth. It now becomes very clear to him that his own youth too is long past: reflection has taken the place of an emotional triumph. He has become horribly conscious of the general fate of mankind, and his own.

III

One group of Horatian odes might be called poems of reflection.[15] They start from a real situation, and attached to it are thoughts moving often far away from the starting-point. Above all, *Odes* 1. 3, 1. 37, 2. 1, and 3. 29 follow this principle of construction. Since their structure was thoroughly investigated by Eduard Fraenkel,[16] I shall discuss only *Odes* 2.1 *Motum ex Metello*.

The first four strophes give the impression that the theme of the poem is Asinius Pollio's reputation as an author and statesman. Horace first talks about a history of the civil war which Pollio is working on, and hopes that, when he has finished it, Pollio will once again write tragedies; in conclusion he mentions his speeches in court and in the senate, and the triumph he has celebrated. But it was not by chance that Horace put at the beginning the theme of the historical work, the civil war since the time of the first triumvirate, and went into what it meant: for this is a theme which moved him deeply, and moves him still. From the fifth strophe onwards he meditates upon it. The massacres which Pollio will describe appear before his mind's eye. In particular he thinks of Cato's death after the massacre at Thapsos and of the bloodshed which that decisive battle cost. This theme leads once more to a crescendo, when in the passionate questions of lines 25-32 he thinks of the Roman blood spilt over the whole globe. So Horace's passionate involvement leads from thoughts about the difficulty of the writer's task, which stood in the foreground at the beginning of the poem, to the vision of the horrifying tragedy itself, which had led Rome to the edge of the abyss. At the climax of the agitated rhetoric Horace breaks off: this tone does not fit his type of poetry.

Odes 3. 11 *Mercuri nam te* and 3. 27 *Impios parrae* present a variation on this type of structure. These odes begin with a

---

[15] Reitzenstein (1963) 77 [*NJ* 27 (1924) 236] observes in *Odes* 1. 3 'das Gleiten des Gedichts aus dem Erlebnis oder Gefühlsinhalt in die Reflexion'.

[16] Fraenkel (1957) 158-61, 223-9, 234-9; cf. Syndikus (1972-3) i. 58-9, 331-9, 345-51, ii. 250-71.

concrete situation, the former with the courtship of a young girl and the latter with the attempt to prevent a girl from travelling overseas. In both cases there follows an extended description of the fate of mythological figures; these stories are supposed to influence the decision of the girl who is being addressed. But, just as the thoughts in the 'poems of reflection' are weighty, perhaps even excessively so, so too these mythological narratives tend to take on disproportionate dimensions.

IV

Another group of odes are structured by ring composition:[17] after the opening section there comes a second part distinctly different from the beginning in content or mood, while a third part leads back again to the beginning of the poem.

One can count the dedicatory poem to Maecenas, *Odes* I. I, among compositions of this type. Horace begins with a festive address to his important friend and protector, but then in a long list he deals with the different routes people take in their lives. The tension which is established between the address at the beginning and the subsequent enumeration is only resolved at the end of the poem: in lines 29 ff., the poet opposes his own way of life to the others, then in the last two lines he turns to Maecenas again and hopes that with his poetry he will win recognition from his patron.

In *Odes* I. 14 *O navis referent* the beginning and the end, lines 1–3 and 15–20, bring imperatives and warnings; in the middle part these warnings are justified by a description of the horrible damage done to the ship. A link is also forged by the fact that even in the descriptive central section the wrecked ship is constantly addressed in an imploring tone.

In *Odes* I. 16 *O matre pulchra* the theme of the first strophe is taken up again in the last two strophes. The poet would like to be reconciled with a girl whom he had previously attacked in mocking iambics. In the middle section Horace laments the fateful consequences of anger in every area of human life. This com-

---

[17] Reincke (1929) 53–62 puts in this group *Odes* I. 15, I. 16, and I. 32; Brink (1971) 453–5 explains *Odes* 2. 10, 3. 26, and 4. I as examples of ring composition, Schrijvers (1973) 150 *Odes* I. I, I. 16, 4. I, and other less convincing examples. Cf. also Cupaiuolo (1976) 55, and the following paper by R. J. Tarrant.

plaint, which in comparison with the actual situation is rather exaggerated, is obviously meant to raise a smile by its somewhat inappropriate tone, and in this way to help the girl forget her anger, just as Horace has forgotten his own.

Odes. 1. 32 *Poscimus si quid* can also be included here. The first and last strophes contain a hymn-like appeal to the Lesbian lyre, the symbol of lyric poetry. This frames the two middle strophes, which muse upon the poet Alcaeus, in whose style Horace wants to compose his lyric poetry.

In *Odes.* 2. 7 *O saepe mecum,* in which after a long separation Horace greets an old wartime friend, the motif of separation and reunion is also reflected in the structure of the poem. At the beginning Horace remembers experiences they shared and dangers they survived together, as well as hours spent drinking in youthful high spirits. After the two middle strophes, which concern the defeat they suffered together at Philippi and their subsequent long separation, the motif of banqueting is taken up again in the closing strophes. In order to establish their companionship afresh, Horace invites his friend to a reunion party. The connection with the earlier period is underlined by the return of all the motifs with which their former youthful excesses were described. Also the tone, which is unusually loud for one of Horace's drinking-poems, unmistakably takes up the mood at the beginning of the poem.

Another good example of ring composition is *Odes.* 2. 10 *Rectius vives.* In the first and last stanzas the poet speaks to his friend Licinius, using in both cases a nautical metaphor. The intermediate stanzas are sententious and, as Brink says, 'a kind of panel framed by two addresses'.[18]

In *Odes* 3. 25 *Quo me Bacche* the poet appeals to Bacchus at the beginning and the end, and imagines he is being taken away into the wilds of nature, there to be inspired to unheard-of new poetry. These sections frame the beautiful simile of an ecstatic Bacchant, who is gazing spellbound over the Thracian winter landscape. The return to the main theme is accomplished very smoothly in lines 14-16, where Bacchus is addressed as the lord of the Bacchants.

The transition in *Odes.* 4. 1 *Intermissa Venus* is achieved by quite different means. At the beginning Horace turns to the goddess of love with a request for mercy: he has recently been attacked once again by a passion which he considers no longer appropriate to his

[18] Brink (1971) 454; cf. Schrijvers (1973) 144.

advanced age. In the large central part of the ode, from the third strophe to the seventh, a contrasting picture of love is painted: love would be far more appropriate for a noble young Roman. When Horace turns to himself again in line 29, his own unsuitable passion seems to have been overcome by contemplating this beautiful image. But, quite unexpectedly, in line 32 the tone of the opening strophes comes back again. In an excited manner the poet describes afresh how he is overcome by the most violent passion, which does not let go of him even in his dreams.

Odes 4. 5 *Divis orte bonis* begins and ends with direct appeals to the emperor in the manner of a hymn. The similar modes of address, *optime custos* in lines 1-2 and *dux bone* in line 37, bind the two parts together just as much as the almost passionate tone does. The three central strophes of lines 17-28 depict the exact opposite. They praise contemporary blessings more objectively; and here Augustus is mentioned in the third person. The transition glides into the middle section: in the detailed comparison of the third and fourth strophes the emotionally charged tone of the opening strophe is reintroduced; but in the fourth strophe, as the comparison is abandoned, Augustus is already referred to in the third person. In lines 29-30 the closing section begins like a continuation of the objective praise of the middle strophes, but then, almost imperceptibly, in lines 31-2 changes to worshipful address in the second person, in the manner of a hymn.

Comparable in structure is *Odes* 4. 14 *Quae cura patrum*. Here too the two opening strophes start in the tone of a hymn with appeals to Augustus, whose power even the Alpine peoples had just experienced. Then, in the next six strophes, these successes are depicted as his stepsons' deeds; at the beginning and end of this section everything is related back to Augustus by the hint that this has happened on the emperor's orders and through the efforts of his troops. From line 33 the closing section of the poem takes up the hymn-like address to the ruler again. Thus it is not so much contemporary successes that are being celebrated as the good fortune of the whole period of rule since the occupation of Alexandria.[19]

The structures which I have dealt with do not exhaust all possibilities for constructing an ode, but they do encompass a wide

---

[19] Reincke (1929) shows that many more poems are composed in three sections, but these are for the most part not examples of ring composition.

range. An important point is that form in the *Odes* is not detach-
able; rather, it is determined by the content of the individual poem.
The train of thought expresses itself through the ode's structure and
style.

3

Da Capo Structure in Some *Odes* of Horace

R. J. TARRANT

T H E craftsmanship of Horace's lyric poetry is universally admired, but the specifically structural element of these poems has so far received less attention than their verbal and metrical features. This may be in part because, as Robin Nisbet has observed, 'those brought up in a non-classical tradition tend to undervalue structural coherence',[1] partly as well because Horace's manipulation of structural patterns can be so unobtrusive as to escape notice. For much of the last century it was indeed not uncommon among critics of Horace writing in English to doubt his interest in structural coherence; not much more than a generation ago Steele Commager still felt it necessary to defend the study of architectural patterns in the *Odes* against a scepticism illustrated by the following dictum of R. Y. Tyrrell: 'no reader of the odes, however careless, can have failed to notice the extraordinary difficulty of discovering in them anything like a connected train of thought'.[2] There is also—to be brutally honest—something inherently unlovely in the procedures of structural analysis even at their best, while in less careful hands the fitting of poems into structural categories can all

I am grateful to many participants in the Corpus conference for helpful reactions to the oral version of this paper; I owe special thanks to Tony Woodman, who *qua est eius humanitate* sent me valuable written comments and bibliographical suggestions, and to Stephen Harrison for his editorial tact and patience. The paper's basic idea was first aired some years ago in a seminar on lyric poetry led by my colleague Gregory Nagy, and I wish to thank him for generous encouragement and advice.

[1] Nisbet (1962) 182.

[2] Commager (1962) 58, citing Tyrrell (1895) 192–3. Commager himself betrayed the residual influence of that view by referring in the same context to Horace's 'seemingly disheveled progress' (59). Critics who condescend to authors in Tyrrell's lordly manner are often fittingly punished: now it is only a careless reader indeed who could fail to see that Horace's *Odes* are as scrupulously worked out in their movement as in their wording. See e.g. the valuable paper by H. P. Syndikus in this volume.

too easily degenerate into Procrustean pigeon-holing.[3] But the fact that structural analysis has at times been insensitively applied does not mean that there is nothing to be gained from this approach, and indeed the Horatian criticism of the past generation has put it beyond dispute that the movement of thought within odes comprises a vital dimension of their artistry and thus of the pleasure they can give.[4] In this paper I shall discuss some examples of Horace's skill in handling just one structural pattern, here called *da capo* arrangement; by focusing on a single pattern which at least in essence seems relatively uncomplicated I hope to illustrate the variety of effects Horace can achieve within an apparently restricted field of play. To quote Robin Nisbet again—one of those characteristically crisp assertions so much cherished by his friends—'to cover ground is a merit in a poet.'[5] All the more so, one might think, when the poet covers ground while adopting a structure that presents the illusion of standing still.

As my use of the musical term *da capo* suggests, the structure I wish to look at is a tripartite arrangement in which opening and closing sections related either in theme or in language or both are separated by a contrasting middle element. (In shorthand notation the three sections can be designated ABA or more precisely ABA', and I shall use the latter term as synonymous with *da capo* in the course of the discussion.) This pattern is obviously related to the structural device known as 'ring composition', of which it may be seen as a particular type, and listing the features that distinguish it within that broader category will help to define my subject more clearly. *Da capo* structure is marked primarily by its ternary shape, in which a single middle element comes between the responding outer sections; by contrast 'ring composition' can be used to describe any structure in which the final element echoes the first, so that ABCA', ABCDA', and A . . . XA' are as much instances of ring composition as is ABA'. In addition, the designation 'ring composition', at least as usually employed, requires only the

---

[3] Neville Collinge's pioneering attempt (1961) to describe the structure of all the *Odes* encountered severe criticism along these lines from Walther Ludwig (1963) and K. F. Quinn (1962). I have often profited from Collinge's work, but his approach tends to emphasize structural patterns common to groups of poems rather than the function of structure in individual poems.

[4] One need look no further than the introductions to numerous odes in Nisbet and Hubbard (1970, 1978) and Syndikus (1972–3).

[5] Nisbet (1962) 194.

appearance of a single verbal or thematic element at both the beginning and end of the text in question,[6] whereas I am concerned with a pattern that involves a more general sense of return to an opening section; in terms of the structural units of Horace's *Odes*, each A and A' unit comprises at least one entire stanza and usually more. As regards function, the difference is one between a closural device (whose effect on the reading of the text as a whole may be limited) and a means of articulating the movement of an entire poem.[7]

For what I would regard as a clear example of the form and an introduction to the questions it raises, consider Catullus 5:

> (A) Vivamus, mea Lesbia, atque amemus
> rumoresque senum severiorum
> omnes unius aestimemus assis!

> (B) soles occidere et redire possunt;
> nobis, cum semel occidit brevis lux,   5
> nox est perpetua una dormienda.

> (A) da mi basia mille, deinde centum,
> dein mille altera, dein secunda centum,
> deinde usque altera mille, deinde centum.
> dein, cum milia multa fecerimus,   10
> conturbabimus illa, ne sciamus,
> aut ne quis malus invidere possit,
> cum tantum sciat esse basiorum.

On this analysis lines 1–3 comprise an urgent exhortation to Lesbia, 4–6 a contrasting middle section phrased in universal terms and marked by indicative verb-forms (the only ones in the poem), and 7–13 a return to the opening theme, which is now stated in a stronger form (with imperatives replacing subjunctives in 7–9) and at greater length.[8] More specifically, 7–9 are a more explicit equivalent of *amemus* in line 1 and 10–13 elaborate the advice given in lines 2–3.[9] In the broadest terms one could describe the

---

[6] For example, in Ovid *Amores* 1. 5 the echo of *mediam . . . dies exegerat horam* (1) in *medii . . . dies* (26).

[7] On ring composition as a form of closure in the *Odes* cf. Schrijvers (1973) 140 ff., esp. 147 ff.

[8] In Carl Orff's setting of the poem in his 'profane cantata' *Catulli Carmina* (1943, a classical companion to the popular *Carmina Burana*), lines 4–6 form a *dolce espressivo* interlude between a vigorous (*con slancio*) opening and an agitated (*mosso*) final section.

[9] Another pointer to the poem's triadic structure is the echo of *unius* (3) in *una* (6), which serves to mark the endings of the A and B sections.

effects of such a structure by saying that the return of the opening
theme in the final section produces a strong sense of coherence
and closure, while monotony is avoided by presenting the opening
material in a varied or elaborated form (this is why ABA' is a more
precise notation than ABA).[10] But this structure also creates other,
less obvious, effects, some of which are worth noting here since
they will recur in my discussion of several Horatian poems. One
might be called the 'signifying' aspect of *da capo* arrangement: the
form is not simply an element external to the poem's meaning, a
mould into which the content of the poem is, as it were, poured,
but is itself an active component of that content;[11] specifically, the
structure is vehicle of the speaker's thoughts and feelings, and thus
an important means by which the reader constructs the speaker's
persona. In the dramatic monologue that Catullus 5 enacts, the
sombre reflections on mortality in the B section (lines 4-6) moti-
vate Catullus' return to thoughts of immediate enjoyment in the
final section and also explain that section's more insistent tone.[12]
Much of the following discussion will focus on Horace's skill in
relating the use made of ABA' form in any single ode to the ethos
of the poem as a whole, and often to *ēthos* in the strict sense,
i.e. the character and outlook of the speaker. A second point of
importance for my discussion is that ABA' structure can evidently
coexist with other ways of describing a poem's arrangement. With
Catullus 5 the issue is one of competing descriptions. Kenneth
Quinn, for example, analyses the poem into an opening section
(1-3) containing three themes (life, love, external opinion), each
of which is then elaborated in turn (4-6 life, 7-9 love, 10-13
external opinion).[13] This description seems to me less illuminating
than the one I have proposed (and somewhat forced in labelling

[10] In pre-classical musical forms that employ *da capo* structure (e.g. many arias
in baroque opera), the repeat usually differs from the initial statement by virtue of
added ornament (whether specifically notated or left to the taste of the performer);
even when an opening section is repeated without alteration, however, the fact that
it is being heard for a second time distinguishes it from the first hearing.

[11] A similar idea is expressed by Yvan Nadeau's concept of *structurae loquentes*
elaborated in several studies of the *Odes*: see Nadeau (1980), (1983), (1986), and
(1989).

[12] When discussing poems written in the first person which do not explicitly
introduce a persona other than the poet, I normally refer to the speaker as Catullus
or Horace simply to avoid the distracting use of inverted commas or constant
repetition of 'the speaker'; no identification of the poet with the figure in the poems
is intended.

[13] Quinn (1970) 108.

4-6 as an elaboration of *vivamus*), but as a convinced relativist
in matters of interpretation I cannot simply declare it invalid.[14]
Indeed, for my present purpose it is less useful to ask which of these
analyses is 'right' than to grant for the sake of argument that both
are equally valid, i.e. plausibly arguable with reference to the text,
in order to pose a more general question: how do two or more
structural analyses of a poem coexist or, more precisely, how does
the existence of more than one possible way of understanding a
poem's structure affect a reader's experience of the poem? In the
case of Catullus 5, it does not seem to me likely that a reader will
experience the poem according to more than one structural
arrangement simultaneously (i.e. during a single reading). With
Horace's *Odes*, on the other hand, I shall try to show that a
reader's awareness of structural multiplicity is often integral to the
poems' intellectual and emotional effect.

    Approximately a dozen odes of Horace can, in my view, be help-
fully described in terms of ABA' or *da capo* arrangement, while
almost an equal number evoke or relate to this pattern without
actually exemplifying it.[15] Some of my alleged examples may be
successfully challenged as being better analysed in other ways; the
essential point for my argument is that the pattern appears often
enough to be recognizable as a pattern for a reader of the *Odes*.[16]
In none of the Horatian instances is the ABA' pattern adhered to
as neatly as I believe it to be in Catullus 5. In particular, Horace
generally avoids a straightforward repetition of the opening theme
in the final section: the poem's language invites the reader to see
the concluding part as a return, but the point to which one returns
is no longer the same as that from which one set out. Twists of
this kind lend themselves readily to ironic play. The most famous
example—too familiar to need detailed discussion—is 'Integer

    [14] Especially since as skilled a reader as Tony Woodman informs me that he finds
Quinn's analysis more persuasive than mine.
    [15] Instances of ABA' arrangement: 1. 16, 17, 22, 28, 31, 32; 2. 7, 10, 14; 3.
9; 4. 1, 4; poems in which ABA' form is evoked or alluded to: 1. 5, 7, 9, 29, (37?);
2. 6, 13; 3. 25; 4. 13, 14. On 1. 37 see n. 26 below.
    [16] Some of the poems I regard as exhibiting ABA' structure were grouped by
Collinge (see Collinge (1961) under the heading 'symmetrical'; 80, 112-14 and
following note). Previously Gerhard Reincke, in a Berlin thesis directed by Eduard
Norden (Reincke 1929), had attempted an analysis of the *Odes* in general in terms
of tripartite structure; Reincke's categories, however, are too broad and too
mechanically applied to be of much help in revealing the effects of structural
patterning on individual odes.

vitae' (1. 22), which opens by stating a premiss in general terms ('Wherever he may go, the virtuous man is protected by his upright nature') followed by a central section offering a proof of the premiss based on an especially striking example. The closing section announces itself as a return by echoing the geographical extremes of the opening, but the strictly logical conclusion ('Place me wherever you may, I shall be safe because of my virtuous nature') is replaced by an ingenuously warped inference from the central exemplum: 'Place me wherever you may, I shall be safe because I sing of Lalage.' Here the relation between thought and its structural embodiment and the *ēthos* of the speaker is especially clear: the skewed logic is a symptom of the sweetly foolish infatuation that Horace affects as speaker while deflating it from his position as implied author. A comparable but subtler humorous twist can be seen in 1. 16 *O matre pulchra filia pulchrior*, whose three distinct units can be designated A 1–4; B 5–21; A' 22–8: the second reference to *iambi* in 24 (recalling 2–3 'quem criminosis cumque voles modum | pones iambis') strongly marks the return of the opening theme after the central disquisition on anger, a section whose inordinate length itself constitutes a playful anger, a stretching of the form. As often, the A' element presents the themes of the opening in expanded and elaborated form: only now does the reader learn that the offending verses had their origin in a lovers' quarrel which the ode is intended to heal. The delayed revelation and the absurdly inflated sermon on anger are not, however, merely jokes played on the reader; they also hint at the ironic outlook of the speaker, who while seeming to accept responsibility for the rift contrives at the same time to imply that the fault really lies with the woman for her excessively violent reaction.

The structural device of an ostensible concluding 'return' which is significantly different from the opening assumes a more serious form in the ode to Pompeius (2. 7).

> O saepe mecum tempus in ultimum
> deducte Bruto militiae duce,
>   quis te redonavit Quiritem
>   dis patriis Italoque caelo,
>
> Pompei, meorum prime sodalium?   5
> cum quo morantem saepe diem mero
>   fregi coronatus nitentis
>   malobathro Syrio capillos.

tecum Philippos et celerem fugam
sensi relicta non bene parmula,   10
    cum fracta virtus et minaces
        turpe solum tetigere mento.

sed me per hostis Mercurius celer
denso paventem sustulit aere;
    te rursus in bellum resorbens   15
        unda fretis tulit aestuosis.

ergo obligatam redde Iovi dapem
longaque fessum militia latus
    depone sub lauru mea, nec
        parce cadis tibi destinatis.   20

oblivioso levia Massico
ciboria exple, funde capacibus
    unguenta de conchis. quis udo
        deproperare apio coronas

curatve myrto? quem Venus arbitrum   25
dicet bibendi? non ego sanius
    bacchabor Edonis. recepto
        dulce mihi furere est amico.

The poem's seven stanzas clearly divide into a 2 + 2 + 3 arrangement, described by Nisbet and Hubbard as 'two groups of two
stanzas to set out the antecedent circumstances' followed by 'a
crowning group of three stanzas' that draw the 'necessary consequences' (on 17 *ergo*). Yet at least as obvious as this logically
orientated structure, and verbally more prominent, is the link
between opening and concluding sections: the festive reception
anticipated in the final stanzas (especially in the details of 21–3)
pointedly replicates the pre-Philippi drinking sessions nostalgically
recalled in the second stanza (6–8, an echo also noted by Nisbet
and Hubbard on 21 'oblivioso . . . Massico'). This use of ABA'
structure implicitly treats Philippi and its aftermath, the subject of
the middle section, as a lamentable but temporary interruption in
the friends' association; the return to the opening theme here
corresponds to Pompeius' literal return to civilian life in Italy.[17]
(It is noteworthy that the poem's two instances of *militia* appear in
the same position in stanzas 1 and 5, in both cases referring to a

---

[17] The fact that the third stanza (the start of my B section) opens with *tecum*,
repeating *mecum* in line 1, underscores the closeness that the battle itself disrupts.
Collinge (1961) 145–9 offers an interpretation of the poem based on a different view
of its structure (1–16 circular movement; 17–28 linear progression).

time firmly in the past.) The connections between opening and concluding sections can be pressed harder: the exotic Syrian *malobathrum* of the earlier drinking-parties (8) is 'corrected' to respectably Italian Massic wine (21), and the drinking that Horace calls for in the closing stanzas is implicitly portrayed as more appropriate, since it is enjoyed at home and in peacetime, than drinking to lessen the tedium of campaigning overseas under Brutus. (Nisbet and Hubbard remark on the ironic deflation of military language in 6-7 'morantem saepe diem mero | fregi', and also perhaps in 'coronatus'; the irony distances both Horace and Pompeius from their youthful adherence to the losing side, by implying that they were not really all that serious about it, that serving with Brutus was more a lark than a cause.) The final stanzas, therefore, do not hold out the prospect of simply regaining former happiness but of replacing it with something better; hence the greater length of the concluding section and its expanded treatment of the theme it shares with the opening are appropriate to the section's corrective purpose. So far I have tried to show how close attention to the poem's structure sheds light on the rhetorical strategy of the speaker, but the overall view of the poem that results does not differ from that found in most discussions: that is, Horace welcomes the return to Italy of Pompeius—apparently a more obdurate Republican than Horace himself—and gently urges him to put aside the difficult past and accept the blessings of the new regime.[18] But by depicting a return (to past friendship) that is simultaneously a departure (from past loyalties), the poem creates an inherently unstable construct. 'Once we used to drink together, now we can drink together again' reduces a complex history to a straightforward occasion for rejoicing; we can admire the tact (or censure the evasiveness) of the approach, but the poem also

---

[18] For a recent and elegant formulation of this view see Murray (1993 edn.) 100: '[the ode] suitably subordinates . . . themes of gratitude to the feast for the return, and to memories of the past, purged by poetic allusion from the taint of treason. . . . On such an occasion the past need not be forgotten, but may be transformed through the poetic vocabulary of the symposium; the poet celebrates a genuine friendship and the lost idealism of his youth, without offending the present age.' On the other hand, Nisbet and Hubbard (1978) 109 express distaste over the 'whimsicality' of Horace's treatment of the past ('it is disconcerting to find him describing so terrible an experience with discreet jokes and elegant allusions'); the comment implicitly accepts the standard reading and on that basis judges the poem to be flawed, but Nisbet and Hubbard's discomfort could also be seen as pointing to an ambivalence built into the ode.

permits and perhaps even invites us to ask how successful this application of selective memory really is. The opening stanzas portray Horace and Pompeius as inseparable companions: *mecum* (1), *cum quo* (6), *tecum* (9). The final section attempts to reassert that bond: Nisbet and Hubbard alertly remark on 19 'sub lauru mea' that *mea* is emphatic and is balanced by *tibi* in line 20; they conclude, 'as in old days "you and I" is once more appropriate'. This is surely the effect the speaker wishes to produce, but does it actually come off? 'Beneath *my* bay-tree' and 'wine-casks set aside for *you*' arguably create a juxtaposition but not a reunion, and Horace's next words are, perhaps significantly, addressed not to Pompeius but to his own servants. His frantic jollity (cf. especially 26–7 'non ego sanius | bacchabor Edonis') has about it a feeling of forced extravagance, as if he is trying to compensate for Pompeius' inability or unwillingness to join in. Horace and Pompeius are indeed together again; but while at one level the poem presents their meeting as a return to happier days, at another it may imply the impossibility of recovering their earlier closeness.

Rectius vives (2. 10) is an ode in which evocation of ABA' structure rather than its actual use is central to the poem's effect; in fact, adroit manipulation of structure is (for me at least) the spice that saves the poem from banality.[19]

Rectius vives, Licini, neque altum
semper urgendo neque, dum procellas
cautus horrescis, nimium premendo
    litus iniquum.

auream quisquis mediocritatem   5
diligit, tutus caret obsoleti
sordibus tecti, caret invidenda
    sobrius aula.

saevius ventis agitatur ingens
pinus et celsae graviore casu   10
decidunt turres feriuntque summos
    fulgura montis.

sperat infestis, metuit secundis
alteram sortem bene praeparatum
pectus. informis hiemes reducit   15
    Iuppiter, idem

---

[19] The importance of structure in this poem and Horace's skill in handling it are given due weight by both Nisbet and Hubbard and Syndikus, though my analysis differs in its specifics from theirs.

summovet. non, si male nunc, et olim
sic erit. quondam cithara tacentem
suscitat Musam neque semper arcum
    tendit Apollo. 20
rebus angustis animosus atque
fortis appare; sapienter idem
contrahes vento nimium secundo
    turgida vela.

The ode is remarkable for being constructed entirely from gnomic or moralizing statements, a fact which itself suggests that close attention should be paid to their arrangement, since movement of thought within an intellectual argument here takes the place more often occupied by an emotional or dramatic scenario. The opening and closing stanzas are overtly linked by being the only parts of the poem addressed specifically to Licinius and also by the sea imagery they share; furthermore, each also prescribes behaviour for a contrasted set of situations ('neque altum semper urgendo neque . . . nimium premendo litus iniquum'; 'rebus angustis . . . vento nimium secundo'). The poem thus gives an initial impression of *da capo* arrangement. But in fact the opening and closing prescriptions are quite distinct: one advises avoidance of extremes, the other adapting oneself to changing conditions; in addition, the specific precepts themselves vary accordingly (don't *always* press out to sea or hug the shore; act *in opposition* to prevailing conditions so as to anticipate eventual change). This shift is accomplished in the poem's central section (5–20), which begins by recasting the dual statement of the opening stanza in even more general terms (5–8), then focuses in on one of the extremes to be avoided (9–12: the prominent are at greater risk, a development of the implications of *invidenda* in line 7); the fourth stanza then introduces what will become the poem's second theme, the need to anticipate and adapt to change. (Having 'mutability' appear as an unannounced second subject is itself surely a piece of structural wit.)

By restating this new theme in the last stanza in language that strongly recalls the opening one, Horace highlights his redefinition of the opening idea by calling attention to the shift of focus within the ode, and also invites the reader to recognize the close connection between the original and the redefined motif: the 'bene praeparatum pectus' will both avoid extremes and adapt itself to changing conditions. Indeed, on a rereading it becomes clear that

the second theme is already potentially present in the opening
stanza: *semper* in line 2 and 'dum procellas cautus horrescis' in
lines 2–3, which at first may seem extraneous to the contrast
between 'altum urgendo' and 'premendo litus', in fact contain in
embryo the motifs of consistency and response to circumstances
that will form the thematic material of the poem's second half.[20] At
this point the reader can see the end of the poem as simultaneously
a return to and a departure from the opening. Another way of
describing the effect is to say that Horace is punning on two structural patterns: the bipartite division suggested by the appearance
of a new second theme just after the midpoint (1–12 = A; 13–24
= B)[21] and the tripartite arrangement implied by the clear echo
of the opening at the close (1–4 = A; 5–20 = B; 21–4 = A).[22]
Neither pattern entirely displaces the other in the reader's mind,
and the interplay between the two reflects the close relationship in
thought between the poem's two main themes.

Such structural punning is hardly unique to *Odes* 2. 10: it can
be seen in a different form in the Soracte ode, whose opening and
closing scenes are diametrically opposed in their physical details
and yet genuinely parallel at the thematic level as images of enjoying the present moment, in keeping with the advice given in the
generalizing central section. In terms of structural notation, the
poem's external referents describe an ABC pattern, in which the
central section serves as a bridge or hinge to a final section that
marks a shift away from rather than a return to the beginning,
while its thematic movement introduces a significant *da capo*
component.[23] A. Y. Campbell, the first critic to make clear the
thematic connection between the opening and closing scenes,
concluded epigrammatically that the ode was a circle, not a

---

[20] The point was grasped by Collinge (1961: 71), but not precisely enough put
by him ('the first four verses present both themes'); cf. Ludwig (1963) 173,
Syndikus (1972–3) i. 401, n. 11.

[21] Syndikus (1972–3) i. 401 ff.

[22] I owe this use of the term 'punning' to describe a play with non-verbal
elements to Christina Kraus, who has applied it to the plot of Euripides' *Herakles* in
a forthcoming article.

[23] For a relatively clear-cut example of ABC structure cf. *Odes* 1. 34 *Parcus
deorum cultor*, which displays, at least on the surface, the sort of progressive,
logical movement that 1. 22 seems to promise but playfully subverts (see above).
An especially striking use of ABC arrangement appears in 2. 13 *Ille et nefasto*, where
the emotional distance between the 'truculent rhetoric' of the opening and the
'serene harmonies' of the close is central to the poem's meaning (cf. Nisbet and
Hubbard 1978: 205).

parabola;[24] we may now adjust this remark to say that it is both
at once, and that its success in combining these two formal move-
ments is a mark of its poetic quality.[25] Now some degree of interplay between ABA' and ABC structure is inevitable in any poem
whose final section suggest a return to the opening, since in terms
of either language or content a literal return (i.e. an exact repetition) is impossible; what is striking is Horace's ability to exploit the
tension between these patterns, so that his readers often experience
the pleasure (one of the most intense poetry can offer) of recognizing two things as similar and at the same time different, as
separate and yet inextricably linked.[26]

Perhaps the most powerful use of *da capo* structure in the *Odes*
appears in the poem that opens the fourth book, *Intermissa Venus*.

> Intermissa, Venus, diu
>> rursus bella moves? parce precor, precor.
> non sum qualis eram bonae
>> sub regno Cinarae. desine, dulcium
>
> mater saeva Cupidinum,   5
>> circa lustra decem flectere mollibus
> iam durum imperiis; abi
>> quo blandae iuvenum te revocant preces.
>
> tempestivius in domum
>> Pauli purpureis ales oloribus   10
> comissabere Maximi,
>> si torrere iecur quaeris idoneum.
>
> namque et nobilis et decens
>> et pro sollicitis non tacitus reis
> et centum puer artium   15
>> late signa feret militiae tuae,

---

[24] Campbell (1924) 224, quoted approvingly by Wilkinson (1945) 131.

[25] As is regularly the case in Horace's finest poems, structural patterning is itself
a reflection of theme: cyclical and linear movement are simultaneously present in
the poem's arrangement just as in our experience of time the circular progression
of the seasons carries us forward on the path from youth to old age.

[26] The Cleopatra ode (1. 37) may also complicate an apparent ABC structure
with suggestions of ABA'. The poem comprises three clearly demarcated sections (1–
12 *ebria*; 12 *sed*–21 *monstrum*; 21 *quae*–32), of which the first and third are virtually identical in length. It is customary to treat the depiction of Cleopatra in the final
section as simply inverting that of the opening (the end heroizing and sympathetic,
the start hostile and denigratory), but in a forthcoming study Michèle Lowrie argues
for a closer connection between these sections than has been recognized.

> et, quandoque potentior
>   largi muneribus riserit aemuli,
> Albanos prope te lacus
>   ponet marmoream sub trabe citrea.   20
>
> illic plurima naribus
>   duces tura lyraque et Berecyntia
> delectabere tibia
>   mixtis carminibus non sine fistula;
>
> illic bis pueri die   25
>   numen cum teneris virginibus tuum
> laudantes pede candido
>   in morem Salium ter quatient humum.
>
> me nec femina nec puer
>   iam nec spes animi credula mutui   30
> nec certare iuvat mero
>   nec vincire novis tempora floribus.
>
> sed cur, heu, Ligurine, cur
>   manat rara meas lacrima per genas?
> cur facunda parum decoro   35
>   inter verba cadit lingua silentio?
>
> nocturnis ego somniis
>   iam captum teneo, iam volucrem sequor
> te per gramina Martii
>   Campi, te per aquas, dure, volubilis.   40

The first two stanzas protest the poet's unsuitability for a new love
and entreat Venus to return to her younger worshippers. A stately
central section of five stanzas proposes as a fitting substitute the
youthful paragon Paullus Fabius Maximus, then with an emphatic
me in line 29 the poem reverts to its opening focus and motifs,
expanding the implications of 'mollibus iam durum imperiis' into a
full stanza. At line 32 the poem seems to have come full circle,
when suddenly Horace's carefully maintained composure breaks
and the poem ends in passionate longing for the unattainable
Ligurinus.[27] As in the odes already discussed, the structural pattern
here is not simply a framework into which the poem's material is

---

[27] The temporary impression of circular structure followed by a strong new forward movement may be compared to Collinge's description of *Odes* 1. 4: 'sixteen
verses employ all possible devices to indicate their symmetry and roundness; twelve
more exert themselves to drive the thought straight along' (1961: 145). In 4. 1 it
seems legitimate to speak of 'false closure' at line 32; for the phenomenon see
Fowler (1989a) 97–101.

fitted but is itself a signifying element in the poem's emotional drama: the clear-cut, almost frigidly controlled, arrangement of the first eight stanzas mirrors and embodies the protective crust of indifference to love that Horace is attempting to sustain, and the pat closure attempted by the ABA' pattern enacts at the level of form the resistance to new and potentially painful experience (poetic as well as erotic) that is in the end swept aside by ungovernable desire. But Horace's exploitation of structure is still more complex than this analysis would suggest. At one level—in this instance roughly corresponding to a first reading—the poem's ending may come as a surprise, overturning the expectations created by the rhetoric and incipient *da capo* movement of its first eight stanzas. But at another, which perhaps becomes clear only on subsequent readings, the final stanzas entail a return to and reinterpretation of the opening, in which Ligurinus is revealed as the earthly counterpart of Venus and the unstated cause of the poet's appeal to the goddess;[28] in that light the poet's struggle against Venus' 'mollia imperia' is shown to be doomed from the outset and the goddess's response to the plea 'parce precor, precor' becomes in retrospect all too predictable.[29] Taking this line of argument further, we might say that from the perspective of later readings it is rather Horace's resistance to Venus that appears anomalous and surprising, and that the ostensibly sudden collapse after line 32 is in fact required to restore normal conditions, to save the poem from an emotionally 'wrong' ending.[30] Such an inference is supported by the poem's use of intertextual and generic allusion. The opening two stanzas evoke Sappho's invocation to Aphrodite (1 L-P) but with a complete reversal of situation and intent: the

[28] 'Venus is, after all, still present in his life in the person of the boy Ligurinus, her emblem' (Putnam 1986: 37). A verbal sign of this connection is the echo of the repeated *precor* from line 2 (addressed to Venus) in the double *cur* of line 33 (addressed to Ligurinus); it may also be relevant that in the language of elegy *parce, precor* can be as readily addressed to a beloved as to Venus: cf. Tib. 1. 5. 7, 1. 2. 97.

[29] Syndikus (1972–3) ii. 289 rightly stresses the intensity of expression in *parce precor, precor*, but I find that it is only *after* reading the poem's conclusion that the helplessness of the words registers with full force.

[30] Davis (1991: 61) observes that Horace's surrender 'rescues . . . Eros . . . from a scandalous abegnation'. To compare small (in scale, at least) with large, there is a similarity between the suspense created by Horace's resistance to Venus and that generated in a Greek tragedy—Sophocles' *Philoctetes*, for example—when the action seems headed for a conclusion that the audience knows is mythologically impossible.

goddess is not bidden to come but to leave (*abi*), it is unnamed
iuvenes, not the speaker, who summon her with prayer, and it is
Venus, not Sappho/Horace, who is 'once again' acting as before
(compare Horace's *rursus* in line 2 with the threefold δηῦτε of
Sappho 15-18).[31] The opening of 4. 1 even more explicitly cites
Horace's own earlier erotic poetry, repeating in line 5 the phrase
'mater saeva Cupidinum' that begins *Odes* 1. 19, in which Venus
compels Horace 'finitis animum reddere amoribus' (line 4). These
echoes make clear the extent to which the poem's attempt to
renounce Venus constitutes a sharp break with Horace's lyric past;
the reader will probably feel intuitively that such an enterprise is
not likely to succeed, and in particular the quotation of 1. 19, an
ode in which Horace makes no attempt to resist Venus' power and
only hopes to lessen its violence, makes his eventual surrender in
4. 1 appear even more clearly foreordained.[32]

It is good Horatian practice to end not on a note of high seriousness but with a graceful descent to a lighter vein. I shall therefore
conclude by looking at one of his most engaging poems, the lyric
dialogue '*Donec gratus eram tibi*' (3. 9).

> 'Donec gratus eram tibi
>   nec quisquam potior bracchia candidae
> cervici iuvenis dabat,
>   Persarum vigui rege beatior.'
>
> 'donec non alia magis   5
>   arsisti neque erat Lydia post Chloen,
> multi Lydia nominis
>   Romana vigui clarior Ilia.'
>
> 'me nunc Thressa Chloe regit,
>   dulcis docta modos et citharae sciens,   10
> pro qua non metuam mori,
>   si parcent animae fata superstiti.'

[31] On these and other connections between *Odes* 4. 1 and Sappho 1 see Putnam
(1986) 39-41 and Nagy (1994).

[32] Davis (1991) helpfully discusses 4. 1 in conjunction with 1. 19 and 3. 26, but
his rubrics 'abortive disavowal' and 'failed renunciation' of eros do not actually
apply to 1. 19 and are debatable for 3. 26—cf. C. P. Jones (1971) 81-3. It is also
useful to compare 4. 1 with the opening poem of Ovid's *Amores*, which resembles it
in general plot, in its programmatic position, and in the appearance of an extended
but futile effort by the poet at dissuading the love-god as its central section (5-20).
Horace's *me nec femina nec puer* (sc. *iuvat*), line 29, finds a particularly close
parallel in Ovid's couplet 'nec mihi materia est numeris levioribus apta, | aut puer
aut longas compta puella comas' (19-20).

'me torret face mutua
   Thurini Calais filius Ornyti,
pro quo bis patiar mori   15
   si parcent puero fata superstiti.'

'quid si prisca redit Venus
   diductosque iugo cogit aeneo,
si flava excutitur Chloe
   reiectaeque patet ianua Lydiae.'   20

'quamquam sidere pulchrior
   ille est, tu levior cortice et improbo
iracundior Hadria,
   tecum vivere amem, tecum obeam libens.'

Here the part played by *da capo* structure is unmistakable (and the musical origins of the term especially apt, since it is hard to speak of this poem without invoking musical analogies). In the opening and closing sections (1-8, 17-24) Horace and Lydia speak of themselves as happily united (a past state recalled in the first two stanzas, a future one anticipated in the last two), while in the contrasting middle section (9-16) each professes to have left the other for a far superior mate. Verbal links reinforce the ABA' pattern, with the trio of comparatives in 1-8 (*potior, beatior, clarior*) balanced by a second set in 21-4 (*pulchrior, levior, iracundior*) and the names of Chloe and Lydia coupled in 19-20 as they were in 6. Finally, the suggestion that opens the final stanza-pair, 'quid si prisca redit Venus?', openly announces the concluding section as a return to the state described in the opening. But in this poem as well ABA' arrangement coexists with other equally real structuring principles. Here that interplay is particularly intricate, since at least two further ways of structuring the poem are clearly at work: the progressive (ABC) movement from past (1-8) to present (9-16) to future (17-24), and the amoebean format that divides the poem into three parallel dialogic exchanges (ABABAB).[33] The result is a poem unique even for Horace in its overt exploitation of multiple structural patterns, but at the same time typically Horatian in using structure as a vehicle for the depiction of *ēthos*. Since the poem consists entirely of words spoken by its dramatis personae, we may and indeed must interpret the arrangement of their speeches as well as their content as manifestations of character. In this respect Horace's poem differs fundamentally from Catullus 45

[33] I am indebted to David West for insisting on the importance of this last point.

Acmen Septimius, with which it is inevitably compared; there the poet's voice, observing and commenting, is even more prominent than those of the overheard lovers. Horace's characters are also remote in temperament from their precursors in Catullus: deeply attached to each other but far too worldly (and wary) to blurt out their feelings, they plot their ultimate reconciliation through a stylized series of moves that flatters their sense of sophistication while allowing each to preserve at least a modicum of face.[34] As Commager nicely puts it, 'Horace's two lovers derive as much satisfaction from their own cleverness as from the end to which it is directed' (1962: 57–8); this self-consciousness has a formal equivalent in the ode's many-layered structural patterning, which makes it a poem that is in a real sense 'about' its own exquisite design.[35]

The symmetries of 3. 9 are conspicuous enough in themselves to call attention to this aspect of the poem, but its placement in the collection may supply another reason for seeing its structure as remarkable. The first book of *Odes* contains more poems in or related to the ABA' pattern than any other single book, which is not in itself surprising given the larger number of poems in that book; proportionally the pattern is found almost as frequently in book 2.[36] What does seem noteworthy is that ABA' structure is almost completely absent from the third book; very tentatively, I would suggest that Horace in arranging the contents of *Odes* 1–3 for publication tried to give a sense of greater structural freedom and fluidity to the final book. (Another structural observation points in the same direction: book 3 contains several odes whose opening sections are—or at least appear to be—only obliquely related to the body of the poem, e.g., 11, 16, 19, 27.) Given Horace's overall avoidance of ABA' pattern in the third book, it is tempting to ask whether its use here—and in so strict a form—is another way of distancing the poem from Horace's usual mode of

[34] Though Lydia scores higher in this regard by suggesting, in 21–3 *quamquam . . . Hadria*, that Horace's inconstancy and foul temper were responsible for their breakup and that she remains well aware of his shortcomings.

[35] Nisbet (1962) 185 ff. compared Horace's poem unfavourably with its Catullan counterpart, complaining that its language was excessively 'processed and de-natured' and its sentiments not 'true to life'. The terms of this judgement could be questioned (starting with 'life'); I would say instead that each poem successfully depicts the *ēthos* of its respective characters. For a stimulating comparison of the two poems see David West's paper in the present volume.

[36] See above, n. 15.

expression, that is, whether the poem's structure is to be viewed ironically in the larger context of the collection. The ode's pert grace, and its portrayal of genuine emotion beneath a smoothly polished surface, have won for it the epithet 'Mozartian';[37] but I wonder if its effect in context is not rather that of Mozart as evoked in, say, *Der Rosenkavalier*, a style recalled with affection but also with a keen sense of its otherness.[38]

Given the topic of this paper, a conclusion that echoes the opening seems *de rigueur*; for brevity's sake, however, I shall not attempt a true *da capo* but only a slight piece of ring composition. Few texts of classical literature are as apparently familiar, or as firmly canonical, as Horace's *Odes*, yet few other texts have profited as much from renewed study in recent years. Much of the impetus for this quickened interest has been provided by the work of Robin Nisbet, and if my remarks in this paper have added in any way to our appreciation of his favourite poet, I happily offer them as an expression of thanks to the teacher to whom I owe so much.

[37] 'It is a blithe Mozartian duet, ending just at the right point where the reader can sense a deepening of feeling' (Williams 1969: 76).

[38] *Der Rosenkavalier* is invoked by Michael Putnam for a different purpose in his discussion of *Odes* 4. 1 (Putnam 1986: 41): 'Ligurinus is to Horace what Octavian is to the Marschallin.'

4

Design and Allusion in Horace, *Odes* 1. 6

M. C. J. PUTNAM

I N the extraordinary sequence of poems that initiates Horace's lyric masterpiece, *Odes* 1. 6, the *recusatio* wherein the poet cedes to Varius the task of celebrating the praises of Agrippa and Caesar, stands out from its predecessors. It is the first poem in the collection to deal strictly with poetics, the traditions and content of poetry. The initial priamel had pitted the poet's vocation as lyric bard, and its dependency on Maecenas, against a series of other *métiers*. It deftly criticizes them to the advantage of only two figures, the singular individual (*est qui*) who breaks the day with wine (and the poem in its midst), and then the bard himself.[1] Likewise the third ode, addressed to Virgil, has been well taken to adumbrate the hazards of the poet's career, embarked perhaps on the treacherous seas of the *Aeneid*. But only in the sixth ode does Horace's speaker address directly the question of what it means to practise the lyric art, especially by contradistinction to his contemporary and friend Varius, who is imagined as about to follow in the footsteps of earlier epicists, primarily Homer.[2] The august topics of military eulogy will be Varius' to pursue. Horace's speaker, who must come close here to being a mouthpiece for the poet himself, he who alone can speak with authority for the grandeur and power of lyric, remains loyal to the slim, Callimachean spirit with allegiance to *convivia* and lovers' spats. (I need scarcely point out the rich self-irony of Horace's stance, given his work in progress, one of the most astonishing collections of lyric verse in the Western tradition.)

---

[1] Dunn (1989) has recently proposed, surely correctly, that the figure at ease near the sacred spring (*Odes* 1. 1. 19–22) is also a version of Horace himself.

[2] Santirocco (1986) 33–6 illustrates how Horace's apologia takes its place smoothly in the intellectual programme of the 'parade' odes which open book 1. It both follows and precedes two odes which deal in large measure with convivial (*Odes* 1. 4, 1. 7) and erotic (*Odes* 1. 5, 1. 8) themes.

Verbal repetition is a main structuring principle of the poem. *Scriberis*, the ode's initial word, is carefully echoed in *scripserit*, the only verb of the fourth stanza, and *nos*, with which the second stanza commences, is repeated with insistence at the opening of the fifth, final strophe. The poet thus puts particular emphasis on the third stanza, which this patterning surrounds centrally, and on the last quartet of lines, which form the climax of the sequence. These central and last strophes are both concerned with present time, with direct lyric intensity which takes us from negative—the speaker's *nec . . . conamur* complemented by the Muse's prohibition (*vetat*)—to positive, to the continuing force of *cantamus*. By contrast with this immediacy, *scriberis* and *scripserit* look to a contemplated future or to a future which has become past. Likewise the subjects of these verbs—Agrippa's 'you', to be heralded by Varius who will take up the task which the speaker refuses, and the yet more distant *quis*—remain removed from the reiterated, authorial 'I' which initiates the final stanza.

  The double use of *scribere* serves another important purpose. These are the only two occasions on which the verb is admitted into Horace's lyric corpus, and its emphatic presence underscores the impossibility, for him at least, of effectuating the encomiastic enterprise which Horace claims to entrust to Varius.³ Writing and its product, the epic of praise, are as foreign to the speaker's

---

³ Nisbet and Hubbard (1970), commenting on line 1, remark that 'The verb is rather prosaic and suits historical epic.' Only in the fourth book of odes does Horace associate writing with lyric by mention of his *chartae* which will celebrate the deeds of Censorinus (*Odes* 4. 8. 21) and Lollius (*Odes* 4. 9. 31). But in the case of both Censorinus and Lollius Horace's speaker is suggesting that only lyric which takes on the attributes of epic will be worthy to tell of their heroism. For them he can adapt epic modes—in this case the notion of writing—to lyric and subtly draw to himself a parallel with Maeonian Homer (*Odes* 4. 9. 5, the only other use of the adjective *Maeonius* in Horace besides *Odes* 1. 6. 2). His purposes in *Odes* 1. 6 are quite the opposite.

  In the *Satires* on the other hand, at the beginning of Horace's career, *scribere*, when associated specifically with poetry, is regularly concerned with the composition of satire. The exceptions are *Sat.* 1. 10. 16 (on the *scripta* of Old Comedy), 2. 5. 74 (on the courting for his money of someone who writes bad 'songs' *scribet mala carmina vecors*—where the anomalous complementarity of *scribere* and *carmina* is to the point), and 2. 1. 16–17, where Horace puts into the mouth of Trebatius, addressing the 'Horace' of the poem, the following suggestion for a poetic undertaking: 'attamen et iustum poteras et scribere fortem | Scipiadam ut sapiens Lucilius.' Since these lines refer directly back to 9–10 'laude | Caesaris invicti res dicere' and anticipate the opening of *Odes* 1. 6 (*Scriberis . . . fortis*), we are no doubt meant to understand that *scribere* refers to the composition of epic.

  Horace's only other association, in the pre-lyric corpus, of *scribere* with a form of

ambitions towards lyric song as *scribere* is to his lexical usage in the *Odes*.[4] The same holds true of the verb *conari*. It too appears only here in Horace's lyric writings. Initiating the poem's negative, focal stanza, it also points, by lexical anomaly, to non-lyric expectations, i.e. to what the speaker pronounces will be attempted by Varius but which he himself cannot aim to fulfil.[5]

The prosaic quality of this eulogistic endeavour is apparent from the very start in the phrase *rem . . . gesserit*.[6] But in more subtle

verse-writing occurs at *Epod.* 11. 2, when the speaker uses the phrase *scribere versiculos* (which he borrows from Cat. 50. 4, where the metre is hendecasyllabic) to refer most likely to the composition of the *Epodes* themselves.

Since throughout the *Satires* Horace also carefully associates his own 'writing' with *sermo*, speech or talk, most prominently at *Sat.* 1. 4. 41-2 'si qui scribat uti nos | sermoni propiora', we can draw the general conclusion that in his work before the *Odes* Horace links satire, epic, and *iambi* (whether his poetry or that of others) with 'speech' and writing. It remains for *Odes* 1. 6 to take the next, obvious step and conjoin lyric with singing and song.

[4] *Canere* and *Cantare* are, of course, closely associated throughout the *Odes* with the production of lyric song, whether the singer be Horace's 'I' (e.g. *Odes* 1. 22. 10, 3. 1. 4, 3. 28. 9, 4. 15. 32), Alcaeus (*Odes* 1. 32. 10), or Pindar (*Odes* 4. 2. 13). The contexts in the *Satires* where Horace employs either of the two verbs are worthy of note: 1. 2. 107, where the lover sings a Latin version of an epigram of Callimachus (*AP* 12. 102 = 31Pf.); 1. 3. 2, of *cantores* of the ilk of Tigellius; 1. 5. 15, describing a drunken sailor singing to his absent mistress; 1. 9. 25, as the bore boasts that his singing might elicit the envy of Hermogenes (Tigellius)—scarcely a recommendation; 1. 10. 43, of the *senarii* of Pollio's tragedies. If, then, the *Satires* associate writing with the genres of satire, comedy, and epic, they link singing with tragedy and elegy.

[5] As commentary on the distinction developed over the course of *Odes* 1. 6 between Varius and 'Horace' we might note a comparable polarity in *Odes* 2. 12 between the 'walking history' (*pedestribus historiis*, 9-10) through which Maecenas will 'tell' (*dices*, 10) the battles of Caesar and the *cantus* (14) which the speaker's Muse bids him sing about Licymnia's beauty (of which task, however, Horace also uses the word *dicere*). (It is not by chance that the poet labels the 'Muse' of his *Satires* as *pedestris* at *Sat.* 2. 6. 17.) The use of *dicere* at *Odes* 1. 6. 5 deserves special consideration. If we are to imagine Horace 'refusing' to write some grander, more Pindaric version of lyric than is his present wont to serve as a medium for the presentation of Agrippa's *aristeia*, then *dicere* complements, and anticipates, *cantamus* (19). If, as I consider far more likely, given such uses of *dicere* as at *Odes* 2. 12. 10 and *Sat.* 2. 1. 10 (see n. 3 above), the verb refers here specifically to the production of epic, then it serves as a careful supplement to the double employment of *scribere*, and both verbs together stand in contrast to *cantamus*, with the writing and 'saying' of epic, in this poem at least, being on one side, the singing of 'slender' verses on the other.

[6] This is the only use of the phrase in the lyric corpus. The closest parallels are both in *Odes* 4. 4, at 18, where we find Drusus *bella gerentem*, and 67-8, where the Claudian race, in Hannibal's prediction, *geret proelia*. At *Ars* 73 *res gestae*, along with *tristia bella*, are the stuff of epic, for which Homer has shown us the metre (74).

ways even the analogy with the greatest of epic writers, Homer, which dominates the major portion of the poem, calls its validity into question. On the surface we are made to see how challenging will be Varius' putative undertaking, as the accomplishments of Agrippa's soldier on sea and land (*navibus aut equis*) find confirmation in equivalent deeds of battling Achilles, Odysseus the seafarer, and 'the savage house of Pelops.' The new Homer is expected to produce an Augustan version of the *Iliad* and the *Odyssey*. But, as critics have begun to ask, are the parallels between Varian epic and Homer really as complimentary as they may at first seem?[7] To phrase the question in general terms: in what ways can an ethical world that battens on anger, duplicitousness, and ferocity in any way be proudly claimed as a proper literary ancestor for the *laudes* of Agrippa and outstanding Caesar?[8] But we must also be specific. Throughout the work of Horace Achilles is known for his anger and stubbornness.[9] We hear of the first trait directly or indirectly in the *Satires*, *Epistles*, *Odes*, and the *Ars poetica*, while *nescius cedere* finds its counterpart in mention of the *pervicacis pedes Achillei* (*Epod.* 17. 14) and in his characterization as *inpiger* and *inexorabilis* at *Ars* 121. But it is one thing to dwell on Achilles' irascibility, another to debase the μῆνιν . . . οὐλομένην, which opens the *Iliad* and sparks its plot, to *gravem stomachum*, whereby an abstraction becomes concrete and the grandly ethical in concept is reduced by metonymy to the heavily physical as passion of mind becomes weight of body.[10]

---

[7] For Horace's alterations of Homer see Nisbet and Hubbard (1970) on lines 6–7 and the detailed analyses of Davis (1991) 36–9 and of Ahern (1991) *passim*.

[8] Horace uses the phrase *egregii Caesaris* (11) elsewhere in the *Odes* only at 3. 25. 4, and *egregius* of no other person except Caesar. Its recurrence is a matter of interest on two counts. First, the echo helps reinforce the chiasmus of poems that begins with the balance of 1. 1 with 3. 30 and extends inward to the linkage between 1. 5 and 3. 26 (on which see C. P. Jones 1971: 82) and beyond. Second, Horace would now seem, as he comes near the end of his masterpiece, to forgo his *recusatio* and to contemplate, under the influence of Bacchus, the stellification of Caesar. But—crucial for the student of *Odes* 1. 6—no *elogium* is yet forthcoming, any more than it could have been near the beginning of book 1.

[9] See *Sat.* 1. 7. 12, *animosus*; *Odes* 1. 15. 33–4, *iracunda . . . classis Achillei*; *Ep.* 1. 2. 13–15, *ira* (twice); *Ep.* 2. 2. 42, *iratus*; *Ars* 121, *iracundus*.

[10] The word *stomachus* (which Nisbet and Hubbard ad loc. correctly define as prosaic) recurs at *Odes* 1. 16. 16 to locate the seat of an emotion which was prominent in the speaker's angry *iambi* but is to be regretted and rejected in lyric's disavowal. This, the only other use of the word in the lyric corpus, precedes by one line mention of the *irae* which destroyed Thyestes. Horace's deliberate misconstruing of Homer is also noted by Commager (1962) 71 n. 25.

Horace's treatment of Odysseus is even more challenging. In this instance the poet offers us a reversal of his usual portrait, which sees the wily hero as *inclitus* (*Sat.* 2. 3. 197), *laboriosus* (*Epod.* 17. 16), *providus* (*Ep.* 1. 2. 19), or *patiens* (*Ep.* 1. 7. 40), famed for his qualities of vision and endurance.[11] But *duplex* is more than an imitation, and debasement, of πολύτροπος, which defines his resourcefulness in the *Odyssey*'s opening verse. The only previous use of the adjective in Latin occurs at Catullus 68. 51, where *duplex Amathusia* defines the Venus who presides over the bitter-sweet aspects of the poet's love, as patron eminence of Lesbia's fickleness.[12] Eleven poems after our present ode we hear, in relation to Odysseus, of 'laborantis in uno | Penelopen vitreamque Circen'. The yearning of two women, 'labouring' as does their inamorato characteristically, for one man, of which Tyndaris is to tell in *Odes* 1. 17, is replaced in *Odes* 1. 6 by the deviousness of the single object of their desire towards them both. So πολυ- becomes *du-* in a carefully numerological sense as the polymorphous wiliness before the vagaries of life's adventures, which typifies the behaviour of the *Odyssey*'s main protagonist, is reduced to one man's erotic 'doubleness' in relation to wife and mistress.[13]

Finally, whether the *saevam Pelopis domum* refers to the fierceness of Agamemnon and Menelaus in the *Iliad*, as the poem's economy might presuppose, or to the savagery of Thyestes, as the presence of Varius and the allusion to the *irae* of Pelops' son (whether this be Atreus or Thyestes) in *Odes* 1. 16. 17 might suggest,[14] we begin and end our précis of Greek heroic myth with the kindred vices of anger and ferociousness. When these defects are combined with Odysseus' chicanery, we are left wondering in what way we are to read this dubious trio and, more pointedly, how they are meant to serve as models to Varius as he prepares to embark on an epic encomium of the Roman lieutenant and his Princeps.

A different set of ambiguities confronts the student of the three principals of lines 13-16, Mars, Meriones, and Diomedes, all drawn

---

[11] Cf. also *Epod.* 16. 60 *laboriosa . . . cohors Ulixei.*

[12] Note especially Venus' portrayal at 17-18.

[13] Horace would no doubt have us compare his lexical choice with Livius Andronicus' premier rendering of πολύτροπος as *versutus* (fr. 1 Morel, from Gel. 18. 9. 5). The man of 'turns' adept at coping with fortune's twists, is seen by Horace here as specifically a creature of folds and layerings, appearances and deceptions.

[14] Both Kiessling and Heinz (1914-30) and Nisbet and Hubbard (1970) ad loc. take the phrase as a reference to the *Thyestes* of Varius, first produced in 29 BC.

specifically from the *Iliad*. We are not now dealing with epitomes of moral dubiety whose grandeur is complemented by allusion to the initial verses of the epics in which they are pre-eminent. Rather, Horace offers us close-up views of major figures in Achilles' epic: the god of war, the charioteer of Idomeneus, and one of the chief Greek warriors. All of these illustrious individuals could again seem, on first glimpse, to furnish appropriate, more particularized models for Varius to follow as he aims to pursue Iliadic affinities in the careers of his Roman heroes, and Horace's *recusatio* only the more underlines their potential suitability as prototypes to help glorify Agrippa's epic accomplishments by contrast with the speaker's apparently far more modest goals.

But once more heroism is called into question. Here it suffers meiosis not from proclamation of troubling abstractions but from the style of presentation. Horace demands that we put aside our preconceptions of Iliadic courage—the *aristeia* of Diomedes in book 5, for instance, or the reiterated prowess of Meriones, on seven occasions called the equal of Ares[15]—and look instead at what he offers: one god and two heroes perceived as passive, Mars protected by an invincible tunic, Meriones blackened by Troy's dust, Diomedes made equal to the gods only by the help of Pallas Athena. The plot of *Iliad* 5 reminds us not only of the dependency of Diomedes on Athena but also that Ares, far from being indomitable, was wounded by that very hero.[16] A look at the only other mention of Diomedes in the lyric corpus, *Odes* 1. 15. 27–8, further illustrates Horace's point here. In this subsequent ode we find Diomedes as the climactic warrior in a list of enemies bent on destroying Paris:

> . . . ecce furit te reperire atrox
> Tydides melior patre . . .[17]

This is another Diomedes, fierce and furious, different from one who relies for assurance of his prowess on the resources of a goddess.

Actually we have known the passive hero from the very beginning of the poem through the word *scriberis*. Different though the

---

[15] ἀτάλαντος Ἐνυαλίῳ ἀνδρειφόντῃ (*Il.* 2. 651; 7. 166; 8. 264; 17. 259); θοῷ ἀτάλαντος Ἄρηϊ (*Il.* 13. 295, 328, 528).

[16] On this point see further Ahern (1991) 305–7.

[17] These passages are the only two in Horace where Diomedes is given his patronymic. He is called *fortis* at *Sat.* 1. 5. 92.

chronological frames of Roman future and Iliadic past may be, Agrippa is imagined to be as obligated to Varius for the continuous remembrance of his heroism in time to come as Diomedes was beholden to Athena in the present action of Homer's epic. And because these two segments of the poem also converge through the repetition of *scribere*, it is appropriate to ask the meaning of *quis digne scripserit*, a phrase in which *digne* puts as much emphasis on quality of expression as *grandia* earlier had placed on magnificence of topic. Fraenkel concludes that the answer to the rhetorical question must be 'no ordinary poet and certainly not I', while Gregson Davis, supplementing D. A. Russell (as quoted in Nisbet and Hubbard) suggests 'only an *alter Homerus* such as Varius has proved to be'.[18] These are not mutually exclusive interpretations. Both assume implicit continuance of the speaker's *recusatio* along with heightened respect for Varius' poetic prospects. But there is, of course, another more subversive way of answering Horace's interrogation, one towards which my reading of the poem thus far has been leading. It would go something like this: 'No poet, not to speak of a poet of the quality of a Varius, could possibly write worthily of epic deeds, at least if they follow Horace's modes of outlining them.'

This interpretation may, in turn, serve to question the whole Varian undertaking itself. What it certainly does is to strengthen still further the poem's forward momentum towards the final stanza, which at last details Horace's own particular spiritual and emotional stance. It begins by direct as well as less apparent co-optations of epic language, now used not for denigration but to give lyric the forcefulness that epic has lost over the course of the poem. *Proelia*, a standard enough metaphor in elegiac contexts for lovers' wrangles, has a rich resonance in a lyric whose essential subject hitherto has been a refusal to write epic. *Cantamus* in this context is likewise double-edged. It is of course a verb regularly used to describe the production of lyric song, but, at least in its basic form, *canere*, it also traditionally, from the *Iliad* to the opening of the *Aeneid*, qualifies the bard's means of producing epic. Horace, therefore, in the course of his poem at once demotes epic to the status of a written art and raises the standing of lyric by using context to give a standard word for the production of lyric the overtones also of epic.

[18] For details see Davis (1987), *passim*.

The word *acrium* receives special stress in this context. Rarely used by Horace where female eroticism is concerned,[19] it regularly appears in situations where epic and epic heroes are the focus of attention. Virgil, for instance, applies it to Aeneas, *acer in armis*, standing over his defeated foe as his epic draws to a conclusion.[20] Within the Horatian corpus it describes the prowess of Deiphobus (*Odes* 4. 9. 22) and Tiberius (*Odes* 4. 14. 13). Horace so designates the *tibia* at 1. 12. 1–2 when heroism becomes its major theme. But there are two instances that are particularly germane to its appearance at the end of *Odes* 1. 6. First, it is one of the adjectives attached to Achilles at *Ars* 121.[21] Secondly, it designates Varius himself in Horace's punning précis of his friend, the poet who, instead of 'saying' it, 'leads' his poem like the leaders of whom he would no doubt tell. He is the contemporary master of epic (*Sat.* 1. 10. 43–4):

> . . . forte epos acer
> ut nemo Varius ducit . . .

Horace takes an adjective which he had elsewhere used to characterize not only one of the chief actors in the present poem but also the writer who heads the poem itself, adept in a genre (so the ode asserts) impossible for Horace to produce, and applies it to *virgines*, fierce with nails trimmed against the youths of their choice. In thus pointedly showing, once again, that he too controls epic language for his own purposes, he slyly demonstrates command over the very medium whose regulation on the surface he disclaims. And once more, in so doing, he re-evaluates epic by converting it to the purposes of lyric. More specifically, by the play on gender he takes Achilles' word and, through it, the *Iliad*'s fundamental figure himself and establishes both him and his bard in a demeaning context. Through this act of debasement he further asserts lyric's control over epic, but he likewise appropriates its energies, literally deployed in the martial achievements of soldier, leader, ships, and horses, to the metaphorical designs of convivial amatory escapades.

We should observe as well the feminization that takes place here. In this world of erotic 'battling' it is young women who, in their

---

[19] The only instance is the description of the freedwoman Myrtale, *fretis acrior Hadriae curvantis Calabros sinus* (*Odes* 1. 33. 15–16).

[20] *Aen.* 12. 938.

[21] Cf. also *acrem militiam* (*Odes* 1. 29. 2; 3. 2. 2); *acer miles* (*Odes* 3. 5. 25).

sharpness, take over the role played by male heroes in the warring
essential to the *Iliad*'s plot. As epic is co-opted into lyric and women
replace men as protagonists on literature's stage, 'reality' becomes
metaphor and the destructiveness of actual war suffers metamorphosis into figuration. It may be Horace's point that with this
magical change the horrific truths which a Varius must face are
devitalized and replaced by the far less pernicious challenge of eros.
It may also be not coincidental that two poems later (*Odes* 1. 8.
13–16) we find Achilles dressed as a woman in a moment of
escape before facing the slaughter at Troy into which *virilis cultus*
would lead him.[22] It should likewise be noted in this context that
in *Odes* 1. 17 it is a woman, Tyndaris, who is imagined as converting Homer to Anacreon, which is to say turning epic's effortful
subjects into the stuff of symposiastic entertainment. The violence
of her lover Cyrus is kept at bay. The only *labor* admitted into the
convivium's ceremony is at once lyricized and metaphoric.

Both structure and lexical usage therefore put enormous stress
on the final stanza, but particular importance is given to the ode's
last word, *leves*, which leads back into the poem in two important
ways. First, through its connotations of lightness and nimbleness it
echoes the initial portrait of Varius as bird of Maeonian song. Our
speaker too can assert a fleetness of style that has its parallels with
Varius' accomplishment. Nor is allusion to Horace's own brand of
heroism absent from the picture. In the last ode of book 2 Horace,
of course, does suffer metamorphosis into a bird (*Odes* 2. 20. 9–12):

> iam iam residunt crucibus asperae
> pelles et album mutor in alitem
>   superne nascunturque leves
>   per digitos umerosque plumae.

But this is a lyric bird who both disowns the Callimachean posture
of *Odes* 1. 6. 9 (we who are *tenues*) through proclamation of the
grander wing on which he will now be borne ('nec tenui ferar |
pinna biformis') and demands for himself not only the superhuman, adventurous posture of Daedalus but also a form of
public acceptance parallel in extent to the sweep of the Roman
empire itself—again a non-Callimachean attitude more akin to the

---

[22] In *Odes* 1. 8 the love of Lydia turns Sybaris away from the ordinary process of
game to reality in the military training of a Roman youth. Lydia's eroticism, the
speaker exclaims with some irony, twists Sybaris into a feminized Achilles who is
sequestered momentarily from epic perils at Troy.

premisses of a writer of epic. The climactic use of the adjective *levis* in *Odes* 1. 6 also helps transform the speaker into his own version of a bird of Maeonian song, absorbing Varius' potential and declaring his own ability to immortalize his subjects.

If Horace's employment of *leves* complements *ales* and closely connects Varius and the speaker, the poem's start and its conclusion, its use also contrasts with *gravem* in the phrase *gravem | Pelidae stomachum* (5–6). Here at least surface Callimacheanism comes into play. The 'light' topics of Horatian lyric are deliberately contrasted with 'heavy' themes that fall to the lot of (in Horace's case) the writer of epic. This distinction is an organizing principle in other odes as well. I think most specifically of the initial poem of book 2, where delineation of, and commentary upon, Pollio's perilous enterprise to tell of the civil wars is distinguished from what would ordinarily be the *ioca* of the poet and his Muse, at play together in Venus' grotto. In particular, the poem is bounded by references to the *gravis . . . | principum amicitias* (3–4), the 'heavy friendships of princes', prime themes for Pollio as he meditates upon a precarious topic conceived in history's weighty mode, and the *leviore plectro* (40), the poem's last words, which call attention to what would ordinarily be the slight, harmless style and content of Horatian verse.[23] Yet in both instances Horace, by brilliant acts of incorporation, proves his own mastery of the perspectives of both epic and historical writing. The 'carefree' lover we see at the conclusion of *Odes* 1. 6 and the lover's 'lighter' *plectrum* which brings *Odes*. 2. 1 to an end for all appearances claim distinction from the addressees of their respective poems and from the portentous sweep of the topics which complement them. In actuality Horace embraces both apparently antithetical subjects in lyrics of extraordinary persuasive power.

This may all seem a highly dour, negative evaluation of the possibilities of contemporary epic and of Varius' pretensions in undertaking it, but the speaker in part mitigates the sting that remains from the initial stanzas by humorously deflecting his final words away from Varius and on to his own incompetence. In his witty act of self-disclosure, 'Horace' is *levis*, lightweight, not committed to, or perhaps not even able fully to comprehend, Roman *gravitas* in action, be it exhibited in heroic deeds themselves or in the

[23] See also Davis (1991) 246–7.

grand words that would add lustre to them in the telling. He is also *vacuus*, empty-headed, unencumbered by obligation to anything of serious ethical or intellectual significance. He is the performer who, in the splendid irony of *Odes* 1. 32. 1–2, prepares to sing

> . . . si quid vacui sub umbra
> lusimus tecum . . .

His *carmen* is mere play, the fruit of someone at ease in the shade, sequestered from the glare of life that would lend any point and value to his poetic endeavour.

But there is a nuance to the adjective *vacuus*, in these and other Horatian contexts, that deepens its value in helping us interpret the conclusion of *Odes* 1. 6. If one side of its meaning looks to the trivial fatuity of Horatian song *vis-à-vis* Varian epic, another speaks to his αὐτάρκεια, to the independence that remains an essential unvarying feature of his moral 'biography' throughout all his work.[24] It is to *vacuum Tibur* that he turns for pleasure in *Ep.* 1. 7. 45, not to the paradoxes open for discovery in *regia Roma* (44). Tibur offers not only release from care and from reliance on others but also freedom for creativity. Horace underscores his point five lines later when he places his *alter ego*, Volteius Mena, *vacua tonsoris in umbra* (50), to become an earthbound version, as it were, of the Apolline bard of *Odes* 1. 32. In this richly provocative reversal of what we expect from Horace, the shade of an urban barber's establishment replaces the emblems of spiritual liberty which Horace regularly draws from country things, and the rustic existence which Maecenas-Philippus foists off on his pawn has disastrous consequences. Mena's 'Sabine farm' is in fact a humble city shop in whose shadow he finds the emancipation of which the benison of his patron would rob him.

It is important that we consider the generic situation in which Horace, *tenuis*, *vacuus*, and *levis*, places himself at the end of *Odes* 1. 6. This Horatian persona, free from the assignments of epic and from the political compulsion that undertaking such a task implies, is a singer of *symposia* and of the loves of the young. Horace here adopts for a posture of escape the traditions of archaic Greek lyric, just as his fellow Augustan poet Propertius uses espousal of the rich inheritance of elegy as excuse not to write epic. But the elegist's two *recusationes*, not incidentally the only two poems that

---

[24] Cf. Préaux (1968) on *Ep.* 1. 10. 49.

he addresses to Maecenas, tell us much about himself but something as well, vicariously, of Horace, poet of *Odes* 1. 6. If I were
to sing of epic and the wars of 'your Caesar', says the elegist to
Maecenas, I would weave you into those deeds (2. 1. 27–30):

> . . . quotiens Mutinam aut civilia busta Philippos
> aut canerem Siculae classica bella fugae
> eversosque focos antiquae gentis Etruscae,
> et Ptolomaeei litora capta Phari . . .

Two things are striking about this list. One is the powerful
metonymy of *civilia busta* placed in apposition to *Philippos*. The town
which harboured one of the major battles of the Roman civil wars
becomes, in the stark hands of Propertius' genius, simply the tombs
of citizens. The second is also a metonymy. The siege, starvation,
and cruel slaughter that we associate with the campaign at Perusia
in the winter of 41–40 BC the poet makes us visualize as over-
turned hearths. Propertius has already brought the hideousness of
the *Perusina sepulcra* before us in the brilliant self-defining σφραγίς
with which he had concluded his previous, first book of elegies.[25]
He gives the occasion special stress again in the *recusatio* that opens
his second book by having poetic and historical order diverge from
each other, i.e. by placing his reference to the events at Perusia
between his allusion to the defeat of Sextus Pompeius in 36 and
his mention of the capture of Alexandria in 30.[26]

In so doing Propertius directs emphasis on to what comes close
to being an explicit reminder of one of the ugliest moments in the
early career of Augustus, one in which his henchman Agrippa took
a prominent part.[27] The elegist falls back on the 'limitations' of his
genre as an excuse for refusal to write an epic on the emperor's
rise to power, yet in so doing he touches in passing on a particularly distressing moment fifteen or so years in the past. Horace, in
sliding finally back into the tenuous vacuity of lyric, is more discreet. Mention of Agrippa alone is hint enough of the problems that
might lie ahead for Varius or for Pollio, whom, in *Odes* 2. 1, Horace
imagines as about to write the history of the civil war with fire still
smouldering in the ashes. Both poets declare their intellectual
independence. For one it is elegy, for the other lyric that is the
true source of power to touch on grave matters while appearing,

[25] See Putnam (1976; 1982), *passim*.
[26] See Nethercut (1971) 413 for the 'disorder' of the subsequent lines.
[27] Cf. Appian *BC* 5. 32.

masterfully, to avoid the challenges that such an enterprise would seem to imply.

There is another continuing dialogue to be discovered in the final stanza. On this occasion Horace is concerned not to create generic frictions emanating from within the poem, paralleled in other poems, or to suggest similarities to, as well as differences from, Propertius, his contemporary writer of elegy. He also provokes an interchange with Catullus. It seems not to have been remarked upon that the words which end Horace's final two lines, *urimur* and *leves*, are the same as those which conclude two adjacent lines in one of the earlier poet's most complex epigrams, poem 72. Catullus begins, we recall, by remarking on how Lesbia continuously said that she 'knew' (*nosse*) Catullus alone and how, at that time, the Catullus of the poem loved her both sexually and as a father loves his sons and sons-in-law, in other words with the essence of piety. The third couplet begins by taking the ambiguous implications of her *nosse* and giving them to the speaker, now meditating on the ramifications of a deeper knowledge:

> nunc te cognovi: quare etsi impensius uror
> multo mi tamen es vilior et levior.

Horace pointedly alters the sense of *levis* from Catullus, where it connotes fickleness and faithlessness, to something akin to 'uncommitted' or 'unconcerned', applied to someone not deeply, certainly not destructively, involved in his feelings of the moment.[28]

Though he may sing of *convivia*, celebrations together, and *proelia*, the posture of Horace's speaker is aloof from the strife of amatory tergiversations, whether he is now aflame or now free from involvement. For Catullus the act of differentiation rests not within himself—now I'm this, now I'm that, as if the facile transition from the one to the other betokened lack of deep emotional concern—but between him and her, between a speaker who is burnt, and therefore cannot be apathetic, and Lesbia, who is *levis* and has no interest in passively suffering love's tortures.

The emotive, romanticist author revels in opposition between self

---

[28] Catullus' striking *impensius* is absent from Horace's imitation. Critics point to Lucr. 5. 964 (*inpensa libido*) as a possible parallel. There is a probable connection with *Aen.* 4. 54. 'His dictis impenso animum flammavit amore', where *impenso* is the reading to be preferred over *incensum*, redundant next to *flammavit* and lacking the further Catullan note in an already very Catullan episode.

and others which may in fact help to define the individuality of
each. The rational classicist manipulates such oppositions from a
distance, analysing them from above the battle. One must be
'light', says Horace's speaker, towards all possibilities. The classicist can tolerate no splits and divisions between a differentiated
here and there, between longing and distance or fidelity and dis-
affection, but looks on himself as untouched by such dualities
because of his gifts of self-control. Mastery of these tensions, which
are focal to Catullus, domination of such differentiations within
oneself, makes Horace into a type of Lesbia but without the Circean
malice which figures so prominently in Catullus' portrait of her.
Lesbia is fickle, the antonym of the poet-speaker who is burnt and
steadfast. Horace's 'we', whether in love or not, is forever *levis*,
avowing unseriousness, not given to consequential involvements.

On the one hand, then, Horace, as a lover who is whimsical
and mercurial, seems to espouse an anti-Catullan stance when we
look solely at the moral and ethical attitudes of each poem. Yet,
on the level of genre, Horace also must be said, by his allusion, to
pre-empt Catullus for his own purposes. Allusion sanctions both
positions. Whatever the distinctions between lyric and epigram,
Horace, by careful reference to his greatest Roman predecessor, is
adopting to himself another 'lesser' genre in order to weave one
more strand into a larger fabric which serves further to distinguish
him from the world of Agrippa, Homer, and potential Varian epic.
As a lover he maintains an anti-Catullan posture of reserve, an
unchanging lightness of mood. As a poet he is lively and nimble,
as willing to appropriate Catullus to his devices as he is to mark
himself off from the heavy themes of war or adroitly to twist the
grandiose, imagined flights of Varius to his own private ends.

Horace appropriates Catullus but in so doing he also both
corrects him and expands on his ideas. He thereby reaffirms the
singular power of lyric to construct dialogues in language, whether
directly or obliquely, whether with Catullus, or Agrippa, or us, his
readers. Just as Varius, modern epicist, must take advantage of
lessons learnt from the study of Homer, so Horace acknowledges
his own education at the school of Catullus. Whatever his
differences from his predecessor, Horace here mirrors the multi-
farious occasions in which Catullus likewise modifies, challenges,
or affirms positions taken with regard to lyric by its earlier practi-
tioners. (I am, of course, using the term 'lyric' in the modern sense,

where there are no metrical restrictions.) Horace, by ending his poem in such a manner, further legitimates the long tradition of lyric interplay among poets and holds that tradition up as equal or, if we yield our imaginations to the poem's forward movement, superior to the illustrious heritage of epic.

And through Catullus comes Callimachus once more. Only one poem, introduced for purposes of *variatio*, separates Catullus 72 from 70, the most directly Callimachean of the epigrams.[29] It is not entirely fortuitous, I suspect, that it too, like Horace's lyric, is very much concerned with the differentiation between the spoken and the written word. For Catullus' speaker, a woman's promises, said and said again, deserve only to be inscribed on wind and water. Writing, like the marriage she falsely promises, indicates a form of permanence, but her words are as evanescent as the lies they carry. For Horace here, by contrast, writing and, on notable occasions, speaking are synonymous with epic while song regularly defines lyric.[30] This would seem to give special rank to Varius' written, and therefore ever-enduring, undertaking. Yet we have seen how Horace turns things around, usurping and intensifying epic's traditional *cano* in *cantamus*. He is also preparing us, in his own case, for the arrival of his own immortality, heralded, in *Odes* 3. 30, not in terms of writing but through words, in the boast of *dicar* and in a future based on the uttered word and reached through the medium of *Aeolium carmen* which he leads in triumph to Italian measures.

[29] Catullus clearly has Callimachus *Ep.* 25Pf. in mind as he writes.
[30] See nn. 3 and 5 above.

5

Horace, *Odes* 3. 7: Elegy, Lyric, Myth, Learning, and Interpretation

FRANCIS CAIRNS

Quid fles, Asterie, quem tibi candidi
primo restituent vere Favonii
    Thyna merce beatum,
        constantis iuvenem fide

Gygen? ille Notis actus ad Oricum   5
post insana Caprae sidera frigidas
    noctis non sine multis
        insomnis lacrimis agit.

atqui sollicitae nuntius hospitae,
suspirare Chloen et miseram tuis   10
    dicens ignibus uri,
        temptat mille vafer modis.

ut Proetum mulier perfida credulum
falsis inpulerit criminibus nimis
    casto Bellerophontae   15
        maturare necem refert;

narrat paene datum Pelea Tartaro,
Magnessam Hippolyten dum fugit abstinens,
    et peccare docentis
        fallax historias movet,   20

An earlier, briefer version of this paper was read at the Horace bimillenary conference, Oxford in 1992 and, in Italian translation, at the Convegno Internazionale di Studio, '*Non omnis moriar*: La lezione di Orazio a duemila anni dalla scomparsa' (Potenza and Venosa, 16–18 Oct. 1992). The text of this lecture appeared unannotated in the proceedings of that conference, published in 1993 under the same title (pp. 66–84). The script published there no longer necessarily represents my views, which may be found in full in the present, canonical version. The present revised and enlarged text owes much to the comments of my Oxford audience, among whom I am especially indebted to Prof. Edward Courtney. I am also grateful to Dr D. L. Cairns, Dr S. J. Harrison, and Prof. David West for their reactions to it in written form. Self-evidently, none of the above bears responsibility for stubbornness or errors on my part.

frustra: nam scopulis surdior Icari
voces audit adhuc integer. at tibi
    ne vicinus Enipeus
        plus iusto placeat cave,

quamvis non alius flectere equum sciens   25
aeque conspicitur gramine Martio
    nec quisquam citus aeque
        Tusco denatat alveo.

prima nocte domum claude neque in vias
sub cantu querulae despice tibiae   30
    et te saepe vocanti
        duram difficilis mane.

20 movet φψ: monet aBEM

I. INTRODUCTION: CURRENT APPROACHES TO ODES 3. 7

Odes 3. 7, which treats the private lives of a couple (Gyges and Asterie) and a would-be interloper (Enipeus), is an intrinsically odd and difficult piece. Its location immediately after the great public pronouncements of the six 'Roman Odes' challenges the reader further. Unsurprisingly, then, although it has generated an extensive secondary literature, for which cf. esp. Owens (1992), no scholarly consensus about its interpretation prevails. Instead, there are at least three conflicting views of it:

(1) Contrary to appearances, Horace is not dissuading Asterie from yielding to Enipeus, but is indirectly encouraging her to do so.

(2) The ode is a cynical and amusing piece. Asterie may be no better than she should be: but the characters are of little consequence anyhow. Hence the ode offers light relief after the solemnity of the six 'Roman Odes'.

(3) Gyges and Asterie are married, and Horace's advice to Asterie recalls his emphasis on marriage in the 'Roman Odes'.

View (1) was, it seems, first advanced by Pasquali (1920: 463–70). It was adopted by Groselji (1953), and reflected by a number of other scholars in the 1960s to 1980s. Finally, arguments in its favour were rehearsed at length by Owens (1992), who documented thoroughly his predecessors' opinions. View (1) claims, in effect, that Horace means the opposite of what he says.[1] For such 'ironic' interpretations to be worthy of consideration, the presence of explicit linguistic evidence of irony or of an unmistakably ironic context, or of both, is required. Since these are absent from *Odes* 3. 7, I shall engage no further with view (1), or with the attempt of Owens (1992) to hold it in tandem with its opposite.

The real choice is between view (2)—the ode is light relief—which seems to command most scholarly assent,[2] and view (3)—the pair are married. Heinze simply assumed view (3): 'Ein liebendes junges Ehepaar' (see Kiessling and Heinze 1914-30: 294); Copley (1956) 64-9 explored it valuably; and Santirocco (1986: 125-8) and Porter (1987: 175-6) have recently revived it. It accords greater seriousness to *Odes* 3. 7, and links it with the 'Roman Odes'. The gap between views (2) and (3) should not, however, be exaggerated. Whichever is preferred, the amused tone of *Odes* 3. 7, its patronizing attitude to its characters, and its part-fantasy scenario, all of which dilute the high seriousness of the 'Roman Odes', must be recognized. But there is a gap; and it is not just *Odes* 3. 7's location which makes it difficult to read as pure amusement. Another consideration was well put by Connor (1987: 205 n. 12) while rejecting the notion that the ode is epigrammatic in its ethos: 'it [*Odes* 3. 7] is a solidly worked-out poem in which the people, and the poet's attitude to them, seem to matter'. This 'solid working out' involves complex generic craftsmanship and conceptual symmetry. Following Copley (1956: 64-9), Cairns (1972: 208-11) analysed *Odes* 3. 7 as a (possibly unique) 'inverse' *kōmos* which also 'includes' an ordinary (i.e. a non-'inverse') *kōmos*. The latter discussion, which also outlined some of the symmetrical interactions of the characters and situations, real and mythical, and which might have given some pause to adherents of view (2), has eluded all subsequent scholarly treatments of *Odes* 3. 7, even the admirably thorough Owens (1992).

Throughout the present paper the case for view (3) will be underpinned. But other aspects of *Odes* 3. 7 will also be treated:

---

[1] For a parallel attempt to argue that a related (cf. below, n. 9) Augustan encouragement to fidelity (Prop. 3. 12) means the exact opposite of what it says, see Jacobson (1976) 161-4.

[2] It is held, for example, by those scholars listed at Harrison (1988) 186 n. 1.

the ode's (known) relationship with contemporary Roman elegy (Sections 2 and 3); its links with the lyric tradition (Sections 4 and 5); its characters and their names (Sections 6 and 7); and the mythographic and learned traditions to which these enquiries offer an entrée (Section 8).

2. *ODES* 3. 7 AND ROMAN ELEGY: THEMES AND LANGUAGE

Many elegiac elements, situational, topical, and linguistic, have been identified in *Odes* 3. 7, mainly thanks to the pioneering work of Syndikus (1972–3: ii. 98–102); cf. also Mutschler (1978) and Davis (1991: 43–50). A major elegiac presence in the ode must now be regarded as indubitable, as must the (partial) portrayal of Gyges and Enipeus as elegiac lovers, and of Asterie as an elegiac beloved. But further precision is required: there is more that is elegiac in the ode than has been identified, but not everything 'elegiac' in it is elegiac *simpliciter*. Again, as earlier commentators have stressed,[3] there are non-elegiac, not to say anti-elegiac, strands in *Odes* 3. 7.

First the subject-matter and *Topik* of *Odes* 3. 7: the separation of lovers by a tract of sea is indeed an elegiac theme (cf. Syndikus 1972–3: ii. 99 and n. 7), but it is not exclusive to elegy.[4] Likewise, groupings of mythological exempla are certainly common in elegy (cf. Syndikus 1972–3: ii. 100 and n. 12), but they are found in other sorts of poetry too.[5] Yet again, *kōmoi* like the 'included' *kōmos* of *Odes* 3. 7. 29–32 are frequent in elegy, but also in many other types of literature (cf. Copley 1956 *passim*). Finally, dramatic and epic parallels for the attempted (or successful) seduction of a male guest by his hostess (stanzas 3 ff.) suggest themselves more readily than elegiac parallels:[6] these first appear in the presumably

---

[3] Syndikus (1972–3: ii. 98–102); Mutschler (1978) 123-6, who forwards Syndikus' enquiry, concentrating on what he sees as Horace's antithesis between Gyges the merchant and Enipeus the soldier; and Davis (1991) 43-50, who explores yet further ramifications of the lyric/elegiac interface.

[4] Cf. e.g. Horace's Galatea ode (3. 27) and the *Odyssey*. On Harrison (1988), arguing for a connection between the latter and *Odes* 3. 7, see below, Appendix 2.

[5] A few examples: Hor. *Epod.* 17. 8–18; *Odes* 1. 28. 7–15; Virg. *Ecl.* 4. 55-9; *Georg.* 2. 454-7; 3. 89-94.

[6] Epic: e.g. Calypso, Circe, Nausicaa/Odysseus, Dido/Aeneas; drama: e.g. Phaedra/Hippolytus, Sthenoboea/Bellerophon.

later *Heroides*;⁷ and the characters involved for the most part come from epic.

What really gives *Odes* 3. 7 its elegiac flavour, and makes these situations and topoi elegiac in context, is the very high proportion of its vocabulary which the ode shares with elegy. To illustrate this, the relevant terms will now be listed, with indications of previous discussions where they exist. Where new items have been added, the definitions of Pichon (1902) are appended. Pichon had, of course, no thought of *Odes* 3. 7; but the fact that so many of his definitions (or parts thereof) are piquantly relevant to the ode is in itself impressive.

1. *fles*: Syndikus (1972–3) ii 98–9; Harrison (1988) 187.

1. *candidi*: Pichon (1902) 98: 'candidus aliquando idem valet ac pallidus, albus . . . sed, proprio sensu, hoc verbum calorem iucundum ac nitidum significare solet'.

3. *beatum*: Pichon (1902) 93: 'beatus dicitur amans amatus'.

4. *constantis . . . fide*: Harrison (1988) 187.

4. *iuvenem*: Pichon (1902) 180: 'substantive ponitur juvenis non-numquam pro marito . . . saepius pro amatore'.

6–7. *frigidas noctis*: Syndikus (1972–3) ii. 99 n. 9.; Quinn (1980) 259; Harrison (1988) 187.

7–8. *non sine multis . . . lacrimis*: Syndikus (1972–3) ii 98–9; Quinn (1980) 259; Harrison (1988) 187.

8. *insomnis*: Syndikus (1972–3) ii. 99 n. 9; Quinn (1980) 259; Harrison (1988) 187.

9–12. *nuntius*: Harrison (1988) 189.

9. *sollicitae . . . hospitae*: Syndikus (1972–3) ii. 100 n. 11; Harrison (1988) 189.

10. *suspirare*: Syndikus (1972–3) ii. 100.

10. *miseram*: Syndikus (1972–3) ii. 100.

10–11. *tuis . . . ignibus uri*: Syndikus (1972–3) ii. 100; Harrison (1988) 189.

12. *temptat*: Pichon (1902) 276: 'temptare saepe est ad amorem sibi conciliandum eniti'.

13. *mulier perfida*: Pichon (1902) 231: 'perfidi dicuntur saepissime qui amantibus datam fidem non servant . . . perfidi quoque ii qui amicis amores suos rapere conantur'.

13. *credulum*: Pichon (1902) 113: 'credere, credulus, plerumque de iis

---

⁷ On the chronology of Ovid's works see McKeown (1987) 74–89. The theme appears in *Her.* 2 (Demophoon and Phyllis), 6 (Jason and Hypsipyle), 7 (Aeneas and Dido), and 16 and 17 (Paris and Helen).

dicuntur qui simulato amori dolosisque verbis nimiam adhibuerunt fidem'.

14. *criminibus*: Pichon (1902) 116: 'crimen dicitur quodcumque vituperari potest . . . sed plerumque crimina sunt aut eae culpae . . . quae ex amore oriuntur . . . sic crimina referuntur ad adulteria'.

19. *peccare*: Harrison (1988) 190.

20. *fallax*: Harrison (1988) 190.

20. *historias*: Pichon (1902) 163: 'historiae sunt saepe amatoriae fabulae'.

21. *surdior*: Pichon (1902) 272: 'surdi quoque homines qui amantes respuunt'.

22. *integer*: Pichon (1902) 174: 'semper ad corpus pertinet, seu de virginitate agitur . . . seu de temporaria rei venereae abstinentia'.

24. *placeat*: Pichon (1902) 234: 'placere dicuntur aliquotiens feminae quae pulchrae habentur . . . saepius placere idem est ac sibi amorem conciliare'.

26. *conspicitur*: Pichon (1902) 112: 'conspicere est cum admiratione intueri, praesertim in voce conspicienda'.

29. *nocte*: Pichon (1902) 216: 'nox perusitatum verbum apud nostros poetas, neque cuius omnia liceat numerare exempla'.

29. *domum claude*: Harrison (1988) 192.

29-30. *neque in vias . . . despice*: Harrison (1988) 192 (but cf. rather below, n. 26).

30. *sub cantu querulae*: Harrison (1988) 192.

30. *tibiae*: Harrison (1988) 192.

31. *et te saepe vocanti duram*: Harrison (1988) 192.

32. *difficilis*: Syndikus (1972-3) ii. 101 n. 17; Harrison (1988) 192.

Two apparently contradictory points about *Odes* 3. 7 and elegy have so far been made: (1) the ode's subject-matter is not, for the most part, uniquely elegiac; and (2) its language is even more elegiac than has been realized. These propositions have been stressed because, as Syndikus has indicated (1972-3: ii. 98-101), we must, in order to understand the ode, perceive how Horace contravenes the elegiac ethos, which he does mainly in the realm of subject-matter. Horace's most important contravention is not, as has sometimes been thought,[8] his assurance to Asterie that Gyges remains faithful to her: the concept that a lover is, and should be, faithful to his mistress is by no means alien to elegy, and Gyges has some features of the elegiac lover. It is rather Horace's dissuasion

---

[8] Syndikus (1972-3: ii. 98-9) concentrates on this point but draws the broader and valuable conclusion: 'Dieses Unterbrechen elegischer Stimmungen ist überhaupt die wiederkehrende Grundfigur der Ode' (99); cf. also above, n. 3.

of Asterie from infidelity to Gyges, because Enipeus, as has been recognized, possesses many more characteristics of the elegiac lover, and the elegiac poet's quasi-magical role is to open the doors of reluctant girls to himself and to fellow elegiac lovers. Two passages of Propertius sum up this role:

> possum ego diversos iterum coniungere amantis
> et dominae tardas possum aperire fores.

> (1. 10. 15-16)

> ut per te clausas sciat excantare puellas
> qui volet austeros arte ferire viros.

> (3. 3. 49-50)

The notion that Horace's advice to Asterie breaches elegiac norms needs to be argued forcibly for two reasons. First, it has been obscured by a subsequent twist of literary fate—Propertius' 'plagiarism' of *Odes* 3. 7 in books 3 and 4. In elegy 3. 12, and again in 4. 3, both 'published' later than *Odes* 1-3, Propertius champions the marital fidelity of a wife 'abandoned' by her husband, who is travelling abroad. But this does not mean that Propertius' attitude is in origin elegiac. On the contrary—and this point will recur—in 3. 12 and 4. 3 Propertius is answering and subverting Horace's exploitation of the same stance for counter-elegiac purposes in this very ode.[9] Confirmation of the anti-elegiac nature of Horace's advice to Asterie comes from another Propertian elegy (3. 20), cited by others to illustrate a different aspect of the ode:[10]

> Credis eum iam posse tuae meminisse figurae
> vidisti a lecto quem vela dare tuo?
> durus, qui lucro potuit mutare puellam!
> tantine, ut lacrimes, Africa tota fuit?
> at tu, stulta, deos, tu fingis inania verba:
> forsitan ille alio pectus amore terat.
> est tibi forma potens, sunt castae Palladis artes,
> splendidaque a docto fama refulget avo,
> fortunata domus, modo sit tibi fidus amicus.
> fidus ero: in nostros curre, puella, toros!

> (Propertius 3. 20. 1-10)

---

[9] On the influence of *Odes* 3. 7 upon Prop. 3. 12 see Fedeli (1985) 398 (introduction to 3. 12).

[10] Cf. Mutschler (1978) 113-14 and n. 13; Harrison (1988) 186 and n. 2.

In 3. 20 Propertius plays a modified Enipeus: he addresses an unnamed girl whose *vir* has left her and gone to Africa. Propertius implies that the man's departure means he has ceased to care for her (1–4); indeed Propertius suggests that her *vir* may already be committing infidelity: 'forsitan ille alio pectus amore terat' (6); cf. the temptation of Gyges in *Odes* 3. 7. Propertius goes on to profess his own *fides*, in contrast to her *vir*'s alleged infidelity, and to invite the girl to sleep with him and so be unfaithful to her *vir* (9–10). The thematic similarities (and differences) are obvious, and they underline the point that Horace's injunctions to Asterie to reject Enipeus are anti-elegiac. Propertius 3. 12 was published later than *Odes* 3. 7, and so might be thought suspect as evidence. But conclusive proof that Horace was controverting an elegiac stance in his dissuasion of Asterie from infidelity comes from another elegy earlier than *Odes* 3. 7, Tibullus 1. 2. There Tibullus urges his mistress Delia to deceive her guards (65 ff.) at a time when her *vir* is absent abroad. Since Tibullus 1. 2 is, like *Odes* 3. 7, a *kōmos*,[11] it is doubly indicative of the 'normal' elegiac attitude being undermined by Horace in *Odes* 3. 7.

The second reason for taking pains to clarify Horace's anti-elegiac stance in *Odes* 3. 7 is that the proximity of *Odes* 3. 10 might also tend to obscure it. *Odes* 3. 10 too is a *kōmos*, in which Horace himself is the unsuccessful komast of a woman whose *vir* is involved with a concubine (15–16). *Odes* 3. 10 will be discussed later; for the moment it may be noted that it has no elegiac content, and so is irrelevant to the interplay between *Odes* 3. 7 and Roman elegy.

3. *ODES* 3.7 AND ROMAN ELEGY: CHARACTERIZATION

How, then, do the dramatis personae of *Odes* 3. 7 fit the interaction between the ode and elegy? First, Gyges: as was observed, although he is Asterie's *vir*, he has some features of an elegiac lover: he is youthful (*iuvenem*, 4);[12] he possesses the *constans fides*

---

[11] Cf. Copley (1956) 91–107; Tib. 1. 2 was cited to different effect by Mutschler (1978) 124.

[12] The elegiac poet-lover's normal self-characterization as youthful is amplified and contrasted with the elderliness of his rival at Tib. 1. 8. 29–50. The scale of this

(cf. 4) of the elegiac lover;[13] and he exhibits his insomnia and tears
(6–8).[14] Finally his *fides* is demonstrated in action in lines 21–2.
But a major counter-elegiac element has already intruded: Gyges is
Thyna merce beatum (3), and wealth is typical of the elegiac *vir*, as
opposed to the 'poor' elegiac lover.[15] One important proviso must,
however, be made: Horace is not, as has sometimes been thought,
portraying Gyges as greedy:[16] in fact, Horace has specifically
cleared Gyges of this charge. As Heinze long ago pointed out (cf.
Kiessling and Heinze 1914–30: i. 295 on line 5), by representing
Gyges as overwintering at Oricos, Horace distinguishes him from
avaricious traders who set sail in winter (cf. e.g. *Ep.* 1. 16. 71).

But how can we be sure that Horace was conscious of the
elegiac and non-elegiac aspects of Gyges, and that he was savour-
ing the paradoxes involved? First of all, Horace exploited the same
youth/age topic to tease Albius, i.e. Albius Tibullus,[17] about his
elegiac poetry in *Odes* 1. 33. 1–4:

> Albi, ne doleas plus nimio memor
> inmitis Glycerae, neu miserabilis
> decantes elegos, cur tibi iunior
> laesa praeniteat fide.

As noted, the elegiac lover's more successful rival is richer but
older. Horace, however, characterizes Albius' rival as younger than
him (cf. n. 12). Notably, here too, as in *Odes* 3. 7, 'youth' is combined with *fides*, but Horace mockingly associates negated *fides*
with Glycera (4). A second ground for confidence in Horace's
awareness of elegiac paradoxes in *Odes* 3. 7 is his apostrophe of
the same Albius in *Ep.* 1. 4. 5–6 'di tibi formam, | di tibi divitias
dederunt artemque fruendi', as rich (like Gyges), as good-looking
(like Enipeus—see below), and (in the previous line, *silvas* . . .

Tibullan treatment of the theme of youth and age may have prompted Horace's
humorous claim in *Odes* 1. 33. 5–6 that Tibullus' more successful rival is younger
than him; cf. p. 73 below.

[13] Cf. e.g. Cat. 109. 5–6; Müller (1952) 43; Fedeli (1980) 85 on Prop. 1. 1. 32,
147 on Prop. 1. 4. 16, 293 on Prop. 1. 12. 8; Nisbet and Hubbard (1970) 177–8.
[14] Insomnia: cf. Hoelzer (1899) 48; Syndikus (1972–3) ii. 99 and n. 9. Tears:
Pichon (1902) s.v. *lacrimae* etc.; Fedeli (1980) 253 on Prop. 1. 10. 2.
[15] Cf. Hoelzer (1899) 64–6; K. F. Smith (1913) 301 on Tib. 1. 5. 47–8, 420 on
Tib. 2. 3. 35; Cairns (1979) 154; Fedeli (1980) 322—(introduction to Prop. 1. 14).
[16] The view can be found as recently as Davis (1991) 48.
[17] Cf. Nisbet and Hubbard (1970) 368 (introduction to *Odes* 1. 33): 'There can
be no reasonable doubt that this ode is addressed to the elegiac poet Albius
Tibullus.'

salubres, 4) as healthy, in contrast to the sickliness often affected by the elegiac lover, on which cf. Fedeli (1980) 163-4.

Next, Enipeus, Gyges' rival: he too is manifestly not a standard elegiac *vir*. He looks much more like an elegiac lover. His sporting activities (25-8) stamp him as young and good-looking (cf. Cairns 1977: 142-5; Syndikus 1972-3: ii. 101 and n. 16). The similar activities of Sybaris in *Odes* 1. 8 and of Hebrus in *Odes* 3. 12 have similar implications, and interestingly Sybaris (probably) and Hebrus (certainly) are also named after river-gods, while Hebrus was, like Enipeus, a swimmer in the Tiber and, like Gyges, worthy of comparison with Bellerophon (*Odes* 3. 12. 8, cf. *Odes* 3. 7. 13-16). The resemblance between Enipeus and the elegiac lover is strengthened by Enipeus' *kōmos*, complete with elegiac *tibia* and with pleas which involve (cf. Cairns 1984*a*) a term central to the history of Roman elegy, *dura*. But again, Enipeus' good looks, like those of Hebrus and Sybaris, are not the phthisic charms of the elegiac lover.

Finally, Asterie: Horace enjoins upon her fidelity to Gyges, something (as noted) tolerable elegiacally if he were simply her elegiac lover but counter-elegiac inasmuch as he is her *vir*. Again, Asterie is urged to be *difficilis* towards her komast Enipeus, despite his *kōmos* with its elegiac apparatus and despite his elegiac reproaches of her as *dura*. Given that Enipeus looks much more like Asterie's elegiac lover, she is being counselled to be the opposite of the elegiac ideal beloved—a girl who is *facilis* and puts up no resistance to the advances of her lover.

Horace's part-espousal and part-rejection of elegiac conventions in *Odes* 3. 7 is yet another example of that absorption and deformation of one literary type by another which is so widespread in Augustan literature.[18] Seemingly there are no limits to the process: epic, e.g. the *Aeneid*, can take over tragedy, elegy (and possibly lyric).[19] Similarly, bucolic can take over elegy, as does *Eclogue* 10, and elegy can assimilate epic (cf. e.g. Viarre 1986), or even go further, as does Propertius 2. 34, which contrives at once to laud and to subvert through elegiacization Virgil's entire *œuvre*— *Bucolics*, *Georgics*, and *Aeneid*.[20] Propertius was adept at this

---

[18] Davis (1991), esp. ch. 1, 'Modes of Assimilation' (q.v.), examines such interactions of Horatian lyric with other literary forms.

[19] Cf. Cairns (1989) chs. 6-7, with the earlier bibliography cited there.

[20] Lines 61-82. I am currently preparing a paper treating (*inter alia*) this topic in connection with Prop. 2. 34.

practice: 3. 12 and 4. 3, where Propertius seizes for elegy the originally anti-elegiac stance of *Odes* 3. 7, have already been mentioned. The motivations for such 'take-overs' range through a spectrum. At one extreme they may be no more than literary games, allowing one type of poetry to display its virtuosity and its 'superiority' over another, amid reminiscences of the supposed Alexandrian 'battle of the books'. In the middle of the spectrum, which is where Propertius 2. 34 may be placed, the purpose and effect are rather to express the free-spirited admiration of a proponent of one metre (elegy) for his colleague in another (hexameter). But at the other extreme the process can be the vehicle for serious observations upon literature and/or life. The factors which suggest that *Odes* 3. 7 may have (partial) serious import also suggest that it is making substantive points through its 'take-over' of elegy. Eliciting them will necessitate further attention to Horace's characters, and especially to their names and to the implications of those names.

4. LYRIC THEMES IN *ODES* 3. 7

In the meantime, however, a balance must be redressed: an account of *Odes* 3. 7 which focused only on its elegiac language and anti-elegiac message would create a gross distortion. The ode is a lyric poem harking back to the *novem lyrici* and exploiting well-exemplified lyric themes. It starts (1–2 *candidi | primo . . . vere Favonii*) with the spring motif commonly found in archaic lyric (cf. Fatouros 1966: 108 *s.v.* ἔαρ and cognates),[21] and clearly regarded by Horace as a typical lyric opening, since he also used it to begin *Odes* 1. 4, 4. 7, and 4. 12. Then the first character to appear in *Odes* 3. 7 is Asterie (1), whose name, partially 'etymologized' in *candidi* (1)—cf. below, Appendix 1—means 'starry'. The reference to *Caprae sidera* (6) reinforces the ode's stellar interest[22] and confirms that the name Asterie harks back to the widespread, but

---

[21] The spring motif, ubiquitous in ancient poetry (cf. Nisbet and Hubbard 1970: 58–9), provided early lyricists (as did other seasonal motifs) with a convenient context and pretext for subsequent injunctions to drink, reflections on death, etc. The spring motif sometimes has erotic overtones, e.g. Sapph. fr. 2 LP; Ibycus fr. 286 *PMG*, although this aspect need not be pressed.

[22] On the 'starry' quality of Asterie and the contrast with the baneful *sidera* of line 6, see Harrison (1988) 186–7 and n. 5, with references to predecessors.

nevertheless still characteristically lyric, ancient comparison of a beautiful or distinguished person to a star or to the sun.[23] Horace clearly saw this concept as at home in lyric, since he used it four times in his *Odes*: here; at *Odes* 3. 9. 21, where he makes Lydia describe a young man as *sidere pulchrior*; at *Odes* 3. 19. 26, where he himself speaks of 'Telephus' as *puro . . . similem . . . vespero*; and at *Odes* 3. 15. 6, addressed to the wife of 'Ibycus' (see below), where he alludes to *virgines* as *stellis . . . candidis*. Among surviving early Greek lyric texts Alcman twice exemplifies the comparison: the first element of his character Astymelousa's name is (perversely) etymologized in fr. 3. 66-7 *PMG* τις αἰγλά[ε]ντος ἀστὴρ | ὠρανῶ διαιπετής.[24] Again, at fr. 1. 62-3 *PMG*, Alcman makes his chorus compare the 'Pleiads' (probably a rival chorus) to Sirius, and he uses the related sun/human comparison a little earlier at fr. 1. 39 ff. *PMG*; on these examples cf. Bremer (1976) 221-2 and Davies (1991) 29 on fr. 1. 39 ff. *PMG*.

Odes 3. 7's last character, Enipeus, is introduced at line 23. The adjective applied to him there (*vicinus* = γείτων) recalls the term used at line 9 of Chloe (*hospitae* = ξένη), and so triggers the reader's recognition of a major, and typically lyric, theme of the ode—'The Near and the Far', with its numerous and influential appearances in Aeolic lyric, Pindar, and Bacchylides.[25] In early Greek poetry the theme often accompanies a moral judgement or dilemma, frequently to do with love; the 'Near' is invariably morally acceptable while the 'Far' is not. Horace exploits this theme in a characteristically subtle way. Neither *vicinus* (23) nor *hospitae* (9) in isolation would have evoked the duality Near/Far; and each term is applied to a different love-liaison. That Gyges should not (as he does not) become involved in an affair with his

[23] The comparison originated in Homer, reappeared in early lyric, and later became widely diffused (see Kost 1971: 164-7, Exkurs: *Sternvergleiche*). Even for Roman elegists it may have retained an archaic and lyric colour: they compare their beloved's eyes but not the beloved herself to stars (see Enk 1962: ii. 60, on Prop. 2. 3. 14). Ov. *Trist.* 2. 167 'tui, sidus iuvenale, nepotes' (addressed to Augustus) and *Ex Pont.* 3. 3. 2 'o sidus Fabiae, Maxime, gentis, ades' relate to a different, political use of the sun/stars image, in which the king/*princeps*/'leader' is the sun and his φίλοι/*amici*/lieutenants are the stars; see Doblhofer (1966) 17-21.

[24] διαιπετής presumably refers to a 'shooting-star'; cf. also Asterie/Delos's falling from heaven in Call. *Hymn* 4 (quoted below, Appendix 1).

[25] Like much of prominence in early lyric, the motif originated in Homer; see Howie (1977) 214-22. Young (1968) 116-20 (appendix 1) lists both lyric and non-lyric manifestations; cf. also Hubbard (1985) 11-27, 35-6, 163. The motif became widely diffused in prose as well as verse.

hospita—'foreign hostess'—is the more standard half of Horace's implication. Horace then makes the defter point that Asterie should not become involved with Enipeus even though he is 'Near'. His nearness thus joins his other attractive characteristics as something which Asterie must prevail over. Enipeus' attractiveness is highly visual: he is a cynosure when riding in the Campus (*conspicitur*, 26), and Asterie is told not to look down (*neque* . . . | . . . *despice*, 29–30)[26] into the streets when Enipeus comes on his *kōmos*. This emphasis is reminiscent of another strong concern of early Greek lyric, with the eyes as the channel through which love enters the souls of lovers.[27]

Horace's stress on the attractiveness of Enipeus is partly responsible for the very existence of view (1), that Horace is encouraging Asterie to yield to Enipeus. But in fact Horace is drawing on another common archaic lyric motif—that of the 'Desirable Inaccessible'. The Greek lyricists, their choric mouthpieces, and their characters often claim (or are said) to be in love with beautiful girls or boys. Claims of conquest are much less frequent. This principle applies to Sappho (cf. Bowra 1961; general index s.v. 'Sappho: and love'),[28] Alcaeus, Ibycus, and Anacreon,[29] as well as to Alcman's choruses, which limit themselves to erotic aspirations. Again, the sports audience that Pindar imagines as admiring beautiful victors (cf. Bowra 1964: 167–70) will hardly have been envisaged by him as going any further. Archaic lyric exploitation of the topos of the 'Desirable Inaccessible' is easy to understand in ancient terms. Beauty in a young man or girl was regarded as a plausible ground for praise; and the most effective way for the lyric poet to convince his audience that the *laudandus/a* was indeed beautiful was to demonstrate that (s)he her/himself or another/

[26] In these lines Asterie is being counselled not to be a παρακύπτουσα, a standard komastic figure: cf. LSJ s.vv παρακύπτω II.2, ἐκκύπτω; Copley (1956) 134–5, 171 n. 24; Cairns (1972) 209.

[27] The widespread lyric examples (see e.g. Davies 1980) range from the explicit, e.g. Sapph. fr. 31. 7 ff. LP—indebted to Homer (see Page 1955: 29 and n. 1)—to the implicit (see Bremer 1976: ch. 4, index 3 s.v. *Liebe*). The concept was also widespread in later classical literature (see e.g. Hoelzer 1899: 38–40; Fedeli 1980: 64, on Prop. 1. 1. 1). It even became emblematic of elegy: cf. Prop. 1. 1. 1, echoing Meleager.

[28] Although outdated in certain well-known respects, this work and Bowra (1964) offer the best extant summaries of numerous aspects of early Greek lyric poetry, made doubly accessible through their excellent indexes.

[29] See Bowra (1961) general index s.vv 'Alcaeus: love'; 'Ibycus: love'; 'Anacreon: love-poems, boys and court convention'.

others were in love with them. But at the same time the reputation of the young beauty had to be protected—and the best way to do this was to state or imply non-gratification.[30]

Odes 3. 7, then, draws heavily on typical themes of archaic Greek lyric, which is hardly surprising given that Horace had aspired at *Odes* 1. 1. 35 (cf. Nisbet and Hubbard 1970 ad loc) to inclusion in the Alexandrian canon of the *lyrici*. Indeed, it is only because *Odes* 3. 7 is so characteristically lyric in its *Topik* and thought that it can successfully 'take over' elegy (cf. above, Sections 2 and 3). As has already been indicated (above and nn. 21, 23, 25, 27), most of *Odes* 3. 7's typical lyric themes are not exclusive to lyric. This creates no problem: such themes self-evidently need not be unique to lyric in order to be deemed specific to that genre. It is of course quite another matter when claims are made, for example, that elegiac concepts are present in a lyric ode (cf. above, Sections 2 and 3). To ignore this distinction would be just as absurd as to deny that Virgil intended *arma virumque* as a specifically epic incipit on the grounds that *arma* also has a specific erotic usage in elegy (cf. Propertius 1. 3. 16) and that among the recurrent stereotypes of elegy is the beloved's *vir*!

5. LYRIC NOMENCLATURE AND ITS IMPLICATIONS

The lyric themes of *Odes* 3. 7 prompt the question whether its characters' nomenclature might also derive from archaic lyric. No firm answer can be given; but two indirect approaches open up in combination some interesting, if elusive, possibilities. The first derives from the partial overlaps of nomenclature between this and other Horatian odes: Asterie and Enipeus are Horatian *unica*, but Chloe and Gyges recur. Chloe also appears in *Odes* 1. 23 (an animal poem probably indebted to Anacreon; cf. Nisbet and Hubbard 1970: 273-4), in *Odes* 3. 9, and in *Odes* 3. 26. In none of these is she accompanied by another character from *Odes* 3. 7. But her cognate Chloris crops up in *Odes* 2. 5 (another animal poem—also influenced by Anacreon?) along with Gyges and Pholoe. The pair Chloris and Pholoe then resurface in *Odes* 3. 15,

---

[30] In lyric girls usually had the extra protection that their lover was female; the complexities of male 'homosexual' ethics in this area are best explored with Dover (1978, esp. 81 ff.).

along with 'Ibycus' (see below). Pholoe also features in *Odes* 1. 33,
already mentioned (above, Section 3) as addressed to Tibullus, and
she is of course also a Tibullan character (1. 8). What, if anything,
does all this mean? Has Horace simply assembled a common stock
of Greek character-names from early Greek lyric and then deployed
them randomly so that they sometimes recur in combination by
pure chance? Or do the Horatian associations reflect, however
dimly, his Greek lyric models?

The second indirect approach to the nomenclature of *Odes* 3. 7—
and one which favours the second alternative—concerns 'Gyges'.
With first syllable long (see also below, Section 7) 'Gyges' is
also, as commentators have pointed out (cf. Harrison 1988: 186
n. 4, citing predecessors), the πολύχρυσος king of Lydia, whom
Herodotus' account (1. 8-15) makes relevant to our *beatus* Gyges
not just through his wealth but also through the wife of his
predecessor, Candaules. She had threatened Gyges with death if
he would not kill Candaules and take his place as king and as her
husband, a tale manifestly analogous to the myths of Bellerophon
(13-16, esp. *casto Bellerophontae | maturare necem*, 15-16) and of
Peleus (17-20, esp. *paene datum Pelea Tartaro | . . . abstinens*,
17-18) in *Odes* 3. 7. At first sight the king might seem to have
nothing to do with the Gyges of *Odes* 2. 5, where the poet's (or
addressee's) beloved, Lalage, is compared in prospect with her now
superannuated rivals: Pholoe, Chloris, and finally (surprisingly
prominent, capping the ascending tricolon, and with an entire
stanza):

> . . . Cnidiusve Gyges,
> quem si puellarum insereres choro,
> mire sagaces falleret hospites
> discrimen obscurum solutis
> crinibus ambiguoque voltu.

> (*Odes* 2. 5. 20-4)

This epicene Gyges is reminiscent rather of a Smerdis or a
Bathyllos. But there is an account of the king of Lydia ignored to
date by the commentators on Horace which partly bridges the gap
between the king and the *erōmenos*. Gyges of Lydia features in the
Histories of Horace's contemporary, the biographer of Augustus,
Nicolaus of Damascus. *FGrHist* 90 F 62 introduces a certain
Smyrniote called, interestingly (cf. below), Magnes, who was good-

looking, talented in poetry and music, well groomed and well dressed, and who went round the cities performing his poetry. Males and females fell in love with this 'poeta vagante'. One of them was Gyges, who made Magnes his παιδικά. For good measure Magnes also seduced women, especially Magnesian women. Their relatives were outraged; and when Magnes was reciting his epic poem celebrating the cavalry victory of the Lydians over the Amazons, a poem which made no mention of the Magnesians, they seized this pretext and beat him up. Gyges then punished the Magnesians by invading their territory and capturing their city. So here is a Gyges of Lydia who, if not an *erōmenos* like the Gyges of *Odes* 2. 5, is at least a homosexual *erastēs*.

Further elements of Nicolaus' portrait of Gyges resonate equally indirectly, this time with *Odes* 3. 7. *FGrHist* 90 F 47 relates how Gyges became king of Lydia, displacing (on this account) a predecessor named Adyattes or Sadyattes. Here Gyges is a handsome young man (3), enrolled by king Adyattes in his bodyguard. Later Adyattes takes a dislike to him and sends him against wild boars and beasts, hoping that he will be killed (cf. the legend of Peleus and *Odes* 3. 7. 17–18). Gyges survives, regains Adyattes' favour, and is sent by the king in a chariot to fetch home the prospective royal bride. But on the way back Gyges propositions the girl while they are riding in the chariot (cf. the story of Pelops' charioteer Myrsilos). This Gyges, then, is a would-be seducer. Unlike the Gyges of *Odes* 3. 7—but like the Enipeus of that ode—he makes an attempt on a 'wife'. Nicolaus goes on to describe the killing of Adyattes by Gyges and his friends.

Could there be a link between Horace and Nicolaus? Two points favour this notion. First Horace, as will appear in Section 8, is almost certainly using a handbook of mythology for *Odes* 3. 7; and Nicolaus' *Historiae* would fit the bill fairly well. The *Historiae* treated not just Gyges but the central myths of *Odes* 3. 7: Bellerophon, Sthenoboea, and Proetus (cf. *Odes* 3. 7. 13–16) at *FGrHist* 90 F 9; and Akastos, his wife, and Peleus (cf. *Odes* 3. 7. 17–18) at *FGrHist* 90 F 55. Second, *Odes* 3. 7 seems to cite a precise source, and even to compliment a contemporary in so doing. In the middle of *Odes* 3. 7 stand the balanced word-pair *refert* (16) and *narrat* (17), the first at the very end of stanza 4, the second at the very beginning of stanza 5. These two words thus occupy the strategic central location of the ode—on its importance

see L. A. Moritz (1968)—and presumably they must be saying
something important. That they are a 'citation' is suggested by
their analogues in Virgil, *Eclogue* 6: *refert*, 42; *adiungit*, 43;
narraverit, 78; there, incidentally, lines 42 and 43 stand at the
centre of an 86-line poem! *Eclogue* 6 is notoriously problematic;
but there is some consensus that Virgil is referring in it to the
work(s) of another poet or poets (cf. Ross 1975: ch. 2, with the
earlier bibliography assembled there). Virgil's 'citations' in lines
42-3 and 78 help to make explicit what he is doing. The value
of *Eclogue* 6 in illustrating *Odes* 3. 7 is further enhanced by an
apparently unobserved allusion (with witty variation) which the
ode makes to the eclogue:

> *Proetides implerunt falsis mugitibus* agros
>
> (*Eclogue* 6. 48)

> ut *Proetum* mulier perfida credulum
> *falsis impulerit criminibus*
>
> (Hor. *Odes* 3. 7. 13-14)

It is well-nigh certain that in *Eclogue* 6 Virgil is citing recognizable
contemporary or near-contemporary poets. But Horace is much
less likely to be citing a contemporary lyric source: he claimed to
be the first in his field; and it is hard to think whom he had to cite
anyway. Horace might of course be alluding to an archaic lyric
poet, in which case few will have picked up his allusion. But it
is at least worth entertaining the possibility that his reference to
historias at *Odes* 3. 7. 20 reinforces his *refert/narrat* citation of a few
lines before and points to Nicolaus' *Historiae*. Nicolaus was greatly
favoured by Augustus, and he and Horace must have been
acquainted.

It could of course be objected correctly that all the myths
involved are common ones, that Nicolaus' Gyges is only tangen-
tially reminiscent of Horace's Gyges, that Horace must have had
lyric precedents in mind too, and that the mythographic hinterland
of the ode is far more complex (cf. also Section 8). But Horace may
nevertheless still be paying a graceful compliment to Nicolaus'
Historiae, even though he had used them only as his starting-point,
much as Cornelius Gallus was supposedly meant to use Parthenius'
Erōtika pathēmata.[31] For behind Nicolaus' Lydian material lies not

---

[31] Cairns (1979) 226 expressed scepticism about over-literal interpretation of the
dedicatory preface of the *Erōtika Pathēmata*.

only Herodotus and Xanthus of Lydia[32] but also the earlier poets
on whom Herodotus certainly and Xanthus almost certainly
drew—and Gyges was mentioned by at least two early Greek poets:
Archilochus (Herodotus 1. 12; fr. 19 West) and Hipponax (fr. 7. 3
Degani). Nicolaus may therefore preserve traces of a variously
romanticized Gyges who originated in archaic Greek poetry and
came from it, diversified and by different routes, into *Odes* 2. 5 and
3. 7. The appearance in *Odes* 3. 7 of two motifs also found in the
king Gyges tradition, but so obliquely represented in the ode as
not to seem derived from the surviving accounts of Gyges, might
support this view. The first is 'night': Herodotus twice refers in his
Gyges story to the coming on of night: ὥρη τῆς κοίτης, 1. 10;
νυκτὸς γενομένης, 1. 12; cf. *prima nocte*, *Odes* 3. 7. 29. Again,
'night' features prominently in Nicolaus' account of Gyges' killing
of Adyattes (cf. *FGrHist* 90 F 47. 8). The second motif is
'Magnesia'. Candaules was said to have paid a large sum for a
painting of the defeat of the Magnesians in battle (Pliny, *Natural
History* 7. 126, 35. 55)—cf. Horace's *Magnessam*, *Odes* 3. 7. 18—
but of Thessalian, not Asian, Magnesia; and Magnes and Magnesia
feature largely in Nicolaus' narrative (cf. above).

What early Greek lyric predecessor(s), then, might *Odes* 3. 7
have had? The partial overlaps of nomenclature discussed above,
and the probable indebtedness of *Odes* 1. 23, and perhaps also
of 2. 5, to Anacreon, might suggest Anacreon (cf. also 2. 5. 22
hospites and 7. 9 *hospitae*). But again, Pholoe and Chloris, who
featured in 2. 5, reappear in *Odes* 3. 15 along with 'Ibycus' (1).
Surely Horace must be pointing to the poet Ibycus as the 'source'
of *Odes* 3. 15? And surely the pairing of Pholoe and Chloris in *Odes*
2. 5 also raises the possibility that (despite its Anacreontic appearance) it is also, in whole or part, Ibycan? And again, could Ibycus
conceivably have inspired *Odes* 3. 7 too?[33] Three further scraps of
Ibycus' work may help that hypothesis; two show his interest in
characters named Hippolyte, and the third reveals that he wrote
about Peleus.

εἶχεν γὰρ [sc. Jason] ἀδελφὴν Ἱππολύτην, ὥς φησιν Ἴβυκος (fr. 301 *PMG*)

πολλοὶ δὲ λόγοι περὶ τοῦ ζωστῆρός εἰσιν. τινὲς μὲν γὰρ Ἱππολύτης, ἄλλοι δὲ

---

[32] Cf. *FGrHist* iic. 233 ff., although the question of contamination with later
sources also arises; cf. *K.P.* s.v. Xanthos 5.

[33] The stellar imagery at *Odes* 3. 15. 6 *stellis . . . candidis* has already been noted
above, sect. 4, in connection with the stellar interest of *Odes* 3. 7.

Δηϊλύκης. Ἴβυκος δὲ ἰδίως ἱστορῶν Οἰολύκης τῆς Βριάρεω θυγατρός φησιν. (fr. 299 PMG)

Π]ηλεὺ[ς] δέπαλα ..[(PMG S 176. 11)

6. THE DRAMATIS PERSONAE AGAIN

Horatian scholarship has generally, and correctly, regarded the characters of *Odes* 3. 7, despite their Greek names, as Roman (cf. e.g. Kiessling and Heinze 1914-30: i. 294-5) But in what sense? Are they merely residents of Rome, or are they, all or some, citizens? The easiest decision concerns Enipeus. He exercises in the Campus Martius—that is, he prepares for his military duties—and he is, in the words of Williams (1969: 70), 'a perfect example of the model Augustan young man, devoted to athletic training and good at it'. He is patently a *civis Romanus*, and his riding may signal his equestrian status.[34] What, then, about Gyges? He is a rich merchant and shipmaster—presumably, since we are not told otherwise—in business on his own account. He is characterized, at least in his relationship with Asterie, by *fides*, and, as Heinze saw (above, Section 3), he is absolved by Horace from excessive greed. There is nothing in this to suggest the non-citizen or freedman. If anything, Gyges is reminiscent of the citizen trader of *Odes* 1. 1. 15-18, who features in Horace's contemporary gallery of Roman occupations. Gyges, then, is also a Roman citizen, and he may also be equestrian.

The social status of Asterie is nowhere made explicit. Two scenarios are possible: the first is that Asterie is a *libertina* with a citizen lover (Gyges) and a citizen suitor (Enipeus). This scenario, which implies view (2), that the ode is light relief, is purely elegiac:

[34] At *Odes* 4. 1. 37-40 Horace describes how he dreams of his *erōmenos* 'Ligurinus' (also featured in *Odes* 4. 10): 'nocturnis ego somniis | iam captum teneo, iam volucrem sequor | te per gramina Martii | Campi, te per aquas, dure, volubilis.' I am grateful to Prof. V. Pöschl for drawing my attention to this passage and for suggesting that (since Ligurinus is not in his opinion a Roman and since he is represented here as running on the Campus and swimming in the Tiber) it shows that Enipeus' citizen (and indeed equestrian) status cannot be deduced from his riding in the Campus, and also calls into question similar judgements about Sybaris and Hebrus. Two responses, possibly valid concurrently, may be made: (1) 'Ligurinus' could perfectly well be a Roman, like Catullus' *erōmenos* Iuventius, since, provided he was obdurate—as Ligurinus is—being loved was not inappropriate for a citizen; (2) the whole thing is a dream, and hence doubly removed from reality.

cf. the situations in which Tibullus, Propertius, and Ovid (all, incidentally, *equites Romani*) claim to find themselves. So, up to a point, it explains the elegiac content of *Odes* 3. 7. But it is not unproblematic: it does not also explain why the ode contains so much counter-elegiac material too; and it reduces the interplay between elegy and lyric to an implicit claim that lyric can safeguard an 'elegiac' relationship better than elegy. This is not a plausible claim to foist upon a lyric poet. Again, if Gyges and Asterie were simply a pair of lovers whose relationship is under threat, and if Asterie were either a non-citizen or at best a *libertina*, then the situation would have no moral implications for Horace's readers. So why is Horace counselling Asterie to observe fidelity towards Gyges? And why is he so concerned about this group of characters in the first place?

The alternative scenario is that Gyges and Asterie are husband and wife, so that Asterie is a Roman *matrona*. There are four advantages to this approach, which amounts to view (3). The first was expressed by Santirocco (1986: 125), namely that on this view *Odes* 3. 7 continues to preach marital fidelity to citizen women—an important theme of the 'Roman Odes'. In this way *Odes* 3. 7 is both transitional and a continuation of the 'Roman Odes'. Second, this approach explains the use which Propertius subsequently made of *Odes* 3. 7's main theme, first in his elegy 3. 12, where the subjects are his senatorial cousin Postumus and Postumus' wife Aelia Galla, and then, in a more attenuated way, in elegy 4. 3, where, as in *Odes* 3. 7, the protagonists are Romans in Greek masquerade. Propertius' exploitations of *Odes* 3. 7 make more sense if he regarded Gyges and Asterie as married *cives*.

Third, if citizen marriage is being upheld by *Odes* 3. 7, its undermining of elegy becomes more meaningful. Elegy, by its nature and self-admittedly, was linked with *nequitia* and *amor*, and was openly antipathetic to the social, moral, and military demands of the *respublica* upon *cives*, which included marriage. On the other hand, Horace's main lyric model was the citizen and soldier Alcaeus. As a deutero-Alcaeus, Horace had just written six odes enunciating the demands of the Roman state, and encouraging his audience to respond to them. It is therefore appropriate for him to target elegy, the enemy of citizen morality, in his transitional seventh ode. The ode's heavily elegiac language makes its target clear, while the startling blend of the elegiac and non-elegiac in its

male characters, together with its thematic evocations of the world
of early lyric, hint that its ethos is non-elegiac, a warning fulfilled
when Horace offers anti-elegiac advice in the final stanzas. Horace,
then, is seizing the moral high ground for lyric, and is denying
moral standing to elegy. The fourth advantage of this approach,
and a further argument for it, is that the myths of Peleus and
Bellerophon, which occupy the centre of *Odes* 3. 7, both involve
marriage. These myths will feature again in Section 7.

7. MYTHICAL NOMENCLATURE

The interpretation of myth, mythical personages, and mythical
nomenclature in ancient poetry is notoriously difficult. A single
figure, event, or name may have countless potential significances
and associations. Hercules, Dionysus, and the Muses are paradigmatic: self-evidently a mere mention of them cannot imply
everything ever associated with them. But what are the sensible
limits of implication?

Odes 3. 7 is a good test case. Its characters bear mythical names:
certainly Asterie, Gyges, and Enipeus, and possibly Chloe.[35] Two
further myths involving Bellerophon and Peleus make their appearance. So what connotations of these mythical figures, and what
elements of their myths, are relevant to the ode? With Horace there
is an additional problem, his inventiveness over nomenclature. In
Odes I. 33, discussed above in Section 3, Albius (Tibullus)'s girl-
friend is called 'Glycera' (2), whereas in Tibullus' elegies she is
'Delia' or (later) 'Nemesis'. Unless Horace knew something unknown to us, 'Glycera' is a Horatian invention, a lyric (?) mistress-
name (cf. *Odes* I. 19. 5, I. 30. 3, 3. 19. 28) substituted for the
correct elegiac name. The Valgius–Mystes combination of *Odes* 2.
9, where again elegy is in question (9), could involve similar ono-
mastic invention by Horace.[36] *Odes* 3. 7 may contain a further
example: 'Chloe' does not really fit any account of the ode

---

[35] It has been suggested that her name reflects a cult-title of Demeter: see
Mutschler (1978) 114-15, 128 n. 15, and below, n. 49. On the names in *Odes* 3.
7 Gruner (1920: 3-4, 20-1, 44, 49) offers basic facts but scant illumination for the
poem.

[36] On Horace's possible inventiveness over nomenclature (including Glycera and
Mystes), see F. Jones (1986). On the ramifications of the name Mystes, see most
recently Davis (1991) 54-60.

previously given; nor can she be integrated with the one offered in this paper. Could Chloe, then, be an odd name out, a wild-card character invented by Horace or taken by him from a lyric predecessor but out of immediate context?

To return to the names from which something substantial can be extracted: as noted (above, Section 5), Gyges, with first syllable long, is also the name of the wealthy (cf. *beatum*, 3) king of Lydia. But in myth and history king Gyges had no connection with Asterie or Enipeus (or Chloe). Could Horace, then, or a predecessor, have conflated the king with the Titan Gyges, the 'hundred-hander' (cf. *RE* s.v. Gyges 3), whose name has its first syllable short? Herodian 2. 678. 27-9 Lenz appears to incorporate a standard ancient grammatical doctrine about the names of the king and the hundred-hander: Γύγης Γύγου καὶ Γύγητος, ἐπὶ τοῦ γίγαντος, ὅτε δὲ ἐπὶ τοῦ βασιλέως τῆς Λυδίας λέγεται σπονδειακόν ἐστι καὶ ἰσοσυλλάβως κλίνεται . . .[37] Horace, like most ancient writers, observes the distinction. He has the hundred-hander at *Odes* 2. 17. 14 and 3. 4. 69 with first syllable short; and he has two 'real' persons called Gyges (*Odes* 2. 5. 20; 3. 7. 5) with first syllable long, and hence named after the king of Lydia.[38]

But there is also ancient evidence that the distinction between the two names was not always observed. Alexander Aetolus *APl.* 172 = Gow-Page 1 (1965: i. 10) ends an epigram with the pentameter θῆκαν Δασκύλεω μείζονα καὶ Γύγεω. We must either rewrite and/or reorder this line radically,[39] or admit that on this occasion king Gyges has short first syllable. There is more: although Herodian's doctrine distinguishes the two names, it shows a general ancient consciousness that the king and the hundred-hander were homographs. Hence any reference to one must instantly have brought the other to mind.[40] A discussion of 'Gyges'

[37] Cf. also Herodian 2. 639. 6 Lenz, and the passages of Alexander Aetolus and of the Nicander scholia quoted below. All were already utilized by M. L. West (1966) on Hes. *Theog.* 149 Γύγης.

[38] The manuscripts read *gigas*, not *Gyges*, at *Odes* 2. 17. 14 and 3. 4. 69. Nisbet and Hubbard (1978) 279, on *Odes* 2. 17. 14 *Gyges*, point out that, while *gigas* could be defended, Muretus' *Gyges* 'is very plausible'; cf. esp. their remark on the particular susceptibility to corruption of *Gyges* 'because of the unfamiliar scansion'. See further Booth (1991) 101, on Ov. *Am.* 2. 1. 12.

[39] Cf. Gow and Page (1965) ii. 28 on past attempts to regularize the quantity by rewriting line 6. None is persuasive, and it is equally illicit to substitute Candaules for Daskylos(es).

[40] A similar and confirmatory mythical linkage is discussed by Geymonat (1978-9) 372 and n. 4.

in the scholia to Nicander confirms the close association between the two names, and it perhaps reveals more: παραὶ Γύγαό τε· ἤτοι Γύγου τοῦ βασιλέως σῆμα . . . ἢ τὴν Γυγαίαν λίμνην λέγει ἀπὸ Γύγου τοῦ ἑκατογχείρου (Σ Nicander, *Theriaca* 633 Schneider). The indifference shown here about whether Γυγαία λίμνη derives from the name of the king or from that of the hundred-hander may suggest that the quantity of 'Gyges' was more widely disregarded in antiquity. Hence Alexander Aetolus' use of the short first syllable for the king (above) was perhaps not as much of an aberration as Gow–Page thought (1965: ii. 28 ad loc.). The suspicion that the distinction of quantity would not in isolation have discriminated adequately for all readers may be strengthened by the ways in which Horace introduces his various Gygeses. When the hundred-hander Gyges appears (*Odes* 2. 17. 14 and 3. 4. 69), Horace, as well as observing the distinction of quantity, adds a further clue: *centimanus*. Similarly, the 'real' Gygeses (with long first syllable) named after the king are distinguished both from the king and from the hundred-hander by *Cnidius* at *Odes* 2. 5. 20 and by *constantis iuvenem fide* at *Odes* 3. 7. 4. A last point: ancient disregard of quantity in puns and etymologies speaks in favour of a general primacy of letters over quantities.[41]

The advantage of associating the Gyges of *Odes* 3. 7 with the hundred-hander Gyges is that Asterie too is a Titan name. The hundred-handers were the children of Earth and Ouranos:

> ἄλλοι δ' αὖ Γαίης τε καὶ Οὐρανοῦ ἐξεγένοντο
> τρεῖς παῖδες μεγάλοι ⟨τε⟩ καὶ ὄβριμοι, οὐκ ὀνομαστοί,
> Κόττος τε Βριάρεώς τε Γύγης θ', ὑπερήφανα τέκνα.
> τῶν ἑκατὸν μὲν χεῖρες ἀπ' ὤμων ἀΐσσοντο,
> ἄπλαστοι, κεφαλαὶ δὲ ἑκάστῳ πεντήκοντα
> ἐξ ὤμων ἐπέφυκον ἐπὶ στιβαροῖσι μέλεσσιν·
> ἰσχὺς δ' ἄπλητος κρατερὴ μεγάλῳ ἐπὶ εἴδει.

(Hes. Theogony 147-53)

They were confined in Tartarus by Kronos, and brought out of confinement by Zeus to help him fight the other Titans. They turned the tide of battle in favour of the gods (Hesiod, *Theogony* 617-819). Now one of the several mythical Asteries also features in the *Theogony*—the daughter of Koios and Phoebe, sister of Leto and mother (by Perses) of Hecate (cf. *RE* s.v. Asteria 6):

---

[41] Cf. Wölfflin (1893); Adams (1981) 200 n. 3.

Φοίβη δ' αὖ Κοίου πολυήρατον ἦλθεν ἐς εὐνήν·
κυσαμένη δήπειτα θεὰ θεοῦ ἐν φιλότητι
Λητὼ κυανόπεπλον ἐγείνατο, μείλιχον αἰεί,
ἤπιον ἀνθρώποισι καὶ ἀθανάτοισι θεοῖσι,
μείλιχον ἐξ ἀρχῆς, ἀγανώτατον ἐντὸς Ὀλύμπου.
γείνατο δ' Ἀστερίην εὐώνυμον, ἥν ποτε Πέρσης
ἠγάγετ' ἐς μέγα δῶμα φίλην κεκλῆσθαι ἄκοιτιν.
ἡ δ' ὑποκυσαμένη Ἑκάτην τέκε, τὴν περὶ πάντων
Ζεὺς Κρονίδης τίμησε . . .

(Hes. *Theogony* 404-12)[42]

Some incidental points may be made here: a later variant myth
recounted that Zeus was Hecate's father, having cuckolded Perses
(cf. M. L. West 1966 on *Theogony* 409); and Zeus also features in
the Pindaric (fr. 52h. 43 ff.) and Callimachean (*Hymn* 4. 36-8)
versions of the legend that Asterie fled from him, fell into the sea,
and became the island of Delos. This emphasis on the sexual
reluctance of the mythical Asterie seems relevant to *Odes* 3. 7,
where Horace is urging reluctance on his Asterie. Again, the fact
that Asterie was an older name of Delos may recall, in this ode
so taken up with elegy, the popularity of Delos-linked names for
the mistresses of Roman elegists: Tibullus' Delia and Propertius'
Cynthia called after Mt. Cynthos on Delos (cf. Randall 1979). But
the most interesting aspect of Asterie/Delos is that (as noted) she
comes from the same mythical ambience as Gyges the 'hundred-
hander'. They are both Titans: in the later mythographic tradition
Gyges is *Titan* (Hyginus, *praef.* 3) and Asterie is *Titani(s) filia*
(Hyginus 53; Lactantius Placidus on Statius, *Thebaid* 4. 95). They
were contemporaries, and, like Gyges, Asterie fought on the side
of Zeus in the war against the other Titans; indeed, Asterie is
represented in battle in the Gigantomachia upon the Altar of
Pergamon, and her name is inscribed there.[43] Our Gyges and
Asterie might therefore be linked through the two Titans of myth.[44]

What, then, of Enipeus? The only relevant mythical Enipeus is
the Thessalian (or Elean)[45] river-god with whom Tyro was in love.

---

[42] On these matters see further M. L. West (1966) 206 ff., on Hes. *Theog.*
139-53, 158, and 336 ff. on 617-719.

[43] See. *RE* s.v. Asteria 65 col. 1782; Simon (1975) index s.v. Asterie.

[44] A further curious link by contrast is that in the *Theogony* Gyges and the other
hundred-handers are οὐκ ὀνομαστοί (148), while Asterie is εὐώνυμον (409). There are
only two other such descriptions in the work: δυσωνύμου (171, of Ouranos) and οὔ
τι φατειόν (310, of Cerberus).

[45] See. *RE* s.vv. Enipeus 2, and 4; Tyro, col. 1870. On the less common variant

Poseidon disguised himself as Enipeus to win Tyro's favours. The myth of Tyro was well known in antiquity;[46] and long ago Festa (1940) suggested that Horace was thinking of Poseidon disguised as Enipeus. Festa's contribution was unfortunately vitiated by his final paragraphs, which indulged in charming fantasies about Asterie holiday-making at Paestum. But his suggestion is surely correct. Otherwise the mythical analogue makes no sense, since Tyro was in love with Enipeus and would not have resisted him. Festa went on to propose that Enipeus was a cult manifestation of Poseidon, and indeed 'Enipeus' is attested as a cult-title of Poseidon at Miletus (see *Σ* Tzetzes on Lycophron 722). Interestingly, Ovid, *Metamorphoses* 6. 116-17 (cf. Bömer 1969-86 ad loc.), reports that Poseidon also used the Enipeus guise to beget the Aleuads. This variant certainly resulted from a confusion in Ovid's sources;[47] but such confusions, further expanding the activities of Poseidon-Enipeus, may have been more numerous.

But there remains a hiatus—between the Titans Gyges and Asterie on the one hand and Enipeus-Poseidon on the other. Again, a variant myth may bridge it: the standard version of Asterie's flight to become a quail or Delos makes Zeus the importuning god; but in another version he is Poseidon. This version appears only in Nonnus; but it crops up in three separate passages of the *Dionysiaca*: at 2. 124-5 and 42. 410, where it is fleeting but definite, and at 33. 336-40, where it is more elaborately related:

> οὔ με διεπτοίησεν ἐρωμανέων ἐνοσίχθων,
> οἷά περ Ἀστερίην φιλοπάρθενον, ἣν ἐνὶ πόντῳ
> πλαζομένην ἐδίωκε παλίνδρομον, εἰσόκεν αὐτὴν
> ἄστατον ἱππεύουσαν ἀμοιβάδι σύνδρομον αὔρη
> κύμασιν ἀστυφέλικτον ἐνερρίζωσεν Ἀπόλλων.

Vian (1976) 171, on *Dionysiaca* 2. 125, referring to Schwartz (1960) 289-90, rightly accepted Schwartz's view that Nonnus' version arose from a muddle within post-Hesiodic catalogues of divine lovers, the objects of their love, and the disguises adopted by

which made Enipeus an Elean river-(god) see Pearson (1917) 270-1; *RE* s. vv. Enipeus 1 and 5; Tyro, col. 1870. For a further reason for thinking that Horace was using the Thessalian version, see below.

[46] See Pearson (1917) 270 ff.; Schwartz (1960) index v, 'Mythologie', s.v. Énipée; Roscher, *Myth. Lex.* s.v. Tyro; *RE* s.v. Tyro. The last (G. Radke) is the best analytic account of Tyro.

[47] See Schwartz (1960) 290-1 (q.v.), who explains such variants as the result of 'slippage' between pairs of mythical lists.

them.[48] But when did this muddle originate? Nonnus might once have been dismissed automatically as a late source of dubious value; but nowadays his capacity to preserve genuine information about Hellenistic poetry is better recognized (cf. Hollis 1976). There is in fact no reason in principle why the Poseidon–Asterie variant should not be Hellenistic and hence have been known to Horace. But it is not necessary to stake an interpretation of the ode on this point. Although it would be gratifying to integrate Enipeus into the Asterie–Gyges complex, it is not essential to do so; and even if Enipeus can be linked with Asterie through the variant myth of the *Dionysiaca*, there remain two aberrant features. First, in Hesiod and elsewhere Asterie's husband is Perses, not Gyges; and second (as was noted), Horace's Chloe does not fit any discernible mythical pattern anyhow. If we were to take her name as reflecting a cult-title of Demeter (see above), a tenuous link might be proposed on the basis that Demeter too participated in the Gigantomachia—and is portrayed on the Pergamon altar (see Simon 1975: index s.v. Demeter). But (naturally) Demeter fought on the same side as Gyges and Asterie, whereas Chloe in *Odes* 1. 6 represents a threat to Gyges and Asterie; and again, if Horace had wanted to refer to Demeter, it is hard to see why he would have called her Chloe in this context.[49]

A last link between Horace's Asterie and Enipeus and the Poseidon-Enipeus myth—one perhaps particularly germane to this ode so full of etymology (cf. below, Appendix 1)—may end this section. As noted, Poseidon-Enipeus' victim in the standard myth was Tyro, not Asterie. Tyro got her name from her 'whiteness', as Sophocles stressed in his plays called *Tyro* (cf. Pearson 1917: 271, 274; *RE* s.v. Tyro, col. 1874). There some emphasis was placed on the contrast between her creamy-white skin and the livid bruises inflicted upon it by her, again aptly named, stepmother Sidero (cf. Pearson 1917: 271, 282; *RE* s.v. Tyro, coll. 1873-4). The Augustans were well aware of all this; Tyro belonged to a traditional grouping of white-skinned or white-legged heroines, and

---

[48] The description of Asterie as νῆσος ἐρήμη in the final appearance of the variant (*Dionys.* 42. 410) confirms this theory, since it would more aptly refer to the nymph Aegina, whose liaison was with Zeus. *Aen.* 3. 73-4 (describing Delos) 'sacra mari colitur medio gratissima tellus | Nereidum matri et Neptuno Aegaeo' (with Servius ad loc.) cannot be pressed in this connection.

[49] Mutschler (1978) 114-15 offers an explanation to do with Gyges' cold nights and his wish for the coming spring.

in this context she was for Propertius *candida Tyro* (2. 28. 51). Is
it entirely an accident that, when etymologizing 'Asterie' in *Odes*
3. 7 (see below, Appendix 1), Horace used the word *candidi* (1)?

8. HANDBOOKS AND FURTHER RAMIFICATIONS OF MYTH

The possibility that Horace made use of Nicolaus' *Historiae* for *Odes*
3. 7 was mentioned in Section 5. Whatever one thinks of this
notion and the arguments in its favour, there are additional
indications that some mythological handbook(s) or other influenced
the ode. Thus, the myth variant discussed above (Section 7) in
which Enipeus-Poseidon pursued the Titan Asterie can only derive
from a muddle in a post-Hesiodic handbook list. So if Horace is
thinking of that variant, a handbook source is indicated. Again, the
Fabulae of 'Hyginus' are a later reflection of the handbooks available to Horace, all of which, except for parts of Nicolaus' *Historiae*,
have perished. The Titan Asterie is the subject of 'Hyginus' ch. 53,
Peleus appears in ch. 54, and ch. 57 treats Bellerophon, Proetus,
and Sthenoboea. Details reminiscent of *Odes* 3. 7 are lacking,
but the grouping of these myths in 'Hyginus' could in itself be
indicative.[50]

A further set of associations between the mythical characters of
Odes 3. 7 may also reflect a handbook source. Curiously, Tyro is
the pivotal figure here too. By Poseidon-Enipeus Tyro had two sons,
Pelias and Neleus. Pelias became the father of Akastos, husband of
Hippolyte; and Hippolyte, who tried to allure Peleus, was none
other than Tyro's daughter by her husband Kretheus. The family
tree is thus (cf. *RE* s.v. Tyro; *Kl.P.* s.vv. Pelias, Peleus):

POSEIDON disguised as ENIPEUS = TYRO = KRETHEUS
                   |
ANAXIBOIA or PHYLOMACHE = PELIAS
                   |
             AKASTOS = HIPPOLYTE ~ PELEUS

This family tree may also help to explain why Horace calls

---

[50] Disappointingly, nothing can be made of the amusing appearance of Enipeus
in Lucian, *Dial. Mar.* 13, on which see Schwartz (1960) 359-60. Similarly, the
presence of two other dialogues (7 and 15) between *Zephyros* (cf. *Favonii, Odes* 3. 7.
2) and *Notos* (cf. *Notis, Odes* 3. 7. 5) is probably mere coincidence.

Hippolyte *Magnessam* in line 18. Nisbet (1989) 87 (q.v.) provided
a part-explanation: *Magnessam* hints (paradoxically) at Hippolyte's
'magnetic' attractiveness,[51] which however fails to win over
Peleus; magnets were associated in antiquity with Thessalian
Magnesia; and magnetic and erotic attraction were analogized. The
adjective may also have a discriminatory function: the River
Enipeus was claimed (cf. above, Section 7) both by Thessaly and by
Elis (cf. Pearson 1917: 270–1; *RE* s.vv. Enipeus 1, 2, 4, and 5,
Tyro col. 1870). *Magnessam* would come down strongly on the
Thessalian side,[52] since placing Hippolyte in Thessaly places her
mother Tyro there too, and so, by implication, locates the River
Enipeus in Thessaly. Such emphasis on Thessaly serves no obvious
purpose in the ode besides introducing the notion of 'magnetism'—
and Hippolyte failed. So the epithet (like the dispute which it
resolved) may be the legacy of a handbook.[53]

There are further, more elusive, indications that *Odes* 3. 7 draws
on a handbook or handbooks of myth. Consider the following:

(1) Bellerophon had a daughter called Laodameia, and one of
the daughters of Akastos and Hippolyte was also called
Laodameia; cf. *Kl.P.* s.v. Laodameia 1, 2.

(2) The Titan Asterie is the wife of the river-god Hydaspes at
Nonnus, *Dionysiaca* 23. 236–7, although elsewhere in
Nonnus, i.e. at 17. 282 and 26. 353, his wife is Astris.

(3) Bellerophon according to one report had an Asterie,
daughter of Hydeas or Hydeos, as his wife. By her he
became the father of Hydissos; cf. *RE* s.v. Asterie 11.

(4) Poseidon is frequently said to have been the father of
Bellerophon; cf. Roscher, *Myth. Lex.* s.v. Bellerophon, col.
758; *RE* s.v. Bellerophon, col. 242; Schwartz (1960) 569.

All one can say about these variants is that they are suggestive.
One might have hoped to say more about the version of the Peleus

---

[51] Cf. also Macarius 4. 54 Ἡρακλεία λίθος· πρὸς τοὺς ἑαυτοῖς τι ἐπαγομένους,
παρόσον καὶ ἡ λίθος ἐπισπᾶται τὸν σίδηρον; the definition of Μαγνῆτις λίθος at
Macarius 5. 79; and the notes at Leutsch and Schneidewin (1839) ii. 172.

[52] Ps.-Acro's suggestion that *Magnessam* differentiates Hippolyte from the
homonymous Amazon, whether right or wrong, suggests a discriminatory function.
Cf. the patronymic *Iasidos* at Prop. 1. 1. 10, which places Atalanta in Arcadia, not
Boeotia.

[53] The reference of *PMG* 1025 (Adesp.) Πελίου τε Μάγνησσαν κόραν (cf. Pfeiffer
1949–53: i. 457 on fr. 708) is obscure: Hippolyte? a daughter of Acastus? a
daughter of Peleus?

story in Apollodorus, *Bibliotheca* 3. 13. 3. Here the would-be
adulterous wife of Akastos is Astydameia, not Hippolyte. She sends
a message to Peleus' wife claiming that he intends to marry
Sterope, daughter of Akastos. Peleus' wife hangs herself; then,
later, Astydameia falsely accuses Peleus. This tale shares with *Odes*
3. 7 the message (or messenger) motif. But in fact it does not
illuminate Chloe's *nuntius* since the contexts in which the two
messages/messengers appear are so different. But the very appearance of the motif in Apollodorus underlines the inappropriateness
of certain naturalistic questions sometimes posed about *Odes* 3. 7,
e.g. 'How does Horace know what is going on in Oricos?', or
'Might Asterie have heard something about Chloe?'

Whatever uncertainties prevail over the role of mythographic
handbooks in *Odes* 3. 7, the essential message of the ode's myths
is clear. They all relate to marriage and to attempted adultery, and
they all imply that adultery is no light matter. Horace's Gyges
reflects on one level the king of Lydia; the would-be adulterous
behaviour of Candaules' wife led to the death of Candaules.
Bellerophon escaped death; but he did not omit to return and take
vengeance on his false accuser (cf. Roscher, *Myth. Lex.* s.v.
Bellerophon, col. 772). Peleus lost his own wife as a result of the
attempt on him; he later avenged himself by killing the wife of
Akastos (cf. *Kl.P.* s.v. Peleus, col. 597). Tyro, the victim of
Poseidon's impersonation of Enipeus, encountered a great deal of
suffering and misery, as did her children, before accounts were
settled in that legend (cf. *RE* s.v. Tyro, coll. 1872–3). Even the
virtuous Titan Asterie had to endure much in her flight from
attempted rape.

9. THE IMPORT OF THE ODE

In this paper view (3) of *Odes* 3. 7 has been espoused—Gyges
and Asterie are married. The ode, then, resumes in less formal
terms the censure of female adultery expressed formally in the
'Roman Odes' and most vividly in the central four stanzas of the
immediately preceding ode (3. 6. 17–32). That has been understood by others;[54] what seems to have escaped notice is that *Odes*

---

[54] i.e the adherents of view (3). The general principle that Horatian 'personal'
odes often make ethical pronouncements was re-enunciated by Bradshaw (1978:
esp. 176) with regard (among other odes) to *Odes* 3. 7.

3. 7 also continues another theme of the 'Roman Odes'. The secure core of the myth of the Titans Gyges and Asterie is that they both fought on the side of Zeus in the Gigantomachy. The 'Roman Odes' also treat largely of Gigantomachy: indeed, the picture of Jupiter as king of kings and lord of the universe at the beginning of book 3, right after the stanza which introduces the entire group of odes, is of *Iovis | clari Giganteo triumpho* (*Odes* 3. 1. 6–7). Then again, *Odes* 3. 4 devotes ten stanzas (42–80), in which the hundred-hander Gyges is also named (69),[55] to the battle of the gods and Giants. The significance of Gigantomachy for the politics, the self-image, and the political and moral aspirations of the Augustan regime is now well understood (cf. Innes 1979; and esp. P. R. Hardie 1986: chs. 3–4). Among Augustan policies, the regulation of citizen marriage and the campaign against (female) citizen adultery were prominent, and they were accorded by Augustus a recurrent importance which seems disproportionate to us until their socio-logical and cultural motivations are grasped. *Odes* 3. 7, which prohibits adultery and which by implication associates the married couple Gyges and Asterie with the allies of Jupiter in his war against the forces of chaos and disharmony, is more than a relaxa-tion of tension. In its continued concern for public morality it is the seventh 'Roman Ode'.

And yet *Odes* 3. 7 also reintroduces the private voice of Horace, and heralds a definite change of mood. It cannot be an accident that, only two odes later (3. 9), Horace is rejoicing in the fickleness of his love, and only three odes later (3. 10) he is portraying himself as a frozen and unsuccessful komast at the door of a Lyce (suggesting *lupa* = *meretrix*?) with multiple would-be lovers (14). Both these odes come from the world of erotic lyric, and they are

[55] At first sight Horace appears to be drawing for *centimanus Gyges* at *Odes* 3. 4. 69 not on the Hesiodic account but on another in which Gyges was the opponent, rather than the ally, of Zeus. However, Gyges might instead illustrate the preceding *sententia*: 'vim temperatam di quoque provehunt | in maius; idem odere viris | omne nefas animo moventis' (*Odes* 3. 4. 66–8), and hence be on the side of the gods here too. With *provehunt* compare the Hesiodic account, which emphasizes that the hundred-handers were brought out of Tartarus by Zeus to function as his allies (*Theog.* 669). *Re* the similar problem with the hundred-hander Aegaeon (= Briareus), who appears as an enemy of Jupiter at Virg. *Aen.* 10. 565 ff., see P. R. Hardie (1986) 154–6; Schlunk (1984) 226–9 has suggested an allegorical solution based on the notion that Aegaeon is 'an impassive and objective force of nature whose function is order, not chaos, and is a symbol of balance in the universe' (228). Such allegorical considerations might help further with the exegesis of Gyges' role in *Odes* 3. 4.

admittedly far removed in feel from the anti-elegiac *Odes* 3. 7.
Specifically, in *Odes* 3. 10 the circumstances of the woman, her *vir*
(15–16), and Horace's involvement with her are much vaguer
than those which surround the characters of *Odes* 3. 7. But
some movement away from the public voice of *Odes* 3. 1–6 has
definitely begun in *Odes* 3. 7. Of course the contrast between the
opening odes of book 3 and those which follow cannot mean that
in *Odes* 3. 9 and 3. 10 Horace was trying to undermine the
Augustan programme of public morality which he had upheld in
Odes 3. 1–7. Similarly, it is impossible to read the 'Roman Odes'
sensibly as insincere; and *Odes* 3. 7 continues in one dimension to
preach their message—effectively, as is shown by Propertius'
attempts to redress the balance and defend elegy in 3. 12 and
4. 3.[56] The contrast between the public and the erotic odes is
literary, not political: the poet who, like Horace, aspires to be
enrolled among the *lyrici* must be more than a concerned citizen
like Alcaeus; he must also be a flighty lover constantly changing
the objects of his affection, in the manner of Sappho, Anacreon,
and of Alcaeus himself. There is neither irony nor hypocrisy in this
collocation: after all, the lyric poet is not married, and neither are
his mistresses. Indeed, Horace could be making the point that the
Augustan moral programme will not stop people enjoying themselves provided they do so within acceptable limits.

Horace, then, shows his most public of faces in *Odes* 3. 1–6: four
odes later, in 3. 10, his most private face is revealed. *Odes* 3. 7,
which combines public and private in its underpinning of marriage,
and *Odes* 3. 8, with its similar though different admixture (a bow
to the *Matronalia*, 1 ff., which renews the theme of marriage,
Horace's private σωτηρία, 6–14, and Maecenas' public *civilis curas*,
16 ff.), deftly manage the transition from one sphere to the other.

---

[56] I am not implying that Propertius was necessarily entirely serious in these
attempts. However, the later poetic careers of Propertius (and perhaps more
significantly of Ovid) may show that, as time advanced, elegy was under growing
pressure to make its own, positive contributions to the 'moral' programme of an
increasingly directive society.

APPENDIX 1

'Etymologies' in Odes 3.7

Like much Augustan poetry, Odes 3. 7 shows interest in ancient pseudo-etymology. This appendix assembles its 'etymologies'.

1. As was mentioned (above, Section 4), line 1 etymologizes 'Asterie' in candidi or, with Diomedes' reading, candida, presumably understood by him as a vocative in agreement with Asterie describing her future joy at the return of Gyges. Etymologies of 'Asterie' are traditional. Pindar fr. 33c. 4–6 relates that mortals call Delos by that name, while the gods call it τηλέφαντον κυανέας χθονὸς ἄστρον; and Callimachus, Hymn 4. 36–8 tells Asterie/Delos that she got her name because she leapt from heaven 'like a star': . . . οὔνομα δ᾽ ἦν τοι | Ἀστερίη τὸ παλαιόν, ἐπεὶ βαθὺν ἥλαο τάφρον | οὐρανόθεν φεύγουσα Διὸς γάμον ἀστέρι ἴση. Latin 'etymological' texts link two cognate words denoting a gem both with 'stars' and with candicans/candida (cf. Maltby 1991 s.vv.):

> asteria. Pliny, Natural History 37, 131: 'asteria . . . contraria soli regerit candicantes radios in modum stellae, unde nomen invenit.'
>
> asterites. Isidore, Origines 16. 10. 3: 'asterites candida est, inclusam lucem continens veluti stellam intus ambulantem, redditque solis candicantes radios; unde et nomen invenit.'

None of this implies that Diomedes' reading is correct; but he too clearly thought that candidus was etymologizing 'Asterie'. Odes 3. 15. 6's stellis . . . candidis confirms that he was right. Stellar etymologies (cf. also above, Section 4, on Alcman's Astymelousa) are one of the lyric-inspired strands in this ode.

2. The 'derivation' of elegia is alluded to in fles (1), in Gyges' tears (8), in Chloe's sighs (10 suspirare, pointing to (e)heu), and Enipeus' querula tibia (30) (cf. Nisbet and Hubbard 1970 on Odes 1. 33. 2, miserabiles; Maltby 1991 s.vv. elegeus and cognates). This etymology further confirms the ode's interactions with elegy.

3. Notus (5) is implicitly derived from νοτίς = umor in lacrimis (8) (cf. Maltby 1991 s.v. notus).

4. Proetus is linked in the Greek etymological tradition with impulsiveness: ὁ δὲ Προῖτος τῇ ἐτυμολογίᾳ προϊτητικός . . . καὶ ὁρμητίας ἀπὸ τοῦ προϊέναι (Eustathius p. 631. 55). Horace wittily alludes per contrariam to this etymology in impulerit (14), where Proetus is 'impelled'.

5. A more elusive etymological interest in the Favonii which will restore Gyges to Asterie at the beginning of spring (1–2) may be indicated by the ancient definitions which Maltby assembles (1991 s.vv. favonius 1 and 2, q.v.). These connect this wind with spring and generation.

APPENDIX 2

Penelope in Odes 3. 7?

Harrison (1988) proposed that *Odes* 3. 7 should be seen in terms of Homer's *Odyssey*, with Penelope as Asterie, Odysseus as Gyges, and the suitors as Enipeus. Horace and his readers were, of course, familiar with the *Odyssey* and, if these analogies had been suggested to them, they would in some measure have recognized them as appropriate. Indeed, their aptness to *Odes* 3. 7 is confirmed by Horace's own reference to Penelope in *Odes* 3. 10. Like *Odes* 3. 7, *Odes* 3. 10 is a *kōmos*, and in it Horace is the failed komast of a 'Lyce' to whom he says 'non te Penelopen difficilem procis | Tyrrhenus genuit parens' (11–12); see also above, Sections 2 and 9. But, for all that, I am not convinced by this proposal, which is, however, too important to be passed over without brief rebuttal. My reasons for scepticism are as follows.

1. The analogies are remote: one suitor (Enipeus) = many suitors; a definite (Bithynia to Rome) and time-limited (returning next spring) voyage for Gyges = an indefinite and unlimited voyage for Odysseus; a single *hospita*, Chloe, for Gyges = several *hospitae* (Circe, Calypso, Nausicaa) for Odysseus. In the case of the crucial central figure Asterie, the analogy with Penelope is disturbingly slight. Penelope is a middle-aged woman with a grown-up son, who determinedly schemes to frustrate her suitors' wishes and who needs no Horace to advise her to do so. Asterie is a young woman, presumably without children, and she may be a new bride. Far from being determined to refuse Enipeus, she is clearly at risk of being seduced by him and greatly needs Horace's counsel against this.

2. Of the two underlying story-types in the ode, the first, the temptation of a male 'guest' by his 'hostess' (often involving the 'Potiphar's wife' motif—cf. Thompson 1958: K 2111) is commonplace. In classical mythology Bellerophon, Peleus, Jason, Hippolytus, and Aeneas instantly come to mind. The second story-type is the attempted (and often successful) seduction of a wife during her husband's absence; here one thinks of ancient examples like Clytemnestra and Aegistheus and Helen and Paris, as well as the Enipeus–Poseidon–Kretheus–Tyro quadrangle.[57] These are successful seductions, as are the cases covered by Thompson (1958) K 1310–25: 'seduction by disguise of substitution', an overlapping type alluded to in *Odes* 3. 7 through the name Enipeus. But women who resist seduction are not uncommon in antiquity either. As well as Penelope (1. 81–96), the *Heroides* include three others: Oenone (5. 133–8), who tells Paris how she holds out against the advances of Satyrs and Faunus; Hermione (8), who

---

[57] On the question whether or not her affair with Poseidon-Enipeus preceded her marriage to Kretheus see *RE* s.v. Tyro, cols. 1870–1.

recounts her enforced and resisted possession by Pyrrhus; and Cydippe
(21. 189–202), who explains to Acontius how she repels the more
innocent advances of the fiancé her father has chosen for her. Two other
Heroides hint more fleetingly at similar themes: 7. 123–4 (Dido) and 15.
15–20 (Sappho). In view, then, of the commonplace nature of such story-
types, limiting the mythico-literary influence upon *Odes* 3. 7 to the *Odyssey*
seems unnecessarily reductionist.

3. The only very specific link adduced by Harrison (1988) between the
Odyssey and *Odes* 3. 7 involves *Icarus/Icaria* (21)—the island—and
Ἴκαρος/Ἰκάριος—Penelope's father. There are two arguments against it,
which may or may not cohere; either of them, however, is enough in itself
to challenge seriously a connection with the *Odyssey*. First, Horace himself
also refers to the island Icarus in his description of the merchant at *Odes*
1. 1. 15–17 (on which see above, Section 3):

> luctantem Icariis fluctibus Africum
> mercator metuens otium et oppidi
> laudat rura sui: mox reficit rates . . .

This suggests that Icarus featured in early Greek lyric descriptions of
voyaging traders and reached Horace through them.[58] Second, Harrison
(1988: 191 n. 28) reports that Adrian Hollis paralleled Horace's *Icari* from
Callimachus, *Aetia* fr. 23. 2–3Pf.: ὡς ἁλὸς ἦχον ἀκούει | Σ]ελλὸς ἐνὶ Τμαρίοις
οὔρεσιν Ἰκαρίης, also in a context of 'paying no heed'. This again points
to a common source for Horace and Callimachus in an early Greek text,
possibly involving a proverb.

4. *Odes* 3. 7 has its full share of myth anyhow: it has characters called
Asterie, Gyges, Enipeus, and Chloe (three of whom have mythical dimensions) and it refers to other myths about Bellerophon and Peleus. But
the ode says nothing at all about the *Odyssey* or about any character or
incident in the *Odyssey*. It is therefore quite unnecessary to drag Penelope
and the *Odyssey* into *Odes* 3. 7.

5. How, then, can the presence of Penelope in two related
contexts be explained—i.e. in *Odes* 3. 10, also a *kōmos*, and in Propertius
3. 12, which is indebted to *Odes* 3. 7? Horace's reference to Penelope at
Odes 3. 10. 11 has two confluent explanations: she became an erotic
exemplum (cf. Harrison 1988: 187–8 and n. 11), and she turned into
a proverb.[59] The latter fact explains her presence in *Odes* 3. 10 most eco-
nomically, since in ancient literature mythical and historical resonances

---

[58] Nisbet and Hubbard (1970) 10, on *Odes* 1. 1. 15, refer to Hom. *Il.* 2. 144 ff.,
and say that the 'the picture is Homeric'; on *Odes* 1. 1. 16 they speak of Horace's
remarks about the trader as derived from popular philosophy. None of this is inconsistent with Icarus having featured in early lyric too.

[59] Cf. Otto (1890) s.v. Penelope 1, who cites, *inter alia*, *Od.* 3. 10. 11; Häussler
(1968) 200, 243.

disappear once proverbial status has been achieved.[60] As for Propertius 3. 12, the explicit *Odyssey* analogy there is not a recognition of *Odyssey* influence upon *Odes* 3. 7 but an independently conceived means of heroizing the journeyings of Propertius' cousin Postumus. Manifestly, Gyges is no Odysseus-type hero in *Odes* 3. 7: his voyage follows a standard trade-route.

6. Of the other more detailed points of resemblance between *Odes* 3. 7 and the *Odyssey* claimed by Harrison (1988), most are commonplaces of erotic situations (or just commonplaces) which could only support a thesis otherwise acceptable. One—an equivalence between Athene as comforter of Penelope and Horace as comforter of Asterie—is strained. Harrison further argued correctly that Penelope became an erotic *exemplum* (see above), and he suggested interestingly that Anacreon may have treated themes from the *Odyssey* in amatory terms. This last possibility could easily be the origin of some apparent, but non-significant, similarities between Horace and Homer.

---

[60] Cf. e.g. Call. 11 Gow–Page (= *AP* 5. 6), where the (by then proverbial) alleged response of the Delphic oracle to the Megarians has only one point of connection with the situation of the abandoned girl—she is now of no account in the eyes of her former lover. All other aspects of the supposed historical event are irrelevant.

6

Reading the Metre in Horace, *Odes* 3. 9

DAVID WEST

WE are often asked how there can still be unsolved problems in Greek and Latin literature despite two millennia of scholarly labour in the field. It is not an easy question to answer but there is no doubt about the fact. Even in our working lifetime there have been substantial advances in the understanding of Horace's poetry, not just rearrangements of old material, not just subjective notions or new terminology or theory, not just the combing of ancient literature for parallels or the combing of the texts for *x*, *y*, or *z*, but genuine and objective improvements. This is in no small measure due to the Nisbet and Hubbard commentaries.

The purpose of this paper is to try to suggest how the sound of the Latin contributes to the poetry of *Odes* 3. 9. First I shall offer an interpretation of the ode, then point to a striking metrical phenomenon, then suggest how this phenomenon is related to the sound of the verse and is therefore part of the effect of the poetry. This is an elusive matter. We are a long way from knowing how Horace would have read his odes but there may be some hope of advance in the fact that this is an amoebaic poem, in which the second speaker is clearly capping the words of the first. Some of the nuances are clear. Does the sound of the verse support them?

The title of this essay is taken from The '*Scholar*' *Me*, an essay by Jack Shepherd in Astley (1991). Here Tony Harrison introduced himself when interviewed by Melvyn Bragg on *The South Bank Show* in 1980 as 'the man who came to read the metre'. I owe this reference and much other help to Rosemary Burton. I am grateful also to Peter V. Jones and Robin Nisbet for reading and criticizing a draft of this essay. The text used is by Shackleton Bailey (1985ᵃ), with the exception of *reiectaeque* for *reiectoque* at 3. 9. 20. There is an excellent treatment of *Odes* 3. 9 in Lyne (1980) 222–7.

I. AN INTERPRETATION OF *ODES* 3. 9

'Donec gratus eram tibi
  nec quisquam potior bracchia candidae
cervici iuvenis dabat,
    Persarum vigui rege beatior.'

'donec non alia magis   5
  arsisti neque erat Lydia post Chloen,
multi Lydia nominis
    Romana vigui clarior Ilia.'

'me nunc Thressa Chloe regit,
  dulcis docta modos et citharae sciens,   10
pro qua non metuam mori,
    si parcent animae fata superstiti.'

'me torret face mutua
  Thurini Calais filius Ornyti,
pro quo bis patiar mori   15
    si parcent puero fata superstiti.'

'quid si prisca redit Venus
  diductosque iugo cogit aeneo,
si flava excutitur Chloe
    reiectaeque patet ianua Lydiae?'   20

'quamquam sidere pulchrior
  ille est, tu levior cortice et improbo
iracundior Hadria,
    tecum vivere amem, tecum obeam libens.'

— 'While I was still attractive to you
and there was no better man to put his arms
  round your white neck,
I was more blest than the king of Persia.'

— 'While you did not yet burn with love   5
for another woman and Lydia did not come second to Chloe,
  the famous Lydia
was more glorious than Roman Ilia.'

— 'Now it is Thracian Chloe who rules me,
expert in sweet measures, skilled in the lyre.   10
  I shall not be afraid to die for her
if the Fates spare my beloved's life.'

— 'It is Calais, son of Ornytus of Thurii,
for whom I burn and who burns for me.
   I shall endure to die twice for him   15
if the Fates spare my boy's life.'

— 'What if the old Venus returns and forces
those who have been parted to join under her yoke of bronze,
   if golden Chloe is being pushed out
and the door stands open to Lydia who was rejected?'   20

— 'Although he is lovelier than a star
and you bob about like a cork and are worse-tempered
   than the surly Adriatic,
I would love to live with you and with you I would gladly die.'

Lydia's first word, *donec* in line 5, picks up her lover's first word.
Her *non alia magis arsisti* caps his *gratus eram tibi*. She trumps his
quisquam potior by making no bones about naming names in line
6, and speaking in the third person to give the semblance of a
report from an unbiased assessor. His last line is thrown back at
him with interest—the wealth of the king of *Persia* is no match for
the fame of Ilia, *regina sacerdos* (*Aen.* 1. 273), ravished by the god
Mars and mother of the founder of *Rome*. Her own name perhaps
hints at a connection with the proverbial wealth of Croesus, king
of Lydia. She is guying his line 4, but trumping it with a broader
hyperbaton, *Romana vigui clarior Ilia* being more spacious than
Persarum vigui rege . . .

   In the third stanza the errant lover, trounced in the east,
switches his campaign to the north. His new beloved is a Thracian,
and she rules him. Lydia has no difficulty with this. *He* may be
ruled but *she* is afire with love and *her* love is returned, *me torret
face mutua*. The mistress who rules *him* is a Thracian and therefore
probably a slave-girl or freedwoman, but *her* inamorato is not a
Thracian but a Thurian, no slave but the son of a named father,
citizen of Thurii, a city built on the site of Sybaris, which was a
byword for wealth and luxurious living. Calais and Ornytus are no
arrivistes. We may remember that the names come together in the
catalogue of heroes who sailed with Jason on the Argo in the first
voyage made by man. Calais, son of the god Boreas, was on the
expedition with Iphitus, grandson of Ornytus (Apollonius Rhodius
1. 207-11). The rest of Lydia's stanza again guys and caps her
lover. He will not be afraid to die for his beloved. She might be
afraid but she would endure her fear and die *twice* for her boy.

Most scholars believe that the lover is meant to be thought of as Horace. Pasquali, for instance (1966 edn.: 408), notes that Horace has already had dealings with a Lydia in *Odes* 1. 8, 13, and 25. Gordon Williams (1969: 76) observes the fickleness and irascibility of lines 22 and 23, which neatly accord with the character Horace is given at *Sat.* 2. 7. 28 *Romae rus optas*, and at *Ep.* 1. 20. 25 *irasci celerem*. Syndikus (1972–3: ii. 110) points to the hint in line 7 that the lover is a poet. Perhaps we should cite also her response in line 16, where *animae* is answered by *puero*. In this context that is a loaded word. Calais is pointedly a youngster, like the *gracilis puer* who is Horace's successor in *Odes* 1. 5, not the old buffer Horace makes himself out to be.

Reeling under this bombardment, he puts out a nervous feeler, *quid si*. He even tries to suggest that he is not entirely to blame for his lapse. A mere man can scarcely hope to resist the goddess Venus and her yoke of bronze. He suggests that perhaps Chloe is being kicked out unceremoniously, *excutitur*, and his door is standing open for Lydia. Here there are two problems. It has been suggested that *excutitur* is used with a hint at unhorsing Chloe or throwing her out of a chariot (*OLD* s.v. 1c), but this sits ill with line 18, where lovers are visualized not as horse and rider but as animals under the same yoke. It is far easier to take lines 19 and 20 closely together, as Bentley does on *Odes* 3. 15. 8, citing Terence, *Eunuchus* 358, 'homo quatietur certe cum dono foras'. Chloe is being kicked out and the door stands open for Lydia. In line 20 Shackleton Bailey accepts Peerlkamp's *reiecto*, imagining that Horace had been shut out by Lydia. But surely it is the other way round. If he is now offering to kick out Chloe, surely he is suggesting that he had once kicked out Lydia. Besides, the righteous anger of Lydia and the sheepishness of Horace throughout the poem suggest that he is the one who put an end to the affair. The emendation is inferior to the transmitted text.

At this Lydia moves into the attack. Horace is not so handsome as Calais, and *ille est* gains emphasis by coming after the enjambment, before the only internal pause in the poem and before the contrasting choriamb, *tu levior*. He is not only fickle, but also ill-tempered in another emphatic run-on, *improbo | iracundior Hadria*. Now, astonishingly, with the battle won, Lydia capitulates. Perhaps we know the poem too well to savour fully the shock when, after all her teasing and bragging and browbeating, she produces her declaration of undying love. This is what Lydia's love is like. There is nothing ironic or implausible about it, and it turns this amusing comedy of manners into a love poem.

2. DIAERESIS IN *ODES* 3. 9

The metre is based upon the choriamb (– ∪ ∪ –). The short lines are glyconics (– – – ∪ ∪ – ∪ ×). The long lines are Asclepiads (– – – ∪ ∪ – – ∪ ∪ – ∪ ×) with obligatory central diaereses. The vertical bars in the text below indicate diaereses, i.e. points where word-endings coincide with divisions between the feet. The numbers on the left are the numbers of diaereses in each line.

2 'Donec │ gratus eram │ tibi	2 'donec │ non alia │ magis
1　　nec quisquam potior │ bracchia candidae	2　　arsisti neque erat │ Lydia post │ Chloen,
1 cervici iuvenis │ dabat,	1 multi │ Lydia nominis
1　　Persarum vigui │ rege beatior.'　　4	1　　Romana vigui │ clarior Ilia.'　　8
2 'me nunc │ Thressa Chloe │ regit,	0 'me torret face mutua
3　　dulcis │ docta modos │ et citharae │ sciens,	1　　Thurini Calais │ filius Ornyti,
2 pro qua │ non metuam │ mori,	2 pro quo │ bis patiar │ mori
1　　si parcent animae │ fata superstiti.'　　12	1　　si parcent puero │ fata superstiti.'　　16
2 'quid si │ prisca redit │ Venus	1 'quamquam │ sidere pulchrior
1　　diductosque iugo │ cogit aeneo	2　　ille est, │ tu levior │ cortice et
1 si flava excutitur │ Chloe	0 improbo iracundior Hadria,
1　　reiectaeque patet │ ianua Lydiae?'　　20	3　　tecum │ vivere amem, │ tecum　　24
	obeam │ libens.'

In the second stanza Lydia, as we saw, is mimicking Horace, and she reproduces his pattern of diaereses (*post Chloen* may be read as a unit). In the first two lines of the third stanza Horace is plodding along with the the words falling exactly into the feet at every possible point until his plangent cry in line 12. In the first two lines of the fourth stanza Lydia is capping Horace and has none of these pedestrian rhythms except the obligatory diaeresis at the centre of the long line 14. Then in lines 15–16 again she reverts to the mimicking mode and apes Horace's rhythms, changing only two words, *non* and *animae*, in order to crush her antagonist. In the last pair of stanzas, in her angry tirade at line 23 once again she throws away all thought of diaereses. In her unexpected capitulation in the last line she speaks for the first time with the full complement.

3. DIAERESES, SOUND, AND POETIC EFFECT

The facts in the last paragraph are observable, but it may still be
argued that since word-endings are not audible these facts are not
part of the sound of the poem. This cannot be true. The proof is in
I. II, a poem in which each line consists of three choriambs,
flanked by bisyllables (– – – ∪ ∪ – – ∪ ∪ – – ∪ ∪ – ∪ ×):

> Tu ne quaesieris, scire nefas, quem mihi, quem tibi
> finem di dederint, Leuconoe, nec Babylonios
> temptaris numeros. ut melius, quidquid erit, pati,
> seu pluris hiemes seu tribuit Iuppiter ultimam,
> quae nunc oppositis debilitat pumicibus mare   5
> Tyrrhenum! sapias, vina liques et spatio brevi
> spem longam reseces. dum loquimur, fugerit invida
> aetas. carpe diem, quam minimum credula postero.

Don't you ask, Leuconoe—the gods do not wish it to be known—
what end they have given to me or to you, and don't meddle
with Babylonian calculations. How much better to accept
whatever comes, whether Jupiter gives other winters or whether
this is our last now wearying the Tyrrhenian Sea on the pumices   5
opposing it. Be wise, strain the wine, and cut back long hope
into a small space. While we speak, envious time will have
flown past. Harvest the day and leave as little as possible for tomorrow.

Here lines 5–6 make the case. The pumice shingle round the Bay
of Naples is wearing out the sea, and this long elemental process
is expressed in a line which has the full complement of diaereses.
We do not know exactly how the line would have been spoken, but
this was incontestably part of the effect of the poem. Ancient metri-
cians divided these metres in different ways, but I. II. 5 is enough
to support the view that such lines were heard as choriambic
(Heinze 1972: 261–73, esp. 265, 271; cf. Bellinger 1957: 103–9).
Doubters may read the only two lines in I. 24 which have two
diaereses, with *Quintilium perpetuus* and *compulerit Mercurius*. We
must therefore listen for similar and more subtle effects in 3. 9.

Horace opens with the obvious pattern of total diaereses, thus
guiding the reader by asserting the metre at the beginning of the
poem. At this point, as we have seen, Lydia is mimicking his
words. She mimics also his rhythms throughout this first stanza,
her most striking departure being in line 7, where *multi* fits into

the first foot and would give the voice a chance ironically to emphasize the magnitude of her fame over the hyperbaton *multi Lydia nominis.*

In the first two lines of the third stanza Horace again starts with coincidence of foot and word. In her reply, in line 13-14, where Lydia is using Calais to trounce Chloe, she keeps only the obligatory central diaeresis in the Asclepiad in line 14. The ardour of their reciprocated love and the splendour of Calais's connections burst the constriction of diaeresis and force us to remember the sound of Chloe's music, flat-footed, totally devoid of any metrical freedom, and boringly monotonous. This is the only line in the poem which contains three diaereses, except for the last line of all, where also, as we shall argue, a particular effect is aimed at and achieved. This, further, is the stanza in the poem which has most punctuation at the end of lines (e.g. in the Oxford text and in Shackleton Bailey's Teubner). It also produces by far the longest string of disyllabic words in the whole poem, seven if we include *Mé nunc.* Each would be spoken with the word accent on the first: *mé nunc Thréssa Chloé régit dúlcis dócta módos.* Musically this is sorry stuff, five-finger exercises, and Lydia contemptuously ignores it. Having soared above Chloe's diaeresis in the first two lines of her reply, in the last two Lydia reverts to mimicry, doing her damage by simple but deadly substitutions, *bis* for *non* and *puero* for *animae.*

Horace never learns, but in the first three lines of the fifth stanza plods on with the maximum number of diaereses and a great string of accentual trochees, this time seven of them: *quid si prísca rédit Vénus díductósque iúgo cógit.* Now Lydia lets fly. Her praise of Calais runs on to *ille est,* then, at the diaeresis, she turns on Horace with *tu levior* and another diaeresis, after which her wrath spills over the line-ending and produces *iracundior Hadria,* the only line in the poem with only two words and her second line with no diaereses, setting the scene for the shock of her last line with its full complement of three dutiful diaereses and its simple, total submission. And yet this is the submission of an independent spirit. She would *gladly* love him and die with him. The point is important to her, as it was to Jupiter at the end of the *Aeneid.* He too capitulated after a quarrel. At 12. 809 Juno reluctantly gives up the struggle, *terras invita reliqui,* but Jupiter at 12. 833 makes the point that he concedes of his own free will: 'do quod vis, et me victusque volensque remitto.'

4. CONCLUSIONS

If this approach has any validity, it could be extended in a study of other poems written in choriambic metres. Take 1. 11, for example. At *scire nefas* the parenthesis fits neatly into a choriamb, and that will have something to do with the tone of voice. *Quidquid erit* in line 3 will enjoy similar articulation. At *quem mihi, quem tibi* the whole phrase forms an antithesis, but the first three words offer a different and striking symmetry in the choriamb which brings the lovers strangely together. In line 5 the endless clash of sea on rock does not end in one line with four diaereses but rolls on into the first choriamb of line 6 to *Tyrrhenum* with its stop in the middle of a choriamb, the only such break in the whole poem. Further self-contained choriambs at *vina liques, dum loquimur*, and *carpe diem* isolate and emphasize these instructions. The three consecutive tri-syllabic commands *sapias, liques*, and *reseces* each end a choriamb, and this rhythm would help the speaker to add an insistent note to his wise advice.

The Roman writers of the Republic are a vastly humorous and witty tribe. Some of this fun is obvious. Plautus, Lucilius, Lucretius, and Cicero spring to mind. Some of it is subtle and savourable, Terence, Horace, and Virgil pre-eminently. How are we to understand the thinking of the Greek professor who recently wrote about Terence's 'clod-hopping rehashes' of Menander? To pin Horace down when he is smiling, the reader has to exercise great care, and final certainty is often not attainable. It is a contention of this paper that the amoebaic structure of *Odes* 3. 9 has offered more confidence than we can usually hope for and that the humour of the poem lies partly in sound:

> Blest pair of Sirens, pledges of Heav'n's joy,
> Sphere-born harmonious sisters, Voice and Verse.

> (Milton, *At a Solemn Music*)

7

Horace, Pindar, Iullus Antonius, and Augustus: *Odes* 4. 2

S. J. HARRISON

ODES 4. 2 has received much critical attention,[1] owing to several evident difficulties. First, what does it mean for Horace to reject imitation of Pindar in a poem which is itself somewhat Pindaric and which appears in a book together with other poems which are notably so (e.g. *Odes* 4. 4 and 4. 14)? Second, how is Iullus Antonius, the addressee, treated? Is he really envisaged as himself composing a poem in a context where Horace is unable to produce one, and if so what kind of poem? Finally, does the poem in fact constitute effective praise of Augustus on Horace's part, and is there a unified sequence of thought which links up the initial section on the poetry of Pindar and Horace (1–32), the middle section on Iullus and the return of Augustus (33–52), and the final vignette of the two differing sacrifices (52–60)? The present treatment will deal with these themes, which form the central concerns of previous discussions, with the aim of producing a coherent and credible account of the poem in its social and literary context.

I. HORACE AND PINDAR

Horace's poem begins with a warning to would-be imitators of Pindar; the great poet is inimitable in his grandeur, force, copiousness, and range, especially for Horace, who is not so ambitious (1–32):

[1] For articles on the poem in the period 1936–75 see Kissel (1981) 1512; subsequent articles are listed by Putnam (1986) 341–8—see also Nagy (1994). Relevant monographs and commentaries are mentioned in the notes which follow. I use the text of Shackleton Bailey (1985*a*). Some of the points which follow expand on a brief section of Harrison (1993).

Pindarum quisquis studet aemulari,
Iulle, ceratis ope Daedalea
nititur pennis vitreo daturus
    nomina ponto;

monte decurrens velut amnis, imbres   5
quem super notas aluere ripas,
fervet immensusque ruit profundo
    Pindarus ore,

laurea donandus Apollinari,
seu per audaces nova dithyrambos   10
verba devolvit numerisque fertur
    lege solutis,

seu deos regesque canit, deorum
sanguinem, per quos cecidere iusta
morte Centauri, cecidit tremendae   15
    flamma Chimaerae,

sive quos Elea domum reducit
palma caelestis pugilemve equumve
dicit et centum potiore signis
    munere donat,   20

flebili sponsae iuvenemve raptum
plorat et viris animumque moresque
aureos educit in astra nigroque
    invidet Orco.

multa Dircaeum levat aura cycnum,   25
tendit, Antoni, quotiens in altos
nubium tractus: ego apis Matinae
    more modoque

grata carpentis thyma per laborem
plurimum circa nemus uvidique   30
Tiburis ripas operosa parvus
    carmina fingo.

The close link of the idea of Pindar's inimitability with the first address to Iullus Antonius in line 2, and the equally close link of the contrast between Pindar and Horace with the second address at line 26, has led commentators to the reasonable conclusion that Horace is turning down a request from Iullus Antonius to write a poem in Pindaric fashion, presumably on the forthcoming return of Augustus, with which the second half of the poem deals (see below).² The common form of the *recusatio* is employed here, as has long been recognized; a summary is given of the kind of poetry which the speaker cannot write, and an alternative author is suggested, in this case Iullus himself (see Section 2 below).³ But the terms in which Horace here refuses Pindaric enterprise closely reflect his own career as a Roman poet, and this seems a paradox. A close investigation is required in order to understand the procedure and meaning here.

In the opening stanzas Horace compares the would-be Pindaric imitator with Icarus, likely to fall from sky to sea, and Pindar himself with a mighty stream. The continuing water imagery is surely significant, stressing that the unwary Pindarizer will perish by drowning either way, in the sea through his own inability to sustain lofty flight, or while unsuccessfully attempting to cope with the rushing river of Pindar's style. The choice of Icarus reflects the ill-fated attempt of the imitator to match the eagle, Pindar's famous characterization of himself as poet,⁴ with false and inappropriate wings. Stress is laid on the force and boldness of Pindar's style and on his apparent disregard of metrical pattern, continuing the stream metaphor (*devolvit, fertur*), and some of the various genres in which he wrote are listed or alluded to: dithyrambs (10-12), hymns (13-16), epinician odes (17-20), and laments, θρῆνοι (21-4).⁵

The characterization of Pindar's style in lines 5-8, as many have noted, reflects not only Pindar's own description of his poetry, but also the terms of Callimachean literary polemic, above all the well-known end of the *Hymn to Apollo*, where in a metaphorical characterization of poetry large bodies of water such as the sea and the River Euphrates are rejected in favour of small but pure streams from which bees may carry water (Callimachus, *Hymn* 2. 105-13).⁶ Horace uses this type of imagery elsewhere in contexts criticizing Lucilius for not matching Alexandrian ideals of well-crafted poetry (*Sat.* 1. 4. 11, 1. 10. 50-1), but here this critical aspect,

---

² So e.g. Kiessling and Heinze (1914-30); Fraenkel (1957) 433 n. 5, Syndikus (1972-3) ii. 296-7.

³ So similarly *Odes* 1. 6, where Varius is suggested as singer of Agrippa's deeds, and *Odes* 2. 12, where Maecenas himself is put forward as writer of the deeds of Augustus; cf. Wimmel (1960) 269.

⁴ Cf. Pind. *Ol.* 2. 88, *Nem.* 3. 80-2, 5. 21; Steiner (1986) 104-8.

⁵ For the details of the catalogue see Freis (1983).

⁶ For Pindar's view of his own poetry as a rushing wave or stream see *Ol.* 10. 10, *Nem.* 7. 12, Isth. 7. 19; for the Callimachean material cf. Wimmel (1960) 61-70, 222-33.

though present, is overshadowed by evident admiration for the
great inimitable Pindar. This Callimachean aspect of the opening of
the section about Pindar is clearly picked up at its close in an
effective piece of ring composition; the stress on *labor* and *parvus* in
27–32 strikes a strongly Callimachean note,[7] and the image of
the bee, though (as we shall see) partly Pindaric, recalls the bees
gathering water at the end of the *Hymn to Apollo*. There is also
a clear link between the Icarus comparison for the would-be
Pindarizer and Horace's low-flying bee. Horace is no Icarus but
rather a Daedalus, keeping low, taking fewer risks, and therefore
escaping safely (cf. Ovid, *Met.* 8. 203–8), and like Daedalus he is a
humble artisan; *operosa . . . fingo*, though this verb is used elsewhere by Horace for poetic composition (*Ep.* 2. 1. 227, *Ars* 331,
382), perhaps recalls Daedalus' outstanding reputation for making
things as well as the bees' moulding of the honeycomb.[8] Horace,
then, appears to be rejecting Pindaric grandeur for Callimachean
literary reasons.

As already suggested, the very Pindaric way in which the
rejected Pindaric themes of lines 9–24 are expressed, in one continuous period of twenty lines, with clear allusions to details in
known Pindaric texts, although paradoxical, is not problematic; this
is what one would expect in an allusion to themes associated with
another writer, which often tend to reflect the style of the original.[9]
This does not in itself weaken Horace's claim of incapacity to
Pindarize. But there are two aspects of lines 1–32 which suggest
that the contrast between the inimitable grandeur of Pindar and
the Callimachean modesty of Horace is far from straightforward.
First, several of the themes in the long Pindaric catalogue reflect
the themes of Horace's own poetry and poetical status, as expressed
elsewhere in his work and even in this very same fourth book of
Odes; second, the two images used to describe the respective poets
in lines 25–32 could equally well apply to either.

At line 9 Horace calls Pindar *laurea donandus Apollinari*. This
could be a simple allusion to the bay-wreath offered to athletic

---

[7] For *parvus* see Wimmel (1960) 83–7; for *labor* see Cairns (1979) 5 n. 20.

[8] For *fingere* of bees and the honeycomb cf. Virg. *Georgics* 4. 179 *daedala fingere
tecta*, where the epithet *daedala* provides an interesting link with *Odes* 4. 2; for
Daedalus' famed skills as craftsman see C. Robert in *RE* iv. 2002. 11 ff.

[9] Cf. e.g. *Odes* 2. 1, full of suggestions of the style of Pollio's *Historiae* (see Nisbet
and Hubbard 1978 ad loc.), or Lucr. 3. 832–7, strongly recalling Ennius' *Annales*
(see Skutsch 1985: 486).

victors at the Pythian Games,[10] whose victories Pindar had celebrated in his *Pythians*, or it might perhaps suggest that Pindar himself won such a wreath in the poetical contests held at the festival—though there is no other evidence for this[11]—but we need to ask why the Pythian Games are selected rather than the Olympic, indubitably ranked first in the ancient world as in the modern, and implicitly accepted as such by Horace himself.[12] The answer is not far to find. In the closing lines of his first collection of *Odes*, Horace had claimed this same Delphic bay-garland from the lyric Muse, having accomplished the ambition expressed in the first poem of the collection (*Odes* 1. 1. 35-6) of achieving equal status with the great lyric poets of the Greek canon (*Odes* 3. 30. 13-15):

> sume superbiam
> quaesitam meritis et mihi *Delphica*
> *lauro* cinge volens, Melpomene, comam.

Thus, Horace's description of Pindar as worthy of the Delphic wreath recalls his own self-characterization in a prominent previous poem. So does the idea that Apollo is patron of the poet, implicit in *Apollinari*; the approval of Apollo for Horace is relevant to *Odes* 1. 31, but is particularly prominent in *Odes* 4. 6, clearly written as a consequence of Horace's role at the Ludi Saeculares in 17 BC (4. 6. 29-30):

> spiritum Phoebus mihi, Phoebus artem
> carminis nomenque dedit poetae.

We should also recall that the *Carmen Saeculare* was written to accompany the sacrifice to Apollo and Diana at the Ludi themselves;[13] it is perhaps not over-fanciful to imagine Horace himself appearing in such a context literally crowned with the garland of Apolline bay.

Horace also characterizes Pindar in his *Hymns* as singing of gods and kings, the descendants of gods, through whose might the

---

[10] Cf. e.g. Paus. 10. 7. 4.

[11] For these contests see Paus. 10. 7. 2-3. The ancient lives of Pindar, found most conveniently in Drachmann (1903) and historically unreliable (see Lefkowitz 1981: 57-66), do not record a Pythian victory for him, though they do allege that he was a special favourite of Apollo at Delphi (Drachmann 1903: 2. 14, 3. 5, 5. 7-8, 9. 7).

[12] Cf. *Odes* 1. 1. 3; *Ep.* 1. 1. 50; Bowra (1964) 162-4.

[13] As is clear from the famous inscription recording the details of the Ludi Saeculares (*CIL* vi. 32323 = *LLS* 5050).

Centaurs and Chimaera were overthrown (13-16). While this is no doubt literally true of these largely lost poems of Pindar (gods and heroic kings are mentioned in the few remaining fragments of the *Hymns*, the Centauromachy does occur as a theme in the unplaced dactylo-epitrite fragment 166Sn., quite possibly from a hymn, and Bellerophon's slaying of the Chimaera is mentioned in an epinician, *Ol.* 13. 90), the mention of monster-slaying kings who are descended from gods might well recall for a contemporary readership the effective king Augustus, *divi filius*, whose defeat of disruptive forces had been compared to the punishing of Giants and other monstrous figures by Horace himself in a poem deriving much from Pindar (*Odes* 3. 4. 69 ff.).[14] This possible hint at Augustus and Horace's own praise of him hardens into a probability in the next stanza (17-20). There Horace is talking of the Pindaric epinicia, but his evocation of the victorious athlete's glorious return (*quos Elea domum reducit | palma caelestis*) must surely have echoes of the current context of writing (see Section 2 below), where the triumphant return of Augustus himself is expected; military and athletic victory are parallel, as happens more than once in Horace's use of Pindaric victory motifs in *Odes* 4, and this seems to be confirmed by 43 *fortis Augusti reditu: fortis* can suggest the prowess of an athlete as well as military courage.[15]

Similarly relevant to Horace's own poetry in *Odes* 4 is the notion that poetry is superior to statuary sculpture as a way of providing permanent commemoration of heroic deeds. This theme is of course also Pindaric, as commentators note (cf. *Nem.* 5. 1 ff., 4. 79 ff.), and is indeed found in other Greek authors, but it is also prominent in late Horace.[16] Horace uses it to praise Ennius at *Odes* 4. 8. 12-20:

> non incisa notis marmora publicis,
> per quae spiritus et vita redit bonis
> post mortem ducibus, non celeres fugae
> reiectaeque retrorsum Hannibalis minae,
> [non incendia Carthaginis impiae]
> eius, qui domita nomen ab Africa
> lucratus rediit, clarius indicant
> laudes quam Calabrae Pierides . . .

And later he uses the motif in his epistle to Augustus, the

[14] Cf. Fraenkel (1957) 273-85.
[15] Cf. Harrison (1990) 34-5.
[16] Cf. Fraenkel (1957) 396 n. 2; Brink (1982) 252.

character whose commemoration is in his mind in this very poem
(*Ep.* 2. 1. 248–50):

> nec magis expressi vultus per aenea signa
> quam per vatis opus mores animique virorum
> clarorum apparent.

Thus this Pindaric motif is also Horatian.

This same ambiguous status also applies to the two images
characterizing the two poets in lines 25–32. The soaring swan
might, like the eagle, be a grand self-presentation of the poet in
Pindar, but does not occur in his extant poems and fragments,
though it is likely to have appeared in a lost poem; its most famous
use, of course, is by Horace of himself at *Odes* 2. 20. So the image
here chosen to characterize Pindar is again one that Horace has
chosen for himself in an earlier and prominent poem. The converse
phenomenon applies to the image of the bee which Horace selects
to describe himself here; as suggested above, this is clearly on the
surface an anti-Pindaric and Callimachean image, implying poetry
which is less grand but more exquisite, but the hovering bee itself
conceals a Pindaric allusion. The usual parallel cited is that of
Simonides 593 *PMG* ὁμιλεῖ δ' ἄνθεσσι μελίσσα | ξανθὸν μέλι
μηδομένα, with *fingo* picking up μηδομένα; but, as Putnam has
recently noted, there is also a specific allusion to a famous passage
of Pindar himself,[17] which, like Horace's poem (and unlike
Simonides), compares the activity of the poet to that of the bee
(Pindar, *Pyth.* 10. 53–4):

> ἐγκωμίων γὰρ ἄωτος ὕμνων
> ἐπ' ἄλλοτ' ἄλλον ὧτε μελίσσα θύνει λόγον.

Plurimum in Horace, if taken with *nemus* rather than *laborem*, as
Bentley suggested,[18] seems to match ἐπ' ἄλλοτ' ἄλλον, indicating the
diversity of the poet's sources and inspiration. Thus, in rejecting
Pindaric poetics and espousing Callimacheanism, Horace actually
uses a Pindaric image for poetic activity.

[17] Cf. Putnam (1986) 56 n. 7. On the image of the poet as bee cf. Wimmel
(1960) 271 n. 2; Waszink (1974).

[18] See Bentley (1869) 232–3: 'mihi contra videtur convenientius, ut ad *nemus*
pertineat . . . ita loqui amant scriptores Latini, *per dolum, per iram, per otium, per
iocum, per necessitatem, per vim*, numquam addito epitheto. Tum autem illud,
plurimum circa nemus, multo opinor nitidius et ποιητικώτερον erit, quam *circa nemus*
nude arideque prolatum.' *Per dolum* appears similarly without epithet at *Odes* 1. 10.
10 *per dolum amotas*; for *per laborem* cf. Sall. *Cat.* 7. 4 'iuventus . . . in castris per
laborem usum militiae discebat'.

The effects of this ambiguity are not immediately clear. Are the evident links between Horace and Pindar as poets simply clever paradoxical details which make no difference to the sundering of the two different poetic styles, or is Horace in fact implying that although Callimachean he is also Pindaric, i.e. that he is capable of either mode? I take the latter view: Horace is not to be taken literally here when he denies his ability to imitate and resemble Pindar. Fraenkel viewed Horace's denial of Pindaric qualities in this passage as insincere and exaggerated, arising from his own worries about praising Augustus;[19] he was right that the *recusatio* must be seen as an elaborate literary pretence generated for the occasion, but I would ascribe a different motivation to it. And it *is* a pretence: Horace is not claiming that the elaborate metres of Pindaric epinician are beyond his powers, as Steinmetz has argued;[20] this is not a question of technical worries—which might indeed have been very considerable—about the possibility of dactylo-epitrite metrical systems in Latin. Nor is Horace claiming an inability to imitate Pindaric style and diction; as Fraenkel and others have argued, he does this effectively in *Odes* 4. 4, 4. 14, and elsewhere. Nor is he claiming an inability to praise Augustus in the high style, as Fraenkel himself thought; this occurs both in the earlier lyric collection of *Odes* 1–3 (e.g. *Odes* 1. 2, 1. 12, 3. 3, 3. 4, and 3. 14) and with particular prominence in this same book (*Odes* 4. 5 and 4. 15). The whole first section of the poem, I would argue, is an elaborate compliment to its addressee, Iullus Antonius, a compliment generated for the occasion; it suits Horace to pretend that he is no Pindar in order to highlight the different abilities of Iullus, but the presence of evidently Horatian elements in the Pindaric catalogue suggests an implication that the poet is perfectly well aware that this is largely a pretence, and lets the reader understand this without endangering his praise of Iullus' 'higher' talents.

2. HORACE, IULLUS ANTONIUS, AND POETIC GENRES

In his forthright and stimulating, if often perverse, account of Horace's *Odes* at the end of *Sappho und Simonides* Wilamowitz takes the view that Horace's attitude to Iullus Antonius in this poem is one of scorn and disdain; he implicitly takes Iullus as the Icarus-

[19] See Fraenkel (1957) 434–6.   [20] See Steinmetz (1964) 12–14.

figure of the opening, and sees Horace as criticizing him as a rash
and over-ambitious Pindarizing poetaster.[21] This view is rightly
rejected by most subsequent critics—it is very difficult to square
both with what we know about Iullus and with the last two
stanzas of the poem—but it does pinpoint a vital question. We
should first be sure of Iullus' status in Rome at the time of the
poem's composition, which will clearly be a relevant consideration.
Odes 4. 2 belongs by general consent to the year 16 BC;[22] the date
is derived from the mention of the defeat of the Sygambri in lines
34-6, a reference to their bloodless retreat, and from the natural
expectation of Augustus' triumphant return, not in fact to happen
for another three years. By this time Iullus Antonius was a person
of some consequence; a son of Mark Antony and Fulvia, born
about 43 BC and too young to take part in the Actium campaign,
he was brought up by Antony's second wife Octavia, sister of
Augustus, and in 21 BC had been married to Marcella, Octavia's
daughter by her first marriage to Claudius Marcellus. Later to be
praetor (13 BC) and consul (10 BC), in 16 BC he was aedile, and
clearly a secure and rising member of the imperial house; in this
he is not unlike other addressees in the fourth book of *Odes*, such
as Drusus and Tiberius, the Princeps's stepsons (*Odes* 4. 4 and 4.
14), or Paullus Fabius Maximus (*Odes* 4. 1), husband of the
Princeps's first cousin Marcia.[23]

Thus Iullus Antonius' high standing and imperial connections
are not in doubt in 16 BC, though he was to fall spectacularly from
grace and be forced to suicide in the scandal of the elder Julia more
than a decade later.[24] It seems unlikely, therefore, that in a poem
of that date, contained in a book which wholesomely flatters
and celebrates the achievements of other young nobles connected
with the imperial house, Horace would pillory Iullus' poetical
over-ambition as Wilamowitz requires. We should rather see the
mention of Iullus as poet as an element of compliment from one
poet to another of higher social status, where that status itself is

[21] See Wilamowitz (1913) 319 and n. 1.

[22] For the dating see e.g. Fraenkel (1957) 432-3; Syme (1986) 398. One dis-
senter is Williams (1972) 47, who prefers 13 BC, but the Sygambrians were
topical in 16 and a distant memory by the time of Augustus' return in 13 after
subsequent Gallic campaigns.

[23] On Iullus Antonius' career and links with other members of the imperial house
as addressees in *Odes* 4 see Syme (1986) 398-401.

[24] See Syme (1986) 90-1.

perhaps more significant than the poetical talent. As Wimmel has stressed,[25] we should not forget that the son of Mark Antony, stepson of the Princeps's honoured sister (cf. *Odes* 3. 14. 7) and chosen husband of his niece, was someone towards whom Horace might feel deference and respect as well as friendship. For a similar combination of social deference and literary respect we might compare the address to Pollio, then proconsul returning from his year in Illyria, at the beginning of Virgil's eighth *Eclogue*,[26] where he is celebrated for both his military achievements and his tragedies, a part of his literary output mentioned by his contemporaries Virgil and Horace as a compliment but almost entirely ignored by later Roman writers.[27]

From these general and sociological observations, which set the context for the argument, we turn to the details of the text. After Horace's self-characterization as a literary bee, he turns to Iullus and to the prospect of celebrating the return of Augustus (33–44):

> concines maiore poeta plectro
> Caesarem, quandoque trahet feroces
> per sacrum clivum merita decorus   35
>   fronde Sygambros,
>
> quo nihil maius meliusve terris
> fata donavere bonique divi
> nec dabunt, quamvis redeant in aurum
>   tempora priscum.   40
>
> concines laetosque dies et urbis
> publicum ludum super impetrato
> fortis Augusti reditu forumque
>   litibus orbum.

---

[25] See Wimmel (1965) 100–3.

[26] I adopt the traditional identification of the unnamed addressee of *Ecl.* 8 as Pollio, against the ingenious arguments of Bowersock (1971) for Caesar (Octavian); it is difficult to believe that the latter could be saluted for his great tragedies given the fiasco of his only known attempt in the genre—cf. Suet. *Div. Aug.* 85. 2 and Tarrant (1978).

[27] The testimony for Pollio's tragedies consists of Virg. *Ecl.* 8. 10, Hor. *Sat.* 1. 10. 42–3 and *Odes* 2. 1. 9–12—all compliments to a powerful contemporary—and a later incidental and slightly disparaging mention (Tac. *Dial* 21.7). As Nisbet and Hubbard (1978) 8 note, there are consequently no post-Augustan compliments for these works, and it is particularly notable that they do not achieve a mention in Quintilian's catalogue of Roman literature, where Pollio is praised as an orator (10. 1. 11), while Accius, Pacuvius, Pollio's contemporary Varius, Ovid, and Pomponius Secundus are picked out as the representatives of Roman tragedy (10. 1. 97–8).

Much has been written on the words *concines maiore poeta plectro* (33), which as it stands must suggest that Iullus himself, unlike the humble Horace, will be up to the occasion and sing of it in a higher kind of poetry. This has been found unacceptable by those who could not stomach the great Horace's yielding to a youthful amateur in the sphere of poetry; Lachmann conjectured *concinet* for *concines* in both 33 and 41, assigning the triumphal celebration to a third anonymous poet of higher powers,[28] while Seel kept *concines* but thought that the whole phrase referred not to Iullus' poetic talents but to his creative organizational responsibilities as aedile.[29] Neither view is at all satisfactory; the anonymous poet is introduced very suddenly and makes little sense, while to refer the phrase to non-poetical artistic endeavour seems to give an impossible meaning to the Latin, even in a metaphorical mode. Iullus is, then, being encouraged to sing in a higher kind of poetry than the humble Callimacheanism just professed by Horace in refusing Iullus' own request. This type of *recusatio*, passing the requested commission back to its author with an assertion that the author himself would accomplish it better, is familiar from *Odes* 2. 12, where Horace, addressing Maecenas and answering an apparent request, rejects the writing of historical epic in favour of handing the material back to Maecenas for treatment in prose.[30]

But what kind of poetry? Most have assumed that the reference is to lyric poetry, and that Horace is encouraging Iullus to produce the Pindaric type of victory-poem which he himself has just refused to provide. But this comes up against an evident objection. The prescription against imitation of Pindar with which the poem begins is specifically made universal (*Pindarum quisquis studet aemulari*), and it seems impossible for Horace to warn off all potential Pindarizers at the beginning of the poem but then turn to exhort the addressee, specifically linked with the earlier warning, to provide a poem of this very Pindaric type himself. One might try to argue that there is no need to refer *maiore poeta plectro* to imitation of Pindar in particular, but if the sphere required is lyric, the register high, and the subject a triumphant return home after victory, then there can be few other models available. A solution was provided by Bücheler in 1889, but it has not been sufficiently

---

[28] Lachmann (1845) 83 (= Lachmann 1876: 617).   [29] Seel (1970) 166-7.
[30] Maecenas' potential prose work need be no more real than Iullus' potential panegyrical epic: see Nisbet and Hubbard (1978) 193.

appreciated by critics.[31] Bücheler picked up an important passage
from the ancient commentary of pseudo-Acro on line 33: 'Iullus
Antonius heroico metro Diomedias duodecim libros scripsit egregios,
praeterea et prosa aliquanta.' The circumstantial details of title,
number of books, and additional prose works make this testimony
plausible and credible, and Bücheler used it to argue that the
greater work expected from Iullus by Horace was not a Pindaric
epinician ode but rather a panegyrical epic.

This seems to me correct, and indeed provable from the details
of our poem, as I will argue shortly. But Bücheler's argument has
largely been discounted, almost entirely because scholars have
found it difficult to believe that *concines maiore poeta plectro* can
refer to epic as well as lyric. On *concines*, it has been argued that
the prefix *con-* certainly refers specifically to choral lyric or has
another special sense,[32] but there are a number of passages where
concinere clearly and unambiguously refers to performance by a
single individual, and it is clear that in poetry at least the compound verb can be used fairly indifferently for the simple form,
perhaps here with some vaguely intensifying sense.[33] Similar
linguistic arguments can be made for *plectro*. Bücheler's critics
point to the three other Horatian lyric passages where *plectrum*
is clearly used of lyric poetry,[34] and suggest that it is simply
inappropriate for epic. But this argument can be countered in two
ways. First, for those who might imagine that the *plectrum* and
lyre-playing have nothing to do with epic poetry in the technical
sense, even a cursory reading of the Homeric poems makes it clear
that archaic Greek epic had some kind of accompaniment on the
lyre, usually played with the *plectrum*.[35] Of course, epic poetry in

---

[31] Bücheler (1889) (= 1930: 161–3). Of subsequent commentators, only
Kiessling and Heinze (1914–30) accept Bücheler's arguments.

[32] Amongst commentators, ps.-Acro glosses *concines* with 'cantabis nobiscum',
Orelli and Baiter (1886) with 'canes ad lyram', Quinn (1980) with 'perform in
totality'. Putnam (1986) 57 rightly points out that the compound appears only in
this poem in Horace, but his view that 'the compound underscores the double sense
of involvement Horace imputes to Iullus, both as part of the ceremony and as
singer, with others, of the exploits it honours' seems to include too much.

[33] Cf. Prop. 2. 28. 38; Ov. *Am.* 3. 9. 24, *Her.* 7. 2.; Stat. *Silv.* 4. 6. 105; *TLL* iv.
53. 82 ff. For the apparently indifferent use of the same prefix in poetry cf. e.g. Virg.
Aen. 10. 783 *Aeneas hastam iacit*, 10. 891 (Aeneas) *conicit hastam*, both attacks on
the same opponent (Mezentius).

[34] *Odes* 1. 26. 11, 2. 1. 40, 2. 13. 7.

[35] For the Homeric material see Barker (1984) 19–32; for the *plectrum* as the
usual instrument for playing the lyre see Barker (1984) 50, 185 n. 12, and 270,

Horace's own time is unlikely to have had any musical accompaniment, but the same is true of lyric poetry itself in the Augustan period; most scholars agree that the references to lyres and musical performance in the *Odes* are formal generic indicators rather than real evidence of Horatian citharody.[36] Second, and much more telling, there are other poetical passages in Latin which clearly class the *plectrum* and the lyre as the equipment of epic. Three of these actually use the comparatives *gravior* and *levior*, possibly in imitation of the Horatian passage, and will therefore repay close inspection.

First, Ovid, *Met.* 10. 149–52:

> 'Iovis est mihi saepe potestas
> dicta prius: cecini *plectro graviore* Gigantas
> sparsaque Phlegraeis victricia fulmina campis.
> nunc opus est *leviore lyra*, puerosque canamus
> dilectos superis inconcessisque puellas
> ignibus attonitas meruisse libidine poenam.'

This is the introduction with which Orpheus prefaces his song which will take up the rest of the book, and which will deal with the usual erotic and metamorphic themes of Ovid's poem. The reference to his previous singing of the Gigantomachy is clearly to epic; the battle of the gods and Giants was undoubtedly epic material in antiquity, and was perceived as such in the Augustan period, as its appearance in *recusationes* makes very clear.[37] This grander epic material is here contrasted with the lighter subjects of love. *Plectro graviore* does seem very close to Horace's *maiore . . . plectro*, and to point to exactly the same thing—epic poetry on epic subjects.[38]

Two passages from Statius make very much the same point about the epic status of the lyre, with which the *plectrum* was necessarily associated. The first is from the *Thebaid*, marking the deaths of the lovers Hopleus and Dymas, the Nisus and Euryalus of Statius' poem, in which Statius refers self-consciously to the

and the mention of lyre and *plectrum* together at *Hom. Hymn* 3. 182–5, 4. 47–54, 499–501, Eur. *HF* 351.

[36] Cf. esp. Heinze (1923) 162–7 (= 1972: 184–8).

[37] Cf. Nisbet and Hubbard (1978) 189–90.

[38] Fraenkel (1932–3) 12–13 airily dismisses the Orpheus parallel on Wilamowitz's inadequate grounds that 'Orpheus is nothing but a citharode transferred to the heroic period' and therefore no epic singer.

episode in the *Aeneid* which constitutes his model (*Theb.* 10. 445–8):

> vos quoque sacrati, quamvis mea carmina surgant
> *inferiore lyra*, memores superabitis annos.
> forsitan et comites non aspernabitur umbras
> Euryalus Phrygiique admittet gloria Nisi.

Here *inferiore lyra* must refer to the *Thebaid*, cast as inferior to the *Aeneid* in the well-known conclusion to Statius' poem, but still very much an epic. The same language can be used of the *Aeneid* itself. In a similar context in the *Silvae*, Statius talks of the Tiburtine villa of Manlius Vopiscus, and of how its owner will be able to regale the local fauna with his multiform poetical talent (*Silv.* 1. 3. 99 ff.):

> hic tua Tiburtes Faunos chelys et iuvat ipsum
> Alciden dictumque *lyra maiore* Catillum,
> seu tibi *Pindaricis* animus contendere *plectris*
> sive *chelyn* tollas *heroa ad robora* sive
> liventem saturam nigra rubigine turbes . . .

This is a particularly interesting passage for our purposes. *Lyra maiore*, using the same adjective as Horace, clearly points to the difference between Vopiscus' poetry and that of Virgil; the reference is to the mention of Catillus, legendary founder of Tibur, in the Latin Catalogue of the *Aeneid* (7. 670), and therefore to epic, classified here as in the *Thebaid* as poetry for the lyre. But note too *Pindaricis . . . plectris*, which would seem at first to support the notion that the *plectrum* belongs to lyric and not epic poetry, until we read on to *chelyn* in the next line, clearly referring to epic again (*heroa ad robora*); *chelys* is used as always as a metonymy for *lyra*,[39] naming the instrument by its tortoiseshell material. Clearly epic and lyric are in the same musical category as appropriate to the lyre, and therefore the *plectrum*, with which the lyre was standardly plucked, can symbolize either genre.

Thus it is clear that *maiore poeta plectro* can indicate a generic ascent from lyric to epic, not merely an elevation within the lyric genre itself. This linguistic indication that Iullus is portrayed as an epic poet may be strengthened by what follows in Horace's poem. As Fraenkel and others have noted, lines 37–44 clearly suggest the themes of the notional poem that Iullus is to write;[40]

[39] Cf. *TLL* iii. 1004. 77 ff.
[40] See Fraenkel (1957) 438; Syndikus (1972–3) ii. 306–7.

my contention is that these are specifically the themes of panegyrical epic. First, the picture of captured tribes appearing in
Augustus' anticipated triumph (34-6), while reflecting what
normally happened on such occasions, also reflects the kind of
praise offered by poets in panegyrical passages celebrating the conquests of the Princeps and his family.[41] Second, the personal praise
for Augustus in lines 36-40 provides clear parallels with the lines
cited by Horace himself in *Epistles* 1 some years earlier, lines which
are clearly from an epic panegyric of Augustus, quite possibly from
the *Panegyricus Augusti* of Varius[42] (*Ep.* 1. 16. 25-9):

> si quis bella tibi terra pugnata marique
> dicat et his verbis vacuas permulceat auris,
> 'tene magis salvum populus velit an populum tu,
> servet in ambiguo qui consulit et tibi et urbi
> Iuppiter', Augusti laudes agnoscere possis.

The two passages share the theme of Augustus' mere presence as
a divine gift to the Roman people. Note too that Horace in lines
39-40 makes the point that no better gift can be given by the gods
to Rome, not even if the Golden Age should return; this again
recalls panegyrical passages in Virgilian epic which talk of the
reign of the Princeps as itself a Golden Age.[43]

Thus, there are solid arguments to the effect that Horace
presents Iullus Antonius here as an epic rather than a lyric poet,
and that the themes imagined for Iullus' poem on Augustus' return
are those of panegyrical epic.

3. HORACE, AUGUSTUS, POETIC OFFERINGS, AND POETIC UNITY

Having described and prescribed what Iullus is to say, Horace
describes his own much less prominent part in the proceedings
(45-52):

> tum meae, si quid loquar audiendum,   45
> vocis accedet bona pars, et 'o sol

---

[41] Cf. e.g. Virg. *Aen.* 8. 720-8 (captured tribes at the triple triumph of 29 BC);
Prop. 3. 4. 17-18 (captives in an anticipated eastern triumph of Augustus); Ov. *Tr.*
4. 2. 21-4 (captured Germans in an anticipated triumph of Tiberius and his sons).

[42] For this and a reconstruction of the *Panegyricus Augusti* cf. Wimmel (1983)
1605-14.

[43] Cf. *Aen.* 1. 286-96 (I take 'Caesar' there to be Augustus) and 6. 791-7.

pulcher, o laudande!' canam recepto
Caesare felix.

†teque dum procedit† 'io Triumphe!'
non semel dicemus, 'io Triumphe!'   50
civitas omnis dabimusque divis
tura benignis.

Horace's ostensible contribution to the proceedings will be non-literary, the words *o sol pulcher, o laudande!* are deliberately trite and represent the reactions of the typical citizen, perhaps (as has been noted) hinting by their trochaic rhythm at the measures of popular songs,[44] while *io Triumphe!* is of course the standard celebratory cry. The reference is solely to the great presence of the Princeps in the triumph, and should not be ascribed to any technical part to be taken by Iullus Antonius in the procession as aedile.[45] The finer details of the triumph lay in the future, in fact some three years in the future, and line 49 should pick up from line 48 the idea of the Princeps's return and concentrate on his actions rather than that of Iullus. Thus Shackleton Bailey (1985*a*) is right in rejecting the *teque* of the manuscripts, which makes Iullus undesirably prominent as the object of popular adulation which should surely be reserved for Augustus, and in reading *procedit* rather than *procedis* (both are attested), again fittingly concentrating on Augustus. A convincing emendation for *teque* has been difficult to find; Pauly's *terque*, a limp echo of *non semel*, seems prosaic in the extreme, Gow's *ioque* gives a sundered half of the traditional triumphal cry, Bentley's *isque* provides a pronominal form otherwise unknown in the *Odes*, and Meineke's *atque* yields a connective which seems weak in this emphatic context. Shackleton Bailey's own suggestion, *usque*, seems better than all of these, adding the significant point that Horace and the Roman population will follow the triumphal procession all the way to the Capitol in their enthusiasm; his parallel from Livy (10. 2. 8 'dulcedine praedandi longius usque a navibus procedunt') may be supplemented by one from Horace himself, *Odes* 3. 30. 7-9, 'usque ego postera crescam laude recens, dum Capitolium scandet cum tacita virgine pontifex', where *usque* is in similar emphatic initial position and again followed by a *dum*-clause in the same sense of 'as long as', though with a future verb.

[44] Cf. Fraenkel (1957) 439; Syndikus (1972-3) ii. 307-8.
[45] As argued by Seel (1970) 167-8.

How are we to interpret Horace's humble position here as merely one of the crowd? This cannot mean that Horace himself is unable by nature to praise the return of Augustus in any fuller terms, for we can see in *Odes* 4. 5 and 4. 15 in this book that he is still capable of doing so, and in *Odes* 3. 14 that he had done so some years before. Again, as with the pretence that he cannot imitate Pindar, this is a pose for literary purposes. Horace defers at least temporarily to the abilities of Iullus, himself a member of the imperial house and a magistrate, and therefore a suitably grand epic poet for this epic occasion; but, as has been noted, Horace is also following other Augustan poets in placing himself as an admiring and ordinary civilian spectator of the military triumphs of the great man, an established form of literary compliment.[46] Horace's classing of himself as one of the populace (*civitas omnis*), neatly marked by the use of first-person plural verbs (*dicemus . . . dabimusque*), is not mere modesty; it too is a compliment, indicating that the whole populace longs for the return of Augustus and will celebrate it in unanimous joy, a point also made at *Odes* 4. 5. 9–16:

> ut mater iuvenem, quem Notus invido
> flatu Carpathii trans maris aequora
> cunctantem spatio longius annuo
>   dulci distinet a domo,
>
> votis ominibusque et precibus vocat,
> curvo nec faciem litore dimovet:
> sic desideriis icta fidelibus
>   quaerit patria Caesarem.

The central point here is that Horace's self-imposed humility (both literary and social) before the greatness of Augustus is itself a form of panegyric, so that in refusing to write grandly about Augustus Horace is actually praising him in a different but equally effective way. This connects well both with the rejection of Pindarizing at the poem's opening and with the thematic anticipation of Iullus' panegyric of Augustus in lines 37–44; Horace, by setting out his own inadequacies and suggesting themes to another, is in fact accomplishing a praise-poem of his own. As Fraenkel puts it, 'Though apparently in passing, he did pay a glorious tribute to Augustus.'[47]

---

[46] Cf. e.g. Prop. 3. 4 and the Gallus fragment; for a good discussion see Putnam (1986) 58–9.   [47] Fraenkel (1957) 438.

That Horace's poetical and social humility is the unifying force in the poem is confirmed by the final two stanzas (53–60):

> te decem tauri totidemque vaccae,
> me tener solvet vitulus, relicta
> matre qui largis iuvenescit herbis   55
>   in mea vota,
>
> fronte curvatos imitatus ignis
> tertium lunae referentis ortum,
> qua notam duxit, niveus videri,
>   cetera fulvus.   60

Here the talk is of sacrifices; these were of course appropriate as a thank-offering for the safe return of a friend, but their emphasis here and prominent closural location suggest that they have a further symbolic value.[48] Of course, their relative sizes reflect the relative social positions of the two, as at the end of *Odes* 2. 17. 30–2, where in commemoration of Maecenas' recovery from illness Horace will offer a humble lamb, Maecenas many victims and a votive temple.[49] But a felt need for balance and ring composition with the opening of the poem and its contrast of poetic styles also argues that these sacrifices and their dramatic differences represent the poetry of Iullus and Horace, which, like the sacrifices, will be offered to celebrate Augustus' return. This view, which several scholars have argued,[50] is supported by the fact that the metaphor of poem as sacrificial animal is well established in Hellenistic and Latin poetry.[51]

The sacrificial animals described, then, should correspond to styles or genres of poetry. The overall contrast is of the grand and the humble; twenty cattle as against one calf. In particular, given the interpretation above of the kind of poetry to be produced, the twenty cattle, ten bulls, and ten cows of Iullus' offering would seem to provide a symbol of the epic register; such extravagance does not reflect normal Roman practice in private sacrifice and is unusual

---

[48] For this kind of symbolic statement about poetry in Horace's *Odes* see esp. Davis (1991), particularly his analysis of *Odes* 1. 38 (118–26), which resembles the last two stanzas of *Odes* 4. 2 in its final position (in that case in its book) and its contrast between two types of activity analogous to poetry.

[49] As noted by Syndikus (1972–3) ii. 310 n. 82.

[50] Cf. Syndikus (1972–3) ii. 310 and esp. Davis (1991) 142–3.

[51] Cf. Wimmel (1960) 270–1. Especially interesting is Virg. *Ecl.* 3. 84–7, where the kinds of animals dedicated clearly reflect and compliment the poetry of Pollio.

except on occasions of national expiation,[52] and the scale and
specific numbers of male and female are more like the sacrifices
found in epic and mythological contexts (e.g. twelve bulls to
Poseidon at *Od.* 13. 180 ff., four bulls and four heifers to the
Nymphs at Virgil, *Georgics* 4. 538–40). Even the language suggests
epic links; for *totidem* in similar contexts of animal sacrifice cf.
Virgil, *Aeneid* 5. 96–7 'caedit binas de more bidentis | totque sues,
totidem nigrantis terga iuvencos', *Georgics* 4. 550–1 'quattuor
eximios praestanti corpore tauros | ducit et intacta totidem cervice
iuvencas'. Such a scale would be appropriate for the epic author
of a twelve-book *Diomedeia*. Similarly, Horace's own offering
represents the type of poetry proclaimed by the poet earlier on;
matching the labouring and carefully constructing bee, we have
the exquisitely coloured calf. This stresses the small-scale nature of
Horace's poetry and its Hellenistic inspiration; the adjective *tener*
may even allude to the erotic and Callimachean world of love
elegy,[53] while some details of the description of the calf are clearly
taken from Moschus' *Europa*, a leading example of the highly
crafted Hellenistic epyllion (compare lines 56–60 with Moschus 2.
84–5 τοῦ δή τοι τὸ μὲν ἄλλο δέμας ξανθόχροον ἔσκε | κύκλος δ᾽
ἀργύφεος μέσσῳ μάρμαιρε μετώπῳ); its varied colour might be taken
to represent the Callimachean literary virtue of ποικιλία, diversity
and variation,[54] though it may also have some sacral associations.[55]

Thus the concluding section presents a symmetry between the
initial contrast of the poem, the grand Pindar against the humble
Horace, and the contrasting poems of Iullus and Horace for
Augustus' return, Iullus' mighty epic against Horace's Hellenisti-
cally crafted lyric. It also stresses Horace's genuine desire to produce
some poetic offering for the occasion, crucial to the complimentary
presentation of Augustus in the poem; the *recusatio* of the beginning is necessitated by the temporary contrast with the high
status and lofty poetry of Iullus, but the poem's conclusion, like the
suggested themes for Iullus' panegyric, stresses that this *recusatio*
does not in any sense constitute a refusal to praise Augustus.
Indeed, the poem which results from this literary debate is itself, as

[52] Cf. Wissowa (1912) 415 n. 5, quoting Livy 22. 10. 7 (300 victims), 45. 16.
6 (50 victims), 43. 13. 7 (40 victims), 30. 21. 10, 40. 2. 4 (20 victims).
[53] Cf. Davis (1991) 142; for *tener* used of elegiac poets and poetry cf. *Ars* 294;
Cat. 35. 1; Pichon (1902) 278.
[54] Cf. Brink (1971) 95.
[55] Cf. Davis (1991) 143; Price (1983) 219.

we have seen, full of compliments to the Princeps; Horace's sacrifice at the poem's end must parallel or even represent the poem itself, small in comparison with larger literary forms, exquisitely shaped on Hellenistic principles, and offered as a modest but genuine tribute to the greatness of Augustus.

8

Horace, *Odes* 4. 5: *Pro Reditu Imperatoris Caesaris Divi Filii Augusti*

I. M. LE M. DU QUESNAY

I. HORACE AND AUGUSTUS

IN the late summer of 15 BC Augustus wrote to Horace from Gaul and requested a poem to commemorate the magnificent victory which his stepsons, Tiberius and Drusus, had won over the Vindelici.[1] The care that was being taken over the representation of this victory and its significance is revealed by the choice of 1 August as the day of victory, the fifteenth anniversary of the fall of Alexandria in 30 BC.[2] The Gallic campaign also provided a focal point for a further refinement and redefinition of the role of Augustus. The war had been conducted under the *auspicia* of Augustus by Tiberius and Drusus acting as the *legati*.[3] Since Augustus had secured through his *pietas* and his special relationship with the gods the divine support without which there would have been no victory, it was Augustus, not Tiberius or Drusus, who was acclaimed as *imperator* for the victory.[4] The importance attached to communicating effectively this carefully nuanced relationship between Augustus and his *legati* is reflected in the coinage of this period. For the first time the acclamation of Augustus as *imperator* is advertised on the coinage, and there is a famous series which shows either one or two figures in military

---

[1] Suet. *Hor.* 20. 5 Klingner.

[2] For the date see Hor. *Odes* 4. 14. 34–40. A land battle which involved no surrender of a city presumably left some scope for deciding on which day the victory fell. It was the *dies natalis* of the temples of Victoria and Victoria Virgo on the Palatine and the day on which the Ara Romae et Augusti was dedicated at Lyons in 12 BC: see Degrassi (1963) 489–90; Fishwick (1987) 97–9, 118; Rich (1990) 211–12.

[3] For *ductu auspiciisque* see Plin. *NH* 3. 136–7; *CIL* v. 7817 = Ehrenberg and Jones (1976) 62 No. 40: cf. Aug. *RG* 4. 2 and Hor. *Odes* 4. 14. 33–4.

[4] Fears (1981*b*) 746–9; Rosenstein (1990) 54–91.

dress (Drusus and/or Tiberius) presenting Augustus with the laurel-branch of victory.[5] A conscious decision had been taken about what the message was to be, and Horace was, very clearly, not the only person enlisted to communicate it. Horace discharged the commission with tact and skill in two magnificent Pindaricizing odes (4. 4 and 4. 14), each partnered in the final collection by a shorter piece for Augustus himself (4. 5 and 4. 15).[6]

As an *amicus* of Augustus,[7] Horace will not have needed the message to be spelt out in detail. The Latin term *amicitia* covers not only friendship, in something like the modern sense of a relationship based on common interests, shared values and outlook, but also includes many features more naturally covered by the modern sense of patronage.[8] *Amicitia* was often, as in the case of Augustus and Horace, an asymmetric relationship between individuals of unequal status which imposed obligations and was cemented by an exchange of gifts and services. Augustus was an extremely wealthy and powerful man, and his gifts were made on a very generous scale. Suetonius records simply that he enriched Horace by one or two acts of generosity (19–20 Klingner *unaque et altera liberalitate locupletavit*). Details are not known but can be inferred. L. Varius Rufus wrote the *Thyestes* for performance on the occasion of the triple triumph in 29 BC, and in a single act of generosity Augustus gave him 1m. sesterces. Virgil had died leaving 10m. sesterces acquired *ex liberalitatibus amicorum*, including, of course, Augustus.[9] The significance of generosity on this scale can be judged from the fact that when Augustus reviewed the senate and introduced a census-rating for eligibility which was eventually set at 1m. sesterces (probably in 18 BC), the purpose was to enhance and define the *dignitas* of the *ordo senatorius*.[10] There was nothing for either party to be ashamed about concerning such gifts: they advertised the generosity of the donor and expressed his judgement

[5] For the acclamation as *imperator* see Barnes (1974) 22; for the coins see Kraft (1978) 321–6; Sutherland (1984) 52 Nos. 162–5; Trillmich (1988) 489, 523.

[6] See Zanker (1988) 223–7. Contrast White (1993) 127–32.

[7] For discussion of what this means see Horsfall (1981); White (1978, 1993). There is no satisfactory way of translating *amicus*: 'friend' underplays the obligations; 'patron' or 'client' overstates them. But it is excessively pedantic always to insist on the Latin word.

[8] See Brunt (1988) 351–81; Saller (1982) 1–40; (1989).

[9] He casually bestowed 100,000 sesterces on a Greek poet he hardly knew: Macr. *Sat.* 2. 4. 31. For Varius and Virgil see Brink (1982) 252; White (1993) 276 n. 22.

[10] See Nicolet (1976); (1984) 91–3, 118–19.

of the worthiness of the recipients. The obligation of the recipient
was to show himself worthy of the gift.[11] The poet could reciprocate with gifts of his own in the form of poems which would be
expected to immortalize the memory of the recipient, his benefactor, and so had a value beyond price.[12] But the obligations of
amicitia were not met by a simple exchange of poems for gifts or
gifts for poems. The *potens amicus* could be expected to provide a
wide range of other supportive services appropriate to his own
position in society and to the needs of the poet. Like any other
friend, the poet was also bound to reciprocate by providing his
support in whatever way he could and in a form appropriate to the
needs of his *potens amicus*. When Augustus requested a poem for
the victory of his stepsons, he demonstrated his high estimation
of Horace's poems.[13] It was Horace's obligation and, we must
suppose, his pleasure to respond positively. To have done otherwise
would have been a disgraceful display of ingratitude. For he
incurred the obligation as a friend and discharged it as a friend.

Augustus and Horace had known each other for more than
twenty years, and in their private communications adopted an
intimate and teasing banter.[14] There is no justification for sup-
posing that their friendship was not as genuine as their relative
positions in society allowed, which is not to deny that Augustus
was immeasurably Horace's social superior in terms of birth,
wealth, power, and prestige.[15] Some fifteen years previously Horace
had told an anecdote which shows how people assumed that he
knew what was going on at the very centre of power (*Sat.* 2. 6.
51–8). They were right. *Odes* 4 shows Horace intimately connected
with men close to the Princeps: Paullus Fabius Maximus (4. 1),
married to a cousin of Augustus, consul in 11 BC, proconsul of Asia
(without the usual interval) in 10 BC; Iullus Antonius (4. 2), a son

[11] See Hor. *Ep.* 2. 1. 245–7 'at neque dedecorant tua de se iudicia atque | munera
quae multa dantis cum laude tulerunt | dilecti tibi Vergilius Variusque poetae.' He
does not explicitly state that he too had received gifts, but it can be safely inferred
that he was one of those whose wishes had been granted: compare *Ep.* 2. 2. 49–52
with *Ep.* 2. 1. 226–8: and see Brink (1982) 295.

[12] See White (1978) 84.

[13] Suet. *Hor.* 20–3 Klingner 'scripta quidem eius usque adeo probavit
mansuraque perpetuo opinatus est, ut non modo saeculare carmen conponendum
iniunxerit sed et Vindelicam victoriam Tiberii Drusique privignorum suorum.'

[14] Suet. *Hor.* 17–19 Klingner 'praeterea saepe eum inter alios iocos "purissimum
penem" et "homuncionem lepidissimum" appellat.'

[15] On the difficulties presented by a *potens amicus* see Hor. *Ep.* 1. 7, 17, 18; cf.
White (1978) 81–2.

of the triumvir but brought up by Octavia, whose daughter Marcella he had married in 21 BC, aedile in 16 BC, praetor in 13 BC, consul in 10 BC—not to mention Maecenas (4. 11), Tiberius, or Drusus.[16] It should not therefore be surprising if Horace shows in the poems of book 4 an advance knowledge of what was to be put into effect only after the return of Augustus from Gaul and Spain.

2. THE DATES OF 4. 5 AND *ODES* 4

The Suetonian *Life of Horace*, drawing on the correspondence of Augustus, provides exceptionally good evidence for the genesis and 'publication' of *Odes* 4.[17] However, the relevant passage is not without its problems. The statement 'eumque coegerit propter hoc [i.e. the request for a poem on the victory over the Vindelici] tribus carminum libris ex longo intervallo quartum addere' is marked as Suetonius' own inference by the words *propter hoc*.[18] It is certainly misleading if it encourages the view that Horace was forced against his will and better judgement to return to lyric.[19] To understand *Odes* 4 it is necessary to acknowledge the significance of being asked to write for an *amicus* as important as Augustus and to recognize that the question of Horace's personal feelings as distinct from those he chose to represent in the poems is simply beside the point. Those who claim to detect lack of sincerity or enthusiasm in the odes of book 4 are well-intentioned but misguided in their attempts to assert the independence of the poet, for Horace makes plain his communicative intention to praise Augustus, and to accuse him of failing to convince his readers of his enthusiasm or sincerity is to impugn his skill.

Suetonius cannot be correct in suggesting that Horace did not start on book 4 until after he had received the request to celebrate the victory of Tiberius and Drusus over the Vindelici on 1 August 15 BC. *Odes* 4. 6. 29-44 and, probably, 4. 3. 22-3 refer to the

---

[16] For these men see White (1993) 224-39; Syme (1986) 396-420.

[17] The book is conventionally and rightly dated to 13 BC: see Fraenkel (1957) 364-5, 410, 449; Becker (1963) 190; Putnam (1986) 23. Williams (1972) 44-9 argues unconvincingly for a date as late as 8 BC.

[18] Contrast White (1993) 43, 115, 127-32, who believes that *coegerit* also derives from the correspondence and whose understanding of the nature and significance of the formal request is different from mine: on *cogere* see Brink (1982) 243.

[19] This view has dogged criticism of *Odes* 4 in a most unhelpful way: see Brink (1982) 546-52.

Carmen Saeculare which had been commissioned by Augustus for performance on 3 June 17 BC, on the last day of the Ludi Saeculares. The most natural inference is that both poems are more or less contemporary with the composition of the *Carmen Saeculare*, and that it was Augustus' request for that poem which provided the opportunity, at least, for Horace to return to lyric. *Odes* 4. 2 confirms that Horace was engaged continuously with the writing of lyric after 17 BC. Some time in the summer of 16 BC news had reached Rome that the Sugambri had crossed the Rhine and invaded Gaul, inflicting a defeat on the proconsul M. Lollius and capturing a Roman legionary standard.[20] Augustus left Rome some time after 29 June, when he dedicated the rebuilt temple of Quirinus.[21] According to Dio (54. 20. 6), as soon as the Sugambri heard that Augustus himself had taken the field they withdrew to their own territory and sued for peace. No fighting actually took place. Even allowing for exaggeration, it is clear that the threat from the Sugambri quickly evaporated. In *Odes* 4. 2 Horace is still looking forward to the return of Augustus and the triumph he will celebrate over the Sugambri.[22] The vows for Augustus' safe return, mentioned by Dio and confirmed by contemporary coins, have already been made.[23] The dramatic date of the poem is thus the moment of Augustus' departure or shortly after. The actual date of

[20] On the date of Lollius' defeat see Timpe (1975) 140; Christ (1977) 185-6; Halfmann (1986) 161 against Syme (1933) 17-19; Syme (1989) 115-16 with n. 14. For sources and further bibliography see Halfmann (1986) 158; Rich (1990) 198-9.

[21] For the dedication of the temple of Quirinus see Dio 54. 19 with Rich (1990) 196; Ov. *Fasti* 6. 795-6; Degrassi (1963) 475. Augustus may even have remained in Rome for the celebration of the Quinquennial Games, which, as they celebrated the victory at Actium, were presumably held on or around 2 Sept.: see Dio 51. 19. 2 with Reinhold (1988) 146-8; 53. 1. 4 with Rich (1990) 133; Weinstock (1971) 310-17; Kienast (1982) 67-8.

[22] The *Fasti triumphales* were inscribed on the Arcus Augusti, which had been decreed in 19 BC and is best known from coins struck between 18 and 16 BC: see Sutherland (1984) 50 Nos. 131-45, 68 No. 359; Nedergaard (1988). They began with the three triumphs of Romulus. Augustus' refusal to celebrate any further triumphs after 29 BC has been attributed to *imitatio Romuli* (see Binder 1971: 166). Perhaps the policy was not formulated until the *Fasti* were inscribed, which would help to explain why Horace still anticipates a triumph for Augustus in 16 BC but does not suggest one for the victory over the Vindelici. That there was a change in attitude to claiming triumphs around this time is also suggested by Dio 54. 11. 6, 12.1-2, 24. 7-8 with Rich (1990) 188-9, 202.

[23] *Odes*. 4. 2. 42-3: *publicum ludum super impetrato . . . reditu*; cf. Dio 54. 19. 7 with Rich (1990) 197; and Sutherland (1984) 57-8 n. 57, 50 No. 146, 68 Nos. 351-38 (e.g. 353, *senatus populusque Romanus vota publica suscepta pro salute et reditu Augusti*).

composition may be identical and must anyway be before the news of the surrender of the Sugambri reached Rome.[24] The second poem in the collection is, as often, one of the earliest pieces.[25]

The latest datable reference is in *Odes* 4. 4 and 4. 14: the defeat of the Vindelici, which is assigned to August 15 BC, the anniversary of Augustus' conquest of Alexandria in 30 BC. If time is allowed for Augustus to communicate with Horace and for Horace to set to work, then 14 BC is perhaps the most probable date of composition. In that year Augustus was in Spain, and the prominent references to Spain, in both *Odes* 4. 14 and *Odes* 4. 5, will have had a topical significance.[26] The view that some of the poems were written after the return of Augustus to Rome utterly fails to convince for want of tangible evidence or compelling grounds. There is nothing in the rest of the book which requires us to think of any later date.[27]

The Suetonian evidence implies that after the victory over the Vindelici Augustus' thoughts started to move towards his return. Tiberius went back ahead of him to hold the consulship in 13 BC, and in part, no doubt, to make preparations. Drusus would not return until the end of that year or the beginning of 12 BC.[28] It seems that Augustus wanted the poems written to celebrate the victory for which he had received his tenth acclamation as *imperator* and which had been achieved under his *ductu auspiciisque*. Although *Odes* 4 and 14, together with their companion pieces 5 and 15, may have been written in 14 BC, they were written with a view to being performed and published in the context of the celebrations that would mark Augustus' quasi-triumphal return.

---

[24] Prop. 4. 6, which is probably also connected to the Quinquennial Games of 16 BC, belongs to exactly the same time: see 4. 6. 77. Cairns (1984*b*) 151–4 argues that the occasion is rather the *dies natalis* of the temple of Apollo on the Palatine (9th Oct.).

[25] That it was not revised in the light of events is clear from *Odes* 4. 14. 51–2: 'te caede gaudentes Sugambri | compositis venerantur armis', which exactly matches Dio's account.

[26] See *Odes* 4. 14. 41 (Cantaber), and 4. 14. 50 and 4. 5. 28 (Hiberia).

[27] Williams (1972) 44–9 argues for a later date for 4. 4, 14, and, particularly, 15. He is effectively refuted by Brink (1982) 553 and Putnam (1986) 23. Bowersock (1990) 389 is inclined to think 4. 14 later than 6 Mar. 12 BC, although Augustus' election as Pontifex Maximus was guaranteed after the death of Lepidus, which Bowersock (1990) 383 places in 13 BC.

[28] See Dio 54. 25. 1 and 33. 1 with Rich (1990) 211–12; and Bowersock (1990) 392. I am inclined to accept Bowersock's suggestion, although Dio does not mention his return before the winter of 12/11.

This conclusion is hardly surprising. *Odes* 4 conforms to a generally observable pattern according to which the publication of a book of poems coincides with a significant date or event in the career of the patron-friend who is the dedicatee. So the triumphal return of Asinius Pollio in 39 BC is marked by Virgil's *Eclogues*; Octavian's ovation for the defeat of Sextus Pompey in 36 BC by Horace's *Satires* 1; Augustus' triumphal return after Actium by Virgil's *Georgics*, Horace's *Satires* 2 and *Epodes*, Varius Rufus' *Thyestes*; the departure of Volcacius Tullus to Asia by Propertius 1; the triumphal return of M. Valerius Messalla Corvinus on 26 September 27 BC by Tibullus 1; Augustus' departure for the east in 22 BC by Propertius 3; the election of Valerius Messalla's son as a *XVvir sacris faciundis* by Tibullus 2 (?); the Ludi Saeculares in 17 BC by Horace's *Carmen Saeculare* and Virgil's *Aeneid*;[29] the Quinquennial Games and the departure of Augustus for Gaul in 16 BC by Propertius 4.[30]

The important thing for the reader of *Odes* 4. 5 to realize is that the dramatic date and setting are different from the date and setting of its intended first performance. The poem purports to be a pressing and urgent invitation to Augustus to return to Italy. In fact all the indications are that it was written to be performed amid the celebrations of his return. This is a variation on the familiar tactic of the encomiast, which is neatly caught by Ovid (*Tristia* 5. 14. 45–6):[31]

[29] See esp. *Aen.* 6. 789–97. I assume that the *triennium* which Virgil is said (Donat. *Vit. Verg.* 126–19 Hardie) to have intended to spend finishing the *Aeneid* was the *triennium* which lay between the departure of Virgil from Italy in the summer of 20 BC (i.e. Virgil's 50th, not 52nd, year) and the 'publication' of the *Aeneid* in the summer of 17 BC.

[30] It is tempting to add 'Horace's *Odes* 1–3 for Augustus' return from Spain in 24 BC'. Prof. Woodman reminds me that the same thought had occurred to Murray (1985) 50 = (1993) 103. *Odes* 1–3 shows a steady sequence of datable references from at least 29 through 24 BC. There is then an awkward gap until the period July–Aug. 23 (from the time Sestius entered his suffect consulship until the death of Marcellus), in which the publication of the *Odes* is generally placed: see Nisbet and Hubbard (1970) xxvii–xxxvii. Perhaps Jerome was wrong to place the death of Quintilius Varus in 23/22 BC. Sestius' suffect consulship in 23 BC is not referred to explicitly in *Odes* 1 . 4, and he may be at most *designatus* at the time of publication, or perhaps he is just being commended by the dedication as a suitable replacement for Augustus. On the election of *suffecti* see Talbert (1984a) 202–7, 242–3. One might compare the way in which *Odes* 4 honours one of the consuls in each of years 13 (Tiberius), 11 (Paullus Fabius Maximus), 10 (Iullus Antonius), 9 (Drusus), and 8 BC (Marcius Censorinus).

[31] Compare Arist. *Rhet.* 1 . 9, 1367ᵇ36; Cic. *De or.* 2 . 333; Quint. *Inst.* 3. 7. 28.

qui monet ut facias, quod iam facis, ille monendo
laudat et hortatu comprobat acta suo.

Horace guarantees the sincerity of the speaker's feelings of joy at
Augustus' return by depicting the longing for his return that had
been felt during his absence and the intensity of the speaker's
desire for his return. By adopting this strategy, Horace shapes and
guides the audience's 'recollection' of its feelings during the absence
of Augustus (regardless, of course, of whether the individual
members of the audience had ever consciously experienced such
feelings before) and so suggests an appropriate response to his
return. The poem is aimed as much at the audience as it is at
Augustus himself.

3. REDITUS IMPERATORIS CAESARIS DIVI FILII AUGUSTI

Augustus returned to Rome, after an absence of three years, on
4 July 13 BC.[32] The only narrative account that we have is provided
by Cassius Dio (54. 25. 2–26. 1). Unfortunately, Dio's account is
demonstrably lacunose, confused, self-contradictory, and in error
in some particulars. As Dio implies, rumours and announcements
of Augustus' approach to the city along the Via Flaminia from the
north will have come in over several weeks in advance of his
actual arrival.[33] Progress will have been slow and stately and
attended by much pomp and ceremony: places along the route will
have turned out to welcome the returning Princeps, to demonstrate
their loyalty, and, no doubt, to petition on matters of local concern.[34]
    Just as it had done previously on the occasion of Augustus'

After a long absence it could be safely assumed that Augustus was eager to return:
cf. Cic. *Pro leg. Man.* 22 'noster autem exercitus, tametsi urbem ex Tigrani regno
ceperat et proeliis usus erat secundis, tamen nimia longinquitate locorum ac desiderio suorum commovebatur. hic iam plura non dicam; fuit enim illud extremum ut
ex eis locis a militibus nostris reditus magis maturus quam progressio longior quaer-
eretur.'

[32] See Halfmann (1986) 159.

[33] It took Augustus at least three or four weeks to progress from Brundisium to
Rome in 19 BC: see Halfmann (1986) 158.

[34] The practice of *adventus* was well established in the Greek world and in the
Roman Republic: see Peterson (1930); Alföldi (1970) 79–118; Pearce (1970)
313–16; Versnel (1970) 387–8; Weinstock (1971) 289–90, 296, 300, 330;
MacCormack (1972); Millar (1977) 28–40; Woodman (1977) 130–6;
MacCormack (1981) 17–89; Woodman (1983) 118–21; Halfmann (1986), esp.
15–29, 111–29, 143–8.

return from Egypt in 29, from Spain in 24, and from the east in
19, the senate met to decide on honours suitable to the occasion.
Each *reditus* recapitulates earlier ones and revives memories
associated with them. So the honours proposed by Cornelius Balbus
on this occasion clearly recall the honours voted by the senate for
Augustus' earlier *reditus*.[35] The proposal of an altar to Fortuna
Redux in the Curia is a variation on the Ara Fortunae Reducis
decreed for the Porta Capena in 19 BC;[36] while the proposal of the
power to provide asylum to supplicants sounds like an extension of
the powers of *auxilium* and appellate *cognitio* voted to Augustus in
29 BC.[37] The final honour which Dio says Balbus proposed in 13 BC
is an ἀπάντησις, a formal welcome by representatives of the SPQR.
In 29 BC it had been suggested that the whole population of the
city should go out to meet him whenever he entered the city.
Augustus expressly declined this honour.[38] Nevertheless, he seems
to have accepted the proposal that the anniversary of the day on
which he had entered the city in 29 BC should be honoured with
sacrifices by the whole population and be held sacred for ever.[39] On
his return in 19 BC an ἀπάντησις was voted by the senate.[40] Dio is
simply wrong when he claims that Augustus gave the magistrates
and others who had come to honour him the slip and entered the
city at night. The reason for his misrepresentation can easily be
guessed, for Dio is known to have suffered from the demands made
in connection with the imperial *adventus*,[41] and he could not have
his model emperor providing precedent and sanction for such
behaviour. But the fact that Augustus recorded the honour in
detail and with evident pride in the *Res Gestae* makes it quite clear
that it was accepted.[42]

[35] Dio is clearly following a source hostile to Balbus, who had celebrated a
triumph *ex Africa* in 19 BC, the last person to do so who was not a member of the
imperial house. He must have been among those to whom Augustus in 17 BC made
the suggestion that those who held triumphs should undertake some public work
out of their spoils to commemorate their achievements (Dio 54. 18. 2).

[36] See Dio 54. 10. 3 with Rich (1990) 186.

[37] See Torelli (1982) 32–3; Reinhold (1988) 149–51.

[38] See Dio 51. 19. 2, 51. 20. 4.

[39] See Dio 51. 20. 3 and Torelli (1982) 30. This was the formal beginning of the
imperial ceremony of *adventus*: see esp. Halfmann (1986) 143–8.

[40] For the return in 24 Hor. *Odes* 3. 14 is suggestive; note especially 13 *hic dies
vere mihi festus* together with Dio 51. 20. 3 τὴν τε ἡμέραν ἐν ᾗ ἂν ἐς τὴν πόλιν ἐσέλθῃ
θυσίαις τε πανδημεὶ ἀγαλθῆναι καὶ ἱερὰν ἀεὶ ἄγεσθαι.

[41] See Dio 77. 9. 5–7 (on Caracalla); Millar (1964) 152, 216; (1977) 33.

[42] *RG* 21. 1 'Ex senatus auctoritate pars praetorum et tribunorum plebi cum

A similar ἀπάντησις was proposed in 13 BC, perhaps including the suggestion that Balbus should lead the welcoming party as Q. Lucretius had done on the earlier occasion.[43] Dio says that the honour was again declined, and this time there is no evidence to contradict.[44] But once again he must be wrong when he says that Augustus slipped into the city under cover of night.[45] This time Dio supports his assertion by reference to a general practice.[46] Suetonius also records this practice, which he includes, instructively, among those which illustrated the *civilitas* of Augustus and distinguished his behaviour from that of more tyrannical emperors (*Augustus* 53. 2): 'non temere urbe oppidove ullo egressus aut quoquam ingressus est nisi vespera aut noctu, ne quem officii causa inquietaret.' It is clear that, unlike Dio, Suetonius does not present this as an inviolable rule. He is thinking only of routine comings and goings during times when Augustus is resident in Italy.[47] People may well have been delighted to be relieved of this burden in connection with routine journeys.[48] But the very fact that Augustus had to go to such lengths even on those occasions to avoid the populace turning out to see him off or to welcome him shows how deeply ingrained this behaviour was.[49] It is quite another thing to suppose that Augustus could have slipped into Rome under cover of darkness after a three-year absence without causing the greatest offence, when everybody had been eagerly

consule Q. Lucretio et principibus viris obviam mihi missa est in Campaniam, qui honos ad hoc tempus nemini praeter me est decretus.' Cf. Dio 54. 8. 3. It should be noted that in 29 the proposal was for all the people to go out (σύμπαντας . . . τοὺς ἐν τῇ πόλει), while in the *Res Gestae* it is some of them (*pars*). That is sufficient consistency for a politician in a changing world.

[43] It is difficult to think what else might lie behind Dio's obscure comment Κορνήλιος Βάλβος τὸ θέατρον . . . καθιερώσας θέας ἐπετέλει ἐπί τε τούτῳ ὡς καὶ αὐτὸς τὸν Αὔγουστον ἐπανάξων ἐσέμνυνετο (54. 25. 2).

[44] Unless it could be shown beyond all reasonable doubt that the scenes on the Ara Pacis do represent the events of the day of its *constitutio*, as argued by Welin (1939). For a bibliography see Settis (1988) 424–5. Add now Bowersock (1990) 390–4, who argues that it represents 'the procession of the imperial family on the day that Augustus became *pontifex maximus* [i.e. 6 Mar. 12 BC]'; Billows (1993), who argues that the scene represents a *supplicatio* on 4 July 13 BC.

[45] The possibility of Dio's being wrong on this point, whether innocently or not, seems not to have occurred to those concerned with the Ara Pacis, who frequently find themselves forced into the most tortuous arguments in order to accommodate Dio.

[46] Dio 54. 25. 4; cf. 56. 41. 5.   [47] Cf. Carter (1982) 176.
[48] Cf. Tac. *Agr.* 40. 3; *Ann.* 3. 33. 4; Wallace-Hadrill (1982) 40.
[49] See Pearce (1970) 316.

preparing for his return for weeks, if not longer.[50] Suetonius (*Augustus* 57. 1–2), in fact, makes it quite plain that it was not his practice on occasions of major significance. For he goes on to talk about how the people showed their genuine affection for Augustus precisely because of his *civilitas*,[51] by the elaborate and spontaneous welcome they gave him when he returned from the province. It would be completely out of character for Augustus to have shown himself contemptuous of such a spontaneous display of affection and loyalty.

The date 4 July 13 BC was the *constitutio* of the Ara Pacis, and this enables us to reconstruct the events of that day with some certainty.[52] Augustus approached Rome from the north, along the Via Flaminia. Exactly one Roman mile from the *pomerium*, where generals returning from war exchanged their military garb for the civilian toga, he was met formally by the SPQR. Here the magistrates, the priests, and the Vestal Virgins performed a sacrifice, in thanksgiving for his safe return, to Pax Augusta.[53] This was the first occasion on which the goddess had been honoured with the new *cognomen* which gave her a special link with Augustus, one which honours him as much as the goddess: for it suggests that it is through him alone and through his actions that the goddess Pax manifests herself.[54] The sacrifice on this occasion no doubt set the pattern for the *anniversarium sacrificium* decreed by the senate.[55] It will have been performed at a temporary altar constructed within a *templum* duly marked out for the purpose.[56] This temporary structure would later determine the orientation, size, and shape of the final altar.[57]

[50] Cf. esp. Cic. *In Pis.* 53–5.

[51] See Wallace-Hadrill (1982) 40—but the entire article is pertinent. Compare the popularity of Germanicus: Versnel (1980) 542–8.

[52] For the nature of *constitutio arae* see Welin (1939), esp. 510, 512 (whose arguments are misrepresented by Torelli 1982: 30, 42); Fishwick (1987) 203–13.

[53] *RG* 12. 2. On the day of the *dedicatio* of the Ara Fortunae Reducis the *supplicatio* was made to Fortuna Redux; on that of the Ara Pacis Augustae it was made to the Imperium Augusti: see Degrassi (1963) 404–5, 538.

[54] On deifications such as Pax Augusta see Wallace-Hadrill (1981); Fears (1981a); Fishwick (1991) 446–74.

[55] This also seems to be the first time in Rome that a god is given the cognomen of *Augustus*.

[56] See Welin (1939) 509–10; Torelli (1982) 35.

[57] Cf. Vitruv. 4. 8. 7–9. 1, where *constitutio arae* denotes the layout or design of an altar and where the importance of advance planning to achieve the required results is emphasized.

The choice of the site was not haphazard. For the Ara Pacis Augustae was to form part of the Horologium Solare Augusti, a monumental horizontal sundial-cum-calendar marked out and inscribed on a large paved area of the Campus Martius. The dimensions and design of the entire monument were precisely dependent on the dimensions of the massive obelisk which was to be imported from Heliopolis in Egypt only a year or more later (12 or 11 BC) on a ship to be especially constructed for the purpose.[58] Moreover, both the obelisk and the Ara Pacis Augustae would be related, with powerful astrological symbolism and with some degree of precision, to the Mausoleum which had been started long before, in 28 BC, and perhaps also to the Ustrinum.[59] The planning of the Ara Pacis and of the Horologium must have been well advanced by 4 July 13 BC, since the size and orientation of the Ara would be determined by the religious proceedings which took place on that day; and, once the site of the Ara Pacis had been fixed, there would be only one place that the obelisk could go.[60] The offer of alternative honours, which Dio (54. 25. 3) tells us were solicited from Cornelius Balbus by Tiberius, can only have been part of a carefully orchestrated ritual of refusal such as regularly accompanied the granting of honours.[61] Yet it is clear from the way that Augustus records the Ara Pacis in the *Res Gestae* (12. 2) that it was

[58] For the Ara Pacis and the Horologium see Buchner (1982; 1988); Rakob (1987). For the transportation of the obelisk see Buchner (1982) 48-9. Buchner calculates that the original overall height of the gnomon (the sundial's pointer) was 100 Roman feet. The pavement area on which the sundial was marked out and on which the Ara Pacis stood covered some 12,000 square metres.

[59] It is not clear when the Ustrinum was marked out. On the site of the Ustrinum see Strabo 5. 3. 8; Jolivet (1989) 94-6; Patterson (1992) 199. For the Mausoleum see Kraft (1967); v. Hesberg (1988). Schütz (1990) raises some doubts about the precision of Buchner's calculations. Schütz wrongly dismisses Buchner's interpretation of Augustus' horoscope (446-9): see Brind'amour (1983) 62-76. Buchner's main arguments seem to stand, and the excavations seem to have confirmed the all-important point that the Ara Pacis was designed and constructed as a part of the Horologium complex: see Buchner (1982) 73-4. What will have determined the symbolic value of the complex is not just mathematical precision but the means used to guide the viewer's sight-lines. For example, it would be helpful to know if the obelisks near the Mausoleum, first mentioned by Ammianus Marcellinus (17. 4. 16), were part of the original design (so Zanker 1988: 76) or added at the time the Horologium was constructed (so v. Hesberg 1988: 246) or later additions (so Buchner 1982: 66). I am grateful to Prof. Snodgrass for discussing these matters with me.

[60] So, tentatively, Buchner (1982) 48, but rightly emphasized by Bowersock (1990) 383-4.

[61] See Wallace-Hadrill (1982) 36-7.

important to him that the honour should be seen as coming from the senate. Moreover, since there is no sign that Balbus was colluding with Tiberius, it must be supposed that the plans were known only to the very close friends of Augustus.[62] For, whoever proposed the Ara Pacis Augustae in the senate, the proposal must have come directly or indirectly from Augustus.[63] At all events, it is quite impossible to believe that the senate designed the Ara Pacis or the Horologium complex.[64] The entire episode brilliantly illuminates the degree of careful planning and the massive effort of co-ordination that could, at least on some occasions, go into the construction of the image of Augustus. It has long been noticed that *Odes* 4 reflects the imagery and ideology of the Ara Pacis Augustae and of public inscriptions.[65] The image of Augustus presented by both the Horologium complex and *Odes* 4 is significantly different in emphasis from that familiar in the 20s BC. Given Horace's position within the circle of the *amici Caesaris* and the chronology of *Odes* 4, this cannot be considered a matter of chance or coincidence. Both Horace and the designer of the Horologium are, in their very different media, consciously promoting a carefully considered new image.

Augustus had accepted his tenth salutation as *imperator* for the victories won by Tiberius and Drusus over the Vindelici.[66] His return retained something of a triumphal quality, and Dio informs us that the *depositio lauri* in the temple of Jupiter Capitolinus was part of the ceremonial.[67] Among his many honours, Augustus

[62] On the role of the senate see Brunt (1984) 437–8.

[63] The names of Iullus Antonius (praetor 13 BC) or Paullus Fabius Maximus (cos. 11 BC) suggest themselves: the latter was responsible for the suggestion, in language that would suit a proposal for the Ara Pacis and the Horologium, that the cities of Asia should start their new year from Augustus' birthday: see Ehrenberg and Jones (1976) 81–4 Nos. 98, 98a.

[64] Contrast Zanker (1988) 123: 'The sacrificial procession on the ara Pacis is a carefully planned reflection of the renewed Republic, designed not by order of Augustus himself, it is important to remember, but of the Senate, to honour itself and the state.' See also Zanker (1988) 3, 107, 283, 291, 338, quoted with approval by Wallace-Hadrill (1989b) 159–60, who argues that Zanker's model is applicable to poetry.

[65] For the Ara Pacis see e.g. Benario (1960); Putnam (1986) 327–9. For the inscriptions see Kiessling–Heinze (1914–30) i. 416; Pasquali (1966 edn.) 178–81.

[66] See Barnes (1974) 22; and for the significance of the fact that the *acclamatio* as *imperator* x is the first *acclamatio* to appear on coins see Kraft (1978) 323–6.

[67] Dio 54. 25. 4 with *RG* 4. 1. Dio's account is plausible enough on this point, but the address to the people on the Palatium may be misplaced, if it took place at all and is not just part of Dio's fantasy about Augustus dashing home to his bed.

records only the total number of *supplicationes*,[68] but the sheer number of *supplicationes* to be accounted for make it quite certain that one was voted in 13 BC.[69] The length of the *supplicatio* on this occasion is not known, but the celebrations probably went on over a couple of weeks and so must have overlapped with the Ludi Apollinares, which ran from 6 to 13 July, and perhaps even the Ludi Victoriae Caesaris (20–30 July).[70] The whole of the summer would be dominated by the celebration of major events in Augustus' career, culminating in the celebration of his birthday on 23 September.[71] Iullus Antonius, honoured in *Odes* 4.2 and consul in 10 BC, was praetor in 13 BC and organized the celebration of this birthday on an especially lavish scale in this year.[72] This was a special year for Augustus, as he then reached his fiftieth birthday.[73] No less importantly, it was the thirtieth anniversary of his *dies imperii* (7 January 43 BC, 'qua die primum imperium orbis auspicatus est': *CIL* xii. 4333 = 100. 25 E.-J.), of his first *acclamatio* as *imperator* (16 April 43 BC), and of his first consulship (19 August 43 BC).[74]

Certain themes, which can easily be seen in the Ara Pacis and the Horologium, were no doubt reiterated with subtle variations throughout the celebrations that dominated the summer of his return in 13 BC. Although the whole complex was in one sense a substitute for a triumphal monument, the emphasis was on *pax victoriis parta* rather than simply upon *victoriae*.[75] And there was an equal emphasis on Augustus as a man of destiny whose deeds had already guaranteed his apotheosis.[76] On the autumnal equinox,

[68] *RG* 4. 2. On the *supplicatio* see Freyburger (1978); Billows (1993).

[69] Note also that the phrase *ob res . . . prospere gestas* is precisely echoed in his own account of his return from Gaul (*RG* 12. 2).

[70] See Degrassi (1963) 477–9, 485–6.

[71] See Degrassi (1963) 489, 493–4, 496, 497, 499, 504, 505, 505–6, 512.

[72] See Dio 54. 26. 1 with Rich (1990) 204 and, for Iullus Antonius, Plut. *Ant.* 37. Celebrations for Augustus' birthday had been voted as an honour in 29 BC (Dio 51. 19. 2; *ILS* 112), but this is the first time there is mention of a public banquet which was decreed *senatus consulto* and therefore presumably not part of the honour voted earlier: compare and contrast Weinstock (1971) 209.

[73] See Buchner (1988) 72 n. 7. Horace emphasizes his own fiftieth birthday at *Odes* 4. 1. 6.   [74] See Degrassi (1963) 392, 442, 499.

[75] See Torelli (1982) 28–9, 32–3; Settis (1988) 416–24. For the parallelism between the Ara Pacis and the Ara Fortunae Reducis see *RG* 11–12 with Welin (1939) 504–10; Torelli (1982) 27–33. For *Pax* see esp. Weinstock (1960) 44–50.

[76] There is an interesting parallel in Tib. 1. 7, where Messalla's triumph is seen as the fulfilment of his personal destiny and the emphasis is upon the peaceful consequences of victory.

Augustus' birthday, the obelisk, which commemorated the conquest of Alexandria on 1 August 30 BC,[77] cast its shadow along the equinoctial line towards the centre of the Ara Pacis Augustae, voted to commemorate Augustus' safe return from the conquest of the Vindelici on 1 August 15 BC.[78] In one of the poems requested by Augustus before his return (*Odes* 4. 14. 35–40) Horace emphasizes the link between the two events, and so provides important confirmation that trouble had been taken to link them before Augustus had returned to Rome: whoever decided that 1 August 15 BC constituted the day of victory over the Vindelici did so to create the parallel.

After entering the city, Augustus attended the senate. His throat was sore, presumably from days and weeks of exchanging welcomes and greetings, as it had been in 29 BC when he rested at Atella before entering the city. In 13 BC the account of his achievements and his proposals for reforming the terms of service in the army had to be read out by a quaestor.[79] The celebrations of Augustus' return seem to have culminated in the theatre.[80] This was a standard feature of the *adventus*, as it gave the people the best opportunity of seeing their leader.[81] It is likely, in spite of the order of Dio's narrative, that the games held in honour of Augustus' return by the consuls, Tiberius and P. Quinctilius Varus, followed quite closely on the *depositio lauri* in the temple of Jupiter Optimus Maximus on the Capitol.[82] The dominant theme, the inter-

---

[77] *CIL* v. 701–2 = *ILS* 91. 'Imp. Caesar Divi f. Augustus . . . Aegupto in potestatem populi Romani redacta Soli donum dedit.' Cf. Macr. *Sat.* 1. 12. 35 (quoting the *senatus consultum* 'cum Aegyptus hoc mense in potestatem populi Romani redacta sit finisque hoc mense bellis civilibus impositus sit . . .'; *Fast. Praen.* 'Feriae ex s.c. quod eo die Imp. Caesar Augustus rem publicam tristissimo periculo liberavit'; Degrassi (1963) 489. Ovid (*Fasti* 1. 711–14) makes the link with Actium rather than the fall of Alexandria: 'frondibus Actiacis comptos redimita capillos, | Pax, ades et toto mitis in orbe mane . . .'

[78] See Buchner (1982) 36, 72; (1988) 242.

[79] See Dio 54. 25. 5–6; Donat. *Vit. Verg.* 95 Hardie; cf. Suet. *Aug.* 84.

[80] Whether the *Lusus Troiae* was also staged to mark this return, as it had been in 29 BC for the dedication of the temple of Divus Iulius (Dio 51. 22. 4), is unfortunately unclear, since Dio (54. 26. 1) associates it with the dedication of the theatre of Marcellus, which is dated more authoritatively by Pliny (*NH* 8. 65) to 7 May 11 BC. The *Lusus* may have taken place as stated, even if Dio is indeed wrong about the dedication. It is a matter of controversy whether the children in eastern dress depicted on the Ara Pacis are Gaius and Lucius dressed for the *Lusus Troiae* or Parthian hostages: see Torelli (1982) 48; Syme (1989) 119–20; C. B. Rose (1990).

[81] See Schuberth (1968) 22–5; MacCormack (1972) 723–4; Halfmann (1986) 118–20.

[82] See *ILS* 88: 'P. Quinctilius Sex f. Varus [pontifex?] cos. ludos votivos pro

dependence of the *salus* of the *res publica* and the *salus* of Augustus, is reflected in the coin legends of 16 BC.[83] One bears on the obverse a bust of Augustus with the abbreviated inscription reflecting the language of a senatorial decree—'Senatus consulto ob rempublicam cum salute imperatoris Caesaris Augusti conservatam'—and on the reverse an image of Mars with the inscription 'senatus populusque Romanus vota publica suscepta pro salute et reditu Augusti'. Another has on the obverse an oak wreath, symbolizing his role as saviour of citizens, and the inscription 'Iovi Optimo Maximo senatus populusque Romanus vota publica suscepta pro salute imperatoris Caesaris quod per eum res publica in ampliore atque tranquilliore statu est', a significant modification of the traditional prayer for the *salus* of the *res publica* (Valerius Maximus 4. 1. 10): 'di immortales ut populi Romani res meliores amplioresque facerent rogabantur.'[84]

Enough has been said to indicate the festive and ceremonial nature of the welcome which had been so carefully prepared for Augustus' return. Everything possible was done to stimulate a feeling of well-being and rejoicing. The whole focus was on Augustus as the saviour of the *res publica*, as the leader whose *pietas* guaranteed victories in wars fought under his *auspicia*, whose victories brought the blessings and bounty of Pax Augusta for the benefit of all, and on whose *salus* their continuation depended.

4. MODULATA CARMINA AND CHORAL PERFORMANCE

Odes 4 was intended to be performed as part of the celebrations of Augustus' return. When he had returned from the east in 29 BC, Maecenas and Virgil had met him at Atella near Naples and together read the *Georgics* to him. This was clearly a private

reditu imp. Caesaris divi f. Augusti Iovi optimo maximo fecit cum Ti. Claudio Nerone conlega ex s.c.'

[83] For the coins see Sutherland (1984) 68 Nos. 351-33, 356-8; Trillmich (1988) 519-20. Wallace-Hadrill (1986) 78 n. 73 makes the attractive suggestion that COMM CONS, inscribed within a *cippus* on the reverse of 357 and 358 (Sutherland) should be read as *communi conservatori* rather than *communi consensu*. This seems to suit the imagery on the obverse of both coins: contrast Trillmich (1988) 488, 519.

[84] There is a similar set of concerns evident in the dedication of statues in 10 BC to Concordia, Salus Publica, and Pax: Ov. *Fasti* 3. 881-2; Dio 54. 35. 2; Weinstock (1960) 49; Degrassi (1963) 433; Rich (1990) 215.

occasion.[85] L. Varius Rufus' *Thyestes* was performed as a part of the triumphal celebrations.[86] Although there is no direct evidence about the way in which *Odes* 4 was presented or the nature of the occasion, there is no doubt that music and song played an important part in the ceremonial of *adventus*.[87]

Suetonius is quite explicit about the nature of the welcome received by Augustus: 'omnes ordines [Augustum] revertentem ex provincia non solum faustis ominibus, sed et modulatis carminibus prosequebantur' (*Augustus* 57. 2). What Suetonius means by *omina fausta* is revealed by the incident he relates at *Augustus* 98. 2:[88] 'forte Puteolanum sinum praetervehenti vectores nautaeque de navi Alexandrina, quae tantum quod appulerat, candidati coronatique et tura libantes fausta omina et eximias laudes congesserant: per illum se vivere, per illum navigare, libertate atque fortunis per illum frui. qua re admodum exhilaratus quadragenos aureos comitibus divisit.' Such *omina fausta* are the impromptu reaction of ordinary people but could on occasion involve improvised chanting.[89] It is clear that the *modulata carmina* are much more elaborate and well prepared and that they constitute a significant and notable honour, apparently modelled on those given to earlier *triumphatores*.[90] They are at least accompanied by music, presumably played on *tibiae*.[91] But the best clue to what might have been involved is Suetonius' account of the honours devised for Caligula by the senate, which obviously had an eye on those previously paid

---

[85] Donat. *Vit. Verg.* 93–7 Hardie. In this way the *Georgics* were presented as a joint gift from the poet and his patron.

[86] See White (1993) 276 n. 22. The appropriateness of relaxing after the rigours of a military campaign was so well established that Horace could represent it figuratively in Odes 3. 4. 37–40; cf. Tib. 2. 5. 1–10.

[87] See Peterson (1930) 69–8; Alföldi (1970) 79–84; Wille (1967) 139; Schuberth (1968) 18–39; Wille (1977) 123–4; Fishwick (1991) 568–71.

[88] For comment and bibliography see Fishwick (1987) 92 n. 56; (1991) 481, 532, 569.

[89] As when the people prematurely celebrated what they thought was the recovery of Germanicus: Suet. *Cal.* 6. 1 *undique concinentium*: '*salva Roma, salva patria, salvus est Germanicus*'. Cf. Sen. *Apocol.* 13 (a parodic *adventus*), and see further Alföldi (1970) 84–8; Roueché (1984) 181–90.

[90] For the distinction cf. Livy 7. 2. 6–7. For a similar triumphal honour granted to Camillus see Dio fr. 23 = Zonar. 7. 21. 11; and for one to Duilius see *CIL* vi. 31611; *Cic. Cato* 13. 44; Florus 1. 18. 10. [II. 2]; [Aur. Vict.] *Viri ill.* 38. 4; Val. Max. 3. 6. 4; Schuberth (1968) 26–7; Wille (1967) 139; (1977) 75; Versnel (1970) 95–6.

[91] For the use of the *tibia* in the *ovatio* rather than the *tuba* see Plut. *Marc.* 22. 6–7. The same reasoning would hold good for the procession accompanying the *depositio lauri*.

to Julius Caesar and to Augustus: 'quas ob res inter reliquos honores decretus est ei clipeus aureus, quem quotannis certo die collegia sacerdotum in Capitolium ferrent, senatu prosequente nobilibusque pueris ac puellis carmine modulato laudes virtutum eius canentibus. decretum autem ut dies, quo cepisset imperium, Parilia vocaretur, velut argumentum rursus conditae urbis' (*Caligula* 16. 4).[92]

At the very least it seems inescapable that *Odes* 4. 5 and others in the same book are intended to evoke the *carmina* that formed a part of such ceremonies. If it is assumed, with the majority of Horatian scholars, that Horace's poems were written to be read or recited and not to be sung either by a solo performer or by a chorus, then it could be argued that this is just part of the dramatic fiction of the poem. But it is difficult to see why one should proceed from this assumption.[93] The ancient view was that lyric poetry was always written with musical accompaniment and choral performance in mind, even if it was sometimes read by lamplight by the scholar/poet or declaimed at a *recitatio*.[94] So Pliny, in justifying the recitation of genres not intended for recitation, declares: 'cur concedant (si concedunt tamen) historiam debere recitari, quae non ostentationi sed fidei veritatique componitur; cur tragoediam, quae non auditorium sed scaenam et actores; cur lyrica, quae non lectorem, sed chorum et lyram poscunt? at horum recitatio usu iam recepta est' (*Ep.* 7. 17. 3).[95]

The only poem of Horace for which we do have unequivocal evidence concerning the nature of the performance is the *Carmen Saeculare*:

> sacrificio perfecto puer. XXVII quibus denuntiatum
> erat patrimi et matrimi et puellae totidem |

[92] Cf. Dio 59. 7. 1; Apul. *Met.* 11. 9.

[93] Murray (1985) 43 = (1993) 94: 'We must not of course enquire how far the poetry of Horace was actually performed within the symposium.' Why not?

[94] See Wille (1967) 234-53 (bibliography: 235 n. 271); (1977) 129-31 (bibliography: 10, 44). Wille collects the evidence, which he hopes will speak for itself, but his presentation of the case is not discriminating. See also Cairns (1984*b*) 149-54; Wiseman (1985) 98-9, 198-206, who have also argued for choral performance.

[95] See also Quint. *Inst.* 1. 10. 20; Cic. *Or.* 55. 183, who says of the language of lyric poetry that *cantu spoliaveris, nuda paene remanet oratio*. The language of Horace is notoriously prosaic: see Axelson (1945) 98-113 and, for *Odes* 4. 5, Radke (1964*c*) 74-5. Although not all of their analyses are valid, it is worth noting that the language of lyric was thought to be characteristically 'prosaic' and could afford to be because it was intended to be accompanied by music.

carmen cecinerunt eodemque modo in Capitolio.
carmen composuit Q. Horatius Flaccus ‖. (*ILS* 5050. 147–9)

There is no reason to assume that this is exceptional.[96] The evidence of the *Odes* themselves is explicit enough as long as we do not dismiss it all as figurative. It is perhaps time to take Horace, e.g. at *Odes* 4. 15. 25–32, as meaning what he says:

> nosque et profestis lucibus et sacris
> inter iocosi munera Liberi
>   cum prole matronisque nostris
>   rite deos prius adprecati
>
> virtute functos more patrum duces
> Lydis remixto carmine tibiis
>   Troiamque et Anchisen et almae
>   progeniem Veneris canemus.

This would, after all, only be another case of the Augustans reviving and modernizing what they believed to be an ancient custom: '⟨sic aderant etiam⟩ in conviviis pueri modesti ut cantarent carmina antiqua, in quibus laudes erant maiorum et assa voce et cum tibicine' (Varro, *De vita populi Romani* fr. 84 Riposati).[97]

One feature which distinguishes *Odes* 4 from *Odes* 1–3 is the prominence of Pindar as a model, particularly for the more elevated poems.[98] Although there is a lively current debate about the nature of Pindaric lyric and whether it is in fact to be conceived of as choral poetry, there is no doubt that Hellenistic commentators generally assume that the speaker of a Pindaric poem is a chorus.[99] It is therefore reasonable to infer that Horace shared this view of the nature of Pindaric poetry and that when he is writing a Pindaric poem we are supposed to think of the speaker as a

[96] It is sometimes said that the metrical qualities of Horace's verse preclude the possibility of actual performance: e.g. Murray (1985) 43 = (1993) 94. But the metre of the *Carmen Saeculare* is not distinguishable from that of other poems in the Sapphic stanza, and it was undeniably set to music and performed by a chorus.

[97] See also Cic. *Brut.* 75; *Tusc. Disp.* 4. 2; Val. Max. 2. 1. 9; Quint. *Inst.* 1. 10. 20. See Dahlmann (1958) 353–5; Murray (1985) 40–4 = (1993) 91–5; Wiseman (1989) 134. For discussion of Murray (1985) 40–4 = (1993) 91–5; for discussion of *carmina convivalia* see Zorzetti (1990) with bibliography.

[98] See Highbarger (1935).

[99] Those contesting the general view that Pindaric poems are written for choric performance are Davies (1988); Lefkowitz (1988); Heath (1988); Heath and Lefkowitz (1991). The conventional position is staunchly defended by Bremer (1990); Burnett (1989); and Carey (1989; 1991). See also Cairns (1992) 10–16. For the Hellenistic view see Carey (1989) 558–9.

chorus. In the *Carmen Saeculare* the choric identity of the speaker
is indicated in the text itself and confirmed by the inscriptional
evidence cited above.[100] But Horace will have been well aware that
many poems which were supposed to be performed by a chorus
and in which the speaker was understood to be a chorus do not
have the speaker explicitly identified as such in the text.[101]

If *Odes* 4. 5 does not seem as obviously Pindaric as 4. 4 or 4. 14,
that is because the chance survival of the *Epinicians* gives us an
excessively limited sense of what Pindaric poetry was like.[102] Pindar
wrote poems in many genres, including paeans and prosodia or
processionals which were performed as part of the Greek counterpart to the *adventus*. These genres continued long after Pindar,
although he no doubt remained the model for later writers.[103]

Choral performances also played an important part in the
cultural life of Augustan Rome. In particular, the pantomime, in
which a solo mime was accompanied by instrumental music and a
chorus, reached new heights of sophistication during the Augustan
period.[104] On appropriate occasions these performances would
reflect current interests and concerns, as is revealed in an anecdote
told by Phaedrus concerning a *tibicen* called Princeps who regularly
accompanied Bathyllus. Phaedrus refers to a performance which
was intended as an *honos divinae domus* in which

> tunc chorus ignotum [sc. Principi] modo reducto canticum
> insonuit, cuius haec fuit sententia:
> 'laetare, incolumis Roma, salvo principe!'
> in plausus consurrectum est.

> (5. 7. 25–8)

It is hardly necessary to emphasize the similarity of the *sententia* of
this *canticum* and that of *Odes* 4. 5. Although Pliny claims to have

---

[100] *Saec.* 86–8 'spem bonam certamque domum reporto, | doctus et Phoebi
chorus et Dianae | dicere laudes.'

[101] A very good case can be made for identifying the speaker in some of Horace's
earliest Pindaricizing odes as a chorus: see Cairns (1971*a*, *b*).

[102] Bergson (1970) 359–62 recognizes the Hellenistic and rhetorical background
but argues for direct influence of Pind. *Pyth.* 8. 96–7 on 4. 5. 7–8.

[103] There is a particularly interesting account of the performance of these types
of poem in the context of an *adventus* of Demetrius Poliorcetes in Athen. 6. 62
Kaibel. It is undistinguished verse, but for the potential of the genre see Bacch.
Paeans fr. 4. 61–80 and compare Melinno's *Hymn to Rome* and the *Paean to
Flaminius*.

[104] One of those credited with these developments is Bathyllus of Alexandria, a
protégé of Maecenas. See Luc. *Salt.* 34; Athen. 1. 20 D–F.

disapproved, he makes it clear in his panegyric for Trajan that
songs and performances of this type became frequent and ever
more elaborate in the first century AD.[105] One of the main occasions
when such performances will have been commonplace is the
reditus or *adventus* of the emperor. There were many opportunities
for the performance of poems from *Odes* 4 on the return of
Augustus, both private and public. There is no good reason to
think that they were not taken.[106]

5. THE POEM[107]

> Divis orte bonis, optime Romulae
> custos gentis, abes iam nimium diu;
> maturum reditum pollicitus patrum
>   sancto concilio, redi.
>
> lucem redde tuae, dux bone, patriae: 5
> instar veris enim vultus ubi tuus
> adfulsit populo, gratior it dies
>   et soles melius nitent.
>
> ut mater iuvenem, quem Notus invido
> flatu Carpathii trans maris aequora   10
> cunctantem spatio longius annuo
>   dulci distinet a domo,
>
> votis ominibusque et precibus vocat
> curvo nec faciem litore demovet:
> sic desideriis icta fidelibus   15
>   quaerit patria Caesarem.
>
> tutus bos etenim prata perambulat,
> nutrit rura Ceres almaque Faustitas,
> pacatum volitant per mare navitae,
>   culpari metuit fides,   20
>
> nullis polluitur casta domus stupris,
> mos et lex maculosum edomuit nefas,
> laudantur simili prole puerperae,
>   culpam poena premit comes.

---

[105] Plin. *Pan.* 54. 1–2; Suet. *Dom.* 4.

[106] Private occasions: Suet. *Aug.* 74, 89. 3. Public occasions: *Ludi votivi*—Dio 54.
27. 1; *ILS* 88; theatre of Marcellus—Dio 54. 26. 1; Ludi Apollinares (6–13 July)—
Degrassi (1963) 477–9.

[107] For the detailed analysis that follows the reader may find it helpful to read
the conclusion of the article in advance.

quis Parthum paveat, quis gelidum Scythen,   25
quis Germania quos horrida parturit
fetus, incolumi Caesare? quis ferae
     bellum curet Hiberiae?

condit quisque diem collibus in suis,
et vitem viduas ducit ad arbores;   30
hinc ad vina redit laetus et alteris
     te mensis adhibet deum;

te multa prece, te prosequitur mero
defuso pateris et Laribus tuum
miscet numen, uti Graecia Castoris   35
     et magni memor Herculis.

'longas o utinam, dux bone, ferias
praestes Hesperiae!' dicimus integro
sicci mane die, dicimus uvidi,
     cum sol Oceano subest.   40

The opening stanza provides a clear indication of the addressee, the
speaker, genre, and dramatic setting. The most difficult to identify
for the modern reader is the speaker. There is a deep-seated
assumption that the speaker of a lyric poem is the author himself.
As we have seen, this is at odds with the general assumption in
antiquity that a lyric poem is intended to be sung by a chorus. The
question therefore needs careful consideration. In his prescription
for the kletic speech Menander Rhetor emphasizes the need for the
speaker to identify himself and say why he has been chosen by the
polis to represent it.[108] Nothing so crude is to be expected in a
Horatian poem. But the reader surely expects to be able to infer the
answers to these natural questions, however minimal and oblique
the clues may be. Of course, Q. Horatius Flaccus is the author of
the poem and we are entitled to ask what he intended to communicate by writing it. But he does not speak here as the *amicus Caesaris*
that he was.[109] Nothing could be further from the tones of this
poem than the tones appropriate to that relationship, which are
so evident in the snippets of correspondence preserved by Suetonius
in his *Life of Horace*. Nor is it adequate to say that Horace is

---

[108] Men. Rhet. 424. 4–6.

[109] Contrast Fraenkel (1957) 440: 'While he [Augustus] was still absent, Horace
wrote the ode (and in all probability sent a copy of it to Augustus) . . . He, like
many others, felt deep anxiety for the safe return of the Princeps, and . . . he now,
unasked and unprompted, endeavoured to express his own feelings and those of his
fellow citizens.' Cf. e.g. Dahlmann (1958) 346–7.

simply playing a role as a representative of the state, as he does, for example, in *Epode* 16 or *Odes* 3.14, in both of which the individuality of the speaker is marked.[110] The contrast with the latter poem is especially striking in view of the similarity of theme and situation.[111]

In *Odes* 4. 5, although everything underlines the representative nature of the speaker, nothing identifies the speaker with the poet. In the only first-person reference in the poem (37–8 "*longas o utinam, dux bone, ferias | praestes Hesperiae*" *dicimus*), the *nos* implied in *dicimus* is defined within the direct speech by *Hesperia* and the speaker is simply identified as representative of the *populus Romanus*. That is a very different thing from having Horace present an individualized version of himself as representative of the *populus Romanus*. It is, however, the opening stanza which most clearly insists on the representative nature of the speaker. There the speaker is expressing the feelings of sadness caused by the absence of Augustus. The emotion gains colour from the assertion that Augustus had promised an early return, and the solemnity of that promise is stressed by reference to the fact that it had been made *patrum sancto concilio*. The point, however is not really to offer a reprimand or rebuke to Augustus, much less to accuse him of having broken his word.[112] Rather the accusation here is intended to convey the emotional state of the speaker.[113] In such a context we expect the speaker to say something along the lines of 'I am very upset at your long absence, especially as you promised me a speedy return.'[114] In view of the ancient assumption that lyric poetry was normally intended to be performed by a chorus, the most natural inference to draw is that the speaker in this poem is a chorus which represents *senatus populusque Romanus*.

The speaker is calling upon the absent addressee to return. The poem is thus identified from the start as a *klētikon* and the conventions of this genre are evoked to provide one of the main contexts which will determine the relevant implications of the details of this

[110] See esp. *Epod.* 16. 66 *Vate me*; *Odes* 3. 14. 27–8 *non ego hoc ferrem calidus iuventa | consule Planco*.

[111] For Augustus' *adventus* in 24 BC as the occasion of *Odes* 3. 14 see Nisbet (1983) 109.   [112] Contrast Radke (1964c) 63; Syndikus (1972–3) ii. 332.

[113] See e.g. Men. Rhet. 396. 3–32.

[114] Cf. Hor. *Ep.* 1. 7. 1–2 'quinque dies tibi pollicitus me rure futurum | Sextilem totum mendax desideror'; Ov. *Her.* 2. 1–2 and 23–4 'hospita, Demophoon, tua te Rhodopeia Phyllis | ultra promissum tempus abesse queror . . . at tu lentus abes; nec te iurata reducunt | numina, nec nostro motus amore redis.'

utterance and their significance.[115] A Roman audience would have
supplied the relevant framework almost subconsciously from its
familiarity with literary examples and models, its rhetorical education, and the experience of the ceremonial connected with the constant pattern of visits, arrivals, and departures which formed such
an important part of the highly personalized socio-political life of
antiquity. The modern reader can obtain a good idea of what those
expectations might have been from a study of other examples of the
genre and from texts such as Menander Rhetor's prescriptions for
speeches of invitation (*klētikon*), welcome (*prosphōnētikon*), and
arrival (*epibatērion*). It has long been recognized that the poem has
certain hymnic features, and it may seem tempting to go further
and classify the poem as a ὕμνος κλητικός.[116] But, as we shall see,
the basic pattern adhered to is that of the *klētikon* addressed to a
ruler rather than to a god. The most important hymnic feature of
the poem is that the speaker is not identified as part of an embassy
but is represented as addressing an absent addressee from afar.[117]
But it seems best to think of Horace as deliberately making use of
the ambivalent and ambiguous area between two closely related
genres in order to convey the ambivalent and ambiguous status of
Augustus between the human and divine.

The primary concern of the speaker in these opening lines is to
convince the addressee that he is missed and that he should return
home. The sense of longing is well conveyed by the juxtaposition
of the phrase *nimium diu* with *maturum reditum*, which is given
emphasis through alliteration and a note of urgency by being
picked up by the imperative, *redi*. The request is grounded in the
addressee's promise to the senate, which is given weight and
solemnity by the intricate pattern of alliteration and assonance.
The basic idea here is a commonplace of the *klētikon*, as we can
see from Menander, who describes the city as 'having long desired

<hr />

[115] For the *klētikon* see Giangrande (1971) 91–2; Cairns (1972) 114; Du Quesnay
(1981) 90–7 with nn. 339–42.

[116] See Kiessling-Heinze (1914–30) i. 413; Syndikus (1972–3) ii. 331. Such a
classification would have the advantage of clarifying the identity of the speaker, for
hymns are normally thought of as being choric.

[117] Contrast Porphyrio on 4. 5. 1: 'populi ac senatus legationibus missis reditum
eius precatum'; ps.-Acro on 4. 5. 1: 'de Augusto scribitur, qui in transmarinis
provinciis diu residens senatus ac populi precibus legatione missa reditum suum
promittens immorabatur'. The embassy they envisage derives from their recognition
of the genre of the poem as a *klētikon* (cf. Men. Rhet. 424. 4–6) rather than dis-
placed historical information (cf. Dio 54. 6. 2–3; 54. 10. 2).

to partake of your great qualities every day' (424. 6–8) and then urges the addressee: 'Hurry quickly with good omens in answer to the city's summons, make haste' (425. 17–19). It is perhaps significant that Menander does not suggest that the speaker should recall the addressee's promise to return, even though such promises were a commonplace in the speeches of departure (the *syntaktikon*) and the wish for a swift return equally a commonplace of the send-off speech (the *propemptikon*).[118] Augustus may or may not have made such a promise on the occasion of his departure but Horace's decision to represent him as having done so is plausible and interesting,[119] especially in view of the elevated and honorific language used to describe the senate.[120]

At the time of his departure Augustus' relations with the senate were in fact under some strain.[121] The marriage legislation of 18 BC had provoked opposition, in spite of the fact that it was in these laws that the senators were first distinguished from equestrians in a move designed to enhance the dignity and authority of the senate. Similarly, the review of the membership of the senate was intended to reduce the numbers further towards the ancient 'ideal' of three hundred and so strengthen the dignity and authority of those that remained. Although in the end Augustus reduced it only to six hundred, this reform too had caused resentment, perhaps because there was such emphasis on removing those who were immoral and irresponsible as well as those insufficiently wealthy. Dio suggests that the invasion of Gaul by the Sugambri provided a welcome excuse for Augustus to leave Rome and allow time for the senate to come to terms with his reforms. Whatever the real reasons, morale among senators was low and there had

[118] See Men. Rhet. 431. 28 and 433. 13 (*syntaktikon*), and cf. e.g. Livy 44. 22. 17 'sacrificio rite perpetrato protinus inde et consul et praetor Cn. Octavius in Macedoniam profecti sunt. traditum memoriae est maiore quam solita frequentia prosequentium consulem celebratum, ac prope certa spe ominatos esse homines, finem esse Macedonico bello maturumque reditum cum egregio triumpho consulis fore.'

[119] Suetonius at *Aug.* 92. 1 may be generalizing from a specific incident: 'si terra marive ingrediente se longinquam profectionem forte rorasset, [*sc.* id observabat] ut laetum maturique et prosperi reditus.'

[120] The phrase *patrum sancto concilio* is unique but an elevated variation on *sanctus senatus*, for which see Enn. Ann. 272 with Skutsch (1985) 455.

[121] See *RG* 8. 2; Suet. *Aug.* 35–7; Dio 54. 13–17. 3, 26.3–9, 35. 1 with Rich (1990) for references to some earlier discussions; Raaflaub and Samons (1990) 433–5; Chastagnol (1992) 31–56. On the senate under Augustus see Talbert (1984*b*); Brunt (1984).

been difficulties in recruiting new senators during the period of Augustus' absence. It was a problem that was still very much alive at the time of his return in 13 BC, and one to which he then gave his urgent attention. Horace represents the relationship with great tact. He emphasizes precisely the view of the standing of the senate that Augustus' reforms were designed to safeguard and perpetuate. He also includes the senators implicitly in the feelings of longing for Augustus' return which would turn to joy when he did. In other words, Horace's poem works, like many of the celebrations devised for the *reditus*, to shape and orchestrate the feelings of both the senate and the people towards Augustus.

Although the addressee is not named until line 16, his identity is clear from the start. *Divis orte bonis* is a poetic elaboration of the patronymic of Imperator Caesar Divi Filius Augustus.[122] The *divi boni* include Apollo, Jupiter, Venus, and Mars as well as the deified ancestor, Aeneas, Romulus, and Divus Iulius.[123] While it is the descent from Aeneas which is emphasized in 4. 6 and 4. 15, here it is Romulus and Divus Iulius: the line is framed by *divis* and *Romulae*.[124] The phrases *Divis orte* and *Romulae custos gentis* pointedly allude to Ennius' description of Romulus as *patriae custos* and *sanguen dis oriundum* (*Annales* 107–8, Skutsch). The word *custos* was never a formal title but was used informally, especially of those who had secured the frontiers by military expeditions.[125] Its occurrence at *Odes* 4. 15. 17 (*custode rerum Caesare*) strongly suggests that it had especial currency at this time. It is therefore no surprise to find one of its rare semi-official uses in the *Feriale Cumanum* in connection with the *dedicatio* of the Ara Pacis: 'eo die ara Pacis Aug. dedicata est. supplicatio Imperio Caesaris Augusti custodis imperi Romanorum . . .'[126]

---

[122] This is standard Horatian usage: see *Sat* 1. 5. 55; 1. 6. 10; 21; *Odes* 3. 6. 33; 4. 6. 31–2. See Brink (1982) 56: '*orior*, often in elevated style . . . indicates a person's provenance (as *diuis orte bonis*)'. Fraenkel (1957) 440 n. 2 is a very revealing piece of special pleading. See also Radke (1964c) 59–60: Syndikus (1972–3) ii. 332.

[123] At this time there is no distinction between *divus* and *deus*: see *Odes* 4. 6. 1–2, *Dive . . . Phoebe*. *Boni* is a standard epithet for *dei* (Appel 1909: 99; Fraenkel 1957: 440–1), perhaps with a view to the supposed etymology of both words: *quod beant, hoc est beatos faciunt* (Ulp. *dig.* 50. 16. 49); *deus dictus . . . quia omnia commoda hominibus dat* (Paul. Fest. 71). See Maltby (1991) 83, 185, 193.

[124] For *Romulae gentis* see *Saec.* 47.

[125] See Béranger (1953) 183–5; Syndikus (1972–3) ii 332–3; Woodman (1977) 136–7.

[126] Degrassi (1963) 279; Radke (1964c) 62. Cf. *ILS* 140. 7–8 'Augusti patris patriae pontif. maxsumi custodis imperi Romani totiusque orbis terrarum praesidis.'

The adjective *bonis* is picked up and intensified by *optime* in the familiar encomiastic convention whereby descendants surpass the achievements of their ancestors.[127] The idea is well illustrated at Ovid, *Metamorphoses* 15. 50-1, where Divus Iulius, already transformed into a star, 'natique videns bene facta fatetur | esse suis maiora et vinci gaudet ab illo'. But *optime*, in combination with *custos*, also points up Augustus' role as the supreme benefactor.[128]

This complex of connections is rich in contemporary significance. Augustus' use of the patronymic *Divi Filius* was not constant: it diminished in the late 20s but comes back dramatically in the following decade.[129] In 44 BC Octavian had set up in the Forum a *simulacrum* of Julius Caesar with a star on its head.[130] After Actium he had dedicated the temple of Divus Iulius on the site where a column inscribed PARENTI PATRIAE had previously stood. It contained a statue of Caesar similar to that erected in 44 BC.[131] A little later Augustus' *Autobiography* revealed that he saw the star not just as a sign of Caesar's apotheosis but of his own destiny.[132] In 25 BC Agrippa had wanted to place a statue of Augustus in his Pantheon. Augustus refused and a statue of Divus Iulius was installed instead, with statues of Augustus and Agrippa in the antechamber.[133] There was another statue of Divus Iulius in the temple of Romulus-Quirinus restored and dedicated by Augustus just before his departure for Gaul in 16 BC. A little earlier contemporary coins link the Ludi Saeculares and the refounding of the city with a comet which was identified with the *sidus Iulium*.[134] On one Augustus is depicted as placing the star on the head of a statue of Divus Iulius. On others there is a striking visual resemblance between the portraits of Augustus and Divus Iulius, as if to stress their filial relationship and to anticipate Augustus' own eventual apotheosis.[135]

---

[127] See Norden (1927) 345; cf. Woodman (1977) 238-9.

[128] See Cic. *Dom.* 144 'propter beneficia populus Romanus [Iovem] optimum . . . nominavit.' See also Woodman (1977) 245.

[129] See White (1988) and contrast Ramage (1985).

[130] Plin. *NH* 2. 93-4; Suet. *Caes.* 88; Dio 45. 7. 1.

[131] See White (1988) 336-8; Suet. *Caes.* 85; *ILS* 72.

[132] See Plin. *NH* 2. 94 'cometes . . . admodum faustus Divo Augusto iudicatus ab ipso . . . interiore gaudio sibi illum natum seque in eo nasci interpretatus est. et, si verum fatemur, salutare id terris fuit.'

[133] See Dio 53. 27. 2-3 with Rich (1990) 163 for bibliography.

[134] See Weinstock (1971) 379; Sutherland (1984) Nos. 37, 38, 102, 337-40.

[135] See Pollini (1990) 352-3, who makes the unconvincing suggestion that this has to do with the fact that Augustus nearly died in 23 BC. It would be better to

Augustus was always concerned to emulate Romulus.[136] Both the house of Augustus and the *casa Romuli* stood on the Palatine as a constant reminder of the link between them. An important illustration of an interest in Romulus contemporary with *Odes* 4. 5 is provided by his prominence on the Ara Pacis and by the rebuilding of the temple of Quirinus, who had long since been identified with the deified Romulus.[137] This was dedicated by Augustus on 29 June 16 BC, just before his departure for Gaul.[138] The temple had been built originally in 293 BC by L. Papirius Cursor, destroyed by fire in 49, and rebuilt by Julius Caesar in 45, when it was furnished with a statue of Julius Caesar inscribed with the words *Deo invicto*.[139] The pediment of the temple depicted Romulus sighting the twelve vultures, an *augustum augurium* for the founding of the city which had been repeated, it was said, on the occasion of Augustus taking the *auspicia* for his first consulship.[140] It was from this *augurium* that the honorific cognomen *Augustus* was derived, which he had chosen after Actium in preference to *Romulus*.[141]

It should also be remembered that the original builder of Quirinus' temple had set up in the precinct Rome's first sundial.[142] It is not known whether Augustus provided a new sundial when he rebuilt the temple or, if he did, whether it was designed to draw attention to Romulus' horoscope.[143] This had been calculated by L. Firmianus Tarnutius, probably in the early 40s, at the request of Varro. Using the old variable or wandering Egyptian calendar, he fixed the date of Romulus' conception as 23 Choiac and of his birth as 24 Thoth, which, in terms of the Julian calendar, means that he was conceived on the summer solstice in 772 BC and born on the spring equinox. This would make his horoscope complement that of Augustus, who, as the Horologium advertised, was

recall that Romulus was 54 at the time of his apotheosis (Plut. *Rom*. 29. 12; D. H. 2. 56. 7); Augustus technically became *senex* in 18 BC and would be 54 in 9 BC. See Trillmich (1988) 520-1 for a different view of these coins.

[136] See Binder (1971) 163-9; Porte (1981) 333-42; Evans (1992) 87-103, 112-18.   [137] See Binder (1971) 168.

[138] Ov. *Fasti* 6. 795-6; Dio 54. 19. 2; Degrassi (1963) 411-12, 475.

[139] See Weinstock (1971) 186-8.

[140] App. 3. 94; Suet. *Aug*. 95; cf. Dio 46. 46. 3.

[141] See Bömer (1958) 68-70; Binder (1971) 272-4; Rich (1990) 148-9.

[142] Plin. *NH* 7.213.

[143] See Plut. *Rom*. 12. For a good discussion see Brind'amour (1983) 240-7; Grafton and Swerdlow (1985) 463-4. For the traditional Egyptian calendar see Bickerman (1980) 40-3, 115-22.

conceived on the winter solstice and born on the autumnal equinox.[144] In 26 BC Augustus replaced the traditional Egyptian calendar with the fixed Alexandrian calendar, in which the traditional names of the months were retained but 1 Thoth always fell on 29 August.[145] If subsequently Romulus' horoscope was interpreted, by accident or design, in terms of the new Alexandrian calendar, it would match that of Augustus: for in terms of the Alexandrian calendar 23 Choiac fell on the winter solstice and 24 Thoth on the autumnal equinox, and so both 'founders' were conceived under Capricorn and born under Libra.[146]

The second stanza reiterates the address, and the vocative *dux bone* picks up both *divis bonis* and *optime custos*, which eases the transition. The term *dux* is a standard way of referring to Augustus in poetry, but it especially suits the return of the *imperator rebus prospere gestis*.[147] It also suggests the popular nature of his support, as at *Res Gestae* 25. 2, 'iuravit in mea verba tota Italia sponte sua et me belli, quo vici ad Actium, ducem depoposcit.' However, the epithet *bone* underlines Augustus' untiring service to the state and anticipates his role as a benefactor in a civil rather than a military capacity.[148] The simple possessive *tuae* picks up the notion contained in *custos* and suggests that the *patria* depends upon him in the same way as a family depends upon the *paterfamilias*.[149] Augustus refused the honour of the title *pater patriae* until 2 BC.[150] Nevertheless, he had accepted the *corona civica* and the honour of having libations poured to his *genius* as early as 29 BC.[151] It is only the formal acceptance of the title that is missing. Its unofficial use is clearly attested much earlier, not only in poetry but also on coins and inscriptions.[152]

---

[144] See Brind'amour (1983) 62-76   [145] See Brind'amour (1983) 24-5.

[146] Bouché-Leclerq (1899) 369 with n. 1 interpreted the horoscope of Romulus in terms of the Alexandrian calendar, and is followed by Bowersock (1990) 387. The error is explained by Brind'amour (1983) 243 n. 8 and by Grafton and Swerdlow (1985) 460 n. 22.

[147] See Béranger (1953) 47-9; Nisbet and Hubbard (1970) 40; Hellegouarc'h (1972) 324-6.   [148] See Hellegouarc'h (1972) 485.

[149] Cf. Hor. *Ep.* 2. 1. 18 *tuus hic populus*; Wickert (1953) 2103-5; Radke (1964c) 65.

[150] See *RG* 35; Suet. *Aug.* 58, where the wording of Valerius Messalla's proposal sounds like a prayer.

[151] Weinstock (1971) 203-4; Alföldi (1971) 67-79, 130-8; Fishwick (1987) 107-8.

[152] See Hor. *Odes* 1. 2. 45, 3. 24. 27; Sutherland (1984) 48 Nos. 96-101 SPQR PARENTI CONS(ERVATORI) SVO; *ILS* 96; *CIL* x. 823; cf. Ov. *Fasti* 2. 129-30; Dio 55. 10. 10.

The stanza conflates three standard encomiastic topoi:[153] the comparison of a return or arrival with the coming of spring after the cold of winter;[154] the appearance or gaze of the ruler; and the comparison or identification of the ruler with the sun.[155] The speaker explicitly 'recalls' the effect of Augustus' earlier returns in the perfect *adfulsit* and implicitly compares their effect with the return of spring: *gratior it dies.*[156] Horace is perhaps playing with the standard etymologies of *dies* and *sol*: *dies dictus quod divini sit operis* and *sol . . . quod solus ita lucet, ut ex eo deo dies sit.*[157] Augustus is a second sun, and his presence will bring a second spring and lend an additional brightness to the day. The adverb *melius* picks up *bone* (5) and *optime* (1) and recalls the formulae of the prayer for the *salus rei publicae* and for the return of the Princeps. In the former the gods were asked 'ut populi Romani res meliores amplioresque facerent' and in the latter 'bonum eventum des, atque in eo statu, quo nunc est, aut eo meliori eum conserves eumque reducem incolumem victoremq(ue) primo quoq(ue) tempore in urbem Romam sistas.'[158] Now the *salus* of the *res publica* is inseparable from the *incolumitas* of Augustus.

The image of the ruler as the sun is particularly associated with the *adventus* or *reditus*.[159] So Horace himself had said in Odes 4. 2. 46–48: ' "o sol | pulcher! o laudande" canam receptor | Caesare felix.' The conventional nature of the topic in this situation is illustrated by Menander Rhetor in his prescription for the speech of welcome (*epibatērion*):[160]

We have come to meet you, all of us, in whole families, children, old men,

---

[153] For *lucem redde* see Cic. *Dom.* 75; Curt. Ruf. 10. 9. 4; and cf. *lux adfulsit* at Livy 9. 10. 2: see Radke (1964c) 63.

[154] See Aesch. *Ag.* 968–9 (the return of Agamemnon); Theoc. *Id.* 12. 3 (the return of a lover); *Pan. Lat.* 5 (8). 10. 4; 8 (5). 2. 2; 9 (4). 18. 4 Mynors; Nisbet (1969) 175; Pöschl (1963 edn.) 7–8. At Theoc. *Id.* 18. 26–7 in an encomiastic passage, the images of dawn after night and of spring after winter are also combined.

[155] See Doblhofer (1966) 86–91; Weinstock (1971) 375–84; Syndikus (1972–3) ii. 333–4; Woodman (1977) 97–8; (1983) 121.

[156] For *gratus* of the return of spring see Odes 1. 4. 1 and, for the Gratiae and spring, Nisbet and Hubbard (1970) 62–3.

[157] See Maltby (1991) 187, 572.

[158] See Val. Max. 4. 1. 10; *AFA* 107 Henzen.

[159] See Halfmann (1986) 58–9, 148–51 for its peculiar appropriateness to the *adventus*.

[160] Cf. Men. Rhet. 378. 10–13 ἀλλ' ἥκεις . . . λαμπρός, ὥσπερ ἡλίου φαιδρά τις ἀκτὶς ἄνωθεν ἡμῖν ὀφθεῖσα; 378. 21–3 ὥσπερ νυκτὸς καὶ ζόφου τὰ πάντα κατειληφότος αὐτὸς καθαπὲρ ἥλιος ὀφθεὶς πάντα ἀθρόως τὰ δυσχερῆ διέλυσας.

adults, priestly clans, associations of public men, the common people, greeting you with joy, all welcoming you with cries of praise, calling you our saviour and fortress, our bright star: the children call you their foster father and their fathers' saviour. If the cities could speak and take the form of women as in a play, they would have said 'O greatest of governors, O sweetest day, on which you came! Now the sun shines brighter, now we seem to behold a happy day dawn out of darkness. Soon we shall put up statues. Soon poets and writers and orators will sing your virtues and spread their fame throughout mankind. Let theatres be opened, let us hold festivals, let us avow our gratitude to the emperors and to the gods.' (381. 7–23)

This last passage not only illustrates and explains what lies behind the second stanza of *Odes* 4. 5, but also evokes vividly the whole ceremonial of the *adventus* to which the original performance rather than the dramatic setting of *Odes* 4. 5 belongs. In the *klētikon* we would expect a stronger emphasis on the darkness and feeling of loss and less, other than in anticipation, of the joys which will attend the return.

While the conventional nature of the material softens the abruptness of the metaphor, the contemporary resonances deepen and enrich the passage. Augustus had long associated himself with Apollo, and identification of Apollo with the sun and of the sun with the ideal ruler were commonplace in Hellenistic literature.[161] Apollo had been prominent in the celebrations of the Ludi Saeculares in 17 BC and again in the following year with the celebration of the Ludi Quinquinnales on the fifteenth anniversary of Actium.[162] In both cases the games were celebrated by the Quindecemviri, to which priestly college Augustus belonged. But the relationship of Augustus to Apollo, ever since the building of his temple on the Palatine (28 BC), was even more special.[163] The *Carmen Saeculare* seems to identify Sol and Apollo (9–12), and it is to Sol that the obelisk of the Horologium will be dedicated.[164]

Horace exploits the conventions of the *prosphōnētikon* and *epibatērion* to make not only the transition from the darkness and

---

[161] For Apollo and Augustus, see Binder (1971) 252–5; Weinstock (1971) 12–15; Zanker (1988) 49–53, 67–8, 85–9; Rich (1990) 133. For the sun in Hellenistic kingship literature see Weinstock (1971) 381 with n. 7; Halfmann (1986) 149 with references in n. 564.

[162] For Apollo and the Ludi Quinquinnales in 16 BC see Sutherland (1984) 69 Nos. 365–6; Prop. 4. 6. See also *Odes* 4. 6.   [163] See Hor. *Saec.* 73–80.

[164] There is an anecdote associating Augustus with Sol which seems to belong to this period (Suet. *Aug.* 79. 1–2).

longing of the first stanza to the brightness of return in the second, but also the subsequent transition to the comparison of the *patria* yearning for the return of Caesar to the mother waiting for the return of her son (9–16).[165] This can be seen as a refined variation on the idea of the πόλις represented as women, which is used repeatedly by Menander in his accounts of typical scenes of welcome.[166]

While the conventions of the genre serve to illuminate the run of thought, nothing can disguise the strong contrast between the elevated grandeur of the second stanza and the intimacy and warmth of feeling in the third and fourth. The image is almost certainly drawn from a lost Hellenistic classic, perhaps one describing the yearning of parted lovers and which served as a model for a splendid piece of post-Hellenistic grotesquerie in which Oppian describes the yearning of the sea bass for the goats who have left the shore and for Ovid's description of the abandoned Phyllis:[167] Horace focuses exclusively on the relationship of the mother and son, and transforms an erotic relationship into a dignified and moving familial one.[168] The plural *desideriis* is unique and striking, especially in conjunction with the collective singular *patria*: all the people are as one in their longing for the return of Augustus.[169] The love of a people for its ruler is conventionally expressed in erotic language, as can again be seen from Menander's prescription for the *klētikon*.[170]

You have captured our city with desire, O best of all governors, and this is the sign you have of her love, that she has sent again to summon you . . . unable to endure a single day; like those who are struck by the arrows of the frenzied loves and cannot bear not to see their beloved, the whole

[165] At line 14 many editors print *dimovet*, but that suggests rather restive, darting glances in various directions: *demovet* seems to be exactly right. See *OLD* s.v *demoveo* 1a; Radke (1964c) 69–70.

[166] See Men. Rhet. 381. 13–15, 417. 32–418. 3. Roma would be represented as just such a female figure on the Ara Pacis. See also Syndikus (1972–3) ii. 335; Doblhofer (1981) 1978.

[167] See Opp. *Hal.* 4. 331–45 (which has both a mother and son and a wife and husband); Ov. *Her.* 2. 120–9; and cf. Hom. *Od.* 16. 17–19—see Radke (1964c) 68. The combination of *Carpathium mare* and *Notus* at Prop. 2. 5. 11–12 and Ov. *Am.* 2. 8. 19–20, also suggests an allusion to an amatory context; but *Carpathium mare* at Prop. 3. 7. 12, where Paetus drowns with his mother's name on his lips, suggests other possibilities, although Putnam's suggestion of direct allusion (1986: 105–6) seems unlikely. [168] Contrast Syndikus (1972–3) ii. 335.

[169] Cf. Radke (1964c) 65.

[170] Similarly in the *epibatērion* (384. 28–31) and in the *propemptikon* (395. 31–2).

city has poured out and come near to bursting in upon you.[171] (428. 19–26)

The conventions serve only to throw into relief the restraint and dignity of Horace's simile. The mother's dependence on her son for support and succour is simply brought out by the juxtaposition of *mater ~ iuvenem*, in such a way as to recall the standard etymology *iuvenis vocatus eo quod iuvare* [*potest*].[172] The sense of separation by time and immense distance is assisted by the rare geographical name *Carpathii* to denote the far eastern end of the Mediterranean, notorious for its dangers.[173] The son is prevented from sailing by the prevailing northerly winds and the *Notus* is seen as *invidus* because it refuses to blow and bring her son home quickly.[174] The mother's hurt and indignation are conveyed by the adjective *cunctantem*, while the longing of her son for his home is reflected in *dulci distinet a domo*. In the next stanza her traditional piety and reliance on the gods to restore her son are brought out in *votis ominibusque et precibus vocat*, a scene suitably set on the *litus*: 'quidam . . . litus ἀπὸ τῶν λιτῶν volunt esse, quia proficiscentes et revertentes solent ibi vota concipere'.[175]

The simile works through a series of parallels and contrasts. The *iuvenis* is absent in the east, Augustus in Spain and Gaul. Yet it will readily be recalled that Augustus had himself been absent longer

[171] It belongs with the image of the ruler as the sun or a star: see Paul. Fest. 75 *desiderare . . . a sideribus dici certum est* [so *desiderium quod sidus abest*, presumably]; Maltby (1991) 183. The conventionality of the language and of the thought here is also illustrated by Martial when he is urging Domitian to return: 7. 5. 1–3. 'si desiderium, Caesar, populique patrumque | respicis et Latiae gaudia vera togae, | redde deum votis poscentibus.'   [172] See Maltby (1991) 320.

[173] Also at *Odes* 1. 35. 7. In view of the etymologies *aequor mare appellatum, quod aequatum cum commotum vento non est* (Varro, *LL* 7. 23) and *fluctus dicti quod flatibus fiant* (Isid. *Orig.* 13. 20. 2), there seems to be some point intended in the emphatic combination *Notus* and *flatu*, with the latter framing the line with *maris aequora*. The main effect seems to be to draw attention to the 'rejected' etymology of *litus*: *qua fluctus eluderet* (Cic. *Top.* 32; cf. *dictum litus quia fluctu eliditur, vel quod aqua adluitur*—see Maltby 1991: 14, 236, 344).

[174] The normal safe sailing period was reckoned to extend from 27 May to 14 Sep., and voyages were only made outside of that period with very good cause and only outside of the period 10 Mar. to 10 Nov. in emergencies: see Casson (1971) 270–3. The journey from Alexandria, which is probably what Horace has in mind, took at least a month, and ships on the spring run often arrived as late as the end of June or early July, i.e. about the same time as Augustus returned to Rome in 13 BC: see Casson (1971) 297–8.

[175] Prisc. *Gram.* 3. 493. 31: see Maltby (1991) 344. Cf. also Livy *Praef.* 13 *cum bonis . . . ominibus votisque et precationibus deorum dearumque*, which is obviously echoing a poetic model: see Radke (1964c) 69.

than a year in the east and from there had returned in triumph in all but name in 19 BC. That previous return was much in people's minds, as is clear from the parallelism between the Ara Fortunae Reducis and the Ara Pacis Augustae. Both were voted as substitutes for triumphal honours; both have separate festivals for their *constitutio* and *dedicatio*; both were situated where the returning armies of the future would re-enter the city: the Ara Fortunae Reducis marking the entrance from the south and east; the Ara Pacis Augustae the entrance from the west and north.[176] In recalling that earlier return, however obliquely, the simile enhances the claims of Augustus to be the greatest conqueror Rome had ever known and well on his way to completing Rome's historic mission.[177] This is also one of the images on the Ara Pacis itself, and the conquest of east and west is one theme of the entire Horologium complex, underlined by the connection between the obelisk, which commemorated the conquest of Alexandria, and the Ara Pacis, which commemorated the pacification of Gaul and Spain.

The simile recalls not just the earlier *reditus* of Augustus but also his departure in 16 BC, as depicted in *Odes* 4. 2 by Horace (42–3 *impetrato | fortis Augusti reditu*). The coin legends recalling the official language of these *vota publica* and the inscription recording the celebration of the votive games have already been noted.[178] The evocation of such *vota publica* by the description of the mother's behaviour in the absence of her son is subtly picked up in the adjective *fidelibus*, which is a word used especially of those who are dependent on the *fides* of some protector or guardian.[179]

The comparison of Caesar to the *iuvenis*, emphasized by the parallelism *ut mater iuvenem ~ sic . . . patria Caesarem*, is evocative. At the beginning of his career Octavian had been contemptuously

---

[176] See Torelli (1982) 27–9.

[177] See Virg. *Aen.* 6. 851-3 'tu regere imperio populos, Romane, memento | (hae tibi erunt artes), pacique imponere morem, | parcere subiectis et debellare subiectos.'

[178] Such prayers follow a clear pattern, and those for Augustus probably closely resembled those for Trajan preserved in the *Acta fratrum Arvalium*: Iuppiter o(ptime) m(axime), te precamur quaesumus obtestamurque, uti tu imp(eratorem) Caesarem . . . ex is locis provincisq(ue), quas terris marique adierit, bene atque feliciter incolumem reducem victoremq(ue) facias earumq(ue) rerum ei, quas nunc agit agiturusve est, bonum eventum des, atque in eo statu, quo nunc est, aut eo meliori eum conserves eumque reducem incolumem victoremq(ue) primo quoq(ue) tempore in urbem Romam sistas; ast tu ea ita facsis, tum tibi nomine coll(egi) fratrum Arvalium bove aurato vovimus esse futurum' (p. 123 Henzen). See further Versnel (1980) 562–70; Scheid (1990) 294, 313-14, 372-80, 405-11.

[179] See Hellegouarc'h (1972) 36–7.

styled *puer qui omnia nomini debet*.[180] His supporters seem to have
coined the designation *iuvenis* in retaliation. He is first so called at
Eclogue 1. 42 by Tityrus, whose lands he has exempted from
confiscation. The next occurrence is at *Georgics* 1. 500: 'Di | . . .
hunc saltem everso iuvenem succurrere saeclo | ne prohibete.' He
has now become the universal benefactor, and the juxtaposition of
iuvenem with *succurrere* makes plain the etymological significance:
iuvenes appellatos, eo quod rem publicam in re militari possent iuvare.[181]
At about the same time Horace uses the same designation in *Satire*
2. 5. 62–4:

> tempore quo iuvenis Parthis horrendus, ab alto
> demissum genus Aenea, tellure marique
> magnus erit . . .

Revenge upon the Parthians (finally celebrated in 19 BC), the god-
sent saviour of the *saeculum*, and the Ludi Saeculares of 17 BC were
closely intertwined concepts, and this perhaps makes less surprising the persistence of this way of referring to Augustus.[182] On the
night after Augustus had departed for Gaul the temple of Iuventas
burnt down.[183] Apart from the designation of Octavian/Augustus
as *iuvenis*, the only known connection is the *supplicatio* offered to
Iuventas on the anniversary of Augustus' assumption of the *toga
virilis*.[184] It was the destruction of the temple of Iuventas that
prompted the vows *pro salute et reditu*.

A sustained allusion to a famous passage of Ennius underlies
the four opening stanzas. This is best considered along with the
commentary and interpretation of Cicero, to whom its survival is
owed (*De re publica* 1. 64):[185]

. . . iusto quidem rege cum est populus orbatus, 'pectora diu tenet
desiderium', sicut ait Ennius, post optimi regis obitum:

---

[180] See M. Antonius (ap.) Cic. *Phil.* 13.24 'o puer, qui omnia nomini debes'; Suet.
Aug. 12. 1 'dicta factaque quorundam calumniatus, quasi alii se puerum . . .' At
Cic. *Att.* 10. 12a. 4, 14. 17a. 2, 16. 14. 2 Octavian is referred to as *iuvenis*,
although Cicero normally uses *adulescens*.

[181] Cens. 14. 2; see Maltby (1991) 320. Cf. Ov. *Fasti*, 4. 675–6 'titulum imperii
tum primum . . . Augusto iuveni prospera bella darent.'

[182] See Simon (1957) 61–4; Weinstock (1971) 196.

[183] Dio 54. 19. 7. The temple itself was rebuilt by Augustus (*RG* 19. 2).

[184] Jointly with Spes: see Degrassi (1963) 523; Fears (1981a) 862 n. 146.

[185] See Skutsch (1985) 255–60, who argues that *diu* and *post optimi regis obitum*
both belong to Cicero, not Ennius. If that is correct, then Cicero must be allowing
his language to be coloured by the wording of the original context, for both *diu* and
optimi are picked up by Horace.

> simul inter
> sese sic memorant: 'o Romule, Romule die,
> qualem te patriae custodem di genuerunt!
> o pater, o genitor, o sanguen dis oriundum!'

non eros nec dominos appellabant eos, quibus iuste paruerunt, denique ne reges quidem, sed patriae custodes, sed patres, sed deos; nec sine causa; quid enim adiungunt?

> tu produxisti nos intra luminis oras.

vitam, honorem, decus sibi datum esse iustitia regis existimabant. mansisset eadem voluntas in eorum posteris, si regum similitudo permansisset, sed vides unius iniustitia concidisse genus illud totum rei publicae.

Cicero is clearly tailoring the poet to his own argument, but it is still significant that he sets such emphasis on the *iustitia* of Romulus. This was the supreme virtue of kings and the most essential to the achievement of immortality.[186] Perhaps Ennius, like Ovid, had depicted Romulus as dispensing justice immediately before his disappearance and apotheosis.[187] The first passage quoted by Cicero describes the reactions of the *populus* to the loss of their king, and their words are addressed to him in his absence. The second was presumably part of a contrast between the brightness of their lives while he was with them and the darkness of the despair in which they now find themselves. It appears that at this point there occurred a comparison of their *desiderium* with that of a child deprived of its parent, as is suggested by Cicero's *orbatus* and Livy's version (1. 16. 2): 'Romana pubes sedato tandem pavore . . . tamen velut orbitatis metu icta maestum aliquamdiu silentium obtinuit'.[188] Horace's substitution of a mother and her son for the children and parents brilliantly conveys not just the helplessness and dependence of the *patria* deprived of Augustus but also his love and respect for the SPQR. The allusion to Ennius seems in fact to underpin the whole poem, for Ennius apparently went on to tell of the apotheosis of Romulus and the cult instituted for him by the

---

[186] Cf. Cic. *De rep.* 6. 16; Hor. *Odes* 3. 3; and see Weinstock (1971) 243–8; Binder (1971) 92–5; Millar (1977) 3–5; Cairns (1989) 19, 64.

[187] Ov. *Fasti* 2. 492 'forte tuis illic, Romule, iura dabas'. In Livy he is addressing the troops.

[188] Other parallels with Livy may also reflect a common source in Ennius: for *desiderium* cf. 1. 16. 5, 'sollicita civitate desiderio'; 1. 16. 8 'desiderium Romuli apud plebem exercitumque facta fide immortalitatis lenitum sit'; for *preces* cf. 1. 16. 6 'petens precibus'.

people.[189] Horace goes one better and tells how the people treat Augustus as a god even while alive. In both cases the concept of *iustitia* as the fundamental virtue of the ideal ruler provides the explanation and justification of their behaviour, as Cicero explains.

It is the *iustitia* of Augustus which provides the transition to the next section (4 . 5 . 17–24).[190] These stanzas present a highly stylized and encomiastic description of Italy.[191] The image of peaceful prosperity derives ultimately from Homer and, particularly, from Hesiod's account of the prosperous πόλις which thrives under a just ruler:[192] the *iustitia* of the good leader secures the blessings of the gods and brings victory in war and prosperity in peace. The imagery employed is conventional and stylized, but, precisely because of this, it is rich in associations.[193] It is a standard part of the *klētikon* to procede from the proem to the description of the place to which the addressee is being summoned and to give an account of it in terms which make it attractive to the addressee.[194] Menander, however, also recognizes a standard procedure in which the speaker 'handles the encomium of the city and of the governor as a unity' (429. 28–30). Similarly, the speaker in *Odes* 4. 5 presents his praises of Italy not only to persuade the addressee to return but also as further implicit praise of the addressee and as further explanation—*etenim* (17) picks up on *enim* (6)—of the request to the absent Augustus to return and restore light to his people. The speaker wants him back both because his presence bathes the world in sunshine and because all the attractions that Italy has to offer flow from him. Italy is what it now is because it

---

[189] Whether or not he identified him with Quirinus: see Skutsch (1985) 245–9 (against an early identification with Quirinus) and 260–3 (on the apotheosis); Weinstock (1971) 176–7 (for an early identification with Quirinus); see further Evans (1992) 103–6.

[190] I would print Faber's *prata* in line 17 rather than the manuscripts' *rura*. The latter gives either an unwanted emphasis on work (Varro, *LL* 5. 40 'quod in agris quotquot annis rursum facienda eadem, ut rursum capias fructus, appellata rura') or a poor joke (*rura . . . rura = rursum*). *Prata* better conveys that the *bos* wanders at ease after its work is completed: Colum. 2. 16. 2 'prata dicta ab eo, quod protinus esset paratum nec magnum laborem desideraret'; Maltby (1991) 494. See Syndikus (1972–3) ii. 337–8; and, for the problem, Nisbet (1989) 93 and contrast Fraenkel (1957) 443 n. 5.

[191] For the division into the blessings of the gods secured by the *iustitia* of Augustus and the effects of his lawmaking cf. Men. Rhet. 361. 17–25.

[192] See Hes. *WD* 225–37; Hom. *Od.* 19. 109–14; Theoc. *Id.* 17. 77 ff.; Cic. *De rep.* 2. 26. 1; Syndikus (1972–3) ii. 337; Woodman (1983) 255.

[193] See Fuchs (1926) 182–205.

[194] Men. Rhet. 426. 7–14; 428. 7–11; 429.

stands under the protection of Augustus. The keynote is struck by
the opening *tutus*, which picks up both *optime Romulae custos gentis* (1-2) and *dux bone* (5).[195] The normal order for dealing with the
achievements of the addressee is 'deeds in war', then 'deeds in
peace', if he is distinguished in war.[196] By reversing the standard
order, Horace's emphasis precisely reflects the decision to 'accept'
the honour of an altar dedicated to the Augustan Pax to be
erected on the Field of Mars rather than any more obviously
triumphal monument.[197]

As has often been noted, the image of peaceful prosperity and
abundance in *Odes* 4. 5. 17-20 finds a striking visual counterpart
on the Ara Pacis Augustae.[198] It should be recalled that during the
20s there had been a series of acute food shortages which had led
at times to rioting. Augustus himself took control of the supply of
grain from 22 BC and distributed massive handouts of grain from
his own granaries in 18 BC.[199] This is why, on both the Ara Pacis
Augustae and in this poem, Augustus and the peace that he has
secured by his victories are presented as guarantees of future
prosperity and abundance. The phrase *pacatum . . . per mare* has its
counterpart in the *Res Gestae* at 25.1 *mare pacavi a praedonibus*.
There the reference is to the victory over Sextus Pompeius in 36 BC,
more than twenty years earlier. In the period 41-36 BC the
blockade of Italy by Sextus Pompeius had caused especially acute
food shortages.[200] But this earlier victory is also recalled on a series
of coins belonging to the years 15-11 BC which bear the head of
Diana.[201] Recollection of Augustus' own earlier victories seems
primarily intended at this time to offset the redefinition of his role
and the new victories of Drusus and Tiberius under his *auspicia*.[202]
But recollection of the defeat of Sextus also serves to recall the food
shortages associated with civil war and Augustus' part in bringing
them to an end.

---

[195] Cf. Hor. *Odes* 4. 14. 43-4. 'o tutela praesens | Italiae dominaeque Romae; *Ep.*
2. 1. 2-3 'res Italas armis tuteris, moribus ornes | legibus emendes'. See further
Béranger (1953) 204-6, 257-60, 266-9; Woodman (1977) 141-2; Brink (1982)
36.   [196] Men. Rhet. 372. 25-8.   [197] Cf. Putnam (1986) 114.
[198] See Benario (1960); Syndikus (1972-3) ii. 340-1; more recently de
Grummond (1990), who identifies the figure as Pax; and Spaeth (1994) 91, who
argues that it is, at least primarily, Demeter/Ceres.
[199] See Dio 54. 1. 1-4; *RG* 5, 18; Garnsey (1988) 227-40; Rich (1990) 172.
[200] See Dio 48. 18. 1, 48. 31; App. *BC* 5. 67-8; Garnsey (1988) 202.
[201] See Sutherland (1984) 53 Nos. 172-3, 175, 181-3; Kraft (1978) 321-8.
[202] See Kraft (1978) 323-4; Trillmich (1988) 522.

The preceding lines are framed by *tutus* and *Faustitas*, both
suggestive of the protection afforded by Augustus through his success as *dux*. Faustitas is a novelty, apparently a poetic synonym for
Felicitas or Fausta Felicitas. These latter two were both goddesses
who received sacrifice, the former on 1 July (perhaps the anniversary of the dedication of her temple in 44 BC by Julius Caesar); the
latter, if different, on 9 October in conjunction with the Genius
Populi Romani and Venus Victrix.[203] Felicitas is an essential quality
of the successful military leader and closely associated with both
the triumph and the *adentus*.[204] It is therefore perhaps more relevant
to recall that there was a *supplicatio* to Felicitas Imperii on the
anniversary of Augustus' *dies imperii* (16 April) and a sacrifice
to Felicitas in the Campus Martius on Augustus' birthday.[205]
Callimachus had prayed to Ceres to nourish peace (*Hymn* 6. 137
φέρβε . . . εἰράναν). Horace stands the idea on its head: Faustitas or
Felicitas stands by metonomy for Pax and borrows the conventional epithet of Ceres, *alma*: for *est a gerendis frugibus Ceres*.[206] Ceres
in turn nourishes the *rura*, which stands by metonomy for *fruges*.
The idea of security guaranteed by arms is even more clear in the
next line, with *pacatum . . . per mare*. Nothing can better illustrate
the general sense than the *omina fausta* of the Alexandrian *nautae*
in Suetonius (*Augustus* 98. 2, quoted above).[207]

The final line of this stanza (20 *culpari metuit fides*) effects a
transition to a description of another aspect of Augustus' *iustitia*,
as is clear from Menander (375. 24-6): 'Under justice you will
speak of his legislative activity, saying that he makes just laws, that
he strikes out unjust laws, and himself proposes just ones.' The
allusion to the civil wars in the reference to Sextus Pompeius is
followed by an account of the beneficial effects his legislative programme has had in restoring the fabric of society. The sequence of

203 See Degrassi (1963) 475, 518. For Felicitas see Weinstock (1971) 84,
113-18, 127. Felicitas Caesaris provided a model for the Augustan Fortuna Redux
in 19 BC: see Weinstock (1971) 126-7. 9 Oct. was also the annual festival for the
birthday of the temple of Apollo on the Palatine.

204 See Versnel (1970) 356-71.

205 Degrassi (1963) 442, 512. The underlying idea is similar to that expressed at
Ov. *Fasti* 1. 701-4, 4. 407-8.

206 Cic *ND* 2. 67; see Maltby (1991) 122. For *alma Ceres* see Lucil. 200 Marx;
Virg. *Georg.* 1. 7. However, one etymology derived *pax a pascendo*: Maltby (1991)
458; cf. Tib. 1. 10. 67 *Pax alma*.

207 See Syndikus (1972-3) ii. 339-40. Cf. Men. Rhet. 377. 13-14 γεωργεῖται μετ'
εἰρήνης ἡ γῆ, πλεῖται ἡ θάλασσα ἀκινδύνως; IBM 4. 1. 894 εἰρηνεύουσι μὲν γὰρ γῇ καὶ
θάλαττα, πόλεις δὲ ἀνθοῦσιν εὐνομίαι ὁμονοίᾳ τε καὶ εὐετηρίᾳ.

thought is illuminated by Cicero, *Pro Marcello* 23: 'Omnia sunt excitanda tibi, C. Caesar, uni quae iacere sentis belli ipsius impetu, quod necesse fuit, perculsa atque prostrata: constituenda iudicia, revocanda fides, comprimendae libidines, propaganda suboles, omnia quae dilapsa iam diffluxerunt severis legibus vincienda sunt.' What Cicero sees as the essential task facing Caesar now that the civil war is over, the speaker in *Odes* 4. 5 represents as having been achieved by Augustus. The sense of *culpari metuit fides* becomes clear only at the end of the following stanza when *culpari* is picked up by anaphora in *culpam poena premit comes* (24). Fides is now afraid to be found guilty because punishment will follow as it properly should: *poena . . . quod post peccatum sequitur*.[208] The Romans have, so to speak, learnt the lesson from the Scyths and Getae that Horace had urged upon them in *Odes* 3. 24. 21-4. That they have done so is because Augustus, when requested by the SPQR on his return from the east in 19 BC to become *curator legum et morum*, had accepted the challenge though not the title.[209] The *leges Iuliae de adulteriis coercendis* and *de maritandis ordinibus* were the result.[210] Like the recovery of the standards from the Parthians and the celebration of the Ludi Saeculares, the moral legislation is part of Caesar's legacy of unfinished business to which Augustus gave increasing attention. In the *Carmen Saeculare*, after the laws had been brought in, the chorus was able to request Diana, as goddess of childbirth, to favour the *patrum . . . decreta* (17-18) and to ask the gods (47-8) 'Romulae genti date remque prolemque | et decus omne'. They then proclaim (57-60) the return of the gods (Fides, Pax, Honos, Pudor, and Virtus, all personifications of traditional Roman virtues), which is associated with the idea of peace and plenty, just as it is in *Odes* 4. 5 with the presence of Ceres, Faustitas/Felicitas, and Fides. The temple of Honos and Virtus had received attention when the Ara Fortunae Reducis was erected in its precinct in 19 BC, and Dio, in the same sentence as he records the Ludi Saeculares (54. 18. 2), records that Augustus moved the date of their festival.[211] The altar to Pax Augusta was 'constituted'

[208] Varro, *LL* 5. 177; Maltby (1991) 481. For *fides* see Hellegouarc'h (1972) 23-35.

[209] Cf. Suet. *Iul.* 41-2. See Syndikus (1972-3) ii. 338. For Augustus and the *cura legum et morum* see *RG* 6; cf. Dio 54. 10. 5-7, 16 with Rich (1990) 187.

[210] There is a huge bibliography on this topic: see Rich (1990) 192 and add Treggiari (1991) 60-80, 277-90; Mette-Dittmann (1991). The most useful for the present purposes are Galinsky (1981) and des Bouvrie (1984).

[211] Rich (1990) 195 for details and bibliography.

in 13 BC. Perhaps the temples or the cult of Fides and Pudicitia were also given attention around this time.[212]

In the *Carmen Saeculare* Horace had carefully attributed the *severae leges* to the senate (17–18). In *Odes* 4. 5 they redound to the credit of Augustus. But there is no inconsistency: the laws were approved by the senate and carried through the assemblies by Augustus using his *tribunicia potestas*.[213] The senate had wanted to honour him after his return in 19 BC by calling them *leges Augustae* and by taking an oath that they would obey them (Dio 54. 10. 6–7). Augustus declined both honours, but they still bore the name *leges Iuliae*. The chorus in 4. 5, representing the SPQR, treats the passage of these laws as illustrating his *iustitia* or the closely related virtue: *moderatio*/σωφροσύνη.[214] Once again, Horace is using a stock theme, as Menander's prescription suggests: 'For temperance (σωφροσύνη) is very closely related to justice. So what will you say there? That because of the ruler marriages are chaste, fathers have legitimate offspring' (376. 2–8).

And again the theme has special contemporary significance. There were not only the *lex Iulia de maritandis ordinandis* and the *lex Iulia de adulteriis coercendis* but also *leges Iuliae de sumptu* and *de ambitu*. These measures went hand in hand with the review of the senate in which moral criteria also played a significant part. There was considerable resistance, and, as already noted, Dio actually suggests that the unpopularity of these measures had been the real reason for Augustus' going to Gaul in 16 BC.[215] This was a matter to which Augustus had to give his attention once the elaborate and extended celebrations of his return were over.[216] It is of importance, therefore, to see that Horace has here allowed no hint of such dissension to emerge. On the contrary, he represents the laws as having already achieved their intended effect.

In *Odes* 3. 6. 17–20 Horace had offered a diagnosis of Rome's recent and present ills:[217]

> fecunda culpae saecula nuptias
> primum inquinavere et genus et domos:
>   hoc fonte derivata clades
>   in patriam populumque fluxit.

[212] Prop. 4. 4 (Tarpeia) is suggestive.
[213] See *RG* 6. 2 and Rich (1990) 192.
[214] For *moderatio*/σωφροσύνη as one of the virtues of Romulus see D.H. 2. 18. 1–2.
[215] Dio 54. 19. 2 with Rich (1990) 196.
[216] Dio 54. 26. 3–9.   [217] Syndikus (1972–3) ii. 338.

He then presents two vividly contrasting pictures: first, the modern wife who has been dreaming of *incestos amores* (23) since childhood and now takes as lovers, *non sine conscio . . . marito* (29-30), *iuniores . . . adulteros* (29), with no regard to their social status or her own dignity; then the young men of old who, toughened by work on the farm and schooled by a *mater severa* (39-40), defeated Rome's greatest enemies. The poem ends with a grimly pessimistic prognosis (45-8). The implication is clear: unless the Romans return to the moral standards of their ancestors, they are finished. They will be unable to sustain their position as rulers of the largest empire ever created; they will be unable to withstand their enemies; they will lose the prosperity that is the concomitant of peace. It is precisely the ills diagnosed by Horace in *Odes* 3.6 that the *leges Iuliae* were designed to deal with.

There was a widespread view in antiquity that marriage and the family provide the essential foundations of the state. It is found in philosophers, poets, and rhetoricians.[218] Whatever threatens the foundations threatens the very existence of the state. Conversely, the stability of the family and the production of children guarantee the prosperity of the state and its capacity to defend itself, and, above all, secure its future. It is no coincidence that this legislation on these matters was introduced in the year preceding the Ludi Saeculares, which mark the end of one age and the beginning of the next, a time very much concerned with looking to a new future and the next generation.

Horace's reference to these laws in *Odes* 4.5 is precise, tactful, and subtly persuasive. The emphasis is upon the *lex Iulia de adulteriis coercendis*. The law dealt with *stuprum* in a way which was scarcely to be distinguished from *adulterium*. It may also have dealt with *incestum*.[219] It is tempting to think that Horace might have wanted *edomuit* understood as meaning 'has driven out of the home': for *domare* was derived from *domus*: *hoc est sub domo et potestate mea facio*.[220] Horace's wording may also reflect the language of the *lex*, if one may judge by the definitions of the ancient etymologists: *adulter . . . eo quod alterius torum polluat; quia*

---

[218] See Woodman (1983) 281-2; Treggiari (1991) 205-27; Cic. *De off.* 1. 54; Calvus fr. 6 Courtney; Cat. 61. 61-75; Men. Rhet. 401. 23-36, 411. 14-18; ps.-Dionysius 262-4 Russell-Wilson; Aphthonius 13A. For the 'marriage legislation' of Romulus see D. H. 2. 4.

[219] See Mette-Dittmann (1991) 40-9; Treggiari (1991) 278, 281.

[220] Maltby (1991) 195.

alterius torum commaculavit, adulterii nomen accepit.[221] Certainly the hendiadys *lex et mos* seems designed to recall the senate's request to Augustus to become *curator legum et morum.*[222] The reference to punishment evokes the series of punishments prescribed by the law, including the apparent innovation of the right of the woman's father to execute the adulterer summarily as long as he also killed his daughter.[223] The words *laudantur simili prole puerperae* brings out the reasons that stood behind the attack upon adultery: the protection of marriage, the creation of legitimate children.[224] There is a striking parallel in the speech attributed to Augustus by Dio when he is addressing those who have complied with this legislation:

I praise you all the more because you have accepted your obligations and are helping to replenish your native land. . . . Is it not a joy to acknowledge a child who possesses the qualities of both parents, to tend and educate a being who is both the physical and the spiritual image of yourself, so that, as it grows up, another self is created? . . . If you are to rule others and the rest of the world is to obey you, there should be a flourishing race of ours; such a race as will in time of peace till the soil, sail the seas, practise the arts, and pursue handicrafts, and in time of war protect what we hold with an ardour which is all the greater because of the ties of blood, and which will bring forth others to take the place of those who fall. (56. 2–4)

Augustus may have spoken similarly when introducing his legislation in 18 BC.

The choral speaker passes from the achievements of Augustus in peace, which illustrate his *iustitia,* to his achievements in war (25–8). Here again it is Menander who provides useful guidance to the sequence of thought:

You will speak of the prosperity and good fortune of the cities: the markets are full of goods, the cities full of feasts and festivals, the earth is tilled in peace, the sea is sailed without danger, piety towards god is increased, honours are given to all in due fashion. 'We fear neither

---

[221] Maltby (1991) 9–10.

[222] See Brink (1982) 37–8; Rich (1990) 187.

[223] Treggiari (1991) 264–77, 282–5, 290.

[224] The wording goes back to Hes. *WD* 235: if men break their oaths and act unjustly their wives will bear monstrous children. In Theoc. *Id.* 17. 44 and Cat. 61. 221–5 the idea that children resemble their fathers is a guarantee of the wife's chastity. See Fraenkel (1957) 444; Syndikus (1972–3) ii. 338. For Horace the restoration of *fides* within marriage is coupled with a return of *fides* generally.

barbarians nor enemies, the ruler's arms are a safer fortress for us than our cities' walls.' (377. 10-17)

But here again the stanza is charged with contemporary significance. In 55 BC the Parthians had captured legionary standards from Crassus. These were restored when Augustus returned in 19 BC and a long-standing humiliation for Rome was at last avenged. It was a success for negotiation and diplomacy rather than for arms, but Augustus had been offered a triumph which he declined and the Parthians are represented in the *Res Gestae* as posing no further threat to Rome.[225] Augustus also mentions the Scythians among those who *nostram amicitiam appetiverunt per legatos*, and that must have happened not long after his return in 19 BC, as it is also celebrated in the *Carmen Saeculare*.[226] They are mentioned together here partly to make the learned point that the Parthi *Scythorum exules fuere . . . Scythico sermone exules 'parthi' dicuntur*, and so not, as others held, *Parthi dicti eo, quod virtute praestent nec habeant pares*.[227] It was the invasion of Gaul by the German Sugambri which had caused Augustus to leave Rome, and Germania receives the more elaborate treatment. As an ancient etymologist explains, the name *Germania* conjures up 'terra dives virum ac populis numerosis et immanibus unde et propter fecunditatem gignendorum populorum Germania dicta est'.[228] Horace is deliberately using language suggestive of the Earth-born Giants who had opposed the gods, a conventional image for the forces of barbarism and chaos ranged against those of order and civilization.[229] Their teeming fecundity underlines the significance of the legislation dealt with in the previous stanza, one purpose of which was to ensure that Rome had the manpower to withstand its enemies.

The stanza ends with the reference to the ending of the threat of war in Spain after some two centuries.[230] The main period of

[225] See Syndikus (1972-3) ii. 339; *RG* 29. 2 'Parthos trium exercitum Romanorum spolia et signa reddere mihi supplicesque amicitiam populi Romani petere coegi.' Cf. 32. 1, 33.

[226] See *RG* 31. 2; Hor. *Sac. iam Scythae responsa petunt.*

[227] See Maltby (1991) 453.

[228] See Maltby (1991) 257, and 228 *fecunda a fetu dicta, quasi fetunda.*

[229] See esp. *Odes* 3. 4. 42-80. The Raeti and Vindelici might also have been thought of as a Germanic people: see Oros. 6. 21. 12. For their barbarity see Dio 54. 22. 1-2 and see *RG* 26. 2 with Brunt and Moore (1967) 81.

[230] The Augustan view is reflected in Vell. Pat. 2. 90, esp. 4 'has igitur provincias tam diffusas, tam frequentes, tam feras ad eam pacem . . . perduxit Caesar Augustus ut, quae maximis bellis numquam vacaverant, eae . . . postea etiam latrociniis vacarent.'

Augustan conquest fell in 26–25 BC, but resistance had continued and war flared up in both 22 and 19 BC.[231] Augustus spent most of 14 BC in Spain completing the pacification of the province and establishing colonies. The ferocity and the stubborn resistance of the Cantabri are now seen as a thing of the past. The reference to Spain fixes the dramatic date of the poem to late 14 or early 13 BC: the threat of war is over and Augustus can now return.

This sense of freedom from the threat of war depends upon the safety of Caesar. The inseparability of the *salus* or *incolumitas* of the *res publica* and Augustus was proclaimed in a senatorial decree that lay behind a coin issued in 16 BC bearing the inscription *Senatus consulto ob rempublicam cum salute imperatoris Caesaris Augusti conservatam.*[232] Similar language no doubt echoed through the prayers to the gods which accompanied the various votive offerings, as may be inferred from a later prayer of the Fratres Arvales *pro salute imperatoris . . . ex cuius incolumitate omnium salus constat.*[233]

The final section of the poem turns from the absent addressee to the welcome that is even now being prepared for his return (29–40).[234] Here again Horace's poem follows the traditional pattern of the *klētikon*, as is clear from Menander:[235]

Add to the epilogue: 'The city already stands before the gates, with whole families, meeting you, greeting you, praying to the gods to see you soon. Do not disappoint her hopes, nor change her expectations into distress. As she used to welcome Apollo . . . so she is waiting for you; poets are ready with works of the Muses fashioned for the occasion, prose writers too: all are ready to hymn and praise you.'[236] (427, 17–27)

But the passage of Ennius dealing with the disappearance and apotheosis of Romulus is also still in play. Livy, following Ennius,

---

[231] See Dio 53. 25. 2–7, 29. 1–2; 54. 5. 1–3, 11. 2–5, 20. 3, 23. 7, 25. 1; Flor. 2. 33. 46–60; Oros. 6. 21. 1–11; Woodman (1983) 264–7; Rich (1990) 160.

[232] See Sutherland (1984) 68 Nos. 356–7; Weinstock (1971) 171–2; but it seems to me that the surrender of the Sugambri rather than recovery from an otherwise unattested illness is the more likely occasion.

[233] See *AFA* 110 Henzen. Cf. Cic. *Pro Marc.* 22 'nam quis est . . . qui non intellegat tua salute contineri suam et ex unius tua vita pendere omnium', 32 'nisi te, C. Caesar, salvo . . . salvi esse non possumus.' See Alföldi (1970) 86–7 n. 4; Syndikus (1972–3) ii. 338–9.

[234] At 4. 5. 31 Shackleton Bailey (1985*a*) 158 proposes *tecta* for *vina*, but see Syndikus (1972–3) ii. 342.

[235] Contrast Syndikus (1972–3) ii. 341, 343, who sees Horace increasingly losing sight of the situation depicted in the opening stanza.

[236] Cf. Men. Rhet. 377. 21–30; 381. 19–23; 417. 32–418. 3. See Price (1980) 29–30 (hymnodes in the cult at Pergamum), 32 (ritual of the *adventus*).

tells how the people recovered from their despair and then prayed
to the deified Romulus: 'deinde a paucis initio facto deum deo
natum, regem parentemque urbis Romanae salvere uniuersi
Romulum iubent; pacem precibus exposcunt, uti volens propitius
suam semper sospitet progeniem' (1. 16. 2–3). In *Odes* 4. 5 the
movement from *desiderium* for the absent benefactor and ruler to
honouring him as a god runs parallel to Ennius' account, and the
context evoked by the allusion to Ennius in the opening stanzas
underpins the coherence of the poem.

The closing sequence begins with the image of the *civis Romanus*
cultivating his land in the manner of the idealized youth of the
past.[237] At the end of the day he returns from cultivating his vine-
yard to enjoy the fruits of his labours. Both his *securitas* and the
fecunditas of his land derive from Augustus, and so he invites him
as a *deus* to join his feast. Through this image the choral speaker
in effect proclaims his representative role: everyone feels the joy
that characterizes a speech of welcome and calls upon the
addressee to be present as a god, in recognition of the benefits he
has conferred upon them all.[238]

The phrase *condit quisque diem* is striking and alludes to Virgil,
Eclogues 9. 46–52:[239]

LYCIDAS

> 'Daphni, quid antiquos signorum suspicis ortus?
> ecce Dionaei processit Caesaris astrum,
> astrum quo segetes gauderent frugibus et quo
> duceret apricis in collibus uva colorem.
> insere, Daphni, piros: carpent tua poma nepotes.'

MOERIS

> Omnia fert aetas, animum quoque. saepe ego longos
> cantando puerum memini me condere soles.

Eclogue 9 is set against the background of the eviction of Italian
farmers to provide land for the settlement of veterans discharged
after Philippi in 41–40 BC. Lycidas is recalling a song Moeris had
sung some years before that which had hymned the new god,

---

[237] See esp. *Odes* 3. 6. 33–44.
[238] For joy as the distinguishing characteristic of the *epibatērion* see Men. Rhet.
382. 1–6; cf. 378. 3; 381. 10, 26–7.
[239] So ps.-Acro; see Fraenkel (1957) 445 n. 3; rightly emphasized by Putnam
(1986) 110–11.

Divus Iulius, as a source of fertility, prosperity, and security. The eclogue depicts the bitter disappointment of those hopes in the ensuing chaos of civil war. The general sense of the allusion is clear enough: Augustus has brought an end to civil war and its concomitant upheavals, and *certa cuique rerum suarum possessio* counted among the blessings he had conferred.[240] But the emphasis upon the security of ownership conveyed by the phrase *collibus in suis* has a more specific contemporary reference.[241]

In his account of Augustus' speech to the senate delivered on his return, Dio reports:[242]

He enumerated his achievements and prescribed the years which citizens should serve in the army and the money which they should receive on discharge in place of the land which they were constantly demanding. . . . The immediate reaction of the soldiers to the announcement was neither delight nor anger since they had gained some but not all of what they had hoped for, but the rest of the population welcomed the prospect of no longer having their property taken from them. (54. 25. 5-6)

The problem of finding a suitable way of rewarding those who had served in the armies without evicting existing owners or tenants had long eluded a solution. Augustus had dealt with it after Actium by paying compensation for the lands he had taken over in Italy. In 14 BC he did the same for lands in the provinces. On his return he introduced this new scheme, whereby the soldiers would receive cash grants rather than land on discharge. The importance of the problem and the significance of its solution are confirmed by the space allocated to it in the *Res Gestae*, where the details are accompanied by the proud claim: 'id primus et solus omnium, qui deduxerunt colonias militum in Italia aut in provinciis, ad memoriam aetatis meae feci' (16. 1). By evoking Virgil's celebrated literary account of the earlier sufferings caused by the settlement of veterans, Horace underlines the significance of this new proposal, of which his audience can have become aware only days if not hours before they heard his poem. Horace must have been aware of the proposal considerably in advance of those outside the most intimate circle of Augustus' friends.

[240] Vell. Pat. 2. 89. 4; Hor. *Odes* 4. 15. 17-20. See Nicolet (1984) 111-12.

[241] Cf. Hor. *Epod.* 2. 3 'ut prisca gens mortalium, | paterna rura bobus exercet suis.'

[242] See *RG* 16; Suet. *Aug.* 49. 2; Brunt (1971) 332-42; Keppie (1983) 82-6, 208-9.

In a kletic hymn articulated by the characteristic anaphora of *te*
. . . *te* . . . *te* . . . *tuum*, the farmer calls upon Augustus as a *deus*
to attend his meal. *Odes* 3. 14 provides a parallel and an instructive contrast.[243] There the individualized speaker ends his welcome
by giving instructions for a private party which underlines and
guarantees the sincerity of his feelings of joy at the return of
Augustus. In *Odes* 4. 5 the chorus portrays each and every one
of the citizens that it represents preparing his own private meal
and his own spontaneous ritual expression of gratitude for the
benefits conferred by Augustus' leadership.[244] This is a private
cult and a spontaneous act of gratitude to a benefactor for the
benefits enjoyed as a result of Augustus' rule.[245] It is an action
characteristic of the people Horace is describing: it was the
ordinary people who had worshipped the Gracchi as gods after
their death; hailed C. Marius as a new founder of Rome and made
offerings of food and libations of wine to him; and honoured M.
Marius Gratidianus, the praetor of 85 BC, with supplications of
incense and wine.[246] But the citizen farmer is also shown universally (*quisque*) complying happily with the honour voted by the
senate to Augustus on his return after Actium, which Dio describes
as follows:[247] 'The priests and priestesses were instructed, when
they offered up prayers for the senate and Roman people, to pray
for him likewise, and both at public and at private banquets everyone was to pour a libation to him' (51. 19. 7).

At mealtimes small statues of the Lares were placed on the table
and with them a statue of Augustus, usually holding a cornu-
copia.[248] The libation, the *grati pignus honoris*, was accompanied by
a prayer which is described by Ovid:[249]

> iamque, ubi suadebit placidos nox umida somnos,
> larga precaturi sumite vina manu,

[243] Syndikus (1972–3) ii. 343–4 notes the parallel but does not note the crucial
difference in conception.   [244] Plin. *NH* 2. 18 *deus est mortali iuvare mortalem.*
[245] See Habicht (1972) 42–3, 45; Fishwick (1991) 436–7.
[246] Plut. *Gracch.* 39. 2–3; *Mar.* 27. 9; Val. Max. 8. 15. 7; Cic. *De off.* 3. 20. 80;
Sen. *De ira* 3. 18. 1; Alföldi (1971) 134–5; Fishwick (1987) 53–4.
[247] See Fishwick (1991) 375–6 n. 2 for discussion and bibliography.
[248] See, most recently, Fishwick (1991) 376, 383 with nn. 36–7 for bibliography; pl. LXXV(*b*).
[249] There is a similar account in Petronius: 'consurreximus altius et "Augusto,
patri patriae, feliciter" diximus. . . . inter haec tres pueri candidas succincti tunicas
intraverunt, quorum duo Lares bullatos super mensam posuerunt, unus pateram
vini circumferens "dii propitii" clamabat' (60. 7–8). See Alföldi (1971) 134 n. 91.

et 'bene vos, bene te, patriae pater, optime Caesar'
dicite; suffuso sint bona verba mero.

(*Fasti* 2. 635-8)

In *Odes* 4. 5 the farmer then honours him with a libation and
sets his *numen* in the company of the Lares.[250] It is generally
assumed that in such cultic acts the statue normally represented
the Genius Augusti, the *deus cuius in tutela ut quisque natus est
vivit*,[251] and that it was to the *genius* rather than the living
Augustus that the libation was made. Neither Dio nor Ovid
bothers to make the theologically correct distinction between
Augustus and his *genius*, and Horace specifies the *numen Augusti*.

The word *numen* is notoriously difficult to define.[252] Ancient
definitions equate it with *potestas* or *imperium*. It is perhaps best
seen as being the quintessential property of a god, that through
which he manifests his power or efficacy.[253] The farmer treats
Augustus like a god because of what he has done and especially
because of the benefits he has conferred.[254] He 'recognizes' that the
felicitas saeculi depends upon Augustus. He also 'knows' that it is
beyond the power of any mere man to bring about such a state of
affairs. He therefore attributes to him superhuman or divine power.
The cult-act of prayer and libation is the only proper way to
express due gratitude to so beneficent a divine power.[255]

The farmer sets the *numen* of Augustus among the statues of his
Lares, and the speaker compares the way in which the Greeks
recognized the divine power of their benefactors, Castor and
Hercules.[256] Yet the Lares were themselves believed to be *animae
. . . hominum redactae in numerum deorum*.[257] Moreover, the *populus
Romanus* had worshipped the living Marius in their homes along
with their household gods and had set up statues of Marius
Gratidianus alongside those of the Lares Compitales and supplicated
them with incense and wine. The reference to Greece therefore

[250] The order of events seems to have been dislocated to convey a sense of excitement: presumably the statues of the Lares and of the *numen Augusti* were brought
out from the *lararium* before the invocation and certainly before the libation.

[251] Cens. 3. I. See Niebling (1956) 329-31; Fishwick (1991) 382-3 with nn.
32-4 for bibliography.   [252] See Fishwick (1991) 375-87.

[253] See Pötscher (1978) 358, 391-2; Fishwick (1991) 383.

[254] See Fishwick (1987) 26, 184.

[255] Cf. *Epist.* 2. 1. 15-17.

[256] See Radke (1964c) 73: for *adhibet deum* cf. Virg. *Aen.* 5. 62-3; for the whole
scene cf. Stat. *Silv.* 4. 6. 32-9.

[257] Paul. 121M. (108L.); Fraenkel (1957) 447; Weinstock (1971) 292.

serves primarily to legitimize the action of the citizen farmer by providing it with ancient and respectable precedent.[258] Both the Dioscuri and Hercules had been used to establish precedent for the deification of Alexander, whose achievements and honours were consciously emulated not just by Augustus but also by Pompey, Caesar, and Antony.[259] But both the Dioscuri and Hercules were important gods for the Romans as well. As long ago as 484 BC the Romans had provided Castor with a temple and cult in recognition of the divine aid given at the battle of Lake Regillus.[260] The temple stood in the Forum Romanum close by the temple of Divus Iulius, dedicated in 29 BC, and the Arch of Augustus which commemorated the *signa a Parthis recepta* in 19 BC and bridged the space between them.[261]

The name of *Magnus Hercules* seems at first to point to Hercules Magnus Custos, especially in view of the designation of Augustus as *Romulae custos gentis* (4. 5. 1–2).[262] But the primary reference must be to Hercules Victor or Invictus, the exemplary conqueror, whose victories rid the world of barbarism and chaos, the embodiment of *virtus* and prototypical *triumphator* whose reward for the benefits he bestowed upon mankind was divinity. It was Hercules Invictus who had provided the model for Alexander Magnus, Pompeius Magnus, and Octavian, who in the years immediately after Actium himself receives the title *Magnus* or *Maximus*.[263] When Augustus returned in 29 BC, the timing of his triple triumph was made to coincide with the sacrifice to Hercules Invictus at the Ara Maxima in the Forum Boarium: it was even contrived that a Potitus Valerius should perform the sacrifice on the arrival of Augustus on behalf of the SPQR.[264] The aetiology of this altar

---

[258] See Doblhofer (1966) 125; Brink (1982) 39.

[259] See Bellinger (1957); Kienast (1969).

[260] Livy 2. 20. 12–13, 42. 5; D.H. 6. 13.

[261] See Zanker (1972) 12–13, 18–19.

[262] So Putnam (1986) 112.

[263] See A. R. Anderson (1928); Fears (1981*b*) 819–22; and, for further bibliography, Brink (1982) 45. For Alexander and Pompeius Magnus see Spranger (1958) 36–44; for Hercules Magnus Custos see Spranger (1958) 33. For *Caesar maximus* see Virg. *Georg.* 2. 170; for *magnus* see Virg. *Georg.* 4. 560; Hor. *Sat.* 2. 5. 63; *Odes* 1. 12. 51; Prop. 2. 1. 26, 2. 7. 5, 2. 31. 2; Spranger (1958) 45. In the event he took the cognomen Augustus: see Erkell (1952) 13–15. On *magnus* see also Mette (1961*b*) and, for its use in acclamations, Peterson (1926) 196–210.

[264] See Dio 51. 21. 2–3; Syme (1979) 260–70; (1989) 228–9. The significance of the name goes unremarked by Dio, but see Livy 1. 7. 12–14; Virg. *Aen.* 8. 269. On Hercules and Augustus see Binder (1971) 141–9, 258–9.

became one of the major myths of Augustan Rome. Hercules had been returning from Spain when he destroyed the monstrous Cacus and established the Ara Maxima. One of his rewards was to be included in the hymn of the Salian priests, another of the honours voted to Augustus after Actium.[265] The association with Augustus was brought to the fore again when Augustus returned from Spain in 24 BC: 'Herculis ritu . . . Caesar Hispana repetit penatis | victor ab ora' (*Odes* 3. 14. 1–4).[266] Hercules also appears on the coinage of 19 BC which celebrates the return of the standards;[267] and at the Ludi Saeculares Hercules Victor was among the gods addressed in Augustus' prayer.[268] The Ara Maxima perhaps served as a precedent for both the Ara Fortunae Reducis and the Ara Pacis Augustae, which were both voted as monuments designed to commemorate victories. The relationship of Hercules Victor or Invictus to Hercules Magnus Custos is unclear.[269] But in view of the fact that the temple of the latter was built or restored by Sulla, and given its position in the Circus Flaminius, it may be assumed that he was also closely connected with the triumph and so with the *adventus*.[270] One of the calendars even records a sacrifice to both Castor and Pollux and to Hercules Magnus Custos on 13 August, the anniversary of the first day of Augustus' triple triumph.[271] In *Odes* 4. 5 Augustus is being urged to return from Spain, and the comparison with Hercules in this context must recall the association of Hercules with all his earlier returns.

In the final stanza the chorus identifies with the *populus* that it represents and utters its own prayer.[272] The phrase *dux bone* reiterates *dux bone* in line 5 and signals the closure of the poem.[273]

---

[265] For Augustus see *RG* 10. 1; Dio 51. 20. 1; for Hercules see Virg. *Aen*. 8. 280–305. See further Binder (1971) 192–4.

[266] For the interpretation of 3. 14. 1–4 see Nisbet (1983) 106–7. For Hercules-Augustus cf. *Odes* 1. 12. 25; 2. 12. 6–12; 3. 3. 9–16.

[267] Sutherland (1984) 64 No. 314.

[268] See Moretti (1984) 370, 375–7.

[269] Hercules is *maximus ultor* at Virg. *Aen*. 8. 201 with obvious reference to the Ara Maxima; Horace prays that Hercules *custos mihi maximus adsis* (*Sat*. 2. 6. 15), in what sounds like a playful allusion to the title Magnus Custos.

[270] See Richardson (1992) 83, 186.

[271] The *Fasti Vallenses*, which Degrassi (1963) 403–4 thinks are just confused, as Ovid gives the date of the festival of Hercules Magnus Custos as 4 June (*Fasti* 6. 209–12). It may also be relevant that Augustus' stepfather rebuilt the temple of Hercules Musarum and dedicated it in 29 BC (Ov. *Fasti* 6. 797–812; Suet. *Aug*. 29. 5).

[272] Both *o utinam* and *praestes* belong to the language of prayer: Appel (1909) 136–7.   [273] Syndikus (1972–3) ii. 342–3.

The preceding comparison of Augustus with Castor and Hercules, both of whom have strong associations with victory, brings out the military connotations of the word *dux* (*dux dictus eo quod sit ductor exercitus*), while *bonus* is used, as often in prayers, to encourage a favourable response and anticipates Augustus' resumption of his role as *dux togatus, custos gentis,* the *de facto pater patriae*.[274]

The emphatic positioning of *longas,* which is emotionally intensified by the following *o utinam,* seems to be intended primarily to convey the sense of 'long awaited' or 'long deferred' and so to pick up on the sense of longing expressed at the beginning of the poem (2 *abes iam nimium diu*).[275] But the adjective may also be taken to convey a wish for many more victories in the future, as a variation on the encomiastic commonplace of wishing for a long life for the *laudandus.*[276] The emphasis falls on the wish for Augustus' return, for it is by returning that he will provide *feriae.*[277] The emotional intensity of the prayer partly accounts for the use of the poetic *Hesperia.*[278] But it is striking that *Hesperia* can be used to denote both Spain, where Augustus is lingering, and Italy, to which the chorus yearns for him to return. Horace is perhaps making use of a dispute over the true significance of the name to make a point. *Hesperia* could be explained as derived from *Vesperus,* the *sidus Veneris,*[279] and Venus is not only *Aeneadum genetrix* but also and in particular the divine ancestor of the *gens Iulia.* If this is what Horace is intending to recall then the point is that Italy, not Spain, is home.

The daily reiteration of the prayer, at sunrise and at sunset, parallels the farmers' earlier libation and prayer to the *numen*

---

[274] For *dux* see Maltby (1991) 198; for *dux armatus* contrasted with *dux togatus* see Cic. *Marc.* 24; for *bonus* see Appel (1909) 99; Hellegouarc'h (1972) 485.

[275] For this sense of *longus* see *OLD* s.v. 14. This seems more likely than stressing that the *feriae* themselves should be long, even though the length of the *supplicatio* was a measure of the honour being voted: Augustus records 890 days of *supplicatio* on 55 occasions: *RG* 4. 2.

[276] So ps.-Acro on 4. 5. 37: 'aut propter continuationem victoriarum longas optavit ferias aut ominando vitam prolixam.' For the 'long may you live' topos see Doblhofer (1966) 53–4; Nisbet and Hubbard (1970) 37; Woodman (1977) 281–2.

[277] See Dyson (1990), and contrast Radke (1964c) 74; Syndikus (1972–3) ii. 342 with n. 77. It is worth emphasizing that at the time of writing this poem Horace is aware that there will be no triumph: contrast 4. 2. 41–60. *Feriae* were voted *senatus consulto* for the *constitutio* of the Ara Pacis.

[278] Enn. *Ann.* 20 Skutsch 'est locus Hesperiam quam mortales perhibebant'; Virg. *Aen.* 1. 530, 3. 163 with Skutsch (1985) 178–9.

[279] Plin. *NH* 2. 36; Maltby (1991) 640.

Augusti. That such prayers were made to the *genius Augusti* is attested by Ovid both for the evening and for the morning.[280] Given the immediately preceding comparison with Hercules, it is natural that the chorus should model its cult-act on that associated with Hercules, to whom sacrifice was also made both in the morning and in the evening.[281] The humorously contrasting adjectives *uvidi* and *sicci* neatly suggest the joy of the worshippers. The worshippers are *sicci* when they make the morning prayers, as soon as they wake at the break of day. It was normal for the Lar or the Genius of the *paterfamilias* to receive the first libation, then the person who had made the libation could drink and only after that the other members of the *familia.*[282] Now Augustus as the ultimate benefactor of each individual and his household takes precedence and is counted among the household gods. The evening prayers were made *secunda mensa,* after the first and main course, during which wine had already been drunk to accompany the food, had been cleared.[283] The prayer was accompanied by a libation of *vina pura,* which was then shared by the worshippers.

The poem ends with the image of the rising (implicit in *mane*)[284] and setting of the sun. This picks up the earlier sun imagery and serves to remind us that Augustus' own return will be like that of the sun, and that he too must return from the west. But the image of the rising and setting sun also serves to complement the earlier allusions to the conquest of east and west, and so reminds us that

> . . . Latinum nomen et Italae
> crevere vires famaque et imperi
> porrecta maiestas ad ortus
> solis ab Hesperio cubili.

(Odes 4. 15. 13-16)

---

[280] See Ov. *Fasti* 2. 635; *Ex P.* 3. 1. 159-66; 4. 9. 105-6, 111-12.

[281] Servius ad *Aen.* 8. 269: '[Hercules] cum ergo de suo armento ad sua sacrificia boves dedisset, inventi sunt duo senes . . . quibus qualiter se coli vellet ostendit, scilicet ut mane et vespere ei sacrificaretur.' In the cult of Dea Dia the Fratres Arvales greeted her *primo mane* and invited her to attend *secunda mensa* in the evening: see Scheid (1990) 478, 487, 504, 509-10, 517-18, 527, 541, 550, 635, 640.

[282] For the Lar see Hor. *Sat.* 2. 5. 14 'ante Larem gustet venerabilior Lare dives'; and for the Genius Cens. 2. 3 'illud etiam . . . observandum quod genio factum neminem oportet ante gustare quam eum qui fecerit.'

[283] Ps.-Acro on 4. 5. 33: 'antiquorum consuetudo talis fuit, ut sublata prima mensa poneretur secunda atque in ea positis pomis infusoque vino libaretur diis.'

[284] Varro, *LL* 6. 4 'diei principium mane, quod tum manat dies ab oriente.'

The emphasis on the divinity of Augustus at the end of the poem should not come as a surprise. The poem started by invoking his divine ancestry and then moved on through the evocation of Ennius' account of the death and apotheosis of Romulus. Then the emphasis fell on the achievements of Augustus, in peace and in war, especially those illustrating his *iustitia*. Finally comes the recognition of his divinity as Augustus is shown to have fulfilled the hopes that people had once had of the new god Divus Iulius. What he has achieved and the effects of his achievements can only be attributed to a divine power. So in the absence of the *praesens deus* the farmer summons to the feast his *numen*.

This private and domestic cult is not identical with the cult of the Genius Augusti and the Lares Compitales, which is a public cult introduced in Italy from about 12 BC and in the city of Rome in 7 BC, with the organization of the *vici*.[285] Nor is it the same as the public cult of the Numen Augusti which was established by Tiberius in honour of the living Augustus in AD 6.[286] Yet neither can it be considered in isolation from these later developments. For it can hardly be a coincidence that, so shortly before the introduction of these public cults, the *populus* is suddenly and prominently represented as honouring the *numen/genius* of Augustus as if he were their *paterfamilias*. The decade in which *Odes* 4 was being written saw an increasing emphasis on the divinity of Augustus. Outside of Italy, the worship of the living Augustus was established at Tarraco, probably in the 20s, and at Lyons in 12 BC.[287] In Rome there was the renewed emphasis on Augustus' relationship with Divus Iulius, which is clearly designed to suggest his own divinity and eventual apotheosis. The introduction of Pax Augusta at Rome marks a significant increased emphasis on the ambiguous position occupied by Augustus between the human and the divine. But Augustus' special status found its most powerful expression in the Horologium complex which proclaimed him as both conqueror and bringer of peace, and as a new Romulus whose apotheosis had

---

[285] Contrast Syndikus (1972-3) ii. 342 n. 76; see Niebling (1956) 329-31; Liebeschuetz (1979) 69-70; Dio 55. 8. 6-7 with Rich (1990) 226-7, with further bibliography.

[286] See *Fast. Praen.*: 'Pontifices augures xv viri sacris faciundis vii viri epulonum victumas immolant numini Augusti ad aram quam dedicavit Ti. Caes'; Degrassi (1963) 401; Fishwick (1991) 378.

[287] For the altar at Tarraco see Fishwick (1987) 172-9; for that at Lyons see Fishwick (1987) 97-9.

been earned by these achievements. The planning of this monument must have gone on through much of this decade and
started well before his return. There are many themes in common
between it and *Odes* 4 in general and 4. 5 in particular. Given
Horace's position as *in numero amicorum Caesaris*, it seems more
likely that this is a result of Horace being a party to the thinking
and planning that went into it than of mere chance. *Odes* 4. 5
helps to define and to promote this new image of Augustus and his
unique position in the state.

6. CONCLUSION

Odes 4. 5 belongs to the genre *klētikon*. The opening stanzas (1–16)
constitute the prologue, in which the speaker issues the invitation
and expresses a sense of longing for the return of the addressee.
The central stanzas (17–28) provide an encomiastic description of
the place to which he is being invited. But since the addressee is
the *custos gentis* and *dux bonus*, and since the place to which he is
being invited is what it is because of what he is and what he has
achieved, these central stanzas also constitute praise of the
addressee, ordered untypically and therefore emphatically as 'deeds
in peace' (17–24) and 'deeds in war' (21–4). Here, as is conventional in the *klētikon*, praise of the the addressee is used to provide
an explanation or justification (17 *etenim*) of the speaker's request
for him to return, of the affectionate longing, and of gratitude for
the benefits he has conferred (7 *gratior it dies*). The final section
(29–40) describes the welcome that is already being prepared
throughout Italy by the *populus Romanus*, who express their
gratitude to their *dux bonus* by treating him as a god in
recognition of his godlike power and the godlike benefits which he
has conferred upon them.

In terms of its genre the poem has two interesting features. First,
there is no account of the journey to be undertaken by the
addressee, and that is a noticeable omission. Consideration of the
likely date of composition for the poem and of the date of 'publication' both suggest that the poem was composed before the return
of Augustus in July 13 BC but always intended for publication
and performance on his return. The omission of the journey topos
would be natural in those circumstances. If the poem was always

intended to be performed after Augustus' return, that would also explain the emphasis on the joy that is felt at his presence rather than the sadness and longing that are felt in his absence. Second, the speaker is not portrayed, as is normal in the *klētikon*, as an ambassador who has been sent on behalf of the SPQR to urge Augustus to return. The request is made to the addressee in his absence and from afar. In other words, the speaker, like the citizen farmer at his meal, summons the addressee as one would a god. This would be quite normal in a kletic hymn, and Horace has borrowed this feature from that closely related genre in order to convey the ambiguous status of his addressee between man and god or, rather, as both man and god. The poem has other hymnic features which serve the same purpose: for example, the opening participle (*divis orte*), the introduction of the justifications for the imperatives by *enim* (6) and *etenim* (17), the intricate patterns of assonance and alliteration, and the anaphora of *te ~ tuum* (32-4). In a hymn the speaker is normally a chorus. That this is also the case in this poem is confirmed by the plurals (38-9 *dicimus*), the role of the speaker as representative of the SPQR, and, given ancient assumptions that lyric was normally performed by a chorus, the lack of any counter-indication.

The poem derives its coherence and the logic of its argument from the familiar pattern of the *klētikon*. It is also underpinned by a sustained allusion to a famous passage of Ennius which related the death or disappearance of Romulus, the sense of sadness and loss that his people experienced when deprived of their *pater patriae*, their praises of the just king they had lost, and their subsequent recognition of him as a *deus* and their decision to institute a formal cult. The allusion constitutes an invitation to compare and contrast the situations of Augustus and Romulus. The inference which we are being invited to make is clarified by the complementary references to Castor (35) and Hercules (36), and to Divus Iulius (1). These past benefactors, who have been equalled or surpassed by Augustus, were only recognized as gods after their death or apotheosis. Augustus, by contrast, is worshipped while he is still alive. The message implied in *Odes* 4. 5 is the same as that stated explicitly in the near-contemporary *Epistles* 2. 1. 5-15: earlier benefactors receive worship and recognition as gods only after their deaths, while Augustus' divinity is fully recognized during his lifetime.

Into the framework provided by this sustained allusion to Ennius Horace works several other allusions. Perhaps in place of a simile in Ennius comparing the grief of the Roman people at the death of Romulus to the grief of children deprived of a father, Horace has substituted the long simile (9-16) comparing the yearning of the *patria* for the absent Augustus to the yearning of a (presumably) widowed mother for the return of her only son, on whom her welfare totally depends. The exact source of this allusion is not known but it seems to have come from a lost Hellenistic classic. It appears that Ennius placed considerable emphasis on the *iustitia* of Romulus in his account of the apotheosis and of what was subsequently said in praise of him. Horace has complemented the allusion to Ennius by working in a sustained allusion (17-24) to Hesiod's classic account of the peaceful prosperity enjoyed by the πόλις which is ruled by just men, in order to praise Augustus for his *iustitia* and to paint an alluring picture of Italy, transformed by its just ruler into a land that enjoys prosperity, security, and good order. Finally, at the end of the poem, there is an allusion to Virgil's *Eclogues* (1 and 9). Through a striking phrase (29 *condit . . . diem*) Horace evokes the scene in *Eclogue* 9 where the hopes that peaceful prosperity and security would be guaranteed by the new god, Divus Iulius, shatter on the brutal realities of the confiscations of land required to settle the veterans of Philippi. At that time Octavian could only act as benefactor to a single individual, as he did to Tityrus in *Eclogue* 1 by exempting his land from confiscation, and Tityrus had expressed his gratitude by instituting for his saviour a private cult. Now Augustus has guaranteed the *securitas* of all and guarantees everyone possession of his land, secure from the threat of external enemies and from civil war. Now everyone responds, not just one individual, by recognizing the *numen* of Augustus and worshipping him, spontaneously and privately, as a god.

The dignified simplicity of *Odes* 4. 5 belies the richness of its literary techniques, the complexity of its *arte allusiva*, and the *doctrina* displayed in the learned play with ancient etymologies (analysed above). Yet to view the poem only in terms of its literary and rhetorical background is to miss much of its essential character. This is an occasional poem, written to be performed, it is argued, by a chorus as part of the celebrations, whether private or public or indeed both, for the return of Augustus on 4 July

13 BC. Features of the poem that may seem at first glance no more than literary commonplaces take on new significance when seen in this context. The abruptness of the solar imagery (5-8) will have been less obtrusive in the context of an *adventus*, and less startling to an audience familiar with the statue of Augustus *habitu et statu Apollinis* (Suetonius, *Augustus* 29. 3) in the portico of the temple of Apollo on the Palatine, on the roof of which there was a statue of Sol, to whom in due course the obelisk that formed the gnomon of the Horologium would be dedicated in commemoration of the victories won at Actium and Alexandria with the assistance of Apollo. The implicit comparison with Divus Iulius will have seemed less oblique at a time when efforts were being made to stress Augustus' status as *Divi filius* and to advertise his claim to have already merited his own apotheosis by his achievements at home and abroad. The comparison with Romulus that permeates the poem will have been more apparent given its topicality: it had been strongly promoted by the imagery on the pediment of the temple of Quirinus rebuilt and dedicated by Augustus just before his departure in 16 BC, and would play a prominent part on the Ara Pacis and in the symbolic messages to be communicated by the Horologium. Even the apparently standard comparison with Hercules gains an emotional charge from the strong associations of Hercules with Augustus' previous triumphal or quasi-triumphal *reditus*, and more specifically from the fact that Hercules' arrival at the site of Rome from Spain was commemorated by the Ara Maxima and the return of Augustus from Spain in 13 BC was marked by the *constitutio* of the Ara Pacis Augustae.

But it is not only contemporary art and architecture which point up the topicality of the poem. Its central theme is the idea that the *salus* of all is bound up in the *salus* of the person of Augustus. This theme echoed through the language of the senatorial decrees concerned with the return, as we know from contemporary coin legends and inscriptions, and through the prayers of the various priesthoods as they offered thanks for his safe return. The day of his return also saw the recognition of a new divinity, Pax Augusta, who manifested herself exclusively in and through the deeds of Augustus. What people were saying on this day about their new divinity or in what terms they anticipated the benefits expected to flow from the institution of the new cult can only be guessed or inferred from the imagery on the Ara itself or from what is now

known of the messages to be conveyed by the Horologium complex
as a whole. Horace exploits to the full the context in which the
poem will be performed. The *adventus* was a time of carnivalesque
festivity, with crowds of people thronging the streets. Baths and
barbers were made available free of charge. The atmosphere of joy-
ful excitement was punctuated by periods of solemn and dignified
civic ceremonial and by inspiring and awesome religious acts of
ritual prayer accompanied by music, libations, and blood-sacrifice.
Horace can rely on the mood of such an occasion. With everything
focused on Augustus, the poet can rely on the audience to pick up
any allusion. He can afford to understate because in such an
emotionally charged atmosphere he can, with the slightest hint,
set off a train of reverberating associations. He also knows that the
audience will want to be part of it all and will be glad to be
'reminded' of their sense of yearning and loss during Augustus'
absence.

He can afford to catch the mood of the moment and represent
Augustus' relationship with the senate as Augustus 'wanted' it to
be rather than reflect the stresses and strains that were the underlying reality of the time. He can even turn to a brilliantly imagina-
tive use Augustus' proposals to end the system of giving land to
veterans on discharge by recalling the havoc and dislocation previously caused by this system as it had been memorably depicted
in Virgil's *Eclogues*, and by using the implied contrast between the
conditions in the years immediately following the death of Julius
Caesar and the present to exemplify the benefits conferred by
Augustus, the ending of civil war and the favour of Pax Augusta.

If the significance of the allusion to the *Eclogues* has been
correctly understood, it has an important consequence: it shows
that Horace was well informed of what was being planned for the
return of Augustus and that he knew of these specific proposals
before they were revealed in the senate. Given what is now known
about the elaborate planning and construction of the Horologium
and the skilful political manœuvring that went into securing
the proposal of the Ara Pacis Augustae as the honour to mark
Augustus' return, it is time to give more credence than has
recently been fashionable to the idea that Augustus' image was
constructed and promoted by his friends only after concerted effort
and careful thought and preparation. The image of Augustus presented in *Odes* 4 is fully in line with that presented in other media.

At the beginning of the decade Augustus' constitutional position had been finally defined and stabilized; there was only the office of Pontifex Maximus to add. Constitutionally he was *primus inter pares*, superior to others in *auctoritas* rather than in *potestas*. This formulation (*Res Gestae* 34. 3) underestimates the effect of the combination of offices and powers that he held, but also explains why in the next decade Augustus is marked off from other men by the accumulation of quasi-divine honours and by the promotion of his claims to divinity rather than by a further increase in constitutional powers. *Odes* 4. 5 makes its contribution to building up this image of Augustus, and that is what makes it a perfectly conceived and perfectly executed *donum adventicium pro reditu Imperatoris Caesaris Divi filii Augusti*.

9

Horace's *Epodes*
The Impotence of *Iambos?*

L. C. WATSON

S E V E R A L recent papers[1] have explored what they see as the 'impotence' of Horace's persona in the *Epodes*. This 'impotence', it is argued, is both physiological and psychological. Three poems in particular are invoked in support of this reading—*Epodes* 8 and 12, where Horace experiences literal *enervatio* in the face of the *vetula*'s[2] sexual demands, and *Epode* 15, which is a finely drawn study of the ineffectual bluster of an abandoned lover. In these papers especial importance is accorded to line 12 of *Epode* 15, *nam si quid in Flacco viri est*, 'as sure as there is any manliness in "Floppy"', where the pun on *Flaccus*[3] comically undercuts Horace's assertion of manly resolve. This verse encapsulates, it might be said, that blend of weakness and assertiveness which is characteristic of the book of *Epodes* as a whole.[4]

[1] Fitzgerald (1988); Oliensis (1991); Schmidt (1977); Babcock (1966). See also Gowers (1993) 287.

[2] For the purposes of this paper, I assume that the *vetulae* of *Epodes* 8 and 12 are the same. This is extremely probable, but not beyond question. The women have in common grotesque old age (8. 1-10, 12. 7 *vietis*), wealth (8. 11-14, 12. 21-4), insensitivity to their raddled exterior, and sexual aggression. But these characteristics are traditional in contexts of *Vetula-Skoptik*, and thus insufficiently distinctive to allow one to state with certainty that both poems deal with the same person. On the question see Carrubba (1969) 43 ff.

[3] The pointed juxtaposition of *viri* and *Flacco* seems virtually to guarantee a play on Horace's name. Sceptics object that by the poet's day *flaccus* had become restricted to the sense 'floppy-eared': cf. Cic. *ND* 1. 80 'ecquos deos silos, flaccos, frontones, capitones arbitramur?'; Varro, *RR* 2. 9. 6; and the play on sense at *Sat.* 2. 1. 18-19. *Flaccus* is, however, to be understood in its root sense of *languidus*: cf. Afran. *Com.* 65 'iam flaccet fortitudo', Apul. *Apol.* 25 'cur vestra oratio rebus flaccet, strepitu viget?' Horace was inordinately fond of *redende Namen* (Vogel 1918: 404-6), and may have been inspired to play on *Flaccus* by the example of the Hellenistic poets, who often pun on their names: for an instance see Bing (1990). Significant names are, however, also a feature of archaic *iambos*: cf Bonnano (1980); Rosen (1988).

[4] Cf. Oliensis (1991) 123. See also Büchner (1962a) 80: '*Desidia* und *virtus*,

These studies are both valuable and thought-provoking. Nevertheless, they call for extensive qualification. In the first place, while it is helpful to invoke the political turmoil and uncertainties of the 30s BC as an explanation for the feelings of helplessness which Horace repeatedly displays in the *Epodes*,[5] these papers referred to have failed to take into account a crucial factor—Horace's debt to archaic and Hellenistic *iambos*, where the poet often demonstrates his fecklessness in the most graphic way possible.[6] Second, it is open to doubt whether *all* the *Epodes* where Horace speaks *in propria persona* are characterized by impotence. This claim, which was made by Fitzgerald in particular,[7] needs to be tested very carefully against certain of the political Epodes. Such a reading in effect imposes a homogeneous persona upon the Horace of the *Epodes*—a proposition which is unsustainable in regard to these poems and indeed the iambic genre as a whole: far from displaying a unified persona, earlier iambists typically adopt a variety of masks, revelling in the display of frequently self-contradictory attitudes.[8] Third, as I shall argue, certain of the epodes, such as poems 3 and 6, exhibit the phenomenon of authorial impotence to a far greater degree than the proponents of this approach have realized. Fourth, the term 'impotence', I shall suggest, is something of a misnomer in regard to certain epodes, or at best betrays a misplaced emphasis in the interpretation of these poems.

---

weibisches Verhalten und *virtus*, stehen auch hier [*Epode* 16] wie sonst in den *Epoden* programmatisch gegenüber.'

[5] See esp. Fitzgerald (1988).

[6] This is especially true in the sexual arena. See Hipponax fr. 95 Deg., which, as Latte (1929) showed, involves a grossly embarrassing attempt to restore the poet's lost virility; fr. 86 Deg., where Hipponax may be interrupted *in flagrante delicto* with a woman, and is certainly the victim of intrusive voyeurism; and fr. 50 Deg. καὶ νῦν ἀρειᾷ σύκινόν με ποιῆσαι, which involves a threatened humiliation, very possibly of a sexual nature (see Degani ad loc. and Miralles and Pòrtulas 1988: 84–5). An interesting parallel to the erotic discomfiture of Hipponax is provided by the sexual incompetence of Margites (West 1971–2: ii. 76), who, like the iambist, is a buffoon figure: for the iambist as buffoon see West (1974) 29. For other passages in which the iambist causes himself to appear in a foolish light see e.g. Hipponax fr. 132 Deg., or Call. *Iambus* 3, where the poet's strictures against a schoolmaster's abuse of his charge are compromised by the revelation that Callimachus himself has an erotic interest in the boy.   [7] Fitzgerald (1988).

[8] See Rösler (1976) 301 ff.; Miralles and Pòrtulas (1988) 136. Cf. also the salutary caution of Cavarzere (1992) 29 ff. against the widespread assumption that the heterogeneity of Horace's *Epodes* can be traced to the Hellenistic passion for ποικιλία. As he notes, this was equally a characteristic of archaic *iambos*.

I deal first with the final point. In *Epodes* 8 and 12 Horace is free with the terminology of impotence. *Epode* 8 opens by quoting the frustrated *vetula*'s question '[You ask] viris quid enervet meas', and concludes by speaking of flaccid and erect organs. In Poem 12 Horace describes himself as *non firmus iuvenis* (a notable oxymoron) and, again reproducing the *vetula*'s words, as *mollis* and *iners*: altogether an inadequate performer by comparison with Coan Amyntas, who is evidently something of a sexual athlete.[9] Given, further, the frequency of the impotence theme in the iambic and satiric traditions upon which Horace is drawing,[10] it is unsurprising that critics have routinely assumed that *Epodes* 8 and 12 have to do with Horace's impotence.[11] This, I suggest, is a misconception.

Impotence, as the term is normally understood, implies that desire outruns performance. Impotence in Greek and Roman literature typically involves the inexplicable failure of male sexual equipment in the arms of a woman (or boy) whom the man greatly lusts after. Cases in point are Petronius' 'Polyaenus', unable to satisfy the beautiful and voluptuous Circe, or Ovid, who, after a sexual fiasco with an unnamed *puella*, asks himself in a fashion at once mystified and aggrieved, 'at non formosa est, at non bene culta . . . at . . . non votis saepe petita meis?'[12]

Desire such as 'Polyaenus' and Ovid felt is conspicuously absent from *Epodes* 8 and 12. What Horace is experiencing in these poems is not a failure to be aroused sexually, but a revulsion which precludes arousal. I am not simply engaging in a verbal quibble here. To speak of 'impotence' cloaks an important issue—one, I suggest, with a far richer potential for embarrassment than a mere bout of sexual incapacity. The issue is this: how on earth has Horace

---

[9] Cf. 16–20 'pereat male, quae te | Lesbia quaerenti taurum monstravit inertem, | cum mihi Cous adesset Amyntas, | cuius in indomito constantior inguine nervus | quam nova collibus arbor inhaeret.'

[10] See Brecht (1930) 55; Buchheit (1962) 87–8; Grassmann (1966) 26, 30–1; Kay (1985) on Mart. 11. 46. For instances in Archilochus and Hipponax cf. Miralles and Pòrtulas (1983) 40 ff.

[11] For this reading of *Epodes* 8 and 12 see most recently Fitzgerald (1988) 185; Craca (1989) 133, 141; Stroh (1991) 173; Oliensis (1991) 123; Cavarzere (1992) 194. Richlin (1992) 118 more judiciously states: 'the narrator's sexual ability remains as strong as ever, but lapses only in the face of a woman he wishes to reject'.

[12] Petron. 126 ff.; Ov. *Am.* 3. 7. 1–2. Cf. *AP* 5. 47, 5. 306; Mart. 9. 66; *AP* 12. 11, 12. 232; *Priap.* 83 Büch. for other cases where desire does not translate into performance.

become embroiled erotically with a hag of almost unparalleled repulsiveness? The poet forces this question on the reader's attention. He does so in two ways.

In the first place, one scarcely expects to find Horace, in *Epode* 12, entangled erotically with a *vetula*. For the preceding poem had lamented, with a good deal of mawkish self-pity, the poet's especial vulnerability to youthful charms (3-4 'amore, qui me praeter omnis expetit | mollibus in pueris aut in puellis urere'), exemplified in his past obsession with Inachia and his present devotion to the girlish Lyciscus, from which he can only be freed, appropriately, by an 'alius ardor aut puellae candidae | aut teretis pueri longam renodantis comam'. Yet *Epode* 12—which as a piece of erotic fiction antedates *Epode* 11[13]—mentions in the one breath Inachia and the *vetula* as Horace's bed partners (15-16). Do not the complaints of poem 11 now ring rather hollow? How has Horace, admirer of youthful beauty, become so embroiled with a *vetula* that she can speak so very proprietorially of him ('Inachia langues minus ac me' etc.)? Why did he not simply represent himself as saying 'no', as Martial did when courted by a hag?[14] It is a little late in the day to object to her gifts and *billets doux* (12. 1 ff.).

There is a further way in which the poet draws attention to the oddity of his entanglement with the *vetula*. This involves the anomalous use which is made of *Vetula-Skoptik* in *Epodes* 8 and 12. In personal poetry abuse of this particular type is usually levelled by the speaker as a parting shot against a woman who has been niggardly of her sexual favours, or refused him erotic access altogether.[15] That is by no means the case here. In the present instance the target of the *Vetula-Skoptik* is only too available sexually, and it is the poet, rather than the woman whom he vilifies, who is recalcitrant (12. 25-6 'o ego non felix, quam tu fugis ut pavet acris | agna lupos capreaeque leones'). This is a striking piece of inversion,[16] which has the effect, *inter alia*, of highlighting the strangeness of Horace's situation—a liaison contracted, for

---

[13] At the time of *Epode* 12 Horace is still involved with Inachia (15 'Inachiam ter nocte potes'), but in 11. 5-6 this liaison is placed firmly in the past ('hic tertius December, ex quo destiti | Inachia furere, silvis honorem decutit').

[14] Cf. 10. 75, and 3. 32. 1 ff. 'an possim vetulam, quaeris, Matronia. possum | et vetulam. sed tu mortua, non vetula es.'

[15] Cf. Nisbet and Hubbard (1970) 289 ff.

[16] Craca (1989) 145 speaks of a 'grottesca "Umkehrung"' of the usual pattern in regard to *Vetula-Skoptik*.

reasons left unexplained,[17] with a hag for whom he professes the utmost disgust: a hag, moreover, of a loathsomeness unparalleled in the annals of *Vetula-Skoptik* up to this point.[18] One can of course see her extreme repulsiveness, so graphically depicted by Horace, as a rationalization of his own sexual inadequacies,[19] as an attempt to outdo the efforts of his predecessors in the arena of *Vetula-Skoptik*, or as coloured by sexual *ennui*. The paradox remains that the woman whom he describes as *nigris dignissima barris*, fit partner for elephants, has established some kind of sexual claim on Horace—which he now seeks to deny—by virtue of past erotic commerce. It is important to be clear on this point. The hag is not simply propositioning the poet, as happens, for example, in some epigrams of Martial.[20] The repulsive description of the contours of her naked body (8. 3–10) can only proceed from autopsy. The poet's sensitivity to the *vetula*'s malodorous hypersexuality (12. 3–12) bespeaks personal experience,[21] as does her chiding of Horace's shortcomings as a lover (12. 15 ff.).

What is the point of all this? On one level Horace is simply carrying on the iambic tradition of associating with degraded women. One thinks here of the *fellatrix* Arete, or of Neobule, who, according to Archilochus, had become 'over-ripe' in consequence of her promiscuity.[22] More importantly, by representing himself

---

[17] Generally speaking, when young men (cf. 12. 3 *iuvenis*) consort with old women a need is felt to account for this. The usual reasons are poverty/providing sex for pay (cf. Ar. *Plut.* 975 ff., *Thesm.* 345, *AP* 11. 65, and Kay on Mart. 11. 29 and 87 intro.). Other explanations are simple perversity of taste (Mart. 3. 76, *AP* 11. 70, Papinius *FPL* Büchner p. 54), an attractiveness which belies the passing of the years (see e.g. Apul. *Met.* 1. 7 'anum sed admodum scitulam' and Herter 1960 90 n. 382), or some special factor such as the new laws of the gynaecocracy in Aristophanes' *Ecclesiazusae*. Here Horace is conspicuously silent about the reason for his involvement with the *vetula*—a case of the less said the better, perhaps?

[18] The *vetula* of Epodes 8 and 12 is outdone in loathsomeness only by her later counterparts in Mart. 3. 93 and *Priap.* 32.

[19] Thus Stroh (1991) 273–4 ('nimirum a se culpam in feminam transfert') and Oliensis (1991) 124, who claims 'impotence, not disgust, is the premise of both poems. In a defensive reversal, the hideousness of the woman is manufactured to excuse the incapacity of the man.' It will be apparent that I consider this a mis-reading of Epodes 8 and 12.

[20] Cf. 3. 32, 7. 75, 9. 37, and 10. 75. 13–14.

[21] According to Slings ap. Bremer, van Erp Talman Kip, and Slings (1987) 40, Archilochus had likewise had sexual relations with Neobule, whose allegedly fading charms he treats so dismissively in the *First Cologne Epode*.

[22] Archil., *First Cologne Epode* 17 ff.; Hipponax fr. 24 Deg. κύψασα γάρ μοι πρὸς τὸ λύχνον Ἀρήτη. For further references in Archilochus to sexually debased women cf. frr. 39 πάντ' ἄνδρα ἀπεσκόλυπτ⟨εν⟩, 42, and 189W. with Gerber (1973) 206–9,

as the butt of sexual taunts by a decrepit bedfellow of stomach-churning repulsiveness, Horace makes himself—as well as the *vetula*—appear both feeble and ridiculous. *Epode* 8 to some degree and *Epode* 12 to a large extent are concerned with portraying the poet as victim.[23]

This victimization assumes a number of forms, most of them relating to the erotic sphere. For one thing, note how the roles of iambist and victim are reversed in *Epodes* 8 and 12. It is the *vetula* who launches the attack,[24] and Horace is put in the position of having to reply, in the poems, to her taunts. A further illuminating instance of role-reversal occurs at the close of *Epode* 12, quoted above. Here, by an inversion of erotic and imagistic norms, the woman becomes the sexual aggressor/predator, Horace her fugitive, defenceless prey. In a particularly droll variation on the conventional pattern in such hunting-similes, which essentially enact pre-intercourse rituals between male and female, Horace continues to fear the *vetula* even after he has surrendered to her sexually. This comes about because she manifests no tenderness towards him, but only sexual aggression. It has often been remarked that satirists and iambists denigrate women—young and old—by objectifying them as body.[25] *Epode* 12, one might whimsically say, is the *vetula*'s revenge, since she subjects the iambist to essentially the same treatment. For her, man exists only in so far as he has the capacity to service her sexual needs.[26]

It is particularly revealing of Horace's status as erotic victim that in *Epod.* 12. 15-16 the *vetula* and Inachia are lumped together as his sexual partners. It would appear that, in the amatory sphere, Horace cannot win—pursued on the one hand by a repulsive γραῦς

probably also frr. 34W. with Gerber (1989); see also Rankin (1977) 64 ff. For degraded women in Hipponax cf. frr. 23, (?) 86, 95, and 107. 34 Deg. On the basis of frr. 20. 2 and 69. 7-8 Deg., it has with some plausibility been suggested that Arete, for whose affections Hipponax and Bupalus vied, was the mother of the latter, and had committed incest with him: see Miralles and Pòrtulas (1988) 49 ff. For a licentious female in Anacreon's iambics cf. frr. 432 *PMG* = West, with Brown (1984).

[23] That the iambic poet, who victimizes others, is himself a victim is emphasized by Miralles and Pòrtulas (1983; and 1988). Cf. also Newman (1990) 73-4 on the poet's 'I' as a figure of fun.

[24] *Epod.* 8. 1-2 'rogare longo putidam te saeculo/viris quid enervet meas'; *Epod.* 12. 13 ff. 'vel mea cum saevis agitat fastidia verbis' and the complaints which follow.

[25] See e.g. Curran (1970), 234-5; Henderson (1989) 10 ff. Cf. also Spelman (1982).   [26] Cf. esp. *Epod.* 12. 16-20, also 8. 1-2, 17-8.

καπρῶσα,[27] in helpless thrall on the other to Inachia, who has just been described in the previous *Epode* as a mercenary and cynical *meretrix*. And things are no better in the other erotic *Epodes*. Whereas in the earlier iambists, including Horace's immediate predecessor Catullus, erotic rebuffs or débâcles were tempered by loudly trumpeted successes or aggressive assertions of virility,[28] Horace depicts himself as a perennial loser in matters of love. *Epode* 14 describes how he is is tortured with love for Phryne, *libertina neque uno contenta*, and contrasts his situation unfavourably with that of his fellow lover Maecenas, who is enamoured of an unnamed beauty who is very possibly the pantomime Bathyllus;[29] *Epode* 15, the only one of the erotic *Epodes* not yet discussed, is worth more detailed consideration, because this poem again confronts us with the phenomenon of the toothless iambist.

In the first place, Horace holds out implicitly to Neaera the threat of divine retribution for breaking her oath of everlasting fidelity to the poet (15. 3 ff.). The threat is empty. Everyone knew that the gods looked with indulgence upon violations of the ἀφροδίσιος ὅρκος, the lover's oath.[30] Horace himself wrote a poem rueing that fact (*Odes*. 2. 8). Therefore Neaera can contemplate Horace's appeal to celestial justice with absolute equanimity. By voicing that appeal, the poet simply makes himself look foolish. Moreover, the oath of everlasting fidelity which Neaera swore (and has now broken) paradoxically reveals that Horace's hold on her affections was always tenuous. For she swore it *at the poet's dictation*:[31] this suggests that she would not have sworn spontaneously. Only a fool would expect faithfulness of a Neaera: her name identifies her as a *meretrix*, and the faithlessness of such women was proverbial.[32] Furthermore, by an amusing twist, the oath which Horace administered to Neaera contained the seeds of its own violation.

[27] On the type see Brecht (1930) 62 ff.; Jocelyn (1980) 199; Richlin (1978) 257 ff.; Grassmann (1966) index s.v. *Vetula-Skoptik*.

[28] Cf. Archil. *First Cologne Epode*, with West (1974) 26 on the poet's claim to have participated in orgies with Lycambes' daughters; also frr. 119 and 152W. (if spoken by the poet); Hipponax frr. 86, 107 Deg.; Semonides fr. 17W.; Catullus 32; and Richlin (1981) on Catullus' outspoken boasts of virility.

[29] For the suggestion see esp. Kumaniecki (1935) 147 ff. Cf. also Orelli on *Epod*. 14. 13-16.

[30] Cf. Virg. *Ecl*. 8. 19-20 'dum queror et divos, quamquam nil testibus illis | profeci, extrema moriens tamen adloquor hora', and Nisbet and Hubbard (1978) on Hor. *Odes*. 2. 8, introduction.

[31] 'in verba iurabas mea'.

[32] See Herter (1957) 1169.

She swore that she would remain faithful to him 'as long as the
wolf was hostile to the lamb and stormy Orion to sailors' (lines
7–8). But do not these images of perpetuity in fact undermine the
very point they seek to establish? The proverbial hostility of wolf to
lamb[33] sits ill with the notion of erotic harmony, wolves have
important figurative associations with sexual predacity,[34] and the
tempestuous seas of lines 7–8 might suggest analogically the
stormy seas of love (cf. *Odes* 1. 5, 3. 26).

In the second half of *Epode* 15 Horace passes from warnings of
divine retribution to threats of the vengeance which he will exact
from Neaera. The logic of these threats, and the language in which
they are couched, combine to make them wholly ineffectual. In line
11 Horace protests, as a good iambic poet should, his determination to pay back Neaera for her mistreatment of him (*o dolitura mea
multum virtute Neaera*). But these protestations are at once torpe-
doed by the pun in the next line on the poet's name, tellingly
juxtaposed with *viri*. 'I will be revenged', says Horace, 'as surely as
there is any manliness in "Floppy" (*nam si quid in Flacco viri est*).'
The impression of weakness conveyed by the name is compounded
by the deliberate ambiguity of *si*. As noted, the conjunction is
ostensibly asseverative in function ('as surely as Flaccus is a man').
But it is simultaneously possible to read *si* as *conditional*, thereby
converting line 12 into a straightforward declaration of weakness:
'*if* there is any manliness in "Floppy" '. Also symptomatic of
amatory irresolution is the highly provisional nature of the threats
which the poet utters against Neaera in lines 13 ff. Horace 'will not
bear' her infidelity. His constancy will not yield to her beauty 'once
it has become odious to him'.[35] He will be revenged 'if anger takes
hold irrevocably of him' (16 *si certus intrarit dolor*). These threats
are not expressed in provisional terms simply in order to give
Neaera the chance to amend her ways. They also disclose a deep-
seated vacillation on Horace's part which makes it highly unlikely
that he will ever make good his promised reprisals. And suppose he
does? Consider the humorous illogic, even fatuousness, of Horace's
position in *Epode* 15. He threatens unconvincingly to sever relations
with a *meretrix* of proven unfaithfulness who has already thrown
him over for another man. The prospect of losing Horace is unlikely

[33] See Otto (1890) s.v. *lupus* 3, 5.
[34] See Luck (1959) 34–7; Ov. *AA* 3. 419 etc.
[35] Reading *offensae* rather than *offensi*.

to strike terror into Neaera's heart. Here again, the iambist cuts a
sorry figure, deliberately setting himself up as a target for ridicule
by laying bare his utter ineffectuality. Having been preyed on by a
vetula, Horace is now made to look foolish by a young woman:
Neaera's name is formed after the Greek νεαρός 'youthful'. The
unhappy poet, it seems, suffers amatory catastrophe with females
of both generations.

Before quitting the erotic epodes, I would add one rider to the
above. In pursuit of the feeble-persona thesis, I have deliberately
treated *Epodes* 8 and 12 from a one-sided perspective. Of course
the *vetula* is made to appear every bit as ridiculous as Horace—
with her unseasonable[36] and insatiate sexuality, her insensitivity
to her raddled exterior, and her absurd and disagreeable mealy-
mouthedness at 12. 13 ff. Such even-handedness in dispensing
mockery suggests an important point: that in the *Epodes* Horace
follows the practice of archaic *iambos* in dealing largely with
characters who are, in Aristotelian terms, not σπουδαῖοι—such
'unserious' characters including, prominently, the iambist himself.[37] (A conspicuous exception to this pattern is of course historical personages such as Maecenas and Octavian.)

I turn now to an epode of a very different character, the
problematical poem 4. In this piece Horace attacks an upstart ex-
slave of worthless character, who parades his new-found wealth
before the indignant passers-by, sits prominently in the fourteen
rows reserved for the *equites* by Otho's law, and—the crowning
indignity—serves as a military tribune in the campaign against
Sextus Pompey's crew of servile insurrectionists. The resemblances
between the upstart and the poet are so close as to be actually dis-
turbing.[38] Horace was a freedman's son, had notoriously been a
military tribune (*Sat.* 1. 6. 47–8), and took his place in the fourteen rows with Maecenas at the theatre (*Sat.* 2. 6. 48).[39] Moreover,
the sneer *fortuna non mutat genus* (*Epod.* 4. 6) has an unsettling
echo in the gibe *Fortunae filius* levelled at Horace himself by the

---

[36] On the disapprobation and mockery which sexual desire in older women
attracted see Herter (1960) 90–1; Henderson (1987) 117 ff.; Halperin (1990) 90;
Kay on Mart. 11. 29, introduction.

[37] See Miralles and Pòrtulas (1983; 1988); West (1974) 29, who states 'for the
purposes of iambus, Hipponax assumes the character of a low buffoon'.

[38] These similarities are noted by Fitzgerald (1988) 182–3 and Oliensis (1991)
118. But both fail to stress how provocative Horace is being in attacking a personage who so closely resembles himself.

[39] Cf. Armstrong (1986), 259 n. 13, 281.

jealous populace (*Sat.* 2. 6. 49). No doubt, if pressed, Horace would respond that there were crucial differences between himself and the upstart: that *he* did not flaunt the improvement in his fortunes, that, thanks to his father, his moral character was sound,[40] and that Horace the freedman's son probably had no business in any case becoming a *tribunus militum* (cf. *Sat.* 1. 6. 49-50). These answers, however, beg the crucial question: given that Horace chose in *Epode* 4 to attack the traditional figure of the parvenu, why did he choose as a representative of the type a person who exhibited such disquieting similarities to himself? Why not, for example, attack an ex-slave who had attained *senatorial* rank? There were various such figures in the 40s and 30s BC.[41] I find it hard to escape the suspicion that Horace is being deliberately provocative, deliberately sailing close to the wind, deliberately courting the charge of hypocrisy (as Archilochus did when he accused Neobule of doing with other men what he persuades her sister to do with him):[42] in short, that in *Epode* 4 Horace is quite consciously putting himself in a false position, quite consciously undermining the validity of his statements and the authority of his persona.

The preceding epode, poem 3, conforms to the general picture which is here being explored. In it Horace once again casts himself in the role of victim—this time, victim of a practical joke played upon him by Maecenas. The latter has, it appears, served the poet a dish which he has seasoned over-liberally with garlic— deliberately over-seasoned, or so Horace affects to believe. The result is an acute attack of indigestion, a motif that apparently goes back to Hipponax,[43] and is at all events well represented in the comic and satiric traditions upon which *iambos* draws.[44] The bulk of the epode is devoted to a ludicrously exaggerated account of Horace's sufferings: the fires which are devouring his insides equal in intensity those which consumed Medea's rival Creusa, or the

[40] Cf. *Sat.* 1. 6. 68 ff.

[41] Cf. Armstrong (1986) 269-70; Treggiari (1969) 61-2.

[42] Or as Callimachus may have intended to do in the literary-allegorical *Iambus* 4. If the poet is in some sense to be identified with the laurel, the tree of his patron Apollo, then by joining with the olive in abuse of the bramble he is exhibiting the pugnaciousness in literary matters which he pointedly disclaimed in *Iambus* 1.

[43] Cf fr. 129c Deg. μή σε γαστρίη [λάβῃ, with Bremer, van Erp Talman Kip, and Slings (1987) 77; fr. 118 ἐβορβόρυζε δ᾽ ὥστε κύθρος ἔτνεος ('de intestinis murmurantibus seu crepitantibus', Deg. ad loc.); and perhaps fr. 171 Deg., with lemma.

[44] See e.g. Ar. *Plut.* 1128 ff.; Antiphanes fr. 177. 3 ff.K.; Machon fr. 9 Gow; Lucil. 136M.; Plaut. *Pseud.* 819 ff.; Cic. *Fam.* 7. 26; Henderson (1975) 199.

rays of the Dog Star over Apulia etc. The poem concludes with an
imprecation against Maecenas, who is responsible for Horace's
agonies. 'If you ever again[45] desire to play me such a trick, may
your girl repel your garlicky kisses and edge away to the other side
of the bed.'

This imprecation is noteworthy for its studied feebleness.
Humorous curses, such as the present one, usually depend for their
effect on a ludicrous disproportion between the triviality of the
offence which gives rise to the curses and the savagery of the
maledictions which ensue.[46] The pattern is exemplified in *Epode* 10,
where Maevius is cursed with a particularly nasty end in retribution for his 'stink' or, very possibly, his bad verse.[47] That pattern
is completely inverted in *Epode* 3. According to the humorous
illogic of the poem, Horace has been 'poisoned' by Maecenas. We
might therefore have expected him to respond with a suitably
ferocious, if comic, imprecation against the guilty party. In fact the
curse which he does produce is remarkable for its toothlessness:
'If you ever do this again [so Maecenas is to get away with
"poisoning" Horace on this occasion], may you suffer a minor
and temporary sexual rebuff.' In one sense, of course, the very
triviality of the curse merely puts the whole laughable affair in perspective after the mock pathos and comic hyperbole of lines 1–18.
On the other hand, not only is a feeble curse something of a
contradiction in terms, but the fact that this issues from an *iambic*
poet is doubly paradoxical, given the devastating power that was
conventionally thought to attach to the words of iambists—witness
the Strasbourg Epode, the biographical tradition concerning the
Lycambides,[48] or the claim, reported by the Mnesiepes inscription,

---

[45] *Epode* 3 makes little sense unless *umquam* in line 19 is interpreted thus. For
this meaning of the word see Watson (1983) 82–3.

[46] See Watson (1991) 133 ff.

[47] Fraenkel (1957) 26 ff. seems to me excessively sceptical on this point. Virgil had
written in *Ecl.* 3. 90–1 'qui Bavium non odit, amet tua carmina, Maevi, | atque idem
iungat vulpes et mulgeat hircos'. The *hircus* of the Virgilian ἀδύνατον may be picked
up at *Epod.* 10. 2 *olentem* and 23 *libidinosus . . . caper*, in an oblique endorsement
of Virgil's judgement. Moreover, Horace might have been thinking of the tradition
which made another poet, Apollonius of Rhodes, the target of Callimachus' curse-
poem, the Ἴβις: for the *testimonia* see Call. fr. 382Pf., further Watson (1991) 121 ff.

[48] For the *testimonia* see West (1971–2) i. 15, 63–4. The trend of late has been
to treat as fiction the tradition that Lycambes and his daughters were driven to
hang themselves by shame at Archilochus' scurrilous attacks. For differing views on
the historicity of this story see West (1974) 27 ff.; Carey (1986); Burnett (1983)
19 ff., a judicious discussion.

that Archilochus' detractors were rendered impotent (E col. 3. 40 ff. Tarditi).[49] The question arises: to what extent is the enfeeblement of the curse in *Epode* 3 emblematic of the ethos of the *Epodes* as a whole?

Closures are particularly important in the *Epodes*. As a rule they help to focus, and in some cases qualify substantially, our understanding of a poem. (*Epode* 2 is an obvious instance of the latter.) I have just noted that *Epode* 3 concludes, not with the expected *fulmen in clausula*, but with a damp squib. In fact a number of the *Epodes* end in a broadly similar fashion with inadvertent declarations of weakness on the part of the speaker, or with the undercutting of his/her *persona*. Examples include *Epodes* 2, 3, 11, 14, 17, and the poem to which I now turn, *Epode* 6.

In this epode, which is directed against a cowardly and venal slanderer, Horace pictures himself first as a trusty sheepdog, then as a bull with horns at the ready, and finally he compares himself to Archilochus and Hipponax, whose attacks on Lycambes and Bupalus drove them to suicide, or so the biographical tradition said.[50] In other words, his threats against his enemy describe a crescendo of aggression. It is therefore a surprise that the poem ends on a conspicuous downbeat: 'If some one attacks me with the tooth of malice,[51] will I weep, unavenged,[52] like a child?' The final line of the poem comes perilously close to bathos, when it compares Horace—even if only to reject the comparison—to a child, the very image of weakness and defencelessness, an idea exemplified in the preceding epode, which described how a helpless *puer* was ambushed by a gang of murderous witches, and amply documented in valuable studies by Herter and Golden.[53] Also noteworthy is the syntactical shape of the final couplet. One might have expected Horace to round off his poem with straightforward

---

[49] It would appear from the inscription, which is very fragmentary at this point, that the impotence was inflicted on Archilochus' behalf by Dionysus. None the less, the tale suggests symbolically the virulent power of the iambist's words.

[50] 13–14 'qualis Lycambae spretus infido gener, | aut acer hostis Bupalo'. For Lycambes and his daughters see n. 48. For the tradition that Hipponax hounded Bupalus to death see *testimonia* 9 ff. Deg.; Miralles and Pòrtulas (1988) 151 ff.; Rosen (1988) 31 ff.

[51] 15 'atro dente'. For the significance of this image in *Epode* 6 see Dickie (1981) 195 ff.

[52] More precisely, 'without avenging myself'. As Morgan (1988) notes, *inultus* is not just passive but also reflexive.

[53] Herter (1961) (in Herter 1975); Golden (1990) ch. 1.

menaces against his antagonist, along the lines of Archilochus' ἐμέο δὲ κεῖνος οὐ καταπροΐξεται (fr. 200W.) or Catullus' *at non effugies meos iambos* (fr. 3). What we get, instead, is a challenge to him couched as a rhetorical question, an intrinsically far less forceful mode of expression. When one considers, further, that the concluding couplet represents Horace in notably *defensive* guise, it would seem that these lines purposefully set out to mute and to undermine the virile and pugnacious ethic of the earlier verses.[54]

Whether or not this reading of *Epode* 6 is accepted, there is one epode, not yet discussed, in which Horace indisputably depicts himself as weak and ineffectual. This is *Epode* 1, the first in the collection. Set on the eve of Actium, the poem poses the question 'Should I, Horace, follow my patron Maecenas to war, as Maecenas is following Octavian, given that I am no soldier (16 *imbellis ac firmus parum*) and can make no material contribution to the campaign (15 *roges, tuum labore quid iuvem meo?*)'. Horace's decision is to accompany Maecenas (lines 11 ff.) because, illogically, he will be less apprehensive for the latter's safety if he is on the spot—just like a mother bird, who is less fearful for her unfledged offspring when sitting with them in the nest, even though she cannot thereby defend them in the event of attack by predators (lines 19–22). This image better than anything else in *Epode* 1 captures the imbellicosity of Horace.[55] Whereas Archilochus on one occasion notoriously threw away his shield[56]—more out of realism than cowardice, probably—but on the whole seems to have regarded himself as a soldier (fr. 2W.),[57] Horace, it seems, protests his *general* unfitness for war.

The poet makes significant capital out of these protestations of unsoldierliness. In a novel development, the traditional weakness

---

[54] For the reasons given, I cannot agree with Dickie (1981) 197 when he states: 'the tone of the threat implied in Horace's asking whether he will weep unavenged like a child is of the same order as such declarations as Archilochus fr. 126 (W.) "I know one great thing, how to take requital, doing terrible harm to one who does me wrong" and to an even greater extent, because of the disavowal of cowardice in it, Archilochus fr. 23. 12–15 (W.) "Do I seem such a coward? I am not born from such. I know how to love one who loves and how to hate an enemy and do him harm."'

[55] According to Schmidt (1977) 402–3, the simile is a programmatic avowal of the weakness of Horace's persona in the book of *Epodes*.

[56] Fr. 5W. In general on this poem see Seidensticker (1978).

[57] The image of Archilochus as ῥίψασπις is tempered by evidence of his active involvement in the civic and military life of his community: see *testimonia* 116, 141, 170, and 5A col. 1. 4 ff. Tarditi; further Graham (1983) 83 ff.

of the iambist's persona is harnessed to overt political statement. In the first place, the central paradox explored by the epode—that Horace will accompany his patron to war notwithstanding his manifest incompetence as a soldier—underlines by inference the depth of his commitment to Maecenas, and by extension to the cause which he serves.[58] Second, the poet ties in the motif of his unsoldierliness to the structure of the poem, in such a way as to trace a very flattering portrait of the Caesarians. *Epode* 1 is built around the balancing pairs Octavian–Maecenas and Maecenas–Horace. Horace stands in roughly the same relationship to Maecenas as Maecenas to Octavian. Horace plans to accompany Maecenas to Actium, just as Maecenas will accompany Octavian.[59] These similarities enable Horace to throw flatteringly into relief important *differences* between himself and Maecenas. Whereas Horace must stand ineffectually on the sidelines, Maecenas will play a significant part in the campaign (1–2 'Ibis Liburnis inter alta navium | propugnacula'). Whereas *infirmitas* renders the poet useless as a soldier, Maecenas will boldly share every danger that his leader faces (lines 3–4). In other words, by highlighting his own professed unsoldierliness, Horace delivers a refracted but very pretty compliment to the bravery, loyalty, and military expertise of the Octavianic side, in the person of his *amicus* Maecenas.

Space does not permit me to discuss any more of the political epodes. I merely note in passing that *Epode* 16 perhaps fits into the schema here proposed. Although Horace there adopts the authoritative tones of the *vates*, and addresses himself to those citizens *quibus est virtus* (line 39), the message relayed by the poem is essentially one of despair, which *could* be seen as indicative of weakness. One final point concerning the explicitly political epodes, and those—most of them—with political content: to what degree, if at all, does the weakness of the iambist's persona compromise the validity of the political lessons which the poet seeks to convey? To this question I have no clear answer.

Let me end with a further *aporia*. If it is the case that, in the *Epodes*, Horace to an even greater extent than has been recognized

---

[58] Kraggerud (1984) 29–30 advances the interesting suggestion that Horace's declaration of loyalty to Maecenas echoes in microcosm the *coniuratio totius Italiae* of 32 BC.

[59] It is unnecessary for present purposes to enter into the vexed question of whether Maecenas actually went to Actium. For bibliography see e.g. Watson (1987) 121 n. 19.

represents himself as feckless, weak, and incompetent, what were his motives for so doing? It is not enough simply to point to the phenomenon. Various possibilities may be touched upon. At one level, Horace is simply carrying on the tradition of earlier *iambos* whereby the poet represents himself in the worst possible light;[60] compare Critias' famous, if misconceived,[61] criticisms of Archilochus, fr. 295W.,[62] or the poet's characteristic affectation of ἀμηχανία.[63] But this is no answer. Is Horace's reasoning that, if he advertises his own shortcomings, this makes it easier to execute the primary task of *iambos*, viz. levelling criticisms at others without appearing arch? Are we dealing here with *iambos* as a compensation for inadequacy?[64] Or with a sophisticated interplay between the artistry of the poet and the incompetence of his persona? Again, given that *iambos* incorporates a large element of performance, are we simply meant to pass artistic and moral judgement on the iambist's persona as we would upon any other dramatic or fictional creation?[65] Is the vacillation and helplessness of the authorial persona meant to mirror the disorders and tensions of the 30s BC?[66] Is Horace striving to create a believable picture of an unremarkable, because not specially virtuous, Roman—that is to say, an individual with whom his readers can readily identify—as a sweetener for the political message which it is his primary intention to convey? Or, finally, is it all just an elaborate literary game— the creation of a complex and demanding poetic world, as Zetzel[67] put it with reference to the contemporaneous *Satires*, book 1?

---

[60] Cf. Miralles and Pòrtulas (1988) 47.

[61] For reasons why the criticism is misconceived see Dover (1963) 209 ff.; Burnett (1983) 27–8; Slings (1990) 26–7.

[62] Critias accuses Archilochus because he spoke most evilly of himself. 'For if the poet, he says, had not propagated such an opinion about himself, we would not have learnt that he was the son of the slave-woman Enipo, or that he left Paros and went to Thasos on account of poverty and neediness, or that after his arrival he became an enemy of the people there, or indeed that he abused friends and enemies alike. Furthermore, he says, we would not have known that he was an adulterer, had we not learnt it from himself, or that he was lecherous and a rapist, and, what is even more shameful than this, that he threw away his shield.'

[63] See Archil. frr. 128. 1, 23. 11 ff.W.; cf. also frr. 88 and 112. 3W. for the motif.

[64] For this approach see Fitzgerald (1988) 189.

[65] For the iambic poet as playing a role—on occasion the role of someone other than the poet himself—see Dover (1963) 206 ff.; West (1974) 27; Burnett (1983) 31–2. Cf. in addition Nagy (1979) 243 ff.; Carey (1986) 66–7; Slings (1990) for a critique of the *Rollenpoesie* thesis in its more extreme formulation. On the performative context of archaic *iambos* see most recently Bartol (1992).

[66] Thus Fitzgerald (1988).   [67] Zetzel (1980) 73.

10

Law, Rhetoric, and Genre in Horace, *Satires* 2. 1

FRANCES MUECKE

T H E reader coming for the first time to book 2 of Horace's *Satires* would meet with several intriguing surprises. The first is the form of the opening satire, a dialogue for which nothing in the previous book has prepared us. For its first few lines this poem seems to be another literary monologue in the style of *Sat.* 1. 4 or 1. 10, but, with the question addressed to Trebatius, it suddenly becomes a dramatic dialogue. The interlocutor's identity is the second surprise. This is a conversation between Horace and a well-known jurist, not the expected opening poem dedicated to Maecenas.

What makes this satire so fascinating and so difficult to pin down is the intersection, or dialogue, it stages between the two perspectives, the lawyer's and the poet's. For the one the problem of satiric writing is legal, for the other it is generic. Trebatius views the problem of satire—that is, its offensiveness—from the lawyer's point of view, while Horace argues from within the poetics of satire. Trebatius is blunt, pragmatic, and unmoved by the subtleties of Horace's analysis of his own position. The poem's neat conclusion diverts attention from the fact that no accommodation is possible between them on the literary and legal questions. The solution comes from the political sphere, which encompasses them both.

One of the purposes of this paper is to argue for the autonomy of these two distinct and independent voices. The punning linking

I am grateful to Stephen Harrison for including this article in the volume (despite my inability to attend the conference from which it arose), enabling me to offer a token of gratitude to Robin Nisbet, who encouraged my first explorations in generic law-breaking and who, whenever consulted since then, has been generous with wise advice.

of literature and law at the end of the satire, through the play on
mala carmina, and the ambiguity of *lex* at its beginning, have
perhaps encouraged an assumption that they are fused, not just
combined, in the satire as a whole. Rudd, for example, spoke of
'the principles of aesthetics . . . cleverly confused with the law of
libel' (1966: 130-1), and Fraenkel stated: 'The dialogue . . . owes
some of its grace to the *blending* of two different elements' (1957:
147, my emphasis). A blender mashes different ingredients and
produces a smooth liquid in which the original elements can no
longer be discerned. Fraenkel did not, of course, intend his
metaphor to be pressed as hard as this. I do it to make my point
clear, and to anticipate my quarrel with Leeman (1982; 1983),
who, by making Horace respond to Trebatius' rhetorico-legal
argumentation, assumes a pervasive interpenetration of the legal
and literary.[1]

Interpreters of this satire—and there has been a lot of interest in
it in the last ten years—tend to take sides. Some take the idea of
legal advice seriously as an indication that legal action against the
satirist was a real possibility, or had even been threatened (most
recently LaFleur 1981: 1812-26). The intermediate view is that,
while the Roman law of libel had to be taken into account,
Horace's satire, being now less controversial than in book 1, was
not likely to bring him into danger of infringing it. Circumstances
have changed, and there is no real problem (Rudd 1966: 128).
Then there are those who regard the consultation with Trebatius
as doing no more than providing a framework for a further
exploration of the poetics of Horace's satire and his relationship
with Lucilius.

The question of the reality of the legal situation spills over into
an assessment of the seriousness of the satire as a whole. Rudd's
lightness and playfulness become Coffey's frivolity. Horace is not
only frivolous at the expense of the law (Coffey 1989: 231 n. 83)
but 'the reader should not be deluded by the brilliance of the
artistry into regarding a fundamentally frivolous piece as a major
contribution to Horace's poetics' (1989: 83). None of this has
deterred further study of the legalities and the poetics. LaFleur
(1981), in his major piece on Horace and the law of satire,

---

[1] Cf. Anderson (1982) 118: 'It is only as we realize that the satirist and
Trebatius converse on two entirely different levels that we sense the force of the
legal metaphor'; Williams (1974) 16.

re-examines the question of the libel laws in the footsteps of
R. E. Smith (1951), and concludes that the danger of legal action
was real (given the uncertain political circumstances of the second
triumvirate and the possibility of stricter enforcement of the law in
'the stabilizing period, after Actium' (1981: 1823), and that
Horace has 'at least felt the threat of legal action' (1981: 1815).
The last point depends on a rather tenuous interpretation of the
names mentioned in lines 47–9. Horace is an enemy of Canidia,
therefore he is also one of Cervius and Turius, but they are perverters of justice (whether real or fictitious), therefore references to
them imply the threat of legal action against the satirist. On the
literary side much effort has been devoted to reading the satire as
a Callimachean *recusatio*. Wimmel (1960) 162 ff. remains the basic
study, but more recently there has been Clauss's idea (1985:
201–2), which I find unpersuasive, that lines 19–20 are a version
of the Phthonos scene at the end of Callimachus' *Hymn to Apollo*.
Incidentally, these same lines have also been given a politico-legal
interpretation as a reference to the tribunician sacrosanctity which
was conferred on Octavian in 36 BC (Bauman 1985: 133).

My own position is that neither the witty language-games
nor the fictionality of the consultation with Trebatius (for it *is*
a fiction), nor the irony of Horace's self-presentation (Anderson
1984; Harrison 1987), prevent us from reading the satire for its
political and programmatic significance. As I shall show, the
rhetoric of the piece makes it more obviously programmatic than
Sat. 1 1. It also appears to manifest an awareness of changes in
contemporary cultural politics.[2]

Rudd's description of 'the principles of aesthetics cleverly confused with the law of libel' referred in the first place to the opening lines of the satire. It is usual to see the fundamental dispute
between the law of libel and the law of the genre encapsulated in
the ambiguity of the word *lex*.[3] Here there are two points which
require closer examination: is one of these meanings the primary
one, and was 'the law of the genre' a metaphor that Horace's

[2] The three references to Caesar in this poem have not been much noticed in
recent discussions of the poetics and politics of patronage, but they all acknowledge
in some way his desire and ability to oversee what the poets say (see Hardie 1990:
180 ff.). Du Quesnay's important article (1984) is confined to book 1 of the *Satires*.
I have learnt much from Feeney (1992).

[3] Fraenkel (1957) 148. Of course, from both points of view satire is inherently
unruly. Part of the fun is that Horace is less of a lawbreaker than his predecessor.

audience could take for granted? The evidence on the latter point is fuzzy. Commentators cite *Ars* 135 *lex operis*. Brink, however, cannot produce anything exactly the same which is earlier, though Cicero did use legal terminology when talking about literary or metrical laws (*De or.* 3. 190; *Orat.* 198). I am prepared to accept the *Ars poetica* as evidence for a general first-century view,[4] in the light of the loss of earlier histories of literature, or poetics, in Latin. The concept of 'the law of the genre', or of a normative poetics, is much older, as has been shown by Rossi (1971). Rossi (1971: 75 ff.) considers the words used for 'genre', but does not explicitly discuss the legal metaphor. He does note, though, the use of τεθμός as a literary technical term in Pindar (e.g. *Nem.* 4. 33-4) and Callimachus *Iamb.* 13. 41 (where the context is missing). It is safe to assume that the concept of a generic norm was taken for granted long before the first century BC.[5] But, I incline to think, this is not the most obvious meaning of *lex* in line 2, and in fact it causes logical difficulties. This does not exclude it altogether, because Horace can introduce punning meanings that are not meant to make sense literally: I think of them as 'shadow' meanings (e.g. *Ep.* 1. 5. 31 *falle clientem*).[6]

If *nimis acer* means 'too biting' it is hard to see how Horace can break the law of the genre through this particular quality, which is one of the defining characteristics of Lucilian satire. Therefore we must agree with Anderson (1982: 117-18) and Leeman (1982: 159) that *lex* is to be taken literally at the beginning, and refers to the law of libel, or we must follow the complicated explanation of van Rooy (1966: 67 ff.), according to whom this law of the genre is the law as re-defined by and in Horace's earlier literary satires, in contrast to Lucilian aggressiveness.[7] I do admit that as we read and re-read the satire and become aware of its generic preoccupations we recognize in *lex* an anticipation of this literary theme.

In what follows I treat separately the legal, rhetorical, and generic aspects of the poem, at least at first. They will come

---

[4] LaFleur (1981) 1813. See D'Alton (1917) 420 ff; Coffey (1989) 5-6.

[5] Cf. Accius fr. 8 Funaioli 'nam quam varia sint genera poematorum, Baebi, quamque longe distincta alia ab aliis'; Colie (1973) 12; *contra* Fowler (1982) 56 and n. 7. On *satira* as a generic term here see van Rooy (1966) 67-8.

[6] This double meaning (cf. *XII Tables* 8. 21) was pointed out to me by R. G. M. Nisbet; see Nisbet and Hubbard (1978) on *Odes* 2. 18. 24

[7] In contrast, Freudenburg (1990) argues for a reading of lines 1-2 predominantly in terms of stylistic and compositional theory.

together from time to time and, I hope, at the end. First, we should meet the second of the characters concerned.

Trebatius Testa is the lawyer in the poem. We are fortunate in that we know quite a bit about him both as a lawyer and as a man, and that this information fills out our understanding of his role in the poem. He was an eminent jurist or jurisconsult. There is no evidence that he ever acted as an orator.[8] For reasons which will become clear, it is important to recognize that there was a clear distinction in Rome between the jurists and the orators or advocates. Orators argued cases in court, without necessarily being learned in legal science. What they had to be good at was rhetoric (cf. Cic. *Mur.* 29), constructing a convincing story about the facts of the case.

In fact, Roman jurists were not lawyers in a modern sense.[9] They did not take payment, represent clients 'in relation both to other parties and to legal authorities', or give partisan advice. What they did was to interpret the law: this involved giving *responsa* (legal opinions), preparing documents, and advising clients on legal procedures.[10] Orators, as well as other individuals, were among those asking for advice, and jurists were sometimes consulted even on non-legal matters, a tradition Horace may want us to remember:

M'. vero Manilium nos etiam vidimus transverso ambulantem foro; quod erat insigne eum, qui id faceret, facere civibus suis omnibus consili sui copiam; ad quos olim et ita ambulantis et in solio sedentis domi sic adibatur, non solum ut de iure civili ad eos, verum etiam de filia con-locanda, de fundo emendo, de agro colendo, de omni denique aut officio aut negotio referretur.[11] (Cic. *De Or.* 3. 133)

For all his lapidary brevity,[12] Trebatius is a vivid presence in the satire. When Cicero recommended him to Julius Caesar in 54 BC, praising his juristic knowledge in enthusiastic terms (Cic. *Fam.* 7. 5. 3 'accedit etiam quod familiam ducit in iure civili, singulari memoria, summa scientia'),[13] he was a young man making his

---

[8] Watson (1974) 107.

[9] Frier (1985) 67 n. 78.

[10] Watson (1974) 101–10.

[11] See Watson (1974) 102. Some of Trebatius Testa's *responsa* have survived. See Watson (1974) 126–7, 129.

[12] Cf. Cic. *Amic.* 1. 1 on Scaevola's *multa breviter et commode dicta*; Bauman (1985) 132.

[13] But see Fraenkel (1957) 145 n. 4, on the 'jocular' tone.

career. Now, in his mid-fifties, he is an established figure,[14] who condescends to turn his mind to the quandary brought to him by an amusing younger man, who knows the right people.

Cicero's letters to him (*Fam.* 7. 5–22) give us an insight into his personality and interests in his younger days.[15] His susceptibility to puns is a trait which may have endeared him to Horace: if he could take a joke he would not have minded a characterization which undercut his solemnity (Rudd 1966: 130–1; Anderson 1982: 43–4). Cicero's letters to Trebatius when he was serving on Julius Caesar's staff in Gaul are full of remarks made simply for the sake of word-play on legal technical terms. On the eve of an invasion of Britain Cicero writes 'tu, qui ceteris cavere didicisti, in Britannia ne ab essedariis decipiaris caveto' (*Fam.* 7. 6. 2), and again 'qui istinc veniunt superbiam tuam accusant quod negent te percontantibus respondere. sed tamen est quod gaudeas; constat enim inter omnes neminem te uno Samarobrivae iuris peritiorem esse' (*Fam.* 7. 16. 3). We also learn from Cicero's letters that Trebatius was *homo studiosissimus natandi* (*Fam.* 7. 10. 2), and once sent Cicero home late from dinner *bene potus* (*Fam.* 7. 22; cf. *Sat.* 2. 1. 8). The dedication to him of the *Topica* in 44 BC (*Fam.* 7. 19; *Top.* 1–5) shows that his friendship with Cicero was a lasting one. Cicero's letters to him imply a shared knowledge of poetry and interest in philosophy that also provides a ground for a friendship with Horace.

Our satire takes the form of a conversation between Horace and Trebatius. Horace asks the lawyer's advice in a rather formal way, even though he does not use the formula which was apparently customary (*licet consulere*: Cic. *Mur.* 28), and I think we should regard the imagined situation as being something between the standard legal consultation (of which we have no account) and the asking of non-legal advice that we heard of from Cicero. To call it a parody may be going too far; the conversation is stylized as a consultation.[16]

Trebatius' role in the fictional consultation is to present the legal

---

[14] As is shown by his speaking 'for Caesar' at lines 10–11. For his role as legal adviser to Octavian see Bauman (1985) 132 ff. In *c.* AD 4 Trebatius was consulted by Augustus on a legal matter (*Inst.* 2. 25 pr.). He also gave an opinion to do with Maecenas' and Terentia's divorce case in 16 BC (Dig. 24. 1. 64).

[15] See Fraenkel (1957) 145 ff; Shackleton Bailey (1971) 99 ff.

[16] Leeman (1982) 160–1 warns against describing it with terminology that implies a trial; 'parody' is Cloud's word (1989: 67).

implications of writing satire, or of a particular kind of satiric writing. As a jurisconsult his main task was to interpret the law and alert his clients to ways of avoiding falling foul of legal provisions. At first Trebatius states his opinion that satire is dangerous and that therefore Horace should give it up, but he does not actually bring in the law of libel until the conversation is nearing its end (lines 81–3).[17]

Trebatius is given much less to say than Horace. He appears right from the beginning as one not to waste words, and a man sure of his own opinion. *Quiescas, aio* are one-word replies—the 'short, sharp bark' of the jurisconsult. His language characterizes him as the lawyer, e.g. *aio* and the legal imperatives used in lines 7 ff. Smith Palmer Bovie's translation (1959: 99) catches the parodic flavour well, if anachronistically:

> To one in default of sleep, I decree as follows:
> Rub well with oil the party of the first part, then swim
> (Transnatate) the Tiber thrice, then habeas your corpus
> Well soaked with wine at night.

The advice Trebatius gives at first—exercise and plenty of wine before going to bed—is pragmatic, though expressed in a high legal tone which clashes with the subject-matter. His next suggestion is that Horace take up an alternative poetic genre, panegyrical epic. It would not offend its audience, and might even win the poet financial rewards from its subject, Caesar. In lines 21–3 Trebatius states why satire is dangerous. If some people, however unimportant, are attacked by name, the satirist becomes unpopular generally. *Laedere*, repeated at 67 *laeso . . . Metello*, is a key word in these contexts, mostly put into the mouths of victims of satire or people taking their part. It means 'to hurt, to do injury, do damage to the good name and social standing of'.[18] This points to the general area that libel comes under in the praetor's edict, the *actio iniuriarum*. Libel and defamation were 'injuries'. This is a difficult point for Horace to answer, and we notice that he does not address it directly at first but goes off on another tack. It is difficult because in some ways it is true, or should be, if the satirist obeys the laws of the genre: satire (by definition) should include fearless

---

[17] Leeman (1982) 162, but I disagree that before this the situation is 'pseudo-juridical'.

[18] It is one of the Latin words for defamation (Manfredini 1979: v).

attacks on named individuals. Horace concludes his long answer with the bold declaration that he will continue to write satire, whatever the outcome. Trebatius replies that this may get him into trouble with the great, a lead in to Horace's claim that he has the favour of the great (just how great comes out with Caesar's name in line 84).

Trebatius' last utterance of any length (lines 79–83) is completely in the persona of the jurist, in style and subject-matter.[19] He quotes a law, with the implication that Horace's satire falls within its scope. Whether a serious reference to any law is intended, and what law this might be, are still matters of dispute. There are really two separate questions here. One is: what law of libel was in force in Horace's day? I follow those who believe it was the section of the praetor's edict, the *actio iniuriarum* just mentioned (*ne quid infamandi causa fiat* . . .: 'Let nothing be done with the intent to defame. If anyone breaks this rule I shall take action against him in accordance with the facts of the case'), which required a private prosecution.[20] The second question is: what law does Horace make Trebatius quote? Most commentators—but significantly not the author of the classic article on the law of libel in Rome, R. E. Smith, nor Manfredini, the latest legal historian to have examined verbal defamation in Roman law—think it is a version of one of the old-fashioned laws of the XII Tables.[21]

The position of the laws of the XII Tables in the late Republic was rather complex. They were not exactly obsolete, but in practice they had been supplanted by the remedies of the Edict. Watson sums up the situation this way:

By the late second century and in the first century BC the jurists were embarrassed by the ambiguity of the code; they preferred not to mention it even when they discussed its provisions; and they tended to interpret it with more freedom than was possibly allowable for other statutes. Orators in court would grandiosely refer to the XII Tables for their moral authority but were conscious of the jurists' hesitations, and did not like to argue too openly from interpretation of the code to interpretation of other provisions. Educated laymen regarded the code with general, if imprecise, approval. (Watson 1974: 121)

[19] It is not 'on a par with 7–9', *pace* Bauman (1967) 252.
[20] See Rudd (1986) 56; Coffey (1989) 231 n. 83; Daube (1951).
[21] Smith (1951) 177 n. 6 argued that it was the *Lex Cornelia de iniuriis*, Manfredini (1979) 106–7 the praetor's edict. The penalty under the XII Tables was death.

Two of the factors Watson mentions may be relevant to
Trebatius' citing of the law from the XII Tables: ambiguity and
moral authority.[22]

While most critics agree that there was a Roman law against
defamation, and that Horace's satire would lose a lot of its point if
there had not been such a law in force, the question of whether
Horace was in any real danger of prosecution is another matter.
The fact is that even those who think such a danger *was* real have
to admit that in the whole of Roman history there are very few
documented cases of prosecution. Kelly (1976: 84) also shows that
the role in general of delict/quasi-delict is 'amazingly small' in the
whole corpus of Roman law. The reasons Kelly gives for this are
interesting and relevant to satire, suggesting that the victim of
defamation was in an impossible double bind. On the one hand,
Romans were extremely sensitive about their personal reputations,
but on the other, they feared litigation and avoided it as much as
possible because it involved an inevitable loss of face, whatever the
matter at issue, since blackening of the opponent's character was
standard practice in courtroom oratory. As Kelly says, 'This Roman
convention of rhetorical abuse presents an amazing contrast with
the notions of personal honour on which the delictal forms of
iniuria are based' (1976: 100). Now, while courtroom invective
was in a sense privileged and not actionable, Kelly argues that the
insults uttered in court were none the less real. I imagine that this
was a powerful disincentive to cases of defamation in particular,
and one reason why the satirists always claimed that their victims
deserved attack. The other factor that should be mentioned is the
role of the social status of the defamer or his protectors in providing immunity from prosecution.[23] The less powerful would get
nowhere against the more powerful.

If we can discount the danger of prosecution in Horace's case,
we should not ignore another real danger for the satirist. The very
act of attack is likely to construct him as an unpleasant personality and win him unpopularity, not only in his victims' eyes, but
more generally. So talking about satire and the law is a metaphorical way of raising the problem of the satirist's relationship
with his audience. This explains the turn in the argument in lines

---

[22] Cf. LaFleur (1981) 1819 n. 74.

[23] Crook (1967) 255; Du Quesnay (1984) 20 n. 10 points out that a reality
neglected by LaFleur is that how much a satirist could say with impunity depended
on how powerful his friends were.

62-70: Scipio and Laelius are 'not offended' in their role as audience of the satire, not simply because it is directed against their political opponents. Different moments of the poem highlight the reactions of different audiences. The opening lines allude to opposed but equally negative critical reactions of readers, in lines 21-3 Trebatius warns of widespread unpopularity, and in lines 60-2 of exclusion from high society as a result of offending an élite audience. Horace counters the latter warning by pointing to the power of the patron, in the end appealing to the judgement of Caesar, now the ultimate audience.[24]

Turning to Horace's side of the dialogue, we see that the antitheses that structure the argument and the rhetorical forms in which it is cast assume generic laws. Horace began the poem by placing himself in a false dilemma. The sorts of criticism to which he claims to be subject would be inevitable for the satirist who followed the precedent of Lucilius too slavishly, for Lucilius (so we hear) did bitterly attack individuals and his style was loose and in need of artistic control. So Horace is being attacked *qua* satirist, not for any faults of his own. Given this, it is logical for Trebatius to suggest he turn to another genre, epic, the implied model being Ennius perhaps, and his panegyric of Scipio (*Var.* 1-3V.[2]). Epic and satire can be presented as opposites on two interconnected grounds, style and purpose. Epic is written about heroes in the grand style, satire about scoundrels in the low style. Trebatius relies on a distinction between poetry of praise and poetry of vituperation that Aristotle put right at the beginning of the development of literature.[25] 'Poetry . . . split up according to the authors' divergent characters: the more dignified represented noble actions and those of noble men, the less serious those of low-class people; the one group produced at first invectives, the others songs praising gods and men' (*Poetics* 1448[b] 24 ff., trans. Hubbard). The idea that character determines, or is bound up with, genre is also assumed by Horace for the purposes of his argument. Yet there is a deeper logic to the suggested substitution of praise for blame that is based on an equivalence between them: 'motifs of blame are often simply the inverse of those of praise' (Davis 1991: 263 n. 1).

In lines 12-15 Horace simultaneously gives a specimen of epic

[24] See Gold (1992) on different levels of audience in Horace's *Satires* and Feeney (1992) 7 ff. on 'the conditions of speech determined by the principate'.
[25] Macleod (1983) 271-2.

style while claiming such writing is beyond him. This becomes a
standard ploy in the rhetorical gambit that he is using here.
Trebatius' next move is one I passed over earlier because, though
the citing of precedent does belong to the legal theme, through its
take-up it belongs to the poetics and politics of the piece. Trebatius
points out that Lucilius praised Scipio for his civic virtues, so that
even if Horace did not want to write about wars he could still
praise Caesar. The reply to this from a literary point of view would
be rather involved. Horace refuses to follow his generic model in
writing panegyrical satire, and his refusal amounts to an implicit
criticism of a definition of satire that is wide enough to accommodate eulogy (Christes 1971: 195 n. 238, 200; Hardie 1990: 183).
His excuse, based on propriety of occasion, includes an example of
the best satire can do in honorific mentions, the vivid picture of
Caesar as a touchy horse, ready to kick out (see Rudd 1966:
256-7). This is in contrast to the epic on contemporary warfare
illustrated in lines 13-15.

Trebatius now produces his explicit warning against satire.
Horace's long reply depends on a different distinction between epic
and satire, one based on its subjective personal character (Macleod
1983: 271-2). This paradoxically self-directed quality of satire, the
fact that it is somehow not written for general consumption but
for private amusement, is another plank in the satirist's defence
against social antagonism or in the face of the law. The picture of
Lucilius 'entrusting his secrets to his books' has in a way been
anticipated by Horace's description of his own practice at *Sat.* 1. 4.
133-9:

> neque enim, cum lectulus aut me
> porticus excepit, desum mihi: 'rectius hoc est:
> hoc faciens vivam melius: sic dulcis amicis
> occurram: hoc quidam non belle; numquid ego illi
> imprudens olim faciam simile?' haec ego mecum
> compressis agito labris; ubi quid datur oti
> illudo chartis.

So, Horace claims, satire is a meditative kind of poetry, a poetry
of ethics, written for the poet's own amusement and improvement.
Its personal nature is also implied in the description of Lucilius'
friendship with Scipio and Laelius, which belongs to their private
lives and to times of unbuttoned relaxation (71-4). The poetics

from within which Horace speaks assumes an interdependence of genre, style, and personality.

Virulence cannot be denied altogether, and comes back after the claim that Lucilius set an autobiographical precedent. It is introduced in a suitably autobiographical way. Horace descends from warlike stock and therefore has an aggressive spirit. So he is a satirist by instinct, and this is why he has chosen to follow Lucilius. However, as critics point out, Horace's satire is not very aggressive in reality, and becomes less so. It seems that he has modified this aspect of the Lucilian inheritance, but, because satire had come to be identified with this attacking spirit, he must keep it in reserve, the 'sword hidden in the scabbard', as he puts it. The rule Horace's satire breaks is invoked through its denial.[26] But note how important a rule it is that he breaks—it is the rule that identifies satire as satire, but also as defamation.

If we can read Horace's justification as a kind of poetics, can we also read it as a kind of legal rhetoric? This is the argument of Leeman's attractive analysis (1982; 1983), which has won ready acceptance from other scholars but which, on reflection, I have come to doubt, and would wish to reject or at least modify. The suggestion is that, by means of his advice, Trebatius is helping Horace to formulate the 'status' of his poetry and his satirical programme, according to the rhetorical 'bases' or 'grounds' (*status* was the basic point on which argument turned, 'the issue' of a case: cf. Cic. *De inv.* 1. 10; *Top.* 91-6).[27] Cicero (*Top.* 92) outlines three ways of arguing for the defence: *status coniecturalis, definitiva*, and *iuridicalis* (see Rawson 1985*a*: 147-8). According to Leeman, these headings are applied here as if in a deliberative, i.e. prospective, case: Horace should not write satire, thus avoiding committing the deed. If he must write, he should choose a different genre (his deed will therefore be defined differently). Finally, his satire has special justification, being defensive, not offensive. Further, there is the 'translative question', the question of which jurisdiction is competent, to which Leeman also draws attention (Cic. *De inv.* 2. 57 ff.), in Horace's hope that his *carmina* will be judged good if brought before the proper court, Caesar!

---

[26] Freadman and Macdonald (1992) 10.

[27] See Rawson (1985*a*) 145 ff. *Status* theory came to Rome through the very influential work of Hermagoras of Temnus (Τέχναι ῥητορικαί, *c.*150 BC), and is often mentioned by Cicero. The term in *Rhetorica ad Herennium* is *constitutio*.

First we should note that the *status* arguments are not explicit. I would not put too much weight on this if they were inherent in the situation, the imagined institutional setting, but it seems to me that they are not. As we have seen, rhetoric and legal science were separate fields.[28] Trebatius is not a rhetorician, and his ignorance in such matters is acknowledged in the dedication to him of Cicero's *Topica*. Aristotle's *Topica* was 'an exciting novelty for him'.[29] People consulted jurisconsults to see whether what they had done or were about to do infringed the law. They would go to a Cicero for the lines of the defence to be constructed (for Cicero's procedure see *De orat.* 2. 102-4). Therefore it seems to me over-subtle to place such rhetorical arguments in the body of the satire and inappropriate to Trebatius' role as jurist. Rather, Horace does not formulate his legal defence until Trebatius has cited the law (before that he argues in terms of literature). Then the lawyer is defeated by Horace's simultaneous production of at least three lines of defence: failing a denial of the deed (his *carmina* exist), he will argue that it has a different definition (*bona* not *mala carmina*), and so was not a case of the crime alleged, and that it was justified (line 85).[30]

From legal rhetoric I now return to the rhetoric of poetry in order to discuss the relationship to generic self-definition of the two programmatic rhetorical structures in the poem, the *recusatio* and the priamel.[31] Both of these devices usually have what might be called a liminal function (they are ways of getting started) and a contrastive function. So pervasive is this rhetoric that it may indeed seem that the poem does nothing more than play with its own introductory nature, until we realize that both *recusatio* and priamel focus its underlying political problem—writing satire after Lucilius in the world of the late 30s BC.

In the *recusatio* (or 'refusal') the poet imagines a situation in

[28] Leeman (1982) 162 does admit that 'relations between rhetoric and Roman law are highly disputed'. Wesel (1967) 137 ff., however, sees very little influence of the rhetorical *status* theory on the jurists' methods. Further, the section of Cicero's *Topica* that deals with *quaestiones* and *causae* is not tailored for Trebatius in the same way as are the examples of topics (Huby 1989: 63).

[29] Rawson (1985*a*) 6, cf. 205-6. On the nature of Cicero's work see Huby (1989) 62-3; Fortenbaugh (1989) 57-8 and n. 12.

[30] Griffith (1970) 63 n. 1 had already suggested that the word-play implied a rhetorical *color*, a 'line to be taken'.

[31] Zetzel (1982) 96 considers the priamel 'an implicit *recusatio*', but treats Augustan *recusationes* as apolitical ('literary conceits') on the basis of a definition of 'political' as 'intended to have a political effect' (89). Davis (1991) 28 ff. views *recusatio* as 'generic disavowal'.

which he is invited to switch to a higher genre, usually epic, and refuses to do so, protesting incapacity, but giving a specimen of the rejected genre before restating a commitment to the one he has actually chosen. The rejected genre is a foil to the chosen one, which defines itself in opposition to it, and so the *recusatio* is an elaborate form of what Anne Freadman calls a 'not-statement' and describes as a 'crucial move whereby . . . a genre—situates itself, claims its own specificity, marks its boundaries'.[32] In *Satires* 2. 1 the *recusatio*, Horace's first, is prolonged beyond its usual compass and has an interesting additional element, Trebatius' negative description of satire in lines 21–3, which postpones the positive statement of commitment we might expect at this point.

Fraenkel saw that Trebatius has the role Maecenas has for Virgil and Propertius: 'it was inevitable that . . . some of Horace's well-wishers who were in close contact with Caesar should have suggested to the poet the writing of an epic to glorify Caesar's achievements' (1957: 149). But we need to ask the question: why Trebatius? Is it because Maecenas' literary influence was not yet fully established, or for the sake of the legal metaphor, or because Trebatius can be depicted as a man for whom literary arguments have no reality, so that he becomes by inversion 'a foil . . . for the assertion of literary values' (Zetzel 1982: 99)? All these reasons have some validity, but it seems to me that the choice of Trebatius points above all to the issue of the dependence of the satiric poet's legitimacy on the world of political power.

There are other things worth noting about this *recusatio*. It is the first Callimachean-style *recusatio* 'to' Octavian (Wimmel 1960: 163). The elements of the Augustan pattern of invitation to write heroic epic, the profession of incapacity, and the demonstration of what cannot be done are all there. There are Callimachean themes, but no specific allusions to Callimachus, perhaps because the poet's own genre provides a model (Thill 1979: 253–4). In the introductory satire to his first book (26) a friend advised Lucilius to write an epic on Scipio's victory in the Numantine War (Lucilius 620–2M.; cf. Christes 1971: 72 ff.), a passage in which Ennius' language was parodied. The dialogue form and the initial subject of the dialogue are Lucilian, in a satire in which Horace reaffirms Lucilius as his

---

[32] Freadman and Macdonald (1992) 108; Davis (1991) 191: 'disavowals . . . are by definition programmatic', 263 n. 2: '*recusatio* and priamel both promote generic disavowal'.

model, but brings the problematic of satire up to date. An important function of the *recusatio* is to allow Horace to place himself in
relation to the all-powerful Octavian, with whom he is not on
intimate terms, defining the new cultural politics by means of the
comparison with Lucilius' friendship with Scipio Aemilianus.

The priamel, as its name, (meaning 'preamble') shows, is also an
introductory gambit. In simplified form it goes 'some like *x*, some
like *y*, I like *z*'. The final statement, the 'cap', is thrown into prominence by the rejected options, the foil. It is easy to see how this
pattern could be adapted to generic differentiation, and one could
cite several other poems of Horace to illustrate this (e.g. *Odes* 1. 7).
The long speech at lines 2–60 begins and ends with priamels. The
first is deliberately low-key and ironic, and implicitly contrasts
Horace's casual choice of his vocation with the grandiose claims of
poets writing in higher genres (Anderson 1984: 38). *Odes* 1. 1 is
entirely constructed on this pattern and is simultaneously grand
and ironic. The second priamel (lines 47–60) is used to negotiate
a return to a more positive view of Horace's own satire through
ironic comparison with the named foils and the fierce animals that
illustrate the law of instinctive attack. The catalogue contains two
perverters of justice and two poisoners. These are possible analogues for the satirist (since satire may be seen as a kind of
correction of crime and also as a kind of poison—*Sat.* 1. 4), but the
point of the comparison is to exonerate this satirist, to show how
inoffensive he really is.[33] The animals also have a poetic relevance,
since there is a tradition of identifying the aggressive satirist with
a touchy horned bull (Hor. *Epod.* 6. 11–12; *Sat.* 1. 4. 34). For
Horace himself the more appropriate image is the watchdog which
barks at line 85. The climax to the priamel, built up in an
elaborate sentence after the promise to be short, is essentially the
same as that of the first: 'I will write.' What sort of writing this
will be we have already been told.

The reader may already have realized that there is yet another
priamel in this poem, that in fact the poem starts as one: *sunt
quibus . . . videar . . . altera . . . pars . . . putat . . .* The climactic
element, the cap, is missing, or rather postponed. As Anderson,
who first noticed the role of this priamel, says: 'when the satirist

---

[33] Anderson (1984) 41; cf. Pierre Bayle quoted by Elliott (1960) 268: 'a satirist
who attempts upon the honour of his enemy with libels, would attempt upon their
life with sword or poison, if he had the same opportunity.'

now asks his friend Trebatius for advice, he is implicitly hunting for a positive viewpoint that will reduce these initial comments to negative and negligible foil' (1984: 37). This positive assessment comes right at the end, and is the agreement that Horace's poetry is good. 'Good' qualifying 'verses' at the end has a double meaning in answer to the two senses of 'bad' (*malus*) which are in play. And these two senses correspond to the two criticisms of Horace which are quoted at the beginning. On the one hand his satire is too savage: that is, it consists of vituperation, the Latin term for which is *maledicere* 'to speak ill of'. On the other hand, it is poor stuff, or 'bad poetry'. In the final reply the aesthetic and ethical senses of 'good' respond to these criticisms. The wording of the law which Trebatius quotes (it too is anticipated by the reference to the law in the second line) is also tailored for this context: bad poetry is not lawful, and neither are malicious verses.[34] Here at least the legal and literary are inextricably mingled.

For all the vitality and ingenuity of this poem, we are left wondering what has in fact been said.[35] The underlying assumption of my discussion has been that identifying the poem's forms and conventions is an essential stage in interpretation (Macleod 1983: 179–80). So, the structure of the *recusatio* enables satire to be distinguished from epic as vituperation, as a kind of 'antibiography' (Rudd 1966: 46), and the priamels frame the topic of satire as defined by the satirist's character. Lucilius' satire was an immediate expression of his whole person, and Horace, for irrefutable personal reasons, follows him. The aim of *Satires* 2. 1 is to display Horace's own poetic temperament—that is, the role and character his own instantiation of the genre requires—through a contrast with and redefinition of his model. The literary law of engagement with a significant predecessor (Juv. 6. 635 *legem priorum*) is offered as an answer to Trebatius' concern with the civil or criminal law. In basing his conceit upon a Lucilian model Horace enacts the rules to which he is implicitly adhering, that the writer must work within the parameters set by the generic model. That this is not the whole truth, however, and that poetry must also reckon with its reception in the world, is Trebatius' side of the story.

[34] See Fraenkel (1925) 184 ff.; Brink on *Ep.* 2. 1. 153; for the opposing view Elliott (1960) 122 ff.
[35] See Brink (1965) 8 on Hor. *Sat.* 2. 6: 'What does the poem add up to? If the question is so put, the answer must be, "nothing".'

11

Pindarici Fontis Qui Non Expalluit Haustus:
Horace, *Epistles* 1. 3

MARGARET HUBBARD

H O R A C E's *Epistles* are perhaps more like letters than has sometimes been thought. There is, however, a respect in which one is
unwilling to liken them to some Ciceronian letters (*Fam.* 1. 19, for
instance): it is disconcerting to envisage the poet's talking for some
time about one subject and then adding a postscript on an uncon-
nected matter. So when in the third epistle the Teubner edition
indents line 30, and when a subtle analysis of the poem's imagery[1]
breaks off at line 29, it seems natural to wonder if they are right,
and to see if one can find a more unified pattern.

When in late 21 BC the young Tiberius was given the task of
leading reinforcements to Augustus' army in Asia by the land
route through Macedonia and Thrace, his staff, we must suppose,
had a stiffening of senior military advisers in case there was a barbarian incursion across the Danube. But those to whom and about
whom Horace was writing were not like that; the staff seems to be
made up of young littérateurs, though there is an agreeable play
with the idea that they have serious military functions. The ice-
bound Hebrus or the Hellespont may be holding them up; so may
the rich plains and hills of Asia. And though there the 'holding up'
was more likely to be the result of touristic enthusiasm or the
general desire for a good time than any military obstacles, they can
still be asked what they are doing about it (line 6):

> quid studiosa cohors operum struit?

The expression is prettily compatible with construction of military
engineering-works to overcome these obstacles, and the image

---

[1] West (1967) 29–39.

seems to continue, across a change of topic, to *diffundit* in line 8, as *diffundere* can describe dealing with a river barrier by diverting it into several streams. But Horace's friends are not *praefecti fabrum*, and their *opera* are of different kinds, to which the questions of lines 7–8 make the transition.

Horace shows no interest in the answer to these transitional questions, but pauses on Titius, who is destined to poetic fame and is bold enough to drink from Pindar's spring. Editors recognize in the next line (11) an allusion to the Pindaric fragment 274 quoted in Quint. *Inst.* 10. 1. 109: 'it does not collect rainwater but gushes with a living eddy'. But none of them except Kiessling–Heinze asks what Pindar's spring might be, and they give the wrong answer in suggesting the common Augustan picture of drinking from the spring of Hippocrene on Helicon. Horace's image is surely more closely geared to what he is talking about. Pindar's spring is not Hippocrene but Dirce, of which he says at *Isth.* 6. 71–2 'I shall give them a draught of the holy water of Dirce that the Muses, gold-robed Mnemosyne's deep-girdled daughters, sent up by the well-built gates of Cadmus', and at *Ol.* 6. 85 ff. 'Thebe, whose lovely waters I shall drink while weaving a multi-coloured song for warrior men'. The allusion to the Theban spring is pressed home by *Thebanos* in line 13.

What Titius was up to defeats imagination, but in lines 12–13 Horace certainly suggests that his ambitions included not just the exploitation of Pindaric topics but the adaptation to Latin of Pindaric metres. That was an ambition incapable of realization, and Kiessling–Heinze can hardly be right in suggesting that at this stage Horace regards it with benevolent approval and that it was only when he came to write *Odes* 4 that he recognized that Pindar was inimitable. In fact his expression here indicates scepticism. The two sentences about Titius' dealings with Pindar are interrupted in line 12 by two quite different questions that more easily admit the reassuring answer 'Very well': 'ut valet? ut meminit nostri?'; and in line 14 the passion and loud boomings of tragedy are offered as a likely escape route.

Horace very well knew what could be done in Latin with Pindar, and he had done it himself in the sapphics of *Odes* 1. 12 and the alcaics of *Odes* 3. 4, and was to do it again in the sapphics of *Odes* 4. 2 and the alcaics of *Odes* 4. 4. And in a quite different genre, I believe that in this epistle too he is, while 'weaving a multi-coloured song for warrior men', teasingly showing how to make use of Pindar, and by no means in Titius' way.

Florus himself is venturesome and versatile (lines 20-1):

> ipse quid audes?
> quae circumvolitas agilis thyma?

In this passage too the imagery, as often in this epistle, is sustained and developed. *Ipse quid audes?* in line 20 is picked up in lines 21-2 with *non tibi parvum ingenium*: Florus has genius enough to be venturesome. Similarly, as David West[2] points out, *quae circumvolitas agilis thyma* is developed by 22 *non incultum est et turpiter hirtum*. West rightly saw that we should not take this to be speaking of irrelevant bramble-covered fields that are a disgrace to the cultivator but of the inferior kind of bee that Virgil describes in *Georg.* 4. 96 ff. ('namque aliae turpes horrent . . .'), the bees that are ugly and shaggy, like the traveller coming from deep dust and hawking earth from his parched mouth. Florus is the other kind of bee, the bright and shiny one, from whom in due season one gets sweet honey.[3]

This bee, moreover, is much more Pindaric than the bee in the overtly Pindaric context of *Odes* 4. 2. 27 ff., and in its activity and versatility recalls rather the bee of *Pyth.* 10. 54, where the choicest of festal songs darts like a bee now to one theme, now to another:

> ἐπ' ἄλλοτ' ἄλλον ὧτε μέλισσα θύνει λόγον

The allusion is characteristically sophisticated: the epithet *agilis* renders the sense of the verb θύνει, the verb *circumvolitas* that of the phrase ἐπ' ἄλλοτ' ἄλλον . . . λόγον. In the lines that immediately follow, the image in line 23 of sharpening one's tongue on a whetstone has one of its most memorable expressions in *Ol.* 6. 82,[4] in the immediate neighbourhood of the second of the two references to Dirce mentioned above. In the next line *amabile carmen*, an expression unique in Horace, also recalls Pindar, not so much the

---

[2] West (1967) 31.

[3] The bee is still in mind at 24 *condis*, ambiguous between 'compose' and 'store'; so West (1967) 34. The maintenance of the image over a change of direction is like that by which the equally ambiguous *diffundit* (8) extends in a different context the image of *opera* (6).

[4] The locution does occur in Cic. *De orat.* 3. 121 'non enim solum acuenda nobis neque procudenda lingua est', in surprising conjunction with Pindar's other metallurgical tongue-metaphor of forging (*Pyth.* 1. 86). Cicero presumably found them conjoined in Greek rhetoric.

μέλος χαρίεν of *Pyth.* 5. 107 that Kiessling–Heinze cite as Pindar's favourite epithet ἐρατός, which is used of songs in fr. 124.1 ἐρατῶν ὄχημ' ἀοιδᾶν and fr. 235 4 αὐλῶν . . . ἐρατὸν μέλος, and also at *Isth.* 2. 31 οὔτε κώμων . . . ἐρατῶν οὔτε μελικόμπων ἀοιδᾶν.

It may be worth bearing these hints of Pindaric *color* in mind when one comes to interpret the next and difficult sequence. Florus is told in lines 23 ff. that whether he is practising oratory or training to be a jurisconsult or composing poetry, he will win first prize: 'prima feres hederae victricis praemia.' The particular prize named is the ivy crown of the poet. And he is then told (lines 25 ff.):

> quodsi
> frigida curarum fomenta relinquere posses,
> quo te caelestis sapientia duceret ires.

'But if you could abandon *frigida curarum fomenta*, you would be (as you are not) following the guidance of a heavenly wisdom.'

If in that sentence one takes *frigida curarum fomenta* to mean 'ineffectual[5] remedies for cares' of an unspecified nature, with *curarum* an objective genitive, then the ineffectual remedies can only be the composition of poetry. The orator and the jurisconsult may relieve other people's cares, though it would not then be very polite to say that the remedies are ineffectual, but no one ever supposed that their activities were a remedy, effectual or ineffectual, for their own *curae*; their activities are their *curae*, not remedies for them. It is only poetic composition that can be supposed to relieve *curae*, and if that is what the phrase means, the limitation of the *praemia* to the ivy crown would then be transitional to this focusing on poetry alone of Florus' possible activities. This is not very satisfactory: in lines 23–4 the three activities have been put on a level by *seu . . . seu . . . seu*, and it is hard to see why law and oratory should be brought in at all if nothing more is to be said about them and only poetry is to be important.

This unsatisfactoriness has prompted an alternative interpretation, taking *curarum* in the sense that μέριμναι has in Pindar, the sense of 'high ambitions', and regarding it not as an objective genitive but as a genitive of equivalence. If it is a genitive of equivalence, the useless remedies are the various high ambitions

---

[5] The notion that, just because Antonius Musa had cured Augustus with cold poultices, *frigida* might in any old context lose its sense of 'unavailing' is a mere red herring.

that Florus entertains, for oratory, law, or poetry, and even though he will achieve success, these high ambitions are useless and should be abandoned. But there are difficulties in this too. Firstly, if the *curae* are themselves the ineffectual remedies, we are no longer told what they are remedies for. A second difficulty is coherence both with what precedes and with what follows.

Take first coherence with what precedes. If Florus were to abandon his ambitions, he would, as he is not, be following the guidance of a heavenly wisdom. What would he be doing instead? Studying philosophy, we are often told. And not only he but all the *cohors* would be urged to do the same. On this interpretation, line 28: 'hoc opus, hoc studium . . . properemus' suggests that 'studying philosophy' is the answer that Horace would have liked to get to his earlier question: 'quid studiosa cohors operum struit?' But this does undermine the earlier part of the poem. Horace's tone has sometimes been teasing, but it has not been the tone of one who suggests that all the literary activities of the *cohors* should simply be abandoned.

Moreover, in the following lines the prescription seems to become far too wholesale. Horace was a man of philosophic cultivation, but not a philosophical fanatic. The study of philosophy can no doubt be useful to one's country (line 29): 'si patriae volumus, si nobis vivere cari.' But if we are all, *parvi et ampli* (line 28), urged to pursue philosophy, and if this pursuit involves the abandonment not only of poetry but of oratory and law by all of us, it is not easy to see how the *patria* is going to be pleased.

Given these difficulties, it is perhaps worth asking whether the whole of the troublesome line 26 should be taken to be alluding to and controverting a favourite theme of Pindar's, the notion of repute, of glory, as the remedy for the effort that leads to high achievement, the φάρμακον κάλλιστον ἑᾶς ἀρετᾶς[6] of *Pyth.* 4. 187, the ἄκος ὑγιηρόν of *Nem.* 3. 18. There may be a particular relevance in the opening of the fourth *Nemean*, where Pindar says: 'The best physician of toils completed is festal cheer; for skilled songs, the Muse's daughters, treat and soothe them. Not even warm water so steeps limbs to softness as songs set in harmony to the lyre.' The

---

[6] The older interpretation (*remedium virtutis*) of this tormented phrase is ably defended by Race (1985). The scholia partly misunderstood the passage, but rightly thought of 'good fame' (φάρμακον θανάτου ἡ ἀρετὴ καὶ ἡ εὔκλεια), and Horace no doubt did so too; the passage can be added to those collected by Lefkowitz (1985).

second sentence of that passage is one of the Pindaric γνῶμαι that was taken into the moralistic tradition, and it is cited precisely in Plutarch's work on peace of mind, the περὶ εὐθυμίας that is frequently invoked to suggest what might have been in the περὶ εὐθυμίας of Panaetius, a book that certainly contributed some elements to Horace's philosophical culture. In περὶ εὐθυμίας 6 Plutarch paraphrases 'songs set in harmony to the lyre' as δόξα, 'repute'. Macleane, whose view is mentioned, though with confessed incomprehension, at the end of Wilkins's admirable note, was therefore perhaps on the right lines when he suggested that the *fomenta* are 'glory and suchlike rewards' that are the assuagements of one's ambitious efforts. On that interpretation *curarum* is again objective genitive like the 'toils completed' of the fourth *Nemean*, which find their assuagement in panegyric song. But these *fomenta* are here presented as *frigida* and useless, quite in contrast to the *Nemean*'s θερμὸν ὕδωρ. If that is right, Florus is being urged to abandon the pursuit of glory, the *prima hederae victricis praemia*. If he did that he would be following a *caelestis sapientia*, not the more mundane σοφία of the poet, the orator, or the jurisconsult.

It might be objected that this aim is too negative to deserve the enthusiasm of line 28: 'hoc opus, hoc studium parvi properemus et ampli.' But this is perhaps not so, if we consider what it is that makes the *fomenta frigida* and what Horace elsewhere thinks of the relation between achievement and repute. Colin Macleod[7] rightly saw a connection between the third and the nineteenth epistles, where that relation is more fully explored. At 19. 32 ff. Horace expresses to Maecenas and to us his pride and joy in poetic creation and poetic repute:

> hunc ego, non alio dictum prius ore, Latinus
> vulgavi fidicen. iuvat immemorata ferentem
> ingenuis oculisque legi manibusque teneri.

The *iuvat . . .* sentence is interestingly different from other similar declarations in Latin poetry. In Lucr. 1. 927–8 (= 4. 2 ff.) the poet's delight is purely in the originality of his poetic creation, and in Prop. 2. 34. 59 ff. and 3. 5. 19 ff. in his activity as a poet or his personal poetic stance.[8] Here in Horace the originality of his

---

[7] Macleod (1983) 265–6.

[8] At 2. 13. 11 ff. Propertius does want applause, but as the applause is that of his mistress alone and the views of the rest of the world are dismissed as irrelevant, his position is hardly the same as Horace's.

achievement, on which Lucretius spends four lines, gets a subordinate and participial expression *immemorata ferentem*, and the main
source of delight is the reception his poems get from the *ingenui*.[9]
Horace is very far from asserting 'his detachment from his public'.[10]
Instead he is avowing not only that the writing of poetry is
serious, but that the ambition to be acknowledged and loved as a
great poet is not an ignoble one. Only the acknowledgement has to
be on the poet's own terms: the praise of the *imitatores*, *servum
pecus* (1. 19. 19) is not worth having, the dispraise of the envious
(36 ff.) not worth contending against.

Not only here but as early as the ending of the first book of the
Satires (1. 10. 81 ff.) Horace takes up the stance of the rightly
ambitious man, of whom Aristotle said at *Nic. Eth.* 1095^b 26 ff.
that he himself acknowledges that excellence is better than
honour, because he wants to be honoured not by anybody for
just anything, but by those who are good and who know him for
being excellent. The rightly ambitious man merges into the man of
high spirit, the μεγαλόψυχος,[11] of whom we are told at *Nic. Eth.*
1124^b 26 ff.:

Necessarily, the high-spirited man will be an open enemy and an open
friend, since concealment implies timidity and so does a concern for
opinion rather than truth; again, he will go in for open speech and open
action, since he is outspoken because given to contempt and is candid
except when he uses irony to the many; moreover, he will be unable to
live with an eye to anyone's opinion but a friend's, since that is slavish.

Such a one is, in Latin terms, *ingenuus* and wants praise only from
the *ingenui*.

About here we can find the answer to the question of what
makes the *fomenta frigida*. To seek repute for its own sake and to
be content to be praised 'by anybody for just anything' provides no
proper assuagement for high ambition. There is nothing negative

---

[9] It is not only here that the thought of poetic achievement at once brings to
Horace the thought of poetic reputation; in the *Ars* too the connection is almost an
inevitable one (113, 154-5, 190, 321, 331-2, 341-6).

[10] Macleod (1983) 279.

[11] Macleod (1983) 274 acknowledges the relevance of the concept and cites *Nic.
Eth.* 1124^b 31 ff. More of the passage than that is relevant to the interpretation of
Ep. 1. 19: when faced with the envious and cavilling critic, Horace 'uses irony to
the many' and speaks of his poems as *nugae* (41), but given the whole characteri-
zation of the high-spirited man, we should assume that he speaks the truth to
Maecenas, and in that truth there is no self-depreciation.

about recommending the grander aim of excellence. If what we are to abandon is not the honourable activities of the orator, jurisconsult, and poet, but a low motive of repute and emulation, then the *patria* can have some reason to be pleased, because that abandonment offers wider possibilities for conciliation with others and harmony with ourselves (line 29): 'si patriae volumus, si nobis vivere cari.'

It is these possibilities that Horace goes on to illustrate with his enquiry about the health of the reconciliation between Florus and Munatius. Once more a repeated image bridges the change of direction (cf. above, p. 220, on *diffundit*, and n. 3 on *condis*); the enquiry renews the medical terminology of *frigida curarum fomenta* with the image of the quarrel as a wound that had knitted, but that may have broken open again without healing (31–2). The image of the wound again has a Pindaric parallel, in a context of breach of friendship and reconciliation: at the end of the fourth *Pythian* Pindar pleads with king Arcesilas of Cyrene to recall from exile the noble Damophilus and tells him (lines 270–1): 'You are a most timely physician . . . One should tend with gentle hand the festering of the wound.' If Horace needed help, the scholia could oblige: 'not', they explain kindly, 'that Arcesilas was a physician, but that Damophilus was suffering from the disease of exile.' In the poem's last words we learn that to reconcile Arcesilas and to persuade him to cure the wound, Damophilus had found in Thebes a fount of immortal song, a *fons Pindaricus* (line 299):

> εὖρε παγὰν ἀμβροσίων ἐπέων
> πρόσφατον Θήβᾳ ξενωθείς

There is perhaps another allusion that helps to tie this last section of the poem firmly to the earlier part. In the comparison of Florus with the bee, both Pindar and Virgil are present (above, pp. 221–2); it may be that Virgil as well as Pindar is present in this section too. The question is that of the image in line 34 *indomita cervice feros*. What animal should we be thinking of? The older commentators, starting with Lambinus, took the reference to be to bullocks; Orelli offers either bullocks or horses (with a reference to the spirited horse of *Ep.* 2. 64–5.), and horses seem to be favoured nowadays. In the second *Epistle*, where Horace is talking about reason controlling anger, the Platonic image of the spirited horse is appropriate; here, where he is talking about the reconciliation of two young men, it would be less so. Munatius and Florus are or should be a pair, and Horace's relation to them is rather that of the trainer of *Georg.* 3. 164 ff., teaching young bullocks in light collars to walk in step: 'coge gradum conferre iuvencos.' If bullocks are what we should be thinking about, the *votiva iuvenca* does not come quite unheralded.

12

Horace and the Reputation of Plautus in the Late First Century BC

H. D. JOCELYN

I. INTRODUCTION

EVERYONE knows that the mature Horace took a poor view both of Plautus and of those contemporary teachers of literature who preferred the old comedies and their like to the ones written by his friend Fundanius.[1] It was the view of a man who could claim some knowledge of the theatre scripts in question.[2] The epistle to Augustus (2.1) laughs at the alleged incoherence of current professorial views of what constituted the best poetic writing in Latin, and in particular at the futility of the conventional criterion of age (lines 50-62).[3] The same epistle later describes early Roman attempts to adapt the Greek genres of tragedy and comedy, patronizing the tragedians and denouncing the comedians (lines 156-76). At both points the comic scripts of Plautus are given a high prominence. In a roughly parallel way the epistle to the Pisos (*Ars poetica*) makes a supercilious allusion to the reputation Plautus still enjoyed for linguistic inventiveness (lines 48-58), an explicit sneer at the reputation the comedian had enjoyed two generations earlier for rhythmical skill and verbal wit (lines 270-2), and a

---

[1] See *Sat.* 1. 10. 37-45.

[2] Students like Dietze (1900), Tschernjajew (1900), Winniczuk (1935), Di Benedetto (1962), and Ronconi (1970) (= 1972: 142-68) may exaggerate a little, but comparison of Horace's hexameter poems with those of Persius and Juvenal shows that he had at least some familiarity with the Latin adaptations of the New Comedy (contrast in particular Hor. *Sat.* 2.3. 259-71 [~ Terence's *Eunuchus*] and Persius 5. 161-74 [~ Menander's Εὐνοῦχος]).

[3] Aristophanes and Aristarchus notoriously excluded the living from their lists of the best poets (Quin. *Inst.* 10. 1. 54). The attitude of the critic always irked the practising poet (cf. Martial 5. 10, 8. 69, 11. 90).

confident assertion that a higher level of perceptiveness now obtained in the best Roman society (lines 272–4).

The two epistles received in antiquity a large amount of commentary from *grammatici* of no mean reputation,[4] although what survives can only be described as exiguous. They interested not a few persons of theoretical bent in the high Middle Ages.[5] During the Renaissance they exercised a widespread influence and continued to do so down to the time of the French Revolution. Part of their attraction lay, I suspect, in the difficulty of attaching a clear specific sense to their more striking statements. Pundits could make them support a considerable variety of general points of view. Horace's slighting references to Plautus were often better known than Plautus' actual works.[6] That remained the case after the *Amphitruo, Asinaria, Aulularia, Captivi, Curculio, Casina, Cistellaria,* and *Epidicus* began to circulate, and even after twelve more scripts became available in the middle years of the fifteenth century.[7] Since the beginning of the nineteenth century the two epistles have attracted almost continuous attention—less, however, for what they say about the principles of poetic composition than for the evidence they seem to offer on the history of poetical taste in the first century BC.

Recently the scholarly consensus reached during the last hundred years about the meaning of certain verses of the epistle to Augustus was made one of the starting-points of a new and interesting account of the early history of the text of Plautus' comedies. Otto Zwierlein published in 1990 the first of a series of volumes arguing that Plautus paid careful attention to the details of the late fourth- and early third-century Attic plays adapted by him for performance at the Roman festivals of his time; that he succeeded in making versions exemplifying the virtues of the Attic plays, particularly in

[4] What is now commonly called the epistle to the Pisos was known in antiquity as the *Liber de arte poetica*. Julius Romanus cited an edition which included it among the *Epistulae* (Charisius, pp. 263. 9, 265. 1–3 Barwick). P. Terentius Scaurus appears to have written at least ten books of *commentarii* on it (Charisius, pp. 263. 11–12, 272. 27–30).

[5] See Curcio (1907; 1913); Monteverdi (1936) 162–80; Munk Olsen (1982) 421–522; Quint (1988); Villa (1992). It must be said that the epistle to the Pisos drew much more attention to itself and its argument than the epistle to Augustus did.

[6] The negative view expressed by Petrarch at *Epist. Var.* 22 (iii. 358 Fracassetti) clearly derives from Horace.

[7] On 15th-cent. knowledge of Plautus see the discussion and bibliography at Jocelyn (1991) 112–13 n. 14.

regard to consistency of characterization and coherence of plot; that stage producers of the late second century with different ideas of theatrical effectiveness added large amounts of new material to Plautus' original scripts; and that our manuscript tradition goes back to heavily interpolated texts rather than to the genuine Plautus. Corruption began early, according to Zwierlein, and Horace already read Plautus in the shape in which we do; Horace failed in consequence, as we allegedly fail in the twentieth century, to perceive the true character of Plautus' comic poetry; earlier critics with purer texts had, on the other hand, recognized Plautus as a successful imitator of the great Attic comedians.[8]

The passages of Horace's *Epistles* relevant to the issues raised by Zwierlein have not always been interpreted as they have been in our own time, and it may be worth the effort to re-examine them. This paper takes up three questions: what did Horace find defective in Plautus' comic writing? what was the state of critical opinion in regard to the Plautine scripts in Horace's adolescence? what did the admirers of Plautus whom Horace ridiculed actually admire? The answers do not destroy Zwierlein's thesis, but they suggest that modification of some of the details may be necessary.

2. *EPISTLES* 2. 1. 168-76

> creditur, ex medio quia res arcessit, habere
> sudoris minimum sed habet comoedia tanto
> plus oneris quanto veniae minus, aspice Plautus   170
> quo pacto partis tutetur amantis ephebi,
> ut patris attenti, lenonis ut insidiosi,
> quantus sit Dossennus edacibus in parasitis,
> quam non astricto percurrat pulpita socco.
> gestit enim nummum in loculos demittere, post hoc   175
> securus cadat an recto stet fabula talo.

Where *Ep.* 2. 1. 168-76 is concerned, Zwierlein interprets Horace in a highly specific way: 'Horaz . . . tadelt den Sarsinaten wegen seiner mangelnden Konsequenz in der Charakterzeichnung (*adspice . . . quo pacto partis tutetur amantis ephebi,* | *ut patris attenti, lenonis ut insidiosi*), wegen seiner Übertreibung des Possenhaften in der

[8] Zwierlein (1990; 1991a; 1991b; 1992). More are to come. I have written about Zwierlein's thesis in Jocelyn (1992) and (1993).

Darstellung der gefräßigen Parasiten (*quantus sit Dossenus edacibus in parasitis*) und wegen seiner allzu lockeren Handlungsführung (*quam non adstricto percurrat pulpita socco*).'⁹ A different, and perhaps more correct, view obtained in the sixteenth century; lines 168-73 were thought to denounce a failure to preserve τὸ πρέπον in the delineation of τὰ ἤθη, while line 174 was linked with line 58, and the sense of both verses related to verbal style.¹⁰

The general drift of the hexameters cannot be disputed: Horace condemns Plautus for not taking enough trouble with his scripts, for being more interested in short-term financial gain than in long-term critical acclaim. The expressions *ex medio . . . res arcessit, habere sudoris minimum, habet . . . plus oneris . . . veniae minus, partis tutetur amantis ephebi*, and *cadat an recto stet . . . talo* have, however, no exact parallels in recorded Latin and probably owe their existence in some degree to Horace's particular linguistic dexterity. Little evidence survives as to how ordinary users of Latin talked about comic poetry in the second half of the first century BC. The modern interpreter has thus to feel his way. The words of lines 170-4 refer on the surface to an actor and his performance, lines 175-6 to the reaction of ordinary theatrical spectators, but at a deeper level the context requires the former to be related to a poet and his script, the latter to a group of critical readers. The close connection which is assumed between writing and performing would have been less surprising to Augustus and Horace's other readers than it may be to ourselves. Poets were believed to have once taken part in the performance of their own scripts both at Athens and at Rome.¹¹ The unique expressions have, if I am right, to be interpreted in a way

---

⁹ (1990) 12.

¹⁰ On lines 168-73 see Estienne (1587) 29: 'aspice quam male tutetur horum partes, quam male comico decoro his in personis serviat.' Cf. the discussion of the passage by Lambin (1561): 'in servando cuiusque personae decoro, & in tuendis senum, amatorum, lenonum etc. partibus . . . singularum personarum parteis tueatur . . . neque Plautus curat suae cuiusque personae decorum tueri ac servare'. On line 174 see the comment of Lambin cited in n. 45 below. In an essay prefixed to the sixth edition of his text of Terence's comedies (Amsterdam, 1618) and often reprinted and discussed during the next two centuries ('ad Horatii de Plauto et Terentio iudicium'), Daniel Heinsius declared that *Ep.* 2. 1. 170-1 censures Plautus' presentation of the ἦθος of the young man in love, in particular that of the Charinus of the *Mercator*.

¹¹ On Thespis see Themist. *Orat.* 26, 316 d; on Livius Andronicus Livy 7. 2. 8. On the part played by the actor's voice and gesture in bringing out ἦθη and πάθη see Cic. *De or.* 3. 214-21; *Q. Rosc.* 20. Noteworthy is the way Aristophanic personages referring to the stage behaviour of figures of tragedy and comedy identify the figure with the poet (*Lys.* 188-9; *Ran.* 12-15).

which plausibly fits both a theatrical and a literary-critical milieu. The interpreter must, furthermore, keep in mind the nature of the demand which *comoedia* is represented as making in lines 169-70.

The words *ex medio . . . res arcessit* in line 168 express a current definition of the subject-matter of comedy: *comoedia communia sectatur*[12] or κωμῳδία ἐστιν ἰδιωτικῶν πραγμάτων ἀκίνδυνος περιοχή[13] or ἡ . . . κωμῳδία πλάσματα περιέχει βιωτικῶν πραγμάτων[14] or *comoedia est imitatio vitae, speculum consuetudinis, imago veritatis*[15] or some other definition not elsewhere recorded.[16] They cannot have anything at all to do with the organization of the subject-matter.[17] *Ex medio* suggests that Horace had in his mind a scaling of persons as much as of activities and events: the persons of comedy would come between the *alti* and the *humiles*, the *graves* and the *leves*, the persons of tragedy and those of popular farce.[18] The use of *onus* in the sense of *difficultas* in line 170[19] points in the same direction:

[12] Porphyrio ad loc. Cf. Gellius 2. 23. 12 'illud Menandri de vita hominum media sumptum'.

[13] Diomedes, *Gramm. Lat.* i. 488. 4-5; Donat. *De com.* 5. 1, p. 22 Wessner. Since Diomedes attributes a definition of tragedy to Theophrastus at 487. 11-12 and couples the two definitions closely at 488. 19-20, the definition of comedy is commonly thought to stem also from Theophrastus.

[14] Σ Dionys. Thr. p. 173. 3-4 Hilgard. Cf. *Gloss. Lat.* i. 128 Lindsay 'comoedia est quae res privatorum et humilium personarum conprehendit . . . est quae privatorum hominum continet acta.'

[15] Cicero ap. Donat. *De com.* 5. 1, p. 22 Wessner. Cf. *S. Rosc.* 47 'haec conficta arbitror esse a poetis ut . . . expressamque imaginem vitae cotidianae videremus'; Manilius 5. 475-6 'Menander, | qui vitae [*Scaliger*: vita *codd.*] ostendit vitam'; Quint. *Inst.* 10. 1. 69 'Menander . . . omnem vitae imaginem expressit.' Aristophanes of Byzantium had asked ὦ Μένανδρε καὶ βίε, πότερος ἀρ᾽ ὑμῶν πότερον ἀπεμιμήσατο; (ap. Syrian. *In Hermog.* ii 23 Rabe).

[16] Cf. Ov. *Rem.* 376 'usibus e mediis soccus habendus erit'; Euanthius, *De com.* 2. 6, p. 17 Wessner 'aliud genus carminis . . . repperere poetae, quae argumento communi magis et generaliter ad omnes homines qui mediocribus fortunis agunt pertineret'; 4. 2, p. 21 'in comoedia mediocres fortunae hominum . . . sunt.'

[17] On this theme see Euanthius, *De com.* 3. 7, p. 20 (on Terence) 'media primis atque postremis ita nexuit, ut nihil additum alteri, sed aptum ex se totum et uno corpore videatur esse compositum.' For briefer references see Anon. *De com.* in cod. E. Aristoph. 12, pp. 8-9 Kaibel, *Comicorum Graecorum Fragmenta*, i (on the poets of the μέση κωμῳδία) κατασχολοῦνται δὲ πάντες περὶ τὰς ὑποθέσεις; Plut. *Mor.* 347 F (anecdote about Menander) ᾠκονόμηται γὰρ ἡ διάθεσις. δεῖ δ᾽ αὐτῇ τὰ στιχίδια ἐπᾶσαι; Euanthius, *De com.* 2. 6, p. 17 (on the νέα κωμῳδία) *concinna argumento*. In the 5th cent. BC Aeschylean tragedy had been criticized as ἀξύστατος. Aristotle discussed at length ἡ τῶν πραγμάτων σύστασις (*Poet.* 7-14, 1450b21-1454a15).

[18] Diomedes' distinction at *Gramm. Lat.* i 488. 14-16—'comoedia a tragoedia differt quod in tragoedia introducuntur heroes duces reges, in comoedia humiles atque privatae ⟨personae⟩'—leaves mime etc. right out of consideration.

[19] So Porphyrio ad loc. Cf. Cic. *S. Rosc.* 10; *Verr.* 2. 3. 4; Anon. *Bell. Alex.* 65. 2; Quint. *Inst.* 1 praef. 3.

the fact that the persons of comedy have less 'weight' than those of tragedy increases, in Horace's view, rather than diminishes the difficulty of the comic poet's task. On what the *sudor* of line 169 is to be expended Horace does not say. In view of the frequency of the antithesis between τὸ ἔργον and ὁ λόγος, τὰ πράγματα and ἡ λέξις in Greek literature, of *factum* and *dictum*, of *res* and *verba* in Latin, and in the absence of any other indication, we are obliged to assume that he was thinking of the poet's need to work at his verbal style.

It is the combination *partis tutetur . . . ephebi . . . patris . . . lenonis* which makes lines 171-2 problematic. The theatrical language regularly applied the plural *partes* to divisions of the dramatic script among the performers.[20] No use of *tutari* is recorded for this register of Latin. In other registers the verb regularly conveys the idea of protection against some external source of harm. The Horatian expression does not conform at all. Of the four passages ranged alongside it by the *Oxford Latin Dictionary* under the rubric 'to preserve unimpaired, maintain (conditions, etc.)', namely Sall. *Iug.* 85. 4, Livy 6. 38. 6, Manilius 3. 430-3, Sen. *Ag.* 110-11, only the third,

> simili tum cetera lucro
> procedent numeros semper tutata prioris
> augebuntque novo vicinas munere summas,
> donec perveniant ad iustae sidera Librae,

has any genuine similarity: the signs of the zodiac which rise in the spring and summer keep the number of *stadia* they are imagined to receive from their predecessors; no one threatens to take them. What interplay there was between the language of astrologers and that of the poet we cannot tell. The Manilian passage does not, in any case, elucidate the Horatian.

Two uses of the base verb *tueri* widespread in the common language, *personam tueri* 'live up to an ideal image'[21] and *beneficium*

---

[20] Cf. Plaut. *Amph.* 62 'hic servos quoque partes habet'; Ter. *Haut.* 1-2 'quor partis seni | poeta dederit quae sunt adulescentium'; 10 'quam ob rem has partis didicerim paucis dabo'; *Phorm.* 27-8 'primas partis qui aget, is erit Phormio parasitus.' For *agere* + status of the personage impersonated see Ter. *Haut.* 37-40; Cic. *Q. Rosc.* 20. The way of speaking was transferred to the impersonations of the comic plots; cf. Plaut. *Mil.* 811 'ut nunc etiam hic agat actutum partis defendas tuas'.

[21] Cic. *Brut.* 80 'atque etiam L. Paullus Africani pater personam principis civis facile dicendo tuebatur', 165 'quo et magistratus personam et consularem dignitatem tueretur', *Phil.* 8. 29 'quam magnum est personam in re publica tueri principis'.

tueri 'live up to the demands of a good turn',[22] are closer to
Horace's unique use of the intensive/frequentative *tutari*[23] and
should be considered to lie behind it. Some critic would have
praised Plautus for meeting commonly recognized expectations in
regard to the utterances of participants in comic actions. Both *tueri*
and *tutari* had of necessity positive connotations; gentlemen used
the verbs to denote behaviour they approved of. The use of *tutari*
instead of the neutral and professional *agere*[24] at *Ep.* 2. 1. 170
corresponded with that of *mandare* instead of *dare* at *Ars* 176–7
'ne forte seniles | mandentur iuveni partes pueroque viriles'. In the
latter passage *mandare* had more solemn connotations than *dare*
would have had.[25] Its use transferred to a professional context the
demands of the Roman gentleman's ethical code. The verb
assignare replaced *dare* with similar effect in Seneca's expression of
an ethical commonplace at *Ep.* 80. 7 'nec enim ullo efficacius
exprimitur hic humanae vitae mimus, qui nobis partes quas male
agamus adsignat.'[26] Where Hor. *Ep.* 2. 1. 171–2 is concerned, the
superficial objectivity of *quo modo . . . ut . . . ut* has even caused
some interpreters to leave open the possibility that Horace was

----

[22] Cic. *Cael.* 7 'meum erga te parentemque tuum beneficium tueri debeo' ('to keep
the service unspoilt'; Austin); *Phil.* 2. 60 'licuitne mihi per tuas contumelias
hoc tuum beneficium sic tueri ut tuebar . . .?' ('to live up to'). Cf. *Att.* 1. 18. 6
'togulam illam pictam silentio tuetur suam' ('lives up to that lovely embroidered
toga of his': Shackleton Bailey); 7. 1. 7 'quo artificio tueamur benevolentiam
Caesaris' ('to act up to Caesar's friendliness': Shackleton Bailey); *Q. fratr.* 1. 1. 30
'in his honoribus tuendis'; Plancus, Cic. *Fam.* 10. 11. 1 'tuum munus tuere'.

[23] In earlier writers, notably Plautus himself, the form in *-to/-tor* often bears the
sense of the base verb, merely varying the tone (see Hofmann and Szantyr 1965:
297–8). This practice occurs in some writers of the late Republic and early Empire,
but not in Horace. The fact that elsewhere Horace gives *tutari* its ordinary sense
suggests that at *Ep.* 2. 1. 171 he gives it a distinctively intensive or frequentative
sense, whatever that sense may have been (unless, of course, he is taking off the
language of the old-fashioned author of the judgement).

[24] Cf. Ter. *Phorm.* 28–9 'primas partes qui aget is erit Phormio | parasitus';
Varro, *Men.* 367 'tragoedum iubeas Amphionis agere partis' (for the transferred use
of the locution see Ter. *Phorm.* 835; of *partes peragere* [Virg.] *Moret.* 51; Ov. *Am.* 2.
15. 26; *Rem.* 383; Val. Max. 5. 8. 3).

[25] Cf. Festus, p. 218. 6–10 Lindsay 'orare . . . pro agere . . . oratores . . . quod
rei publicae mandatas partis agebant'. Contrast Ter. *Haut.* 1–2 'quor partis seni |
poeta dederit quae sunt adulescentium'; Livy 24. 7. 4 'uni ex eis [participants in a
conspiracy] . . . partes datae sunt ut . . .'

[26] For the idea of life as a kind of stage-play in which each is allotted a role
to play see Plato, *Phileb.* 50 B; Bion fr. 16 Kindstrand (Teles ap. Stob. 3. 1. 98);
M. Antonius 3. 8, 12. 36; Epict. *Ench.* 17; Cic. *Cato* 5, 64, 70, 85; *Fin.* 1. 49;
Sen. *Ep.* 77. 20; Suet. *Aug.* 99. 1; Apul. *Flor.* 16, p. 66 Oudendorp.

conceding a virtue to Plautus.[27] The difficulty disappears if we suppose that he was referring sarcastically to a well-known critical judgement in favour of the comedian and taking up in some way the very wording of the judgement.

All this does not, however, tell us what the expectations were in regard to the *ephebi amantes*, the *patres attenti*, and the *lenones insidiosi* of everyday life, whether for the actor in performing his part of the action or for the poet composing the relevant part of the script. According to Zwierlein, Horace condemned Plautus for a failure to achieve consistency of characterization. This was very much the view of Richard Heinze,[28] who cited the praise given to Terence by Euanthius (*De com.* 3. 4, p. 19 Wessner 'custodivit personarum leges circa habitum, aetatem, officium partes agendi nemo diligentius a Terentio custodivit') and Donatus (ad *Andr.* 447 'mire servatum est in adulescente libero τὸ πρέπον et in amatore τὸ πιθανόν, nam et honesto iuveni non congruebat versipellis vultus et amatorem absurdum fuerat ingenii celare tristitiam').[29] It is diffi cult, however, to relate such a failure in composition to a failure in performance. If the script attributed something implausible to a young man in love, to a parsimonious old man, or to a scheming slave-dealer, the actor could do little about it. Unfortunately, the force of Porphyrio's interpretation of *quo pacto partis tutetur—hoc est: quam indecenter, incongrue*—has to be guessed at.[30] My own

---

[27] Lambin (1561) cited an earlier view: 'alii enim putant Plautum reprehendi ab Horatio, hoc modo. vide, quam negligens sit Plautus in servando cuiusque personae decoro, & in tuendis senum, amatorum, lenonum, &c partibus: vide quam parum sit accuratus. atque ita, *quo pacto* interpretantur, quam male, quam non accurate.' Kiessling (1884–9: vol. iii) interpreted *quo pacto* as 'wie schlecht'. Lambin came down, with some hesitation, in favour of the very opposite kind of interpretation and was followed by Torrentius (1608); it should nevertheless be noted that Lambin and Torrentius had Horace blame Plautus for attention to τὰ ἤθη at the expense of verbal wit and elegance.

[28] In his 1914 revision of Adolf Kiessling's 1889 commentary (I have not seen that of 1908). Also cf. Becker (1963) 203; Ronconi (1970) 29 (= 1972: 157; cf. Ronconi 1979: 502–3). Brink's note is ambiguous. Heinze's view was Ritschl's ('die sorglose Durchführung der Charaktere': Ritschl 1876: 541 [= 1877: 156–7]).

[29] See also the general recommendation at Hor. *Ars* 126–7 (cited by Desprez 1691) and the criticism of Euripides for making the murderous Medea weep (arg. *Med.* ii p. 138 Schwartz). Heinze replaced the two very hesitant interpretations offered by Kiessling.

[30] Porphyrio has neither *indecenter* nor *incongrue* elsewhere. For *decenter* see the scholia on *Odes*. 2. 1. 22, 2. 4. 13–14, 3. 27. 17–18; *Ep.* 1. 1. 36, 1. 2. 59–60; for *congrue* that on *Ep.* 2. 2. 192. Neither these passages nor those involving *indecenter* (Cornutus ap. schol. Veron. ad *Aen.* 5. 488; Servius auct. ad *Aen.* 4. 163)

guess is that Porphyrio thought Horace condemned Plautus for stylistic rather than compositional ἀπρέπεια, i.e. for a lack of congruity between his language and both the social type and the ἦθος of the person he was trying to represent,[31] for a failure to keep distinct the ways in which the young citizen, the old citizen, and the foreign businessman spoke,[32] and for a failure to relate their respective utterances plausibly to amorousness, parsimony, and deceitfulness.[33] It is easy to imagine corresponding defects in performance, whether in enunciation[34] or in gesture.[35] Sixteenth-century critics took lines 171-2 very much as I guess Porphyrio to have taken them. They were on the right track.

Dossennus was the name of a personage, given to gluttony[36] and doubtless very obese, who frequently figured in a type of farce still performed in the Oscan language in Horace's day.[37] Atella, the home town of Dossennus, symbolized crudity of manners as Athens did refinement.[38] The actor playing Dossennus would have been compelled by his mask and costume[39] to move on stage in a gross and vulgar way. The accusation levelled against Plautus in line 173 must be, therefore, that when he wrote a part for the *parasitus*

---

and *incongrue* (Dona. ad *Eun.* 798; Servius ad *Aen.* 4. 171, 4. 486, 6. 34, 8. 571) in commentary on other authors help to tie down Porphyrio's meaning at *Ep.* 2. 1. 171.

[31] See Hor. *Ars* 89-118, 220-50.

[32] See [Plut.] *Mor.* 853 d; Quint. *Inst.* 10. 1. 69 'mire custoditur ab hoc poeta decor'.

[33] On τὸ ἦθος etc. in the criticism of comedy see Dio Prus. *Or.* 18. 6; Donat. ad *Andr.* 560, 637, 875; ad *Eun.* 14, 15, 48, 214, 310; ad *Ad.* 61, 149, 176, 238, 304, 308, 407, 413, 492.

[34] Cf. the advice on the reading of comedy in the schoolroom at Dionys. Thr. 2, p. 6. 9 Uhlig, Σ ad loc. pp. 20. 10-12, 172. 27-173. 2, 306. 15-307. 7 Hilgard; Auson. *Protr.* 45-50, p. 23 Green. On the role given by the ancients to the voice in ὑπόκρισις see Eustathius ad Hom. *Od.* 4. 279, p. 1496. 47-9.

[35] On the stage-actor's gestures see Cic. *De or.* 3. 214-21; Quint. *Inst.* 11. 3. 91, 178-82; Macr. *Sat.* 3. 14. 11-12. Cicero brings the actor, as well as the poet, into his discussion of oratorical *decorum* at *De or.* 1. 129 and *Or.* 69-74. The 3rd-cent. AD Cassius Longinus advises the trainee orator to study the performances of tragic and comic actors (*Rhet. Graec.* i/2. 196) and defines ὑπόκρισις as μίμησις τῶν κατ' ἀλήθειαν ἑκάστῳ παρισταμένων ἠθῶν καὶ παθῶν καὶ διάθεσις σώματός τε καὶ τόνου φωνῆς πρόσφορος τοῖς ὑποκειμένοις πράγμασι (p. 194).

[36] See Varro, *LL.* 7. 95 (K. O. Mueller: ad obsenum *cod.*).

[37] See Strabo 5. 3. 6, p. 233 Casaubon.

[38] Cf. Cic. *Fam.* 7. 1. 3.

[39] Plaut. *Rud.* 535-6 is generally held to refer to the performance of an Atellan piece. For the use of masks by the Atellan performers see Festus, p. 238. 12-20, s.v. *personata*.

edax the result was something more appropriate to the well-known Atellane personage than to an Athenian gentleman down on his luck.[40] Comparable is the way Gellius criticizes Caecilius' presentation of the old man of Menander's Πλόκιον complaining about his jealous wife: 'alia nescio qua mimica inculcavit'.[41] Euanthius' praise of Terence and implied criticism of the other Republican comedians is also relevant: 'illud quoque inter Terentianas virtutes mirabile, quod eius fabulae eo sunt temperamento, ut neque extumescant ad tragicam celsitudinem neque abiciantur ad mimicam vilitatem.'[42] Neither of these passages ought, however, to be placed above the context of Horace's 'quantus sit Dossennus edacibus in parasitis'. Heinze replaced Kiessling's 'als was für ein Vielfraß sich Pl. in der Zeichnung des Parasiten erweise' with 'wie Plautus statt des immer eßlustigen Parasiten der griechischen Komödie die plumpe Karikatur der Vielfressers aus der Atellane gibt'. Zwierlein follows him with his talk of 'die Übertreibung des Possenhaften'.[43] Brink seems to me to get closer to the truth when he talks of 'the primitive and unartistic bearing' of Plautus' parasites. I should prefer, however, to relate the accusation to gross and vulgar language thought inappropriate to the parasite in particular and to comedy in general. 'Primitiveness' was something Horace attributed rather to the taste of some contemporary critics.

Pulpitum percurrere has an obvious literal sense, as does *non astricto socco*. One easily visualizes the actor running across the stage platform, having neglected to pull his slippers on tight, and perhaps even falling over.[44] It is more difficult to see at what apparent defect in Plautus' comic writing Horace aims his words. Heinze takes *soccus* as symbolizing the whole way of writing comedy and sees in line 174 'einen Tadel der *neglegentia*'.[45] Brink

---

[40] On the παράσιτος of Attic comedy see Nesselrath (1985) 88–121; (1990) 309–17; Brown (1992) 91–107. [41] 2. 23. 12. (adduced by Heinze).

[42] *De com.* 3. 5, p. 20.

[43] Cf. J. C. B. Lowe's arguments (1989) that Plautus added details which exaggerated the element of gluttony in the character of some of his parasites and that the παράσιτος of Attic comedy was regularly driven less by greed than by poverty and hunger.

[44] Cf. the *saltatio* described at Plautus at *Pseud.* 1273–80. For *soccus* of an individual comic personage's footwear see Plaut. *Cist.* 697 (of a slave); *Epid.* 725; *Persa* 124; Ter. *Haut.* 124.

[45] Earlier, on line 170, he preserves Kiessling's phrase 'Die Saloppheit der Komposition'. Lambin interpreted the verse as 'quam laxo, ac dissoluto socco fabulam peragat, id est quam negligenter, ac dissolute fabulas scribat'. Heinze's view was again Ritschl's ('die Lockerheit der Composition'; see above, n. 28).

on the other hand introduces again the notion of primitiveness: 'his comedy disordered, primitively unartistic'. He sees, as did Heinze, a link with lines 57–8 'dicitur . . . Plautus ad exemplar Siculi properare Epicharmi': 'sarcasm at the expense of the literary critics is likely, but the details are uncertain'. We should have expected a third particular criticism rather than such a general all-embracing one. Zwierlein suggests a criticism of the way Plautus shaped the dramatic action. Two objections can, however, be made against this suggestion. One would be that there is little correspondence between sloppy acting and incoherent plot-construction. The other would be that the kind of labour of correction urged by Horace upon dramatists could hardly affect a plot faultily constructed at the outset.

We are still, I should suggest, concerned in line 174 with the representation of comic types. It is now, however, a question of πάθος rather than ἦθος.[46] After the *ephebus amans*, the *pater attentus*, the *leno insidiosus*, and the *parasitus edax* comes the *servus currens*. No other personage could be represented as running on stage.[47] What Horace criticizes is the style in which the *servus currens* describes the occurrence that has caused him to arrive in such haste, perhaps more particularly the metrical pattern imposed on his words and phrases. Again we must return to the sixteenth century for a proper understanding.

Line 176 refers at the metaphorical level to a performance of a Plautine script and its reception in the theatre. *Recto talo* was, to judge by Persius 5. 104, pretty certainly a phrase of the common language. Ter. *Phorm.* 9–10 'quod si intellegeret, quom stetit olim nova, | actoris opera mage stetisse quam sua'[48] shows the theatrical background of Horace's *cadat an recto stet fabula talo*. The use of *cadere* could, like that of *stare*, have come from the theatre[49]—its absence from our record means nothing—or it could have been fashioned by Horace himself. The activities of gambling and wrestling ought not to be invoked.[50] At base, however, Horace can

---

[46] For τὸ πάθος etc. in the criticism of comedy see Varro, *Gramm.* fr. 40 Funaioli (Charisius, p. 315. 3–23); Donat. ad *Andr.* 131, 301. Note the general Stoic definition of literary πρέπον reported by Diogenes Laertius 7. 59: λέξις οἰκεία τῷ πράγματι.

[47] For the stock *servus currens* see Ter. *Haut.* 31, 37; *Eun.* 36.

[48] Not, however, *Hec.* 15, where *stare* is opposed to *exigi*.

[49] Note the use of *iacere* in theatrical criticism by Caesar (ap. Donat. *Vit. Ter.* 7, p. 9).

[50] Lambin cites Cicero's reference at *Fin.* 3. 54 to the gambler casting a *talus*. Heinze (not Kiessling) and Brink cite the wrestling metaphor at Cic. *Or.* 98.

only refer to some objectively assessable quality of the script. The whole of the preceding discussion indicates that it was a question of the adequacy or inadequacy, in regard to the representation of τὰ ἤθη and τὰ πάθη, of the Latin poet's verbal style, perhaps of the presence or absence of *vis*, of forcefulness.[51]

3. PRE-HORATIAN CRITICISM

It is also Zwierlein's view that Horace's assault on Plautus was something novel, the result both of his reading of highly interpolated texts of the comedian's scripts and of a change under way at his time in the way poets looked at their craft. Now even if I have successfully eliminated inconsistent characterization, unrealistic caricature of stock types, and incoherent plot-construction from the charges brought against Plautus at *Ep.* 2. I. 170–6, the general argument of the epistle to the Pisos indicates that Horace would not have been loath to bring such charges had a suitable occasion presented itself. On the other hand, it is hardly credible that a single positive estimate of Plautus prevailed before Horace's time, that negative judgements were entirely lacking. There are in any case, I should argue, unmistakable traces of such judgements in our record.[52]

In the prologue of the *Andria* (18–21) Naevius, Plautus, and Ennius are treated as supreme models in the organization of plots:

> qui quom hunc accusant, Naevium Plautum Ennium
> accusant quos hic noster auctores habet,
> quorum aemulari exoptat neglegentiam
> potius quam istorum obscuram diligentiam.

Terence throws the *neglegentia* of these poets defiantly in the face of his rivals. We may wonder, however, whether the *diligentes* themselves had not already explicitly attacked their predecessors, using the very word *neglegentia*.

---

[51] Cf. Caesar's criticism of Terence's style, ap. Donat. *Vit. Ter.* 7, p. 9 Wessner, 'lenibus atque utinam scriptis adiuncta foret vis'; Anon. *Rhet. Herenn.* 4. 16 'qui in mediocre genus orationis profecti sunt, si pervenire eo non potuerunt, errantes perveniunt ad confine genus eius generis . . . dissolutum, quod est sine nervis [verbis *codd.*] et articulis . . . fluctuans, eo quod fluctuat huc et illuc nec potest confirmate neque viriliter sese expedire'; Hor. *Ars* 26–7 'sectantem lenia [levia *v.l.*] deficiunt animique' (talking of the χαρακτῆρες τῆς λέξεως, the middle one of which was thought appropriate to comedy: Varro fr. 322 ap. Gellius 6. 14. 6).

[52] Blänsdorf (1974) concentrates on the positive aspects of the picture.

The author of the epigram on Plautus cited by Varro in his work *De poetis* refers admiringly to personified *Numeri innumeri*:

> postquam est mortem aptus Plautus, Comoedia luget,
> scaena est deserta, dein Risus Ludus Iocusque
> et Numeri innumeri simul omnes conlacrimarunt.[53]

The sense of *Numeri innumeri* has puzzled many. I should suggest that the epigrammatist made a paradoxical use of *innumerus* (i.e. in the sense of ἄρρυθμος) in defiance of some critic of Plautus' rhythmical structures.[54]

A feature of the biography of Plautus known to Varro[55] was the comedian's alleged interest in making money. Many commentators on *Ep.* 2. 1. 175-6 have suggested that the biographical detail instigated Horace's explanation of his lack of artistic care. We could as well suppose that one of the elements with which the original biographer worked was a hostile judgement on an aspect of Plautus' art.

Varro himself found Plautus' treatment of ἤθη to some degree defective, or at least inferior to that of other comic writers. In the fifth book of his *De sermone Latino*[56] he declared: 'ἤθη nullis aliis servare convenit quam Titinio, Terentio, Attae.' Plautus' name is significantly absent from the list.

A fragment of Varro's Menippean satire *Parmeno*[57] reports a comparison made between Caecilius, Terence, and Plautus: 'in quibus partibus in argumentis Caecilius poscit palmam, in ethesin Terentius, in sermonibus Plautus'. Friedrich Ritschl connected this with Horace's report of opinions held in his time about the same three comic poets.[58] The connection made by Ritschl has dominated subsequent discussion despite the scepticism guardedly emitted by

[53] Fr. 59 (Gellius 1. 24. 3). Skutsch (1972) conjectures *flent* in place of *dein*, Courtney (1993) 48 resurrects Orelli's deletion of *est*.

[54] Auson. *Protr.* 46-8, p. 23 Green 'et amabilis orsa Menandri | evolvenda tibi: tu flexu et acumine vocis | innumeros doctis accentibus effer' seems to refer to the rhythmical variety of Menander's trimeters (cf. Es. A. Hephaest. p. 115. 9-16 Consbruch θέλουσι [sc. οἱ κωμικοί] δοκεῖν διαλελυμένως διαλέγεσθαι καὶ μὴ ἐμμέτρως). That of Plautus' senarii was much greater and would have aroused similar comment.

[55] Fr. 88 (of the *De comoediis Plautinis*, from Gellius 3. 3. 14).

[56] Fr. 40 (Charisius, p. 315. 3-23).

[57] Fr. 399 Bücheler (Nonius, p. 374. 5-7).

[58] See his edition of the *Vita Terentii* in Reifferscheid (1860) 525 (= Ritschl 1877: 264). Ritschl makes no mention, however, of the judgement on Plautus.

Dahlmann in 1962[59] and firmly asserted by Brink in 1963[60] and in 1982.[61] Zwierlein takes *in sermonibus* as 'in der Dialogführung', being perhaps a little more careful than Kiessling, who declared in relation to Horace's 'dicitur . . . Plautus ad exemplar Siculi properare Epicharmi' that 'was die alten Kunstrichter an Plautus rühmten, war die Kunst seines Dialogs: *palmam poscit . . . in sermonibus Plautus . . .* es ist die rasche Lebhaftigkeit seiner Rede, welche an den Fluß der Trochaeen Epicharms erinnerte und der Vermutung, Plautus habe sich den großen sizilischen Dichter zum Muster genommen . . . die Unterlage bot'[62] or Leo, who wrote about 'der rasche und feurige Dialog, der Varro veranlasste, Plautus *in sermonibus* die Palme zu geben'.[63]

If the fragment is looked at coolly in isolation, the phrases *in argumentis* and *in ethesin* give no difficulty whatsoever. $\dot{\upsilon}\pi\dot{o}\theta\epsilon\sigma\iota\varsigma$/$\mu\hat{\upsilon}\theta\sigma\varsigma$/*argumentum* and $\ddot{\eta}\theta\eta$ were regular topics of dramatic criticism. 'Die Dialogführung' was not. There exists no corresponding noun in Greek or Latin; not even the late *diverbium*[64] could be so used. With *in sermonibus* Varro must have had $\lambda\acute{\epsilon}\xi\iota\varsigma$ in mind, the language which Plautus used in all parts of comedy, in monologues as well as dialogues. The plural form jolts when set against Varro's report of Aelius Stilo's view of *sermo Plautinus*[65] or against the title the former gave his work on Latinity, *De sermone latino*. Its use could, however, be attributed to a search for concinnity.[66] Whether Varro put the judgements on the three comedians forward in his own voice or attributed them to some other personage of his *satura* cannot now be known. It was in any case an individual set of judgements, designed to challenge those who heard it: *poscit palmam* means 'ought to be given the prize', not, as Nonius Marcellus suggests, 'receives the prize'. Plautus was not, it is clear, wholeheartedly approved of at the time in which the *satura* was set either for the construction of his plots or for the characterization of his personages.

---

[59] Dahlmann (1962) 63–4. Cf. Dahlmann (1953) 30–2, 60–1; Geller (1966) 48–51.   [60] Brink (1963a) 176–81.

[61] Brink (1982) 110–11.

[62] Kiessling's statement was kept by Heinze. Skutsch (1897) 1190 wrote merely of 'der Dialog'.   [63] Leo (1913) 138.

[64] Diomedes (*Gramm. Lat.* i. 491. 22–4) or his source would seem to be misinterpreting a technical term (*deverbium*).

[65] Fr. 321 (Quint. *Inst.* 10. 1. 99).

[66] Some late writers use the singular of a phrase or even of a word. Horace appears to use the plural with the sense of $\lambda\acute{\epsilon}\xi\iota\varsigma$ at *Ars* 69.

4. EPISTLES 2. 1. 57-9

> dicitur Afrani toga convenisse Menandro,
> Plautus ad exemplar Siculi properare Epicharmi,
> vincere Caecilius gravitate, Terentius arte.

We may now look again at Horace's account earlier in the epistle
to Augustus of some literary critic's praise of an aspect of Plautus'
comic writing.[67] Since Ritschl brought the fragment of Varro into
the debate the content of line 58 has been taken very closely with
that of line 59 and kept to some extent separate from line 57. Even
Brink makes at times a firm distinction between 'Afranius and the
Togata' and 'the Palliata of Plautus, Terence, and Caecilius',
although at other times he seeks to blur it.[68]

When it suited him Varro marked out two comic genres, the
fabula togata and the *fabula palliata*.[69] He had no difficulty, however,
in putting the authors of the two genres in the one category for
the purpose of comparison: fr. 40, for example, joined Titinius and
Atta with Terence. Horace was aware, and could have made use,
of the distinction, but nothing in lines 57-9 or its wider context
compelled him to do so. With the fragment of Varro's *Parmeno*
out of the way, a disinterested reader of lines 59-62 cannot but
group together the two epic poets Ennius and Naevius, the two
tragedians Pacuvius and Accius, the two comedians Afranius and
Plautus, and the further two comedians Caecilius and Terence. It
makes no moment that, whereas the younger Afranius precedes
the elder Plautus, in the other pairs the elder poet comes first. The
sense of *dicitur . . . ad exemplar Siculi properare Epicharmi* has never
been elucidated even to the full satisfaction of the elucidator. Brink
takes more seriously efforts to relate the statement to style and
metre than others have done, but concludes: 'the matter is still
open for discussion'.[70] He even moots the replacement of transmitted *properare* with *superare*. That would, however, leave the area
of the victory quite unspecified. Progress can be made, in my view,
by considering the comparison of Plautus with Epicharmus more

---

[67] An individual must have formulated the phrase. To whom Horace refers is
another question.

[68] Contrast Brink (1982) 107, 108 with 90, 103-4.

[69] See fr. 306 (Diomedes, *Gramm. Lat.* i. 489. 16-18).

[70] Brink (1982) 109-10, 419-20.

closely together with that of Afranius and Menander than with that of Caecilius and Terence.

There has never been any difficulty in translating literally *dicitur Afrani toga convenisse Menandro*—e.g. 'the toga of Afranius, it is said, would have fitted Menander'—or in suggesting the actual sense—e.g. 'Afranius' plays about the Latin bourgeoisie rank with those composed by Menander about the same part of Attic society.' That leaves it unclear, however, what in particular the two poets were valued for, what corresponded in their case to the *doctrina* of Pacuvius, the *altitudo* of Accius, the *gravitas* of Caecilius, the *ars* of Terence. A parallel question has to be asked concerning Plautus and Epicharmus: in what quality did they rival each other?

The answer lies, I submit, in the area of the distinction made by Terence at *Haut.* 35-40 between the *fabula stataria* and the sort of play whose roles demanded from the actor a lot of physical movement and vocal exertion:

> adeste aequo animo, date potestatem mihi
> statariam agere ut liceat per silentium,
> ne semper servus currens, iratus senex,
> edax parasitus, sycophanta autem inpudens,
> avarus leno adsidue agendi sint seni
> clamore summo, cum labore maxumo.

The commentators on Terence of late antiquity frequently make or extend the same distinction: e.g. Euanthius, *De com.* 4. 4, p. 22 'comoediae autem motoriae sunt aut statariae aut mixtae. motoriae turbulentae, statariae quietiores, mixtae ex utroque actu consistentes'; Donat. ad *Andr.* praef. 1. 2 'haec maiori ex parte motoria est'; ad *Eun.* praef. 1. 2 'itaque ex magna parte motoria est'; ad *Ad.* praef. 1. 2 'huius tota actio cum sit mixta ex utroque genere, ut fere Terentianae omnes praeter Heautontimorumenon, tamen maiore ex parte motoria est; nam statarios locos perpaucos habet'; 24. 2 'aut ipsi senes in statario charactere partem aperient, in motorio partem ostendent. nam duo agendi sunt principales modi, motorius et statarius, ex quibus ille tertius nascitur, qui dicitur mixtus'; 299 'hic locus secundum artem comicam servum currentem exprimit et nuntiantem mala maxima itaque pars scaenae motoria est'; *Hec.* praef. 1. 2 'est autem mixta motoriis actibus ac statariis'; *Σ* Bemb. *Haut.* 36 'aut statariae dicuntur †personae† aut motoriae. statariae dicuntur ubi personae tranquillae sunt, motoriae autem ubi sunt procaces servi mali.' A passage of the *Brutus*, 116 'volo enim ut in scaena sic etiam in foro non eos modo laudari, qui celeri motu et difficili utantur, sed eos etiam quos statarios appellant, quorum sit illa simplex in agendo veritas, non molesta',[71] suggests that in Cicero's time the distinction was applied to actors. We have Horace applying it in lines 57–8 to poets.

The mention of the *toga* in line 57 draws the hearer's attention to more than the class into which some critics placed the plays Afranius wrote. I have already argued that Horace ignored in lines 57–9 the division of *comoediae* into *palliatae* and *togatae*. The *toga* was a heavy and voluminous outer garment much more difficult to arrange on the person of the wearer than the simple rectangular Greek ἱμάτιον. A Roman citizen wore it, or was expected to wear it, on all public occasions of any solemnity. It prevented undignified haste of movement and would have tended to discourage noisy forms of utterance.[72] It was the stately aspect of the plays of Afranius that Horace had primarily in mind. No other extant writer comments on this aspect. Seneca, however, remarks on the *severitas* of the sentiments expressed in *fabulae togatae* and puts the genre midway between tragedy and comedy of the Greek type.[73] Donatus notes the absence from the *togatae* of slaves cleverer than their owners.[74] A parallel emphasis on the quietness, if not the stateliness, of Menander's plays is perhaps to be seen in the verses in which Cicero compares them with Terence's versions:

> tu quoque qui solus lecto sermone Terenti
> conversum expressumque Latina voce Menandrum
> in medium nobis sedatis vocibus effers,
> quiddam come loquens atque omnia dulcia dicens.[75]

> vocibus] motibus *Barth*

The use of the verb *properare* in relation to Plautus in Horace's following verse similarly has to do both with a norm of social behaviour and with the kind of situation and personage to which Plautus' plays seemed to give prominence. Persons of high status

---

[71] At 239 the adjective *statarius* is applied to an orator not given to vigorous gesture.

[72] Increasing neglect of tradition in dress worried the emperor Augustus (Suet. *Aug.* 40. 5). For the dignity of the *toga* see the proverbial remark at Martial 2 praef.

[73] *Ep.* 8. 8.   [74] *Eun.* 57.   [75] Ap. Donat. *Vita Ter.* 7, p. 9.

cultivated in public a slow and steady manner of progress from one point to another. Only a slave had to do his business at a run.[76] Modern observers have frequently remarked on the importance given by Plautus to servile and related roles and on the liveliness of scenes of his plays in which slaves, parasites, sycophants, and the like appeared. Nothing comparable is recorded from ancient discussions except the case in question, but that may be an accident. The ancient tradition on Epicharmus is similarly exiguous, and too little survives of his actual dramatic writing to allow modern scholars even to guess at what roles had the greatest prominence. Nothing stands in the way, however, of believing that the Sicilian poet's mode of presenting the slave and the socially subordinate person, whether a citizen or a metic or a slave, sometimes attracted critical notice.

What the literary critics admired in Afranius and the Attic Menander would have been the way their respective styles matched the kinds of personages they most liked to bring on stage. Their choice of words would have been emphasized. Where the arrangement of words and metrical patterning in particular were concerned, Afranius had, as far as we can see, more in common with the older Latin playwrights than with Menander.[77] The achievement of a parallel degree of stylistic decorum would have coupled Plautus and the Syracusan Epicharmus in the eyes of the critics. The latter was admired in many circles for his φιλοτεχνία[78] and was thought to have written in Doric as much out of a belief in its superiority to other Greek dialects[79] as out of necessity. There is certainly no way in which the notion of 'quickness' can be associated with the choice of words. On the other hand, some types of poetic rhythm, and particularly the iambic and the trochaic, the basic rhythms of comedy, had the reputation of being 'quick'.[80] Unfortunately, not enough of Epicharmus' iambics survive for us to institute a meaningful comparison between his practice and either Menander's or Plautus'. Metrical patterning did, however,

---

[76] See Ar. *Nub.* 964–6; Plato, *Charm.* 159 B; Alexis com. fr. 265, *PCG* ii. 170 Kassel–Austin; Plaut. *Poen.* 522–3; *Alex.* 42. 2.; Servius auct. ad *Aen.* 1. 46.

[77] Cf. *Gramm. Lat.* vi. 79. 1–6.

[78] See Anon. *De com.* in cod. E Aristophan. 4, p. 7 Kaibel.

[79] See Iamb. *Vit. Pyth.* 241.

[80] See on the iambic rhythm Hor. *Ars* 251–2; Sacerdos, *Gramm. Lat.* vi. 518. 12–20; Terentianus Maurus 1383; on the trochaic see Arist. *Rhet.* 3. 8, 1408[b] 36–1409[a] 1; on both Aristides Quintil. *Mus.* 2. 15, p. 83. 3–4 Winnington-Ingram.

offer at least one point of comparison with Plautus. The number and variety of Epicharmus' metres were considerable and excited notice. Theocritus' epigram on the Syracusan poet[81] employed three trochaic tetrameters, two iambic dimeters, and five Reizian cola. We have in late grammatical writing two references[82] to theory associating the metrical structures of the Latin poets with those of fifth-century Attic comedy. Horace's talk of an *exemplar Epicharmi* would, I suggest, have been related to another theory making Syracusan comedy their metrical model. The 'quickness' of the Syracusan rhythms suited, I suggest, in the view of the critic denounced by Horace, the situations and persons Plautus most liked to present.

Brink points to a verbal similarity between Horace's *dicitur Afrani toga convenisse Menandro* and a statement composed by Afranius himself, doubtless for a *prologus*, regarding his relationship with his comic predecessors, Greek and Latin:

> fateor. sumpsi non ab illo modo,
> sed ut quisque habuit, conveniret quod mihi,
> quodque me non posse melius facere credidi,
> etiam a Latino.[83]

Brink wonders 'whether Horace's archaist did not deliberately refer to the old playwright, adroitly lifting Afranius' *conueniret* to express his own aesthetic judgement'.[84] If there is anything in that idea, it may also be the case that the 'archaist' seized upon *properare* as a word almost obsessively favoured by Plautus' personages[85] in order to characterize a salient feature of the poet's style.

5. CONCLUSION

Securing assent to a positive interpretation of almost any passage of Horace is a difficult task. I hope I have at least succeeded in undermining any confidence that may exist in the possibility of

---

[81] (*AP Pal.* 9. 600).

[82] *Gramm. Lat.* vi. 78. 19–79. 6, 564. 7–20.

[83] 25–8 (Macr. *Sat.* 6. 1. 4).

[84] Brink (1982) 107–8.

[85] The verb occurs in 16 other places in Horace's writings in more or less its literal sense. Plautus has it disproportionately more often than Terence (99 times in 21 plays [not all complete] ~ 16 in 6).

establishing on the basis of the epistle to Augustus a firm outline of the history of Roman literary taste in the first century BC. Neither Horace nor any man of his generation was, in my view, the first to find fault with aspects of Plautus' comic writing. Lines 57–8 did not allude to praise of Plautus for the formation of his scenes of dialogue. Lines 170–2 did not attack him for inconsistency of characterization, or line 173 for exaggerating the features of a stock personage, or line 174 for leaving loose threads in his plots. The epistle tells us nothing about the state of the text of the comedies at the time of its writing, nothing as to whether Horace read the twenty-one 'Varronian' plays in the shape in which they have come down to ourselves. Both the praise reported and the blame asserted have to do with features of style which are difficult, now that Latin is a dead language, to get hold of and thus of no real service to anyone seeking to distinguish the false from the genuine in the Plautine paradosis.

13

Horace and the Aesthetics of Politics

D. P. FOWLER

THE attitude of Horace to the Augustan regime—'Horaz und Augustus'—is one of the perennial themes of Horatian criticism. As E. Doblhofer commented in his book *Die Augustuspanegyrik des Horaz in formalhistorischer Sicht*, critics have often divided on national lines:

Der deutsche Untertan mit seinem Respekt vor der Obrigkeit und der Staatsmacht, der individualistische, angelsächsische Demokrat und der Italiener der neuen Republik, der es Augustus büßen lassen möchte, daß der Faschismus seinen Duce mit dem Princeps gleichsetzte—sie haben wohl alle ihre Spuren auch in der Horazinterpretation hinterlassen und das Bild gefärbt, das man sich von dem Verhältnis Horazens zu Augustus machte.[1]

As often in the rhetoric of *Rezeptionsästhetik*, these attitudes are set against Doblhofer's own methodology, which is depicted as more historical and scientific than its rivals. He examines the Greek panegyrical tradition in relation to Horace's praise of Augustus, and argues that where the commonplaces are found in bald and unoriginal form we have no reason to see personal engagement,

Rather than the usual acknowledgements, which in this case would be extensive, I should like to offer a memory of my first supervision with Robin Nisbet. I came into his room in Corpus, with that vast desk covered with books and papers, the radical youth prepared to have my brilliancies tempered by a dusty philologist of the old school. But we sat not at the desk, but in those high-backed chairs either side of the fire: and after we had been talking for ten minutes or so, I found that I was the one who was saying things like 'I've never thought of that' and thinking 'Isn't that going a bit far?' What I learnt from Robin (as earlier from Colin Macleod) was above all precisely always to take one's ideas further than one thought one could: as soon as one got something straight, to widen the focus and complicate it all again, looking beyond Latin to Greek, beyond the classical world to other periods, and beyond the discipline of classics to other approaches. All that, and the prose rhythm of Cicero too: riches I shall never forget.

[1] Doblhofer (1966) 13.

but where Horace is clever, he must be sincere: 'Je weiter er sich jeweils von der Tradition entfernt und loslöst oder je selbständiger er sie umschafft, um so "aufrichtiger", so wollen wir schließen, preist er den Herrscher'; '. . . stehen . . . neben den überlieferten, geläufigen Topoi andere Ausdrucksformen des Herrscherlobes, so werden wir dem Dichter eigenes Suchen nach eigenem Ausdruck— und damit auch eigene Überzeugung zubilligen müssen.'[2] So, for example, when Horace makes fun in *Satires* I. 7 of Persius' praise of Brutus, the hackneyed topoi reveal the absurdity of the panegyric:

> laudat Brutum laudatque cohortem:
> solem Asiae Brutum appellat stellasque salubris
> appellat comites excepto Rege; canem illum
> invisum agricolis sidus venisse. (23-6)

When, however, Horace compares Augustus to the sun in *Odes* 4. 5, this is much more *geschmacksvoll*, and therefore sincere:

> lucem redde tuae, dux bone, patriae:
> instar veris enim vultus ubi tuus
> adfulsit populo, gratior it dies
> et soles melius nitent. (5-8)

Others, of course, have found this stress on Augustus' meteorological control more of a *reductio ad absurdum*: and it is hard to see how it could be defended against this except by appealing to the accepted topoi of panegyric—in which case our criterion for sincerity disappears. The argument here is absurd,[3] but my purpose is not to criticize Doblhofer's particular thesis: his book is extremely valuable for its detailed treatment of the panegyric tradition. Rather, it shows how any concern for 'sincerity' or even 'authenticity'[4] is a blind alley. Here, for instance is a Horatian passage in praise of a later Duce, from E. Balbo's *Augusto e Mussolini* (Rome, 1937—or should we say 'Anno XV'?):

Dal seno fecondo della Rivoluzione stessa che risuona e si protende nel futuro, sorgerà l'epico Cantore che narrerà per l'eternità il Fascismo e il suo Duce.

Dirà che i campi fertili, i pascoli opimi, che ampi si rispecchiano negli occhi glauchi degli armenti e le città nuove: Littoria, Sabaudia, Pontinia, Aprilia e tante altre, emersero, come per improvviso miracolo, dalle acque indomabili e mortifere di lande sconfinate.

Dirà che la terra, restituita alla sua naturale funzione, redenta dalla

---

[2] Doblhofer (1966) 16, 84.   [3] See Nisbet (1969).   [4] Cf. La Penna (1963).

bonifica integrale, sottratta all'esoso egoismo dell'interesse particolare, assumendo funzione sociale, fu potente fonte di ricchezza nazionale, oasi di sanità fisica e morale, e le genti rurali ebbero il primo posto nei ranghi e dignità di uomini.

Canterà l'epopea e il rinnovamento del popolo italiano, le legioni vittoriose che portarono i segni del littorio nelle lontane e barbare terre del Africa orientale e dirà che, deposte le armi, le dissodarono e civilizzarono.

Il mito narrerà alle genti e alle epoche venture che un giovanetto irrequieto, dal volto umano e coi segni del genio, sospinato da una forza interna e illuminato da una luce celeste, strumento della volontà divina, protetto da una forza occulta, si partì dall'officina paterna per compiere un prodigio.

Con travaglio di lotta e di pensiero, di sofferenze e di privazioni, liberò l'Italia dagli uomini piccoli, innalzandola ad una potenza mai raggiunta.

Did Mr Balbo really mean this? It is not that we could not spin a yarn about whether this was sincere or not, but that to examine this language in those terms looks like a wasted opportunity. What surely matters here is what is said, not why it was said: the discourse of Fascism, not the beliefs of Fascists.

This move from questions like 'Did Horace or Ovid like Augustus?' to 'What is the relation that we construct between Horatian or Ovidian discourse and that of other contemporary systems?' is a familiar one in contemporary criticism. What comes next tends to take two forms. Either, in the manner of the so-called New Historicism, it is shown how the dominant 'official' discourse encompasses and dominates all other systems, or, in the manner[5] of deconstruction, it is shown how the inevitable contradictions in those systems prevent any stable dominance.[6] What I want to do in this piece is firmly in the older and more conservative second tradition: I want to show that the contradictions in the traditions which are drawn on in Horace's works make panegyric of Augustus an impossibility. (This is actually a milder version of the wider claim that panegyric is always in a sense 'impossible', which I endorse but for the moment shall not defend.) My presentation of the choice between historicism and oppositionalist criticism as a sort of whim might look like cynicism, and there is a sense in which I

---

[5] Cf. Woodman and Powell (1992) 258 n. 14.

[6] For the contrast cf. Dunn (forthcoming): 'whereas post-structuralists, in rejecting the aesthetic unity of new Criticism, celebrated various subversions of unity, authority, and ideology, cultural criticism tends to find a new, overriding order in the cultural system that shapes and determines literary production'.

believe that which tactic you take is a matter of personal preference. The ideological climate is also, however, a factor: if everybody else is heading for the one pole, one has a duty to go the other way. But anyone who opts to take apart Horatian panegyric rather than putting it back together has to resist all the more strongly the seductions of essentialism. If we find that the Horatian attempt to accommodate Callimacheanism and Epicureanism to praise of the great is unsuccessfully self-contradictory (as we shall), we must beware of contrasting that with an ideology of our own which without contradiction plainly reflects the reality of the matter: because there is no such 'master narrative' to tell of Augustus or anyone else. There is no escaping contradiction for any observer historically situated in a society with as complex an inheritance as our own (or the Romans'). The *best* we can hope for is some 'energizing contradictions' in the phrase of Charles Martindale, writing of Virgil:

Virgil's myth potently mediates, or massages, a necessary 'contradiction' within the spiritual ideal of Rome, which is simultaneously the *caput rerum*, the metropolis which Augustus found brick and left marble, and an idyll of primitivism and rural simplicity, sweet especial rural scene. On this reading there is not so much conflict as the (attempted) *erasure* of conflict, in the interests of Roman identity and Augustan ideology. Rome is both an empire of unsurpassed might and yet, at heart, a simple country community. (Compare some myths of modern America, at once superpower and land of the lone cowboy.) Ideologies, in other words, may hammer together energising 'contradictions', which are not then felt as contradictions.[7]

But the recognition that if we want to set ourselves up as rebellious iconoclasts against the myths of power we are in the grip of an enlightenment myth ourselves whose foundations are no more secure need not lead to the abandonment of the oppositionalist tradition. Even Martindale cannot quite bring himself to leave out the 1960s flashback of that little '(attempted)' qualification. It is still as valuable an occupation to take apart what others have hammered together as to forge new chains.[8]

My title, 'Horace and the Aesthetics of Politics', is of course a nod in the direction of Walter Benjamin's famous dictum that

---

[7] Martindale (1993*b*) 51. Cf. Fowler (forthcoming), and Tom Cole's piece in the same volume.

[8] There are some suggestive reflections on non-positivist oppositional reading in Sharrock (forthcoming).

Fascism renders politics aesthetic while Communism responds by politicizing art.[9] The tag is meant partly just to make the general point that Horatian politics is bound up with Horatian poetics: it is in that union that I shall seek my deconstructive opening. But I also want to take seriously the Fascist view of the ruler as artist. This has many ramifications in ancient culture: one thinks, for instance, of Richard Gordon's identification of public sacrifice as the ultimate aesthetic act under the Empire.[10] I want to stress the importance of this for panegyric. Recent studies of the Renaissance have laid great stress on the property of 'magnificence' in the ruler's display, and its roots in Aristotle's doctrine of μεγαλο-πρέπεια,[11] and many aspects of this topic have of course received treatment in Paul Veyne's *Bread and Circuses*.[12] Essential to Aristotle's account in the *Nicomachean Ethics* is the point that μεγαλοπρέπεια differs from simple liberality in size: it is *big* spending, a sublime act, particularly on public matters, though Aristotle allows that it may also apply to semi-private events like weddings:

Those for whom we regard it as right and proper to make such donations are people with suitable incomes derived from property acquired by their own exertions or inherited from their ancestors or relations; or they may be persons of good family or high distinction or otherwise specially qualified. For all these are important advantages and take a high place in the estimation of the public. Now to these requirements the magnificent man answers perfectly, and it is in just such displays of magnificence that this virtue finds scope, as we have noted, these being the grandest and most highly esteemed forms it can take. But magnificence may be displayed also on unique private occasions, such as a marriage or something of that sort which may happen to excite public interest or attract people of importance, or parties to celebrate the arrival or departure of friends from abroad, or the exchange of complimentary presents. For the magnificent man reveals his character in spending not upon himself but on public objects; his gifts are a sort of dedication. It is also like him to furnish his house in a way suitable to his means, for that gives him a kind of distinction. And it is his way to spend more on things that are made to last than on things that are not, for it is the lasting things that are most beautiful and noble . . .[13]

---

[9] Benjamin (1968) 244.   [10] Beard and North (1990) 193 (and *passim*).

[11] See esp. Fraser Jenkins (1970); further bibliography in Green (1990) at 98 n. 2. On the related concept of greatness as μεγαλοψυχία see Held (1993), esp. 102–7; much of interest is promised in a forthcoming book by Carlin Barton on honour in the Roman world.

[12] Veyne (1990), esp. ch. 1 (7–8, 14–18) and ch. 4 (347–8).

[13] *NE* 4. 2, 1122ᵇ29 ff., trans. J. A. K. Thomson.

But magnificence has to be appropriately controlled: ὁ δὲ μεγαλο-
πρεπὴς ἐπιστήμονι ἔοικεν· τὸ πρέπον γὰρ δύναται θεωρῆσαι καὶ
δαπανῆσαι μεγάλα ἐμμελῶς, 'the magnificent man is like someone
with knowledge, because he can observe what is appropriate and
spend large sums with care' (4. 2, 1122ᵃ34–5). ἐπιστήμων here
is variously translated by modern interpreters as 'connoisseur'
or 'artist': Aspasius in his commentary glosses it τεχνίτης and
compares a cobbler and a painter.[14] Stewart (1892) develops the
picture in his note on 1122ᵇ14: 'The result produced by the
liberal man is merely a κτῆμα—something that is materially useful
to the recipient, and has its market value, whereas the result produced by a magnificent man is of the nature of a work of art. It is
θαυμαστόν—"displays genius and imagination".' Now I am not
concerned with how much of this can be read back into Aristotle's
en passant comparison, merely to note that praise of the sublime
acts of the great inevitably involves an aesthetic attitude towards
them, and leads easily to the view of the great as men of 'genius
and imagination', Balbo's Mussolini leaving his father's workshop
'per compiere un prodigio'.

One further aspect of this fetishism of wealth and power is the
central trope of all *Herrscherpanegyrik*, the ruler as superhuman,
the ruler as divine.[15] God too is an artist, of peculiar sublimity: his
works are wonderful, and worthy of praise. God as king—as in the
pseudo-Aristotelian *On the Cosmos*[16]—or the king as god—as in
Pythagorean writings[17]—alike produce Great Works. How could
any mortal artist hope to compete with such perfection? The way
I pose that question immediately brings to mind the *recusatio*. The
poet cannot compete with regal and divine artists: it is not his to
thunder, but theirs. So, at the end of the *Georgics*, Virgil contrasts
his lowly achievement with that of Augustus:

> haec super arvorum cultu pecorumque canebam
> et super arboribus, Caesar dum magnus ad altum
> fulminat Euphraten bello victorque volentis
> per populos dat iura viamque adfectat Olympo. (4. 559–62)

[14] Aspasius, *CAG* xix/1. 105. 2 (cf. also Heliodorus, *CAG* xix/2. 69. 22).

[15] For an excellent recent discussion of some aspects of this see Feeney (1991),
especially the chapter on Ovid.

[16] See esp. 5, 396ᵃ33 ff; 6, 399ᵃ15 ff.

[17] e.g. ps.-Ecphantus *On Kings* ed. Thesleff (1965) 79 ff. (cf. Delatte 1942; Thesleff
1961: 65–71). On the caution necessary in relation to the use of this material cf.
Murray (1968) 676–7; Stevenson (1992) 435.

And similarly Tibullus contrasts himself as a love poet with Messalla:

> te bellare decet terra, Messalla, marique,
> ut domus hostiles praeferat exuvias:
> me retinent vinctum[18] formosae vincla puellae,
> et sedeo duras ianitor ante fores.   (1. 1. 53–6)

The direction of my argument will I hope be plain. If we start to think of the deeds of the Great and the Good in aesthetic terms, as rival artists, then poetics have a potentially political import. Caesar thunders on the Euphrates: but isn't that bad art, combining thunderous bombast with the tumid Assyrian river?[19] Isn't Greatness itself suspect? The polite tones of the *recusatio*, it is a cliché to say, conceal a poetic manifesto in which the small-scale genres are actually *preferred* to sublimity on aesthetic grounds: where does that leave the artistic achievement of the Great Leader?

I take the task of panegyric for a writer like Horace to be to keep us from asking those questions, to keep the aesthetic preference for a particular type of poetry separate from the political endorsement of a particular ruler. And I take it to be an impossible task, if we face Horace not with a reader eager to co-operate in this process but with one prepared to accept linkages 'across the grain'. In the end, such an 'alert' reader cannot in good faith escape making the connections we are told to avoid. In the rest of this paper I want to look at exactly how the attempt is made to direct and control our aesthetic judgement of Augustus, and at why it fails. The first argument might simply be that I have manufactured this connection between poetics and politics by my notion of the ruler as artist, and that there is no reason to foist this on Horace. In fact, however, it has often been observed that one of the most distinctive features of Horace's work is a union of Callimachean poetics with Epicurean stress on the simple life: the union, as Mette put it in one of the best treatments of the topic,[20] of *genus tenue* and *mensa tenuis* encapsulated in *Odes* 2. 16:

---

[18] I should prefer the *victum* of Voss and Mueller, which does not duplicate *vincla* and which suits the contrast with Messalla's conquests. Either way, the poet is always a loser, the great man always a victor.
[19] I accept the link with Callimachus' *Hymn to Apollo* noticed by Thomas and Scodel (1984); cf. Clauss (1988).
[20] Mette (1961a). Cf. Syndikus (1972–3) i. 454; Bramble (1974) 156–73 ('Grandeur and Humility'); Nisbet and Hubbard (1978) on *Odes* 2. 16. 38.

vivitur parvo bene, cui paternum
splendet in mensa *tenui* salinum
nec levis somnos timor aut cupido
    sordidus aufert.   (13-16)

te greges centum Siculaeque circum
mugiunt vaccae, tibi tollit hinnitum
apta quadrigis equa, te bis Afro
    murice tinctae

vestiunt lanae: mihi parva rura et
spiritum Graiae *tenuem* Camenae
Parca non mendax dedit et malignum
    spernere vulgus.   (33-40)

The simple life that is represented by Horace's table is mirrored in the simplicity of his poetics, the refusal of sublime inspiration represented by his *spiritum . . . tenuem*. The *locus classicus* for this union of Callimacheanism and Epicureanism is *Satires* I. I:

        vel dic quid referat intra
naturae finis viventi, iugera centum an
mille aret? 'at suave est ex magno tollere acervo.'
dum ex parvo nobis tantundem haurire relinquas,
cur tua plus laudes cumeris granaria nostris?
ut tibi si sit opus liquidi non amplius urna
vel cyatho et dicas 'magno de flumine mallem
quam ex hoc fonticulo tantundem sumere.' eo fit,
plenior ut siquos delectet copia iusto,
cum ripa simul avolsos ferat Aufidus acer.
at qui tantuli eget quanto est opus, is neque limo
turbatam haurit aquam neque vitam amittit in undis.   (49-60)

The person who refuses to risk drowning in the great swollen river of sublimity is making a decision which is at once poetic and philosophical: and thereby political too.[21] As John Bramble put it in another of the standard treatments of this alliance of art and life: 'As we might expect given the principle of correspondence between style and character, letters and Bios, the exponent of the lower forms correlates his attitude of scorn for physical enormity with abhorrence from the grandiose and inflated in literature. Anything *grande*, *magnum*, *pingue* or *tumidum* is automatically shunned.'[22]

---

[21] On the Callimachean elements here see conveniently Freudenburg (1993) 187-90.   [22] Bramble (1974) 158. Cf. Gowers (1993), esp. 40-6.

Then again, in *Odes* 1. 35, Horace prays to Fortune to keep Augustus safe for future conquests:

> serves iturum Caesarem in ultimos
> orbis Britannos et iuvenum recens
>   examen, Eois timendum
>   partibus Oceanoque rubro.   (29–32)

But how does this act of imperialism sit with the urge to live *intra naturae finis?* More consistent are the calls to retirement Horace makes to Quinctius in *Odes* 2. 11:

> quid bellicosus Cantaber et Scythes,
> Hirpine Quincti, cogitet Hadria
>   divisus obiecto, remittas
>   quaerere nec trepides in usum
>
> poscentis aevi pauca,   (1–5)

or to Maecenas in 3. 29:

> tu civitatem quis deceat status
> curas et urbi sollicitus times,
>   quid Seres et regnata Cyro
>   Bactra parent Tanaisque discors.
>
> prudens futuri temporis exitum
> caliginosa nocte premit deus
>   ridetque, si mortalis ultra
>   fas trepidat.   (25–32)

If it is good to be a Callimachean Epicurean, to honour small things and respect the boundaries of the simple life, how can it also be good to hitch one's wagon to the star of sublimity and greatness?

Now, the very examples I have chosen will, I hope, suggest a number of objections. I am not making the proper distinctions here: I am reading anachronistically, because I have not tried to see the perceptual filters which would have enabled the ancient audience to distinguish between, for instance, a merchant's crossing the sea for gain and the legitimate expansion of the Roman empire. Is that not the point of Juno's injunction in *Odes* 3. 3, that if Rome avoids the greed that Troy represents, it will conquer the world?

> horrenda late nomen in ultimas
> extendat oras, qua medius liquor
>   secernit Europen ab Afro,
>   qua tumidus rigat arva Nilus,

> aurum inrepertum et sic melius situm,
> cum terra celat, spernere fortior
> quam cogere humanos in usus
> omne sacrum rapiente dextra.   (45-52)

And that *tumidus* of the Nile[23] suggests another point: should not
we see the Roman expansion as a civilizing and *taming* action,
which restores boundaries rather than removing them, which
defeats arrogance and bombast like Operation Desert Storm?
Compare, for instance, Horace's injunction to Valgius in *Odes* 2. 9:

> desine mollium
> tandem querellarum et potius nova
> cantemus Augusti tropaea
> Caesaris et rigidum Niphaten,
>
> Medumque flumen gentibus additum
> victis *minores* volvere vertices
> *intraque praescriptum* Gelonos
> *exiguis* equitare campis.   (17-24)

Augustus will make good Callimacheans of the Geloni if it kills
them.[24]

Moreover, if one looks to the philosophical side of Horace's
ideology, one can see this as a special case of a more important
objection. It is not just that the Epicurean good life for Horace is
compatible with the epic achievements of the Boss, the latter
ensures the former. As Matthew Santirocco remarks of *Odes* 3. 14,
public and private are 'not so much juxtaposed as interrelated. The
day can be festive for Horace precisely because Caesar rules the
earth.'[25] The topos is implicit in *Odes* 3. 29, where the reference to
Maecenas' *curae* is a tribute to his power (and that of his master),
and explicit of Augustus more than once: so most baldly in the last
of the *Odes*:

> custode rerum Caesare non furor
> civilis aut vis exiget otium,
> non ira, quae procudit ensis
> et miseras inimicat urbis.   (4. 15. 17-20)

---

[23] Cf. 4. 3. 8 'regum tumidas contuderit minas' etc.
[24] Similarly, when Augustus defeats the Euphrates at the end of *Aeneid* 8, is that
not a victory for style *and* civilization over the inappropriate thunder of anarchy? If
Callimacheanism is about control rather than wild inspiration, may it not go rather
well with Fascism and its neo-classical rejection of *entartete Kunst*?
[25] Santirocco (1985) 130.

Moreover, if we stress Horace's Epicureanism, is not this perfectly Epicurean? The Epicureans favoured monarchy as a political system precisely because it enabled the ordinary citizen to stop worrying about politics and get on with life.[26] Let Caesar run the country, and have another drink:

> quis Parthium paveat, quis gelidum Scythen,
> quis Germania quos horrida parturit
> fetus, incolumi Caesare? quis ferae
>   bellum curet Hiberiae?
>
> (*Odes* 4. 5. 25–8)

Is it not reasonable for Horace to join in the prayer at the end of this, the most Fascist of his *Odes*?

> longas o utinam, dux bone, *ferias*
> praestes Hesperiae.   (37–8)

Infinite power flows down, infinite responsibility flows up:[27] the consequences are well drawn by Syndikus,[28] but an Epicurean does not have to view them with distaste:

Früher fühlte sich jeder Römer für den Staat und dessen Wohl verantwortlich; in unserem Gedicht und noch mehr zu Beginn der Epistel II. 1 wird diese Verantwortung ganz dem Kaiser anheimgegeben. Der Bürger genießt nur noch die Früchte einer segensreichen Regierung, im Grunde ist er nicht mehr selbstbewußter *civis Romanus*, sondern ein zufriedener, dankbarer Untertan. Der Staat hatte begonnen, dem Römer etwas Fremdes zu werden, nicht mehr Sache der Öffentlichkeit, sondern Sache des Kaisers,[29] der das Regiment ganz an sich gezogen hatte.

Being on holiday all the while sounds rather nice.[30]

---

[26] Cf. e.g. Kleve and Longo Auricchio (1992) 226: 'The Epicureans emphasised private life as an ideal: *bene vixit qui bene latuit*. One lost one's peace of mind if one meddled in the dispositions of the mighty. Epicurean rhetoric was meant for peaceful learning and panegyric. There was no need for the despot to expect flaming speeches for freedom from that part . . .' For a different emphasis in relation to Epicurean politics see Fowler (1989*b*).

[27] The Leadership Principle: 'unquestioned authority of the leader, combined with fullest responsibility'—Hitler (1937) 137 (and often quoted unconsciously in modern textbooks of management): but cf. 117 against the 'passive obedience and childlike faith' typical of monarchy.

[28] Syndikus (1972–3) ii. 345.

[29] On the 'privatization' of the public sphere under Augustus cf. Feeney (1992).

[30] The epistemological consequences of this Augustan abandonment of responsibility have been brilliantly sketched by Alessandro Schiesaro in respect of the move away from an aspiration to independent knowledge (as seen in the *De rerum*

Now I do not at all deny that these mechanisms exist to keep separate what I have tried to confuse, nor that my attempt to break these barriers is in a sense unhistorical. My claim is that from a different point of view such readings involve bad faith, that they necessarily entail turning a blind eye to obvious analogies. I am inclined to believe in fact that these analogies were more present to the ancient consciousness than is often supposed, but that is not part of my claim here. The problem with the Epicurean defence of kingship is that it enables government, but not panegyric. The Epicurean will be happy(-ish) in a moderate dictatorship, but she will not want to be boss, nor will she admire the king: and in this, of course, Epicureanism and Stoicism can come together:

> nil admirari prope res est una, Numici,
> solaque, quae possit facere et servare beatum.
> hunc solem et stellas et decedentia certis
> tempora momentis sunt qui formidine nulla
> inbuti spectent: quid censes munera terrae,
> quid maris extremos Arabas ditantis et Indos
> ludicra, quid plausus et amici dona Quiritis,
> quo spectanda modo, quo sensu credis et ore?

> (*Ep.* 1. 6. 1–8)

In a familiar tactic, Horace's use of *plausus et amici dona Quiritis* is meant to point the reader away from the Boss to the Great and Good of the Roman Republican tradition, but it doesn't work. One can of course stress that the Great Man is resistant to this sort of thing: I have no doubt that many would have seen Augustus in the opening of *Odes* 3. 3, for instance (as the recall of *Sat.* 2. 1 suggests):[31]

> iustum et tenacem propositi virum
> non civium ardor prava iubentium,
> non vultus instantis tyranni
> mente quatit solida neque Auster,

natura) to the scepticism and abandonment to authority represented in his view by the *Georgics*: cf similarly Schiesaro (forthcoming) on the *Eclogues*: 'It is not the analogical science praised by Lucretius that can help Tityrus, but a form of knowledge which depends on mutually reinforcing bonds between social and religious powers, a form of knowledge, in sum, that ultimately recognizes its subordination and learns how to "know the gods" . . .' There are, naturally, other ways to read the *Georgics* and *Eclogues*.

[31] *Sat.* 2. 1. 16–20 'attamen et iustum poteras et scribere fortem . . .'

> dux inquieti turbidus Hadriae,
> nec fulminantis magna manus Iovis:
>   si fractus inlabatur orbis,
>   inpavidum ferient ruinae.   (1–8)

Another familiar tactic of monarchs is to depict themselves not as men of power but as men still struggling, standing up to a hostile world rather than bossing others about: a Regulus figure.[32] But when the line-up on the other side is a *tyrannus*, a *dux*, and the great hand of thundering Zeus, it is very difficult not to reverse the comparison. Syndikus notes this, and argues that the reference in line 3 makes it impossible to refer the lines to Augustus:[33] but when he goes on to deny any 'politische Bedeutung' to the lines at all because of their Greek content, he may be doing what Horace wanted him to do, but he is whistling in the dark.[34]

The traces of the Lucretian deconstruction of the terminology of political honour and power[35] are everywhere in Horace, and they are too powerful to be kept away from the *Capo dei Capi*. The cover is easily blown, as Propertius made clear when he dealt with the topics of foreign adventure and trade that Horace tried to keep separate:

> Arma deus Caesar dites meditatur ad Indos,
>   et freta gemmiferi findere classe maris.
> magna, viri, merces[36] . . .   (3. 4. 1–3)

A great deal of traditional classical scholarship is about building fences between apparently continuous concepts: the rhetoric is full of 'we should not think here of . . .' or 'there is no reference here to . . .'. There are good reasons for this in a laudable desire to be historical, but it produces the danger of an oppressive arbitrariness. When Horace says to Sallustius Crispus in *Odes* 2. 2:

> latius regnes avidum domando
> spiritum quam si Libyam remotis
> Gadibus iungas et uterque Poenus
>   serviat uni.   (9–12)

---

[32] For the identification of Regulus in *Odes* 3. 5 with Augustus see Doblhofer (1966).

[33] Syndikus (1972–3) ii. 38 n. 22: 'Die verbreitete Ansicht, die beiden ersten Strophen zielten bereits allein auf Augustus, widerlegt sich durch v. 3 von selbst.'

[34] The Greek tradition of resistance to tyranny was of course anything but inert in Rome: cf. Berve (1967) ii. 737–8; Philostr. *Vita Apoll.* 7, esp. 7. 2.

[35] Cf. Fowler (1989*b*) 134–45.

[36] Attempts to defuse the force of *merces* founder on Lucan 2. 255 'castra petunt magna victi mercede': see the whole context.

Nisbet and Hubbard on line 10 give us a long list of things not to think about:

As in several of the above parallels, the large land-owner is here seen as a kind of king (cf. 12 *serviat*); thus Horace can draw a contrast with the true kingship of the wise man. L. Müller thought that he meant a literal kingdom, but the target is Roman plutocracy rather than people like Juba (who in 25 B.C. was given a new domain in Mauretania). On the other hand Horace is unlikely to be alluding to African properties that Sallustius might have inherited from his great-uncle (*procos. Africa Nova, 46–5*); so hyperbolical a reminder of the historian's malversations would be unnecessarily indiscreet.

That anyone could connect *regnes* and *serviat* with Augustus' dictatorship is so unthinkable that it is not even worth arguing with. But Nisbet and Hubbard want this to have a contemporary meaning, and so point us away from real kings to Roman plutocrats. Horace of course at the end of the poem makes clear the reference to kingship:

> redditum Cyri solio Phraaten
> dissidens plebi numero beatorum
> eximit Virtus populumque falsis
>   dedocet uti
>
> vocibus, regnum et diadema tutum
> deferens uni propriamque laurum,
> quisquis ingentis oculo inretorto
>   spectat acervos.   (17–24)

But if we keep rulers in mind, and respect the need for contemporary reference that Nisbet and Hubbard acknowledge, how can we avoid looking to Augustus? I would not deny that Horace is trying to keep us off that tack, but it is not necessarily the critic's job to reproduce bad faith: sometimes we should expose it.

I want to look at one more example before summing up, and answering a final objection. The example I take is Tony Woodman's discussion[37] of *Odes* 3. 1, and in particular stanzas 2–6:

> regum timendorum in proprios greges,
> reges in ipsos imperium est Iovis,
>   clari Giganteo triumpho,
>   cuncta supercilio moventis.

---

[37] Woodman (1984).

> est ut viro vir latius ordinet
> arbusta sulcis, hic generosior
>   descendat in campum petitor,
>   moribus hic meliorque fama
>
> contendat, illi turba clientium
> sit maior: aequa lege Necessitas
>   sortitur insignis et imos,
>   omne capax movet urna nomen.
>
> destrictus ensis cui super impia
> cervice pendet, non Siculae dapes
>   dulcem elaborabunt saporem,
>   non avium citharaeque cantus
>
> somnum reducent: somnus agrestium
> lenis virorum non humilis domos
>   fastidit umbrosamque ripam,
>   non Zephyris agitata Tempe.   (5-24)

I do not want to get embroiled in the problems of the structure of the poem, but to use Woodman's interpretation as another example of this line-drawing that I have criticized. He is concerned to show that *Odes* 3. 1 is 'both a response to, and an advertisement for, the views of Augustus himself' (94) and accordingly sees no hint of criticism in the figures of stanzas 3-4 *est ut viro vir . . .* etc: they are rather to be contrasted with the impious man of stanza 5 and the later figures of the merchant and property speculator. They represent an idyll of Republican society as restored by Augustus after 27, an encouragement to the landowning classes to believe the words of the Lord. The problem again with this is that the tools of moral philosophy that Horace is wielding are too powerful to allow a conscientious reader with any degree of imagination to stop where Woodman wants her to. For Woodman, it is axiomatic that the man who *latius ordinet arbusta sulcis* is a 'blameless landowner', and indeed his blamelessness is used to reassure us that the politicians of the third stanza are equally free of criticism: he has therefore to deny any link with 2. 18. 24-36, well compared by Syndikus:

> revellis agri terminos et *ultra*
>   *limites* clientium
> salis avarus? pellitur paternos
>   in sinu ferens deos

> et uxor et vir sordidosque natos.
> nulla certior tamen
> rapacis Orci fine destinata
> aula divitem manet
> erum. quid *ultra* tendis? *aequa* tellus
> pauperi recluditur
> regumque pueris, nec satelles Orci
> callidum Promethea
> revexit auro captus.

Although the thought in *Odes* 2. 18 is expressed much more strongly, the philosophically evocative stress on respect for boundaries is at least superficially very similar—similar enough for commentators to cross-refer us to each passage. How does Woodman stop this? Then again, he is emphatic that 'the *impius* is in no sense to be identified with any of the four powerful men mentioned in stanzas 3–4'[38] in contrast to judgements like Syndikus's, which stress the criticism latent in Horace's descriptions of 'ordinary' life:

In den Augen des Horaz hat übergroßer Reichtum eine besondere Affinität nicht nur zu einem unvernünftigen, sondern zu einem schlechten Leben: Er verlockt zu einem Überschreiten der dem Menschen gesetzten Grenzen, innerhalb deren allein ein rechtes Leben möglich ist. Doch selbst wenn das Characteristicum des Frevelhaften hier nicht hinzukäme, wäre Horaz der Meinung, das menschliche Leben sei um so mehr von Sorgen erfüllt, je höher einer gestellt ist, und um so mehr er den Schlägen der Tyche ausgesetzt ist.[39]

But attached to the last word of each of Syndikus's statements is a footnote directing us to the relevant passages of the *Odes*:[40] what forbids us following up these footnotes? Finally, what of the really dark secret of these lines, the thing we must not at all costs be allowed to think? Isn't the king of stanza 2 like the Big Boss Man? Woodman notes that calling peoples *greges* is not like calling the ruler a shepherd,[41] but takes refuge in an appeal to the oracular style against Syndikus's point that 'Gewaltherrscher, die über Menschen wie über Vieh gebieten, können für einen Römer nicht Glieder einer guten Ordnung sein' and that *timendorum* makes it

---

[38] Woodman (1984) 91.
[39] Syndikus (1972–3) ii. 18–19.
[40] 2. 18. 23; 3. 3. 49–2; 3. 16. 11 ff.; 3. 24. 35–40; 3. 16. 17–88; 2. 10. 9–12.
[41] Woodman (1984) 185.

difficult to see a reference to the Good Shepherd.[42] But of course for Syndikus *there is no question of* referring this to Augustus: *it would not occur* to anyone at Rome to see him as a king, after all, though Hellenistic kingship theory occasionally comes in handy for footnotes. Jupiter who is over all kings in the second stanza *clearly has nothing to do* with death who affects everyone in the fourth stanza and the sword which hangs over the unfortunate in stanza 5. And it is vital that we appreciate that the reference there is *only* to a rich man like the property speculator we shall meet a little later on: *Siculae dapes must not be allowed* to bring to mind that the story involves the Sicilian tyrant Dionysius. It would be *quite inappropriate* for a commentator to quote here Cic. *Tusc.* 5. 57–3, where the story is told to illustrate the miseries of dictatorship: 'Satisne videtur declarasse Dionysius nihil esse ei beatum, cui semper aliquis terror impendeat? Atque ei ne integrum quidem erat, ut ad iustitiam remigraret, civibus libertatem et iura redderet: iis enim se adolescens improvida aetate irretierat erratis eaque commiserat, ut salvus esse non posset si sanus esse coepisset.'[43] That does not sound much like Augustus, does it?

Let me now sum up, and deal with that promised objection. My main point is that the inheritance of Epicurean and Stoic moral philosophy on which Horace draws throughout his work, particularly when conjoined with Callimachean poetics to produce a Callimachean ethics, makes it impossible to produce successful panegyric. Whatever attempts are made to control the force of the tradition, they flounder on its power. It is possible to collect any number of passages praising the Augustan state, as Doblhofer does: it is possible to show how subtly Horace tries to conceal analogies from us, how clever he is at supergluing over the cracks. But to take the edifice apart does not require a crowbar: it shatters at the first touch—if one chooses to let it. A poet like Horace, in his historical situation, cannot successfully praise a dictator like Augustus. But there is a more interesting objection to what I have been saying than merely to argue back in turn for an integrative, 'historical' reading in which the contradictions and tensions are subsumed again in a totalizing ideology. I have been treating Horace as if he were a Callimachean in aesthetics and an Epicurean in politics, to parody Eliot's famous self-definition. But he cannot be

[42] Syndikus (1972–3) ii. 16 n. 59.
[43] Cf. *RE* s.v. *Damokles*; Boeth. *Cons.* 3. 5. 6 with Gruber ad loc.

simply either of these. In his essay 'Horaz und Kallimachos', which has tended to be overshadowed by the later more detailed treatments of Horatian Callimacheanism, F. Wehrli had pointed to passages like *Ep.* 2. 2. 120-1 as evidence that Horace went beyond the restrictions of Callimacheanism:

> vehemens et liquidus puroque simillimus amni
> fundet opes Latiumque beabit divite lingua.

Die Kallimacheische Alternative ist hier überwunden mit der ausdrücklichen Feststellung, daß hinreißende Gewalt und Reinheit, das heiß vollkommene Form, sich nicht gegenseitig ausschließ: Horaz bekennt sich also zu einer monumentalen Dichtung ab dem Höchsten.[44]

If Pasquali usefully reminded us of Horace's Hellenistic intertexts, recent criticism has stressed that he is also a classicist.[45] Horace imitates Pindar as well as Sappho and Anacreon: his model is the *engagé* Alcaeus. He drinks wine as well as water; and if we are stressing the Lucretian background and its emphasis on *vivere parce*, we might also note the way in which Lucretius had inserted into his Callimachean manifesto the insistence that he deserves the crown *quod magnis doceo de rebus* (1. 930). Rather than using Horace's moralized poetics to deconstruct his politics, maybe we could use the politics to uncover a different Horace hiding beneath this pose of exquisite modesty. There was always a potential for disagreement in the alliance of Callimacheanism and Epicureanism: *frui paratis* is not a slogan that Callimachus would have taken to, and while Lucretius was able to appropriate the trackless paths to Epicureanism, the essence of the message Epicurus brings back from his journey through the universe is one about fixed and certain *termini* (albeit with its own intimations of sublimity). Maybe Horace is more of a Marinetti than he pretends, with a secret longing for sublime excess and Greatness with a capital 'G': maybe he is a better Fascist than I have allowed. *Odes* 2. 20, for instance, clearly offers us a very different picture for the *simplici myrto nihil allabores | sedulus curo* of the last poem of *Odes* 1:

> Non usitata nec tenui ferar
> penna biformis per liquidum aethera
>   vates neque in terris morabor
>   longius invidiaque maior
>
> urbis relinquam.   (1-5)

[44] Wehrli (1945) 74.   [45] Cf. Feeney (1993), esp. 45.

> iam Daedaleo notior Icaro
> visam gementis litora Bosphori
> Syrtisque Gaetulas canorus
>   ales Hyperboreosque campos;
>
> me Colchus et qui dissimulat metum
> Marsae cohortis Dacus et ultimi
> noscent Geloni, me peritus
>   discet Hiber Rhodanique potor. (13–20)

If *non usitata* might be seen as Callimachean in its rejection of Epicureanism, *nec tenui* turns on both: this is no 'middle flight' but an 'advent'rous soaring', an act of that *superbiam quaesitam meritis* to which he will return in *Odes* 3. 30.

Now it would be a mistake to read either 2. 20 or 3. 30 as simply here prophesying a Great Future for Horace. Even in the midst of his sublime rapture, Horace in that much-discussed phrase *Daedaleo notior Icaro* (if it is right) has, as Nisbet and Hubbard note, drawn back from 'the hazard of his ambition': his great and glorious fame in *Odes* 3. 30 will spread—all over Puglia and Basilicata. But such irony can always be read collusively.[46] For all this apparent restraint, it is possible if one chooses to trace in Horace, as in other Augustans, what Alessandro Schiesaro has termed a 'Bacchic Poetics' in which sublimity and inspired excess transfigure the tropes of Callimacheanism and the *furor* of the inspired poet is a guilty will to power. The pieces can be arranged very differently from the pattern I first constructed. Rather than doing a Wilkinson and taking the ethicized poetics as central, we could with Fraenkel give pride of place to the politics, and see the respect for greatness there as exposing the tensions within the poetics, rather than the other way round. We do not have to jump either way, of course: we can stay with both as themselves held in tension. But that looks a dull and cowardly way out. To jump with the sublime Horace is—with self-reflexive appropriateness—the more heroic act: more of the traditional picture of the unpretentious, ironic Horace has to go, more of the English Horace has to be jettisoned. That is too bold for me, and I would rather go with the Horace of 1. 38 (taken straight). Safe in what a recent study[47] has called 'un spazio privato, protetto, autodifensivo—*angulus* oraziano', Horace can look not up to, but down on, the Great and the Bad.

---

[46] Cf. Martindale (1993a) 14–15.   [47] Ferri (1993) 12.

14

Second Thoughts on Three Horatian Puzzles

C. O. BRINK†

To the present company of all companies I would have wished to offer something more substantial than what I have to offer—second thoughts on three puzzles. Even so, second thoughts are of the essence in this job, and there are still troubles on the way.

I. TOPOGRAPHY AND PROSODY OF THE 'OPPIDULUM' *QUOD VERSU DICERE NON EST* (HORACE, *SATIRES* I. 5. 87)

My first puzzle touches both topography and prosody, which makes it trickier than either would be on its own. Can we put a name to that little town which Horace leaves unnamed in the *Iter Brundisinum* (*Sat.* I. 5. 87), *quod versu dicere non est*? Here I have to plead guilty of acts of both omission and commission in discussing this passage in the *Proceedings of the Cambridge Philological Society* a few years ago[1]—fully so as regards topography, because I did not have the information I might have had, and more than a little as regards prosody, where I had the information but failed to act on it.

As for the former, I overlooked, and had to be reminded by a Swiss colleague, H. Haffter, that the topography had been largely clarified before I even put pen to paper and that the lie of the land rather disproved my assertions. The publications I—and indeed others—had overlooked are by Gerhard Radke, one of the few experts on the ancient Italian road system.

Charles Brink died while this book was in the final stages of preparation for the press. *virum doctissimum humanissimumque amisimus.*

[1] Brink (1987) 30.

Radke, last and most fully in *Rheinisches Museum* for 1989,[2] has pointed out that there are two major problems of topography which stand in relation to each other; and so consequently do their solutions. Horace's party has left Beneventum and at line 77 his familiar mountains of Apulia come into sight: 78–80 'et quos | numquam erepsemus, nisi nos vicina Trivici | villa recepisset'. The problem therefore is not, or not chiefly, whether the villa belongs to a person called Trivicius or Trivicus, or adjoins a place called Trivicium or Trivicum; that is unknown and the question is probably not answerable. The first problem that does require an answer happens to be rather: is the location of the villa identical with, or at least close to, the modern place similarly called Trevico? This, it will appear, is unlikely, although most modern scholars before Radke have believed it possible (certainly including myself). Hence Problem 2: can the unscannable *oppidulum* be identified, allowing for the distance of an easy ride of 24 Roman miles (line 86). Many, again until Radke, thought that the answer to this was known but came to grief (including myself) over the distance. Radke, whose sketch-map may be consulted at Radke (1989) 64, usefully notes the main distances in Roman miles.

To be brief, in antiquity, just as now, the road to Brundisium divided after Beneventum. One ran from that place through the territory of the Peuceti to Tarentum and then across the heel of Italy, as it were, away from the Tarentine gulf, in fact from Tarentum itself, to Brundisium. That was known as the Via Appia, although of course it was much later than the early parts commemorating Appius Claudius. The other, first Via Minucia, later Traiana, ran from Beneventum in a north-easterly direction via Canusia to the Adriatic coast and then along the coast via Rubi, Barium (now Bari), and Gnatia, to Brundisium. Because it is Horace who mentions these places (lines 94 ff.), we know that his party went by that coastal road. Doubts concern only the route immediately after Beneventum, which may have been between the two arteries but closer to the north-eastern one, to account for the coastal places that Horace mentions.

This consideration alone suggests the answer to our Problem 1: can the *Trivici villa* be identified with the similarly named modern

[2] See Radke (1989), esp. 63 ff.; also (1959) 336 n. 57; (1964*b*) 230 with n. 113; (1964*a*); (1967).

place, i.e. the small town now called Trevico?[3] The near identity between their Latin and Italian names would of course be quite usual; thus virtually every place mentioned by Horace in this part of the journey comes in this category. If you look at the few lines from 91 to 104, you will find examples from Benevento to Canosa, Bari, Egnazia, and Brindisi, i.e. Latin Beneventum, Canusium, Barium, Gnatia, and Brundisium. But equally there are numerous instances where a place-name has vanished or changed location. Now it is one of Radke's merits that he ruled Trevico out. One glance at the map shows that to reach it the traveller has to turn right, east, and, in difficult mountainous country, go a long way off that north-eastern route which we have already learnt from Horace his party took. Trevico, then, has to be ruled out because it is in the wrong direction and Horace's 24 miles (line 86) do not produce that unscannable *oppidulum* on which the poet remarks—our Problem 2.

In passing I note the two places which commentators had favoured for the *oppidulum*. Ancient scholarship[4] settled for (A)equum/-us Tuticum/-us near Beneventum. That is in the right direction, but fails because it is much more than 24 miles from the modern Trevico (if Trevico is still the place), quite apart from the scanning of the name, which is not quite impossible (even if not elegant) in dactyls. Modern scholarship, as reported in *RE*,[5] has favoured Ausculum, which is further east, and I argued for it in my paper of 1987. But it will not do. Like Trevico, it is in the wrong direction and, as Radke computes, it is more than double the mileage of 24 which Horace prescribes, again quite apart from the fact that as 'Asclum' it is not entirely unscannable. What one should have looked for all the time is a place near enough for the journey to Canusium (line 91), and then from it project back the 24 miles Horace mentions as the distance between the *Trivici villa* and the *oppidulum*. For the further topography of the *villa* I have to refer to Radke.[6]

---

[3] Trevico is marked on the Italian *Carta Automobilistica*, fo. 19, in a hilly position off Strada Statale 91 bis, the next sizeable place being Castel Baronia, Strada 91. The ancient commentators provide dubious information: Porph. ad 79-80 'Trivici oppidum ⟨in⟩ fine Campaniae est'; ps.-Acro ibid. (Vc) repeats Porphyrio, but a different version (Γ etc.) has 'hoc Trivicium prope Apuliam est.'

[4] Porph. ad 87-8 '(A) equum Tuticum significat, cuius nomen exametro versu compleri non potest'; ps.-Acro ad 87 derives from Porphyrio.

[5] C. Hülsen in *RE* ii (1896), 2558 s.v. *Ausculum*.

[6] Radke (1989) 71-2.

These computations led Radke to find the *oppidulum* at a small place on the Via Traiana (Minucia) called Herdoniae, now Ordona. This had been suggested by two nineteenth-century scholars[7] (possibly others), but since they failed to make Radke's computations they did not persuade their colleagues. Now however, I believe, we ought to allow ourselves to be persuaded, and look at the prosody of the new name suggested by topography.

Learned jocularity concerning the exclusion of metrically faulty words is known from Hellenistic literature. Lucilius may well have introduced it into Latin; anyhow a fragment, often cited though unexplained, offers the first known Latin instance.[8] It is to this instance that Porphyrio, in his commentary on the *Sermones*, ties the Horatian passage.[9] Both in Lucilius and in Horace the joke comes in an 'off' genre, *satura*. But not much later Ovid is seen to extend it to elegiac writing, *Ex Ponto* 4. 12. 10 ff., in some banter on the scansion of the addressee's name *Tuticanus*. As for *Herdoniae*, it is the plural that seems to be properly used in ordinary language, including topography.[10] The singular is indeed what Radke calls it, 'literary': thus in Greek;[11] in Latin employed eight times in

---

[7] Schütz (1881) on Hor. *Sat.* 1. 5. 86; but, unconvincingly, he assumes a scansion *Herdŏnēa* (Greek Ἑρδόνεια) in spite of Sil. It. 8. 567 *Herdōnĭa* (which would correspond to Greek Ἑρδωνία). In the decade after Schütz *Herdoniae* was defended by Grasso (1893–6) i. 146–7 ii. 9 ff. with better, though still not fully conclusive, argument, since he continued to identify the ancient *Trivici villa* with the modern Trevico.

[8] Cf. F. Marx's note (1904) on Lucilius frr. 288–9: 'servorum est festus dies hic, | quem plane (h)exametro versu non dicere possis.'

[9] The beginning of Porphyrio's comment was cited at n. 4 above. He continues: 'Hoc autem sub exemplo Lucili posuit, nam ille in sexto saturarum sic ait', and there follow frr. 228–9M. (see preceding note). The name of Lucilius' *servorum . . . festus dies* is still controversial. A different mode from that of Lucilius and Horace, namely between Greek and Latin prosody, is discussed by Housman at Manilius 2. 897.

[10] Thus the plural *Herdoniae* is on record at *CIL* ix. 1156, as Radke noted under *Herdoniae* in *Der Kl. Pauly*, but not, as he believed, in *CIL* ix. 689 and 690, which are merely inscriptions found in the place now called Ordona but do not appear to contain the ancient place-name. The plural is used also in the *Itinerarium Antoninianum* 116. 2 (*Itin. Rom.* i, ed. O. Cuntz, 1929 p. 16) 'item ab Equo Tutico Hydrunto ad . . . Erdonias', but the text at *Itin. Burdigalense* 610. 5 (ibid., p. 100) is not fully established. Again the plural *Erdonias* is used in the *Ravenn. Anon. Cosmographia* 4. 34 (*Itin. Rom.* ii, ed. J. Schnetz, 1940, p. 73) but the parallel list in the *Geographia* of Guido 45 (ibid., p. 123) offers *Erdona*.

[11] Always, it seems, at any rate in the passages that have reached the dictionaries. As for orthography, editors of course differ: for Ἑρδωνία cf. n. 7 above. I regard the spelling with omega as preferable. I have noted Strabo 6. 3. 6, 282, where the author mentions Ἑρδωνία as a place on one of the roads from

Livy.[12] So if we may now believe that Herdoniae was the *oppidulum* Horace had in mind, it is of some interest that that must be the plural. A century or so later Silius Italicus appears to require no such convention of either jocularity or genre in order to accommodate this name even to high narrative verse: [*quos*] *obscura incultis Herdonia misit ab agris* we read at 8. 567, the 'literary singular' which would cancel Horace's joke.[13] The puzzle and its solution are perhaps of greater interest methodologically than their own inherent weight might suggest. For it is not enough to make the unnamed place fit in with topography (which most of us got wrong and then did not acknowledge when it was put right by Radke); it also fits a tiny feature of Horace's style, which I hope I have now made clear; the plural makes the joke work; Livy's and Silius' 'literary' singular would have spoilt it.

2. A PUZZLE IN LITERARY HISTORY: WHAT IS THE EVIDENCE FOR LATIN SATYR-DRAMA? HORACE, *ARS POETICA*, 220-50

My second puzzle attaches entirely to literary history. There is again some reason for asking a question: what is the factual basis of Horace's remarks? On this occasion he makes demands, indeed celebrated demands, for a renewed, refined Roman satyr-drama, represented as advice addressed to himself as *Satyrorum scriptor*

Beneventum; Appian, *Hann.* 48 Ἐρδωνίαν ἐπολιόρκει; Polyaen. *Strateg.* 6. 38. 7, a correction justified by the context in the edition of Wölfflin and Melber (1886), later repeated; Ptol. *Geogr.* 3. 1. 63 Ἀπουλῶν Δαυνίων μεσόγειοι . . . Ἐρδωνία . . . Κανύσιον (361. 1-8 Curtz).

[12] Livy 25. 21. 1; 25. 22. 14; 27. 1. 4 twice; 27. 1. 6 twice; 27. 1. 14; 27. 2. 1; for orthography the editorial vulgate in Livy is *Herdonea* etc.

[13] J. Delz kindly reminds me that this is not the only passage where Silius makes a place-name scannable by the simple device of turning the plural into a singular. Thus at 8. 477 *Faesulae* (as Münzer, *RE* vi. 1965, 20 ff., points out) appears as *Faesula*, and at 8. 365 *Antemnae* (as again noted by the writer in *RE* i. 2350. 26 ff., Hülsen) as *Antemna(que)*. The latter case is mentioned also in Neue and Wagener (1902) 714, where, however, *Faesula* is disregarded though *Faesulae* appears, and *Herdoniae* (-*a*) finds no mention at all. The variation, in place-names, of plural and singular is an interesting thing; it deserves more scrutiny than it seems to have got, unless I have culpably overlooked competent discussions. P. Michael Brown's new edition of Horace, *Satires*, book 1 (1993), in the Classical Texts published by Aris & Phillips, has just reached me. In his note on the passage he succinctly states the problem which I attempt to resolve in this paper.

at *Ars Poetica* 220-50, a large section of the poem. What I am offering here, however, is not a disquisition on literary history, but one or two small philological points, correcting what I have said in volumes i and ii of my *Horace on Poetry*, and querying some corrections of my remarks.

Attempting to be critical, I overstated the case, as happens even though it should not. In volume i I stated,[14] rightly I believe, that Horace seems to mean what he says about the viability of the genre. But I overstated the case against Roman satyr-drama, instead of allowing that there is some evidence, but that it is weak. Worse still, I argued that recitation, not actual performance, was the compromise that might meet both Horace's notion of viability and the lack (or near lack) of Roman evidence. In volume ii I withdrew this compromise but while still, and rightly, adhering to Horace's notion of viability, I repeated the point about lack of evidence.[15]

Now once again, as over my first puzzle, an external reader helped me to advance the argument. An American friend, John D. Morgan, drew my attention to a passage in Vitruvius, which I knew, although I had not entirely appreciated its bearings. Indeed, useful though the passage might be, its difficulties strike me now as not entirely soluble with the means at our disposal. At 5. 6. 9 Vitruvius talks of painted scenery in the contemporary theatre. If this context is correctly transmitted at the end of chapter 6, and thus separated from *in Graecorum theatris* at the beginning of chapter 7, the author's remarks would apply to the Roman theatre, and satyr-drama would be one of its genres: the Roman scenery would presuppose the Roman genre.[16]

Scenery in the Roman theatre, Vitruvius tells us, is threefold (*genera sunt scaenarum tria*): *tragicum*, with columns and other royal ornament, *comicum*, with private houses, balconies (*Maeniana*), etc., and *satyricum*, 'decorated with trees, caves, hills, and other things rural of the kind met with in an ornamental landscape scene'.[17]

---

[14] Brink (1963*b*) 228.

[15] Brink (1971) 274-5.

[16] John D. Morgan draws attention to the Leipzig dissertation of Neukirch (1833), where, at p. 19, the Vitruvian passage is regarded as a fixed point in the argument on Roman satyr-drama. That would be true—if it is what Vitruvius really says.

[17] The Latin of the third Vitruvian genre (at 5. 6. 9) is as follows: 'satyricae [sc. scaenae] vero ornantur arboribus, speluncis, montibus reliquisque agrestibus rebus

But is this really the scenery of a Roman theatre, as Vitruvius seems to be saying? Some experienced and quite critical scholars have tried to disprove it, but tend to be forgotten for their pains. Thus E. H. Fiechter in his study on the architectural development of the ancient theatre[18] sought to dispel some of the muddle that arises when the above *genera . . . scaenarum tria* are insufficiently separated from the *tres species ornationis* that come earlier (in paragraph 8). C. Fensterbusch, editor and translator of Vitruvius,[19] says clearly that the three kinds of scenic decoration (in paragraph 9) cannot be combined with the elaborate architectural background of the Roman theatre. The *genera . . . scaenarum tria* are in fact Greek, and Fensterbusch suggests that the whole of the paragraph (9) in which they occur should be transposed from chapter 6 to the end of the chapter dealing with the Greek theatre, viz. 7.[20] This is by no means improbable, although the new location of the passage is not easy to enforce; the same holds good if the proposal is that the passage be moved to the end of chapter 8, which concludes the subject of *scaena*.

It appears, therefore, that the Vitruvian passage 5. 6. 9 would be a strong piece of evidence for Roman satyr-drama if it could be securely established as Roman. We have seen, however, that this cannot be done. We can do no more, I believe, than list the passage with a critical question-mark, as a possible pointer to Greek scenic decoration.

A lively paper on Latin satyr-drama by T. P. Wiseman appeared in a recent issue of the *Journal of Roman Studies*, 'Satyrs in Rome: The Background to Horace's *Ars Poetica*'.[21] There the author rightly argues that my earlier compromise of recitation cannot be

---

in topeodi speciem deformati.' For *topeodis* see *OLD* s.v. *topeodes*. For the final word I conjectured *deformatis* to agree in case with *agrestibus rebus*, not, as transmitted, *deformati* with *ornatus* earlier in the sentence. Later, however, I found the conjecture in Valentin Rose's text, 2nd edition (1899), where the editor had carried it from his first edition of 1867 and traced it to that indefatigable 16th-cent. emender of Vitruvius' text, Iocundus of Verona, a professional architect.

[18] Fiechter (1914) 117.

[19] Fensterbusch (1976) 552 n. 292, referring to his earlier paper (1936), where in turn Fiechter (1914) and Bulle (1928) are cited. Fensterbusch still took it for granted—which we cannot do—that Vitruvius' reference to satyr-drama in any case rendered the passage suspect, 'since satyr-drama was not established in Rome'.

[20] Bulle (1928) 272 favoured a transposition of paragraph 8 as well as 9 of Vitr. 5. 6. Fensterbusch (1936) agrees as to paragraph 9, but convincingly vindicates 8.

[21] Wiseman (1988). For further discussion see Rudd (1989) 30-2.

entertained: Horace talks of actual stage performance; but then, as
Wiseman acknowledges, I had come to that point myself in my
second volume.[22] But what Wiseman does not quite do is to give
to Vitruvius' testimony whatever weight it may deserve. Although
he notices the passage elsewhere,[23] he fails to reckon it among his
pieces of direct evidence, or possible direct evidence. On the other
hand, he gives too much weight to the rest of the direct evidence
and far too much to the indirect, which points to Roman satyrs but
not, or not necessarily, to satyr-drama.

Not mentioning Horace, whom, if possible, we want to prove
right or wrong, I can find no more than four pieces of direct
evidence—or three if we omit Vitruvius, whom we have all but
rejected. The second is Cicero writing to his brother Quintus in
Caesar's British camp in 54 BC:[24] 'Συνδείπνους Σοφοκλέους, quamquam a te actam fabellam video esse festive, nullo modo probavi.'
No one knows what *actam* can refer to, scarcely to 'acting'
Sophocles' satyr-play in the situation; Bücheler wrote *factam*—not
impossibly, though it does not readily explain Cicero's disapproval,
however expressed.[25] But whatever it refers to, can a Sophoclean
play testify to *Roman* satyr-drama as a living genre? This largely,
if not entirely, eliminates the Cicero passage. I turn to the third
piece of evidence, which at least is something Roman, provided it
is satyr-drama. It comes from the voluminous writer under
Augustus, Nicolaus of Damascus. In a named book of his *Histories*[26]
he dilates on Sulla's sense of fun, φιλόγελων γενόμενον, and his
delight in μίμοις καὶ γελωτοποιοῖς. His humour is said to be shown
also by his authorship of 'satyric (or satyr-like) comedies', σατυρικαὶ
κωμῳδίαι, composed in Sulla's native language, τῇ πατρίῳ φωνῇ.
What 'satyric comedies' are no one really knows, although not
everyone will say so. They are, however, highly unlikely to be
satyr-plays—not even satyr-plays in the low style of comedy, as

---

[22] Brink (1963b) 228.

[23] Wiseman (1988) 12.

[24] Cic. *QF* 2. 16 (15). 3.

[25] *nullo modo* is transmitted; Shackleton Bailey (1980) considers the possibility of
bono modo, 'moderately'.

[26] Nicolaus Damasc. ap. Ath. 6. 78, 261 C = *FGrHist* 90 F 75 Νικόλαος δ' ἐν τῇ
ἑβδόμῃ καὶ ἑκατοστῇ τῶν Ἱστοριῶν Σύλλαν φησὶ τὸν Ῥωμαίων στρατηγὸν οὕτω χαίρειν
μίμοις καὶ γελωτοποιοῖς φιλόγελων γενόμενον, ὡς καὶ πολλὰ γῆς μέτρα αὐτοῖς χαρίζεσθαι
τῆς δημοσίας. ἐμφανίζουσι δ' αὐτοῦ τὸ περὶ ταῦτα ἱλαρὸν αἱ ὑπ' αὐτοῦ γραφεῖσαι
σατυρικαὶ κωμῳδίαι τῇ πατρίῳ φωνῇ.

Wiseman suggests, the sort of thing he thinks Horace is tilting against.

σατυρικαὶ κωμῳδίαι could possibly be Atellan farces, though the name would be odd. In 1985 Elizabeth Rawson[27] compared Diodorus,[28] where one actor called Saunio or Sannio (Samnio), and described as a σατυρικὸν . . . πρόσωπον and γελωτοποιός, 'buffoon', is distinguished from another called 'comedian', κωμῳδός; she noted that 'Sannio' as a name is linked with Atellan farce.

Indeed it is not impossible, in spite of Nicolaus' stage context, that there is no mention of a stage play at all but that Sulla is credited with Roman *satura*; cf. Hor. *Sat.* I. 4. I ff., linking *satura* with Old Comedy, and much later Joannes Lydus, *De magistratibus* I. 41, describing the *satura* of Lucilius and his followers, Horace, etc., by τὴν σατυρικὴν ἐκράτυναν κωμῳδίαν. It is not very helpful to say[29] that Nicolaus knew what σατυρικός meant, being a Greek speaker. The above theory and terminology that link the Greek and Latin genres may well be Greek.

The fourth and last piece of evidence known to me is a note by Porphyrio,[30] three titles defined as satyr-plays and ascribed to the first and major writer of *Atellanae*, Pomponius: thus *Atalante*, *Sisyphus*, *Ariadne*, to which Wiseman would like to add *Marsyas* and *Satura*.[31] That, however, tells us no more than that travesty of myth was well represented, which we knew anyhow; and that Porphyrio or his authorities spotted some coincidences among *Atellanae* with the titles of old Greek satyr-plays. It does not tell us that those plays were satyr-plays, or how they were related to the main body of *Atellanae*.

In brief, then, Wiseman seems to me to overstate the weight of the direct evidence, and fascinating though the indirect evidence is, it tells us, as I pointed out, more about satyrs in Rome than about Roman satyr-drama. So a puzzle the matter remains, and it is a pity that we cannot get more out of Vitruvius for Roman satyr-drama than we seem to be able to do.

---

[27] Rawson (1985*b*) 98.

[28] Diod. 37. 12. 1–2 κωμῳδὸν ἐπὶ τῆς σκηνῆς ἀγωνιζόμενον . . . . · . . . ἡ τύχη σατυρικὸν τῷ καιρῷ τούτῳ πρόσωπον εἰσήγαγεν. ἦν γάρ τις Λατῖνος ὄνομα μὲν Σαυνίων (? Σαννίων) γελωτοποιὸς δὲ καὶ χάριτας ὑπερβαλλούσας ἔχων εἰς ἱλαρότητα κτλ.

[29] As does Wiseman (1988) 2.

[30] Porph. and Hor. *Ars* 221 'Mox etiam agrestis satyros nudavit: hoc est: satyrica coeperunt scribere, ut Pomponius Atalanten vel Sisyphon vel Ariadnen.'

[31] Wiseman (1988) 3.

3. A PUZZLE IN LITERARY AND POLITICAL
HISTORY: DID MAECENAS GO INTO RETIREMENT?

My third puzzle involves history, both literary and political: did Maecenas go into retirement? The large amount of evidence would call for a much longer treatment; brevity, however, might concentrate the mind. What makes the matter still a puzzle?

Professor Peter White, of the University of Chicago, has been a little unlucky with this controversy. He had come to dispute what looked to him like a doctrine shared by two scholars who, as he points out, have been known to disagree quite strongly on matters Horatian, Professor Gordon Williams and myself. Those matters, doubtless, will bear further discussion; but this is not the time or place. Concerning the retirement of Maecenas, however, when White's brief paper of 1991 was on the point of going to press[32] he discovered that one of us, Gordon Williams, had changed his mind. Maecenas, Williams now thought, so far from losing influence in literary policy because he had fallen from grace, had in fact given up by long-standing arrangement when his services were no longer required; from grace, apparently, he had never fallen.[33]

This change of mind did not satisfy Peter White. The recent reassessment of Maecenas' status was welcomed, but surprise was expressed that the view taken by Williams of Maecenas' literary role had not really changed since the 1960s. (As for my own views, it is only by page-number, not by argument, that White sets them aside, although a whole chapter of my third Horace volume seeks to offer what may appear to be a more extensive critical account of Augustan literary chronology than to my knowledge is at present available elsewhere.[34]) Consequently, White spends what remains of his space on an attempt to persuade us, no longer that there was no change in Augustus' demeanour towards Maecenas so far as politics went, but that Williams was in grave error in recognizing a change in Augustus' or Maecenas' interference with the poets, whatever the motivation. There was no such change, he thinks. Augustus interfered all the time, Maecenas playing a secondary part.

[32] White (1991).
[33] Williams (1968) 4-5, 86-8, etc.; (1990) 228-75.
[34] Brink (1982) ch. 6 (pp. 523-72).

To me it seems that Peter White really runs together two quite diverse and separate things. What the poets did in their poetry (not to mention what they had done to them by their patrons) is one thing; what the patrons themselves did in the large world of affairs is quite another. Whether and how these contexts are linked is yet another. Scholars primarily concerned with philological or maybe literary interpretation will find some way into the first and, perhaps, the second of these contexts. Political historians will see a more direct route to the second. They may produce strong enough evidence for the view put forward by Syme or others. The view would then be that certain political events resulted in depriving Maecenas of his overriding position, together with Agrippa, in the power structure, though that happened in a scarcely spectacular fashion. It would consequently not be unreasonable to link with the putative political change the observable and by no means putative change from a first poetic period in which Maecenas is the central patronal influence and Augustus, in spite of his occasional incursions, a remote saviour figure, to a second period (not long after Virgil's demise) in which neither Maecenas nor anyone else appears to intervene between the poets and Augustus. Or suppose that the historians produce enough evidence for the contrary view and there was no such change, and Tacitus in a famous chapter of the *Annals*[35] and others were mistaken. That will take some doing, but if it succeeds, what of it? It still leaves us with two different approaches to poetry, with a watershed about 18 BC, with Maecenas receding and Augustus taking a new role, and with the poetry changing, one might almost say, accordingly. Those changes are *in situ* and not removable. That the baby of the political poetry which is also non-political, has to be thrown out with the murky bathwater of politics strikes me as a *non sequitur*. White equates Augustus' occasional and haphazard incursions during the earlier patronal period, which both Williams and I describe as indirect, with the direct or near-direct influence of the later. That is equating unlike with unlike. I have actually

---

[35] Tac. *Ann.* 3. 30. 3–4 on C. Sallustius Crispus, the historian's nephew, adopted by him, who modelled himself on Maecenas. Tacitus observes: 'aetate provecta speciem magis in amicitia principis quam vim tenuit. idque et Maecenati acciderat, fato potentiae raro sempiternae, an satias capit aut illos cum omnia tribuerunt, aut hos cum iam nihil reliquum est quod cupiant.' For assessment of credibility it should be noted that Tacitus is not concerned to assert facts rarely recognized, but to assert motives for facts generally taken as established.

made a specific case as part of the early setting for every one of Augustus' occasional interventions on which White places so much emphasis, and I find no disproof of those arguments.

15

Horace's *Moyen de Parvenir*

R. G. MAYER

HORACE chose to cast a bright light upon facets of his own career and social position in all of his poetry. He does not talk about himself out of egotism, though he is undeniably proud of his social, as distinct from his poetic, achievement. As he says crisply at *Odes* 2. 18. 10–11, 'pauperem . . . dives | me petit'. He uses this social success to guarantee his literary achievement later in his life when he boasts that his works are in the hands of the *ingenui* (*Ep.* 1. 19. 34). The rise in life that Horace thus glancingly describes is meant to serve as an example. He believed that the poet's social role is the improvement of his fellow citizens; he ought to advise his readers (*Ep.* 2. 1. 125–31, *AP* 343–4), and an agreeable way of helping us to better our lot, if we choose to, is to show how the poet himself managed it. So, for instance, in the *Satires* he recounts how tactful was his introduction to Maecenas, and how circumspect the great man was in bestowing his favour (*Sat.* 1. 6. 49–64). The ninth satire implicitly praises the liberal society that Maecenas had gathered around himself, a society free from petty ambition.[1] No doubt the account is heavily edited to produce an ideal, but men live by ideals and poets work to realize them imaginatively for less favoured mortals. The autobiographical element in Horace's poetry may usually be seen as exemplary, for the reader's benefit and, at times, amusement.

Horace's background was, as he does not blush to avow, humble. His father had been a slave,[2] but he achieved his freedom

[1] Shackleton Bailey (1982) 17 reckons that Maecenas himself is something of a *parvenu*; but his grandfather had been prominent in Roman society (see Syme 1939: 129 n. 4).

[2] Salmon (1967) 369 n. 4 suggests that he may have been enslaved on the reconquest of Venusia in 88 BC during the Social War. But see Williams in this volume (Chapter 16).

somehow or other before the poet's birth (he was therefore *ingenuus*). Though not rich, he was determined that his son should have the best possible education. Since that was not available at Venusia, he removed his child to Rome, and personally conducted him to the most expensive schools (*Sat.* 1. 6. 71–82), a remarkable undertaking. His purpose is clear: to improve his son's mind as well as his station in life, though Horace reckons his father would not have minded if he had resolved to follow in his footsteps (*Sat.* 1. 6. 85–7). Ambition of an honourable stamp was a strong impulse in Horace's father. After schooling in Rome, Athens; again, this is the sort of training usually given to the sons of the aristocracy. One of Horace's fellow students at the time was Cicero's son, and we know how large an allowance he had.

An exciting visitor interrupted Horace's studies in Athens. Brutus, on his way to Asia in 43 BC, stopped there to recruit young officers. One of the men he secured was Horace. Now his decision to join Brutus' army admits of many interpretations, no one of which necessarily rules out any others. Like many young men, he may have sought the excitement of the camp and the opportunity to travel in security. He may also have had a genuine attachment to Brutus' political cause, though it would be prudent not to assert this as fact.[3] The military tribunate, on the other hand, could serve to introduce a young man to public life, though it rarely led very far.[4] One thing is fairly certain: he was not given the commission for any proven military skills. Presumably Brutus liked the look of him. Most important is the fact that by becoming a *tribunus militum* Horace established his rank of *eques*.[5] One thing at least that Horace achieved was complete social respectability. His father had been a freedman, but he had become the social equal of, say, his future benefactor, Maecenas. Unfortunately, Horace picked the loser, and so suffered some loss of property after the defeat at Philippi in 42 BC. He had the funds, however—and perhaps the support of a powerful individual—to buy himself a treasury secretaryship (*scriptum quaestorium*), and this lucrative post he may have held for the rest of his life (*Sat.* 2. 6. 36);[6] what is more, he

[3] Syme (1939) 254 n. 1.   [4] See Suolahti (1955) 186–7.
[5] See Taylor (1925). This crucial step in his social rise is regrettably overlooked by Fraenkel (1957) in his otherwise scrupulous account of the poet's life.
[6] Jones (1960) 154, 156 discusses the equestrian status of *scribae* and the purchase of the office. That patronage was also required is the view of Badian (1985) 347 n. 7, but see Damon (1992) 243–4; for more on *scribae* see Badian (1989).

takes pride in the honourable improvement of his financial position (*Sat.* 2. 6. 6). It is worth asking (not that a ready answer appears) whether in these circumstances he actually needed further financial support. It is certainly remarkable that, as he presents the rest of his life to us, the existence of other sources of income is eclipsed by the reliance upon a benefactor for security and contentment, Maecenas.

Maecenas' friendship was secured, not on Horace's initiative, but through the recommendation of two fellow poets, first Virgil and then Varius. It must be stressed that Horace himself describes the business (*Sat.* 1. 6. 54-5) so as to emphasize its protracted propriety; Maecenas did not ask for a second visit for a considerable time. We may consider by contrast Philippus in the seventh epistle, who picks up the charming auctioneer Mena without formal introduction and immediately makes a pet of him (not surprisingly, the friendship proves a calamity for the humble *praeco*).[7] Horace was not thrust upon Maecenas, by himself or by any others. The sketch of Horace's social rise as described in Professor David Armstrong's recent study therefore needs to be redrawn.[8] It is not at all unfair to call him a most successful *arriviste*, but a 'ruthless and self-seeking social climber' he arguably was not. Nor should his ambition be deemed 'cold'. He was, like many other Romans, keen on success and self-advancement, but for him the decisive factor was always how courteously one pulled the strings binding society together. If Horace had really been cold and ruthless, like the poetic pest of the ninth satire, would he not have induced his friends to mention him to Maecenas? Yet he does not admit to having done so. Now the point is not what actually happened then (and Virgil and Varius were still alive to give the lie to any misrepresentation of events), but the presentation of an ideal of courteous behaviour as exemplified in the poet's own life. The best course is to leave it to others, and above all to secure a preliminary recommendation or two. The ninth epistle is a kind of model character reference, in this case for a friend seeking a position in the *cohors amicorum* attending Tiberius. On another occasion, in the twelfth epistle, Horace recommends Grosphus to Iccius; general advice about recommendation crops up in *Ep.* 1. 18. 76-85. It is an important social issue that becomes a poetic theme.

---

[7] See now Berres (1992).
[8] Armstrong (1989), esp. 5, 20, 24-5.

Further considerations suggest that Horace's career was not coldly ruthless. As Syme observed after reviewing the addressees of the *Odes* and *Epistles*, Horace does not appear anxious to solicit the eminent.[9] Or again, we know from Suetonius (and *not* from himself) that he was invited to become Augustus' secretary. An unslaked ambition would have leapt at the chance. But Horace refused to climb higher and declined the offered post, a move in harmony with his reiterated endorsement of the doctrine of 'contentment with what is enough'. As Sir Theodore Martin observed in his engaging study of the poet,[10] this argues for sincerity and independence. He knew when he had achieved a sufficiency of wealth and prestige, and prudently stopped aspiring. No ruthlessness in that, surely.

Armstrong also stresses the selfishness of ambition. The Romans, however, did not view it in so harsh a light. In the first place, some ambitions they regarded favourably, even the philosophical among them. Seneca, for instance, applauds the honourable social and financial advance of his friend Lucilius, indeed, he regards it is a sort of self-fulfilment.[11] Horace found no fault with the ambitions his father entertained for him and took costly measures to realize. Second, it was assumed that a good man worked not just for himself but also for his friends and relations, the 'trickle-down' effect. In the seventeenth epistle, which will occupy us in a moment, he makes it plain that the career Scaeva is contemplating benefits not only himself but also his friends, family, and associates: all are included in the simple word *tuis* at line 11.[12] The letter of recommendation already mentioned, the ninth epistle, is an example of the sort of benefit that someone like Horace, more nearly placed to the founts of patronage, could direct towards a deserving friend who is seeking to improve his status. Selfishness should not be assumed to be the dominant ingredient in the aspirant's

[9] Syme (1986) 386.

[10] Martin (1869) 181–2; Martin deserves attention in a matter like this just because, as official biographer of the Prince Consort, he knew what risks to personal independence compassed the man of letters at court.

[11] See *Ep.* 19. 3 'in medium te protulit ingenii vigor, scriptorum elegantia, clarae et nobiles amicitiae' (the same could be said of the young Horace); *NQ* 4 praef. 14–15.

[12] It is worth observing in this context that Virgil puts into Hades the avaricious—a great number—who failed to set aside something 'for their own people': *Aen.* 6. 610–11 'qui divitiis *soli* incubuere repertis | nec partem posuere *suis*'. Servius says that *suis* means *cognatis, adfinibus*; so surely does *tuis* in Horace.

make-up; it was expected in Rome that one also gave one's friends a lift if they needed it. It was presumably in that spirit that Virgil and Varius brought Horace to Maecenas' notice. The difficulty here seems to be that the modern scholar, especially the North American or northern European, is not well placed to understand a social system that runs entirely on personal contacts. In the Rome of Horace, however (and in many other parts of the world today), success depended upon the use one made of the people one regarded as friends; indeed, the verb *utor* can mean 'to be on friendly terms with someone'.[13] One had to secure the support of individuals and offer it oneself at every turn (consider, for example, the scene described at *Sat.* 2. 6. 38-9, where Horace is urged to secure Maecenas' seal on a document). Thus, ambition became an issue for debate among philosophers and historians; it had its good side and, more obviously, its bad. To be sure, *ambitio* was a vice in the main—Horace, as C. O. Brink has pointed out, always delimits the concept with a critical epithet.[14] But it is the excess of a virtue, the desire to improve one's standing by honourable means. Once again, Horace turns a social issue into the raw material of poetry.

To sum up this brief assessment of Horace's career, W. Y. Sellar was right when he said that Horace had an ambition to live with people of distinction and that he cultivated more carefully and valued more highly the qualities which fit men for life than those which secure distinction in literature.[15] His friend Virgil, by contrast, clearly preferred a life retired from high society; he was a pure poet, whereas Horace was also a man of the world and wanted some of the things that only the upper level of society had to offer. The issue then became for him one of method moralized—in what way the aspirant was to conduct himself so as to achieve his goals without forfeiting self-respect and independence. Horace's watchword is 'accommodation', as he describes it in the first epistle (line 19): 'mihi res, non me rebus subiungere conor'. He must induce his circumstances to conform to himself by turning them to personal advantage. Horace, then, like the Roman citizen in general, had to balance the aspiration towards self-determination (what the philosophers called αὐτάρκεια) against the need for help from above, help which involved obligations.

---

[13] See *OLD* s.v. 9b, and cf. *Ep.* 1. 12. 22 *utere Pompeio Grospho*, 1. 17. 2, 13, 14.
[14] See Brink (1982) on *Ep.* 2. 2. 400.
[15] Sellar (1892) 14, 20.

At this point it might be suggested that Horace's experience as a Roman poet (as he had come to see by the time he was composing the first book of *Epistles*) exactly reflected his experience as a citizen. Latin literature had developed and prospered in avowed imitation of literary models provided by Greece. A more dependent literature than the Roman cannot be conceived; indeed, so dependent was it that we find Horace unexpectedly enlarging its imitative character by trying to derive the one native literary form, verse satire, from the Athenian Old Comedy (*Sat.* 1. 4. 1–8). Imitation notwithstanding, the Roman poet could only secure lasting success if he found an authentic voice. So he was faced with a particular variant of the dilemma that he encountered as a citizen, self-sufficiency against dependency, or, in literary terms, how to reconcile the search for originality in composition with the demands of a literary system founded upon the imitation of masters (foreign and domestic). Horace addressed himself to this issue directly in the *Ars Poetica*. In the first book of *Epistles* he preferred to submerge the literary issue within discussions of the role of independence in Roman society as a whole. The last five epistles, 16–20, seem to be carefully grouped together to reinforce his perceptions. Let us consider them now.

The sixteenth epistle, to Quinctius, is a search for a valid, but generally unrecognized, definition of the *vir bonus*. Horace finds the merely public and social definition of the good man to be inadequate rather than entirely wrong; he offers his own assessment of it in the course of the letter. But in criticizing the popular notion of goodness in men he notes that it often takes no account of the inner disposition, which may be hypocritically vicious. In order to emphasize the low moral status of, say, a greedy man, he equates him with a slave: 'qui melior servo, qui liberior sit avarus . . . non video' (*Ep.* 1. 16. 63–5). That traditional figure of ancient moralizing, the intrepid but grasping merchant, is none the less condoned within society for his usefulness, but, Horace insists, it is the bare usefulness of the slave (*Ep.* 1. 16. 69–72). Thus, the *vir bonus* can only be one who is fully independent in a moral sense; the slavish man, like an actual slave, is not a free moral agent, and can be left out of consideration.

The next epistle, to an unknown Scaeva, is something of a critical *locus conclamatus*, so contradictory are the impressions it has left on readers. Some assume that Horace did not like his correspondent. They derive his name from the adjective *scaevus* and suggest that it means 'gauche'; Professor Niall Rudd actually translates the name so. (It should, however, be recalled that the Latin noun *scaeva*, from which the cognomen might as easily be derived, means 'a favourable omen').[16] Or it is reckoned that the letter hints at a certain disagreeability in Scaeva's character.[17] The tone of the letter as a whole has been condemned. Fraenkel candidly says that it is upsetting, extraordinary, and cynical; the ambition of Scaeva to attach himself to some great man he regards as base.[18] Others, equally perturbed by the doctrine, protect Horace's character by finding the letter's tone ironic or humorous.[19] D. R. Shackleton Bailey has described it as half-cynical, half-mocking, and he calls the relationship Horace envisages for Scaeva sordid.[20] Despite this chorus of disapproval, the poem's attitude to social behaviour has not always lacked admirers.

A. Noirfalise (1952) wrote a sympathetic but neglected couple of pages on the tone of the poem and its intimate connection with the following one. A. S. Wilkins said in his introduction to it that its gist is not much more than this: 'a cynic's life is not necessarily the best and modesty is the best policy'; for his part he considered the doctrine far from degraded, if not ideally elevated.[21] Lucian Müller too felt that its contents were taken too much to heart by many, nor did he agree with those who believed that the poet could talk down to or despise his addressee.[22] Moving yet further back in the tradition of comment to a time when social relations were arguably somewhat more like those in Horace's Rome, we find the influential eighteenth-century translator C. M. Wieland offering a balanced assessment of Horace's attitude to Scaeva's

[16] The origin of the name is of course debated; see Schulze (1904) 369–70 (Etruscan origin), 419; and Kajanto (1965) 243 ('left-handed').

[17] So most recently Moles (1985) 46–7, who, however, does not find the letter cynical or humorous.

[18] Fraenkel (1957) 322; this judgement is recalled by Jones (1993) 10.

[19] e.g. Williams (1968) 14–17, who concludes that Horace 'is not giving serious advice' in the last part of the poem; this view is endorsed by Jones (1993) 10. But Williams does not side with those who reckon that Horace despised Scaeva for servile tendencies.

[20] Shackleton Bailey (1982) 60; at 64 he speaks of Horace 'displaying an awareness of the seamy side of clientship in XVII and XVIII'. That is true in so far as Horace warns his addressees against giving so much as a hint of inappropriate ambitions.   [21] Wilkins (1886) 202.

[22] Müller (1891–1900) ii. 134: 'Man hat den Inhalt . . . meist viel zu tragisch genommen.'

position (even though he has recourse to some unsupported guess-work).[23] A century earlier, André Dacier had heartily endorsed the poem's sentiments and its sensible doctrine on what he called the ὁμιλιτικὴ ἀρετή ('la science du monde'); this scrupulous doctrine he reckons to be the fruit of Horace's own mature experience.[24] Before trying to establish from the text, if that is possible, which of the available critical responses is fairest to Horace, let us momentarily cast a glance at a later man of letters who had in his youth been an outsider wanting in, the American Henry James (so similar are many aspects of his career to Horace's that he will often be referred to in the rest of this paper).

James had started his European career in Paris, but associated only with his fellow artists there. This produced a drought in his inspiration because society at large remained closed to him. So he moved to London. During his residence there in the 1880s he is on record as saying that securing a place in society was a legitimate object of ambition. Another American, but a failed *arriviste*, Hoppin, related that James had his disenchantments, especially the need while visiting country houses from Friday to Monday to give up personal independence and to be agreeable morning, noon, and night. James felt that one should go into society only if one is in the mood (he might have been paraphrasing the opening of the seventeenth epistle).[25] This desire to lay siege to society is to be expected in would-be men of the world, but we grow uncomfort-able when it manifests itself in artists, whom we seem still to expect to hold aloof from high society. Yet some men of letters, among other artists, may be driven to battering at society's gates in order to realize their creative powers. For some of them social aspiration is not so much an end in itself (though of course it may be that) as an artistic imperative. Horace and James needed 'the world' just because it was to be the theme of their writing. High society may also provide an author (along with his livelihood) with his pre-ferred audience, as Horace boasted at *Ep.* I. 19. 34; it is significant that it is Maecenas' approval he seeks for his lyric poems, not that of his fellow poets (*Odes* I. I. 35-6). Virgil's spirit, by contrast, fed on the countryside and on heroic myths; his preferred readers seem to have been his fellow poets. But Horace's imagination was

---

[23] Wieland (1801; 1986 edn.) 261-2; his editor, M. Fuhrmann, draws attention to his good sense (p. 1122).   [24] Dacier (1709) 92-4.

[25] Edel (1987) 223; for Hoppin see Edel (1987) 236.

stimulated (at times repelled) by the realities of social life among
the rich and prestigious. So he had to make a pact with 'the
world', and he describes the virtue of such a procedure in the
exemplary anecdote of Aristippus and Diogenes which forms an
apologia for the life of those dependent upon the great.

Aristippus is at the outset the preferred role model; Horace will
demonstrate why his is the 'potior sententia' (*Ep.* 1. 17. 17). He
was normally content with what he had (*fere praesentibus aequum*),
but was prepared to aim higher (*Ep.* 1. 17. 24 *temptantem maiora*).
The leading trait of his character is its adaptability to any role he
chose to play (*Ep.* 1. 17. 29 *non inconcinnus*). Horace artfully tips
the balance further in his favour by evoking the language of
Roman social intercourse when he has Aristippus say *officium facio*
(*Ep.* 1. 17. 21). The cynic Diogenes, by contrast, is dismissed at the
close of the anecdote with the curt epithet *ineptus*, 'misfit' (line 32);
this too recalls the language of social censure, for it describes the
person who habitually misconceives what the situation requires.
He is the born outsider. But he is also a hypocrite, or at least self-
deluded in that he claims self-sufficiency (*Ep.* 1. 17. 22 *nullius
egentem*),[26] while nevertheless taking handouts. The point is clear.
No one is absolutely independent. We are all members of a society
and so need each other for something, however trivial. The question then arises: with which part of our own society do we choose
to associate (assuming we live in an open society which admits of
a measure of free association)? It is that question which Horace
tries to answer obliquely within the anecdote. Aristippus, who
admits his dependency (but in terms of duty, *officium*), has chosen
to associate with kings; Diogenes, who blinds himself to the facts
of life, is unwittingly subordinate to the masses (*populus*), who
support him with charity. But the defence of what was, after all,
Horace's own way of life cannot end there.

He goes on from the anecdote to give a larger account of the
aspiration to improve one's lot. Now, that this was acceptable to
Roman social practice is clear from Cicero, who says in the *De
officiis* that a richer man should give gifts of money to one less well
off who aims to better himself socially (2. 18. 61–3, especially *ut
altiorem gradum ascendant*). Horace looks at the issue from the point
of view of the less well off. Indeed the letter of recommendation for

---

[26] In the circumstances *nullius* should be taken as masculine 'no one' rather than
neuter 'nothing'.

Septimius, to which allusion has already been made, also shows
that Horace approves of aspiration; if he did not, he would hardly
have supported his young friend's suit with Tiberius. To return
to the seventeenth epistle, Horace pointedly asks whether or not
the successful aspirant acted manfully (38 *viriliter*). The adverb
emphasizes method, how we go about it, and it seems also to hark
back to the search for a definition of the *vir bonus* in the previous
letter. This emphasis on method harmonizes with the too often misunderstood opening of the letter, where Horace repeats Scaeva's
question which elicited the poem as a reply: '*quo* tandem *pacto*
deceat maioribus uti' (*Ep.* 1. 17. 2).[27] The emphasis there too is
on 'how' and on the honourableness (*deceat*) of the enterprise.
Ambition he takes in his stride; it is rather our management of it
that counts. Thus the timid man who fails to aspire is condemned
as a weakling (*Ep.* 1. 17. 40 *parvis animis et parvo corpore*; the
repetition of the epithet underscores the contempt). Such people
had better not try at all, since the cultivation of the great ones of
society calls for diplomacy and effort. Professor Nisbet and Miss
Hubbard are refreshingly aware of the normal Roman view that
association with the great was a distinction[28] (an apt sidelight
is cast on this assumption by Velleius Paterculus, who proudly
records that his fellow candidates for the praetorship were noble-
men and members of the priestly *collegia*).[29] That Horace shares this
attitude is further confirmed in a late lyric, the invitation to one
Vergilius, who is described as *iuvenum nobilium cliens* (*Odes* 4. 12.
15). To be sure, this poem's tone is as misunderstood by some
modern readers as is that of the seventeenth epistle; T. E. Page got
it wrong, but E. C. Wickham knew that the phrase was intended
as a compliment.[30]

The reward of successful clientship was the enjoyment with
one's superior friend of the good things of life. That was what
Aristippus secured: tasty meals, fine clothes, a horse to ride. These
comfort and console us for the inevitable miseries and disappoint-
ments of life. Yet the man who would be at home in the world

[27] *Tandem* is commonly used to introduce questions, and can be picked up when
they are reported indirectly; see *OLD* s.v. 1b. It is for this reason that I assume that
Scaeva is presented as having asked Horace for advice.

[28] See their note on *decus* at *Odes* 1. 1. 2.

[29] See 2. 124. 4 and Syme (1958) 759.

[30] Nisbet and Hubbard (1978), however, find the poem humorous in their note
on *Odes* 2. 20. 6, as did Orelli, and Syme (1986) 397; this view does not appeal.

must not repudiate his integrity. And it is personal integrity above all else that Horace seeks to preserve, and encourages his addressees to preserve, during their siege of society. Aristippus claims to play the hanger-on 'for his own sake' (*Ep.* 1. 17. 19 *scurror ego ipse mihi*; the pronouns enhance the sense of deliberate and independent choice). Diogenes, who is at war with the world, none the less panders to the common people to secure his bread and so loses in Horace's eyes all respectability (he never was really independent). After all, the Cynic's integrity proves so brittle that the loss of his filthy rags would cause it to crumble. Diogenes is unexpectedly wedded to mere externals. Aristippus, who has a core of solid worth, is no different whatever he wears. Horace suggests that what we need while besieging society is the flexible integrity of an Aristippus.

The poem is, then, in effect an apologia for Horace's own way of life. The autobiographical strain in his poetry is not only exemplary but at times also defensive. This is perhaps more apparent in his earlier poetry, published at a time when Horace was first coming into notice and needed to answer his personal critics. The sixth satire of the first book is a case in point; in it Horace makes clear that he has no intention of climbing higher than he is, and, as we have seen, he stresses the honourable means by which he achieved his present position. The fourth epode attacks an upstart *tribunus militum*, so as to maximize the difference between the poet and the freedman. A defensive note is less prominent in the *Epistles*, perhaps because the poet's own position is more secure, but it is still there, especially in the seventeenth letter. We should recall that in its origins ancient autobiography often was apologetic.[31]

To round off the analysis of this poem, it will be worth contrasting the advice of Erasmus with Horace's, for his doctrine must strike anyone as repugnant. Erasmus's own social position was not so very different from Horace's. In order to support himself at a time when the only secure institutions, the monasteries, were hardly eager to foster the study of literature, he had to look for patronage. His constant fear, however, was that the acceptance of presents from prelates and monarchs must compromise his

---

[31] See the *Oxford Classical Dictionary*[2] s.v. *Biography, Roman*, sect. 2. In discussion Prof. Jasper Griffin drew attention to the defensive tone, which I here try to account for.

independence.[32] The upshot was that he lived in financial straits for much of his life (this was due in part to his less than Horatian lifestyle). In his later middle age he was in just the position that Horace was at the time of the writing of the *Epistles*, and he used his own experience to advise younger men who needed to rely on grandees for their support. He reaches the same conclusion: be adaptable and preserve your independence. But to this he adds a dash of cynicism in his detailed instruction that goes well beyond the urbanities of Horace.[33] He urges, for instance, a complete lack of trust in others and a concealment of true thought and feeling. In a word, he says, be dead to shame and assume a mask. Here we may well see a truly cold ruthlessness. Horace's own *moyen de parvenir* could not have been more different, because he enjoins a more difficult disposition, a supple yet frank independence. We see this set out in the eighteenth letter, to Lollius.

Lollius is actively pursuing a career; he has served as a soldier under Augustus in Spain (*Ep.* I. 18. 55-7). He has to that extent already arrived; if, indeed, he is the son of M. Lollius, the consul of 21 BC, then he finds himself in the very swim of things.[34] But his position is none the less subordinate (Horace seems to sense that Roman society is being turned into a royal court, centred upon a single princely family). He has the problems not of one on the rise, but of the courtier.[35] (And again, if he is the son of the consul, his nobility is recent, which might expose him to all sorts of snubs in the hierarchy of Roman society.) So almost the first thing that Horace says to his young friend is that affability, the mean between toadying and truculence, is a virtue in social relationships. If Lollius wants to maintain his position he will need to be accommodating in an agreeable way. (To glance into the next century, this

---

[32] The early chapters of Froude (1894) emphasize Erasmus's financial difficulties and his reluctance to commit himself to a patron or a benefice. This all goes to show how exceptional Maecenas was.

[33] The letters referred to by Froude (1894) 304-5 (= *Ep.* 600 in the Leiden edition of 1703) are especially chilling. Soberer is the advice to Cann at p. 351 = *Ep.* 1832 in Allen and Allen (1906-58); one would like to think this is because Cann was coming to England, not the imperial Court.

[34] It used to be assumed that Lollius was either the son or at least a very close relation of the consul. This view was opposed by Groag (1927) on grounds of tone and content which ought not to have convinced R. Syme; see Syme (1978) 185 n. 4; (1986) 396. I am grateful to Prof. M. H. Crawford for discussing this matter with me.

[35] My own view of Lollius' position is anticipated by La Penna (1992).

is surely the *comitas*, 'social tact', which some praised in Germanicus and which Tacitus found worthy of praise in Seneca.[36]) The note is sounded at the outset with the warning word *inconcinna* (line 6); truculence is inharmonious (the word helps us recall Aristippus in the previous poem). The need to be yielding is stressed at lines 43 and 44: *cessisse, cede*, words embedded in the story of Zethus and Amphion. This myth is as usual paradigmatic, and the cultivated poet Amphion shows true brotherly feeling in yielding. Lollius must learn the lesson, and fall in with his superior friend's wishes, which after all are creditable to both men. (We are never told who the superior friend is, but clues point to a princely personage, for he is someone who enjoys a re-creation of the battle of Actium in a country fish-pond; *Ep.* 1. 18. 61–4.)

Lollius seemed to need advice on treading the narrow path of true independence within a hierarchical aristocracy now transforming itself into a royal court. The nineteenth letter looks at the issue in the narrower but more personally Horatian context of literature. Here the Roman writer is faced, on the one hand, with the tradition of imitating the literary masters of the past and, on the other, with the need to set his own distinctive stamp (the Greeks called it 'character') upon his work. Horace sees the clumsy imitator (poor Celsus in the third epistle might turn out to be such a one) as over-dependent upon a model or else dazzled into aping its faults. The result of misunderstanding the correct approach to imitation is servitude: *servum pecus* (*Ep.* 1. 19. 19) is his withering dismissal of such buffoons, and it recalls his demotion of the so-called *vir bonus* to the level of a slave at the end of the sixteenth letter. The high road to literary success is rather to be found within the tradition itself, if rightly understood, in figures such as Sappho and Alcaeus, who managed so to manipulate their model (as Horace views the relationship), Archilochus, that they produced fully independent masterpieces (*Ep.* 1. 19. 26–31). That is the path Horace successfully trod, and so, in his usual exemplary fashion, urges upon his readers (it does not matter if we are not poets, since the message can be adapted to suit any needs).

The last epistle, the twentieth, continues reflections upon slavery and freedom in the writer's experience. Horace now addresses his book of newly assembled letters in the person of a home-bred slave,

---

[36] *Ann.* 2. 13. 1; 2. 72. 3; 13. 2. 1.

pining for liberty and low amusements. The author owns and controls his productions only so long as he keeps them under lock and
key. Once he publishes them, they secure their freedom, but must
also take their own chances and certainly endure rebuffs (even as
the author himself endures disparaging comment; cf. *Ep.* 1. 19.
36). The author loses control, his creatures secure a life of their
own. Freedom costs something, but the price must be paid if the
artist is to have what he most craves, recognition. Henry James's
experience again mirrors Horace's. As an artist he imposed upon
himself the most exacting standards, and yet he yearned for the
popularity of a Kipling (whose art he of course acknowledged) or
an Edith Wharton. His own work could never have secured such
widespread appeal, but he kept hoping. Horace seems to be no different. He knows his work will suffer at the hands of the malicious,
but he also wants it to be in the hands of the *ingenui*. The
inconsistency of his position is past resolution, so the book is let go.

It is in this last letter of the collection that he makes his most
explicit boast that he had found favour in peace and in war with
the chief men of the city (*Ep.* 1. 20. 23), an accomplishment to
be classed among his *virtutes*. It is this pride in his purely
social achievement (he leaves the poetry out of account at this
point) which we need to understand. Perhaps since the age of
Romanticism we have expected our artists to hold aloof from the
world, to be at odds with it, to suffer at its hands. What, then, do
we make of a Rubens, whose art secured him the friendship of
kings (a fact proudly affirmed on his tombstone)?[37] The world's
esteem and friendship have not always been slighted by artists, and
they are not immature or sordid (as unworldly scholars fancy) for
courting social success, especially if they use their position, as
Horace clearly did, to improve the lot of their friends as well.

To revert for a moment to the eighteenth epistle, Horace
concluded it by assuring Lollius that he would have time enough
for going his own way. When would that time come? In the previous letter Horace had said that it was not only the rich who have
their delights, and that the obscure can live well (*Ep.* 1. 17. 9–10).
This reminder is more insistently pressed upon Lollius (who is at

---

[37] In St James's Church, Antwerp: 'Appelles dici meruit atque ad regum
principumque virorum amicitias gradum sibi fecit.' Rubens, to be sure, was
domi nobilis, but the improvement in his status could not pass unrecorded as an
achievement.

the top already with his money, success, and superior friends, all secured while he is yet young). The letter to him closes with a picture of Horace content upon his estate, out of the rat race. So once again Horace's autobiographical notices serve as an example. Lollius too may in due course seek to remove himself from the world. There is no disgrace in that, above all for one who has improved his position through his own character and achievements. The emphasis upon retirement as the fruition of success in the world is clear from the first epistle, where Horace compares himself to an old gladiator or racehorse.

Maecenas had given Horace a farm in the Sabine country (it was surely not, however, his only estate), and that farm became a symbol of success and worldly fulfilment. But to enjoy it Horace had to be away from Rome, and as he admits in the eighth epistle, he cannot do without Rome altogether. Now in this he is again like James, who retired from the hubbub of London to Lamb House in Rye. Yet James always came back to town for that so necessary rush of adrenalin induced by social intercourse. (It is also interesting to observe how similar the elderly James is to the Horace of the time of the *Epistles*, for both write letters to much younger men who combine a position in society with an interest in writing; both are passionately concerned to improve the artistic quality of contemporary literature and to rescue it from the second-rate complacency of the salon.) We might also think of Alexander Pope, another writer of humble birth whose talents secured him the friendship of the great. He too, after achieving worldly success through his poetry, retired from London, but not to the back of beyond, rather suburban Twickenham. These three subtle artists needed the town with its racy glamour to invigorate their fancy. Their retirement is only partial, never complete. Horace admits this, but the countryside becomes increasingly necessary, and in the epistles serves as a symbol of achieved independence. He summed up his feeling in the phrase *vivo et regno* (*Ep.* i. 10. 8), where each verb has a strong sense: in the countryside he feels most truly alive and in control of his own affairs. That is the theme of the seventh epistle, which now deserves notice.

Horace apologizes to Maecenas for deceiving him about the time of his next visit to Rome. He must still stay away and begs not to be pressed (he does not suggest that he has yet been pressed) to return to the life that Maecenas still has energy for, the life of pleasure. The letter describes in various ways the dangers of dependency for one who does not know when he (or she) has had enough or when he is well off. The greedy vixen gets stuck in the grain-bin; the auctioneer Mena thinks wrongly that he and the countryside will agree with one another. Telemachus is a more positive example (owed to Homer, our moral guide from the second epistle), since he knows what is not suitable to his circumstances. The lessons to be learnt from this letter are many, but they all flow from the writer's experience of his own society. They are not abstract theories about conduct, deduced from some rationally established goal. Horace, like everyone else, wanted to be in charge of his own life, but for a Roman to do that he needed a considerable measure of material well-being, to secure which required the help of richer, more highly placed friends. Horace does not aspire to get out of life as much as he can, but only what he needs; he formulates his ideal of society in that which he described to the pest as having been gathered about Maecenas (*Sat.* I. 9. 48–52), a society in which each member had his own role to play unhindered by those of greater wealth or learning (this was not the society of the salons, where mutual compliments were exacted: *Ep.* 2. 2. 95–103). To achieve such goals requires self-discipline and a check upon desires. In Horace's case it also needed the existence of enlightened patronage, as found in the figure of Maecenas.

The seventh epistle is dense with lessons about the relation between friends of unequal financial and social resources. These lessons are to be learnt by superior and inferior alike. The wealthy man's chief duty must be not to press his friend, who will feel bound by gratitude to comply (not that it is hinted that Maecenas has pressed). This crucial lesson is encapsulated in the phrase *lenibus imperiis* (*Ep.* I. 18. 45); his bidding should be mild, the sort with which the inferior will not find difficulty in complying. Thus, Horace feels a confidence that when he asks for leave to be absent from Maecenas' circle, it will be granted; indeed, so confident is he that he does not even ask for it in so many words (*Ep.* I. 7. 4–5). He is free.

The first book of *Epistles* is avowedly admonitory. In it the poet aims to fulfil a task he believes appropriate to his calling. At the same time he is himself still learning (*Ep.* I. 17. 3 *docendus adhuc*), so his advice comes better from the stores of his own experience than from some untried theory. This is just where philosophy fails.

It is not apparently founded on experience, but on theory, which at its best can be usefully applied to the way we live. But all philosophical systems have their special blind spots, none covers all the possibilities or suits all temperaments. Only experience will prove a reliable guide. That is why Horace, in comparing himself to a retired gladiator, says that he is *satis spectatum* (*Ep.* I. I. 2); he has sufficiently proven his worth, and not just as a poet. Thus, the advice he will give has passed the test in his own life. That life must therefore become the theme of his poems yet again, but not in the old forms. In order to review and assess his achievements and advise others on the way up, Horace could not simply recycle the satirical *sermo*. Once again his poetry is made to reflect his life. Just as he had achieved social independence after the long haul up through the ranks, so he at last achieved a literary freedom: he invented a poetic kind unknown to the Greeks and barely exploited by the Romans, the verse epistle, to be the vessel of a new poetry of experience. Indeed, now both as man and as artist he was wholly free.

16

Libertino Patre Natus:
True or False?

GORDON WILLIAMS

I OFFER this paper as a tribute to my friend of forty years, Robin Nisbet. The topic is particularly appropriate, since it was to Robin Nisbet that I first suggested this hypothesis in 1957, a few weeks after Eduard Fraenkel's great book appeared. On that occasion, as on many others, Robin gave me helpful advice and suggestions, though I did not then pursue the idea. It was only many years later that I discovered that Niebuhr had anticipated me in a single sentence in a lecture on Horace.[1] The idea was also put forward in a brief footnote by E. T. Salmon in his book *Samnium and the Samnites* (1967).[2] I tried the idea very informally on an audience at a Liverpool Classical Seminar led by Francis Cairns in 1981, and again on an audience at a lecture in the Institute of Classical Studies in London in 1986; and I am most grateful to both audiences for helpful comments.

I

We know about Horace's father: Suetonius tells us, and, if that were not sufficient, Horace tells us himself. His father was an ex-slave, a *libertinus*. In fact, however, Suetonius had no other source of information; his wording clearly shows that he was interpreting quite literally what the poet says in *Satires* I. 6—a normal procedure for ancient literary biographers when other sources failed.

I am very grateful to friends and colleagues for reading this essay and making useful suggestions, especially to Ramsay MacMullen, Elizabeth Meyer, and Susan Treggiari.

[1] Niebuhr (1848) 133.   [2] Salmon (1967) 369 n. 5.

Yet it is routinely taken as an unquestionable fact that Horace's father had been a slave. So the interesting question becomes: where did Horace's father come from? Otto Seeck in 1902, who did not think highly of Horace's poetry, compared him with Heine and asserted that the father was a Jew.[3] This thesis had been argued extensively by Guglielmo Braun some twenty-four years earlier;[4] he traced many parallels between Horace's poetry and various books of the Old Testament, and he concluded that the poet's father was an enlightened Jew from Alexandria. He even interpreted one of Augustus' jokes at the poet as a reference to his circumcision. Karl Mras set himself to refute this in a paper published the year after the anniversary of the poet's 2,000th birthday in 1935.[5] But Mras then went on to assert that the father was clearly a slave from Asia Minor or Syria. He started from an examination of the rare word *flaccus*—which refers to large pendulous ears, characteristic of certain breeds of dog—and quoted Rudolf Martin, who published a second edition of his handbook of anthropology in Jena in 1928. After an analysis of length of ears in various peoples, Martin concluded: 'The longest ears are found in Mongols and in the Semitic peoples' (1928: i. 572). So, not a Jew, but from the Middle East and, in particular, from 'the Eldorado of slave-hunters and slave-dealers, Asia Minor and Syria' (1928: i. 73). He then went on to demonstrate a close affinity between the attitudes and outlooks of Horace and Lucian.

II

But the so-called 'fact' needs to be called into question. Was Horace's father really what we mean by a slave in Italy? Horace tells us quite a lot about his father and, though what he tells us is likely to be tailored to his particular purpose in each passage, much of it sounds very odd about a former imported slave. The status of his father as a *libertinus* depends on a phrase that is repeated three times in one poem. It is a metrically discordant phrase that draws emphatic attention to itself: *libertino patre natum* (*Sat.* 1. 6. 6, 45, 46). In all occurrences the phrase is used in a way that can only properly be signalled by enclosing it in quotation-marks: that is, the words do not represent the poet's own description of himself,

---

[3] Seeck (1902) 134.   [4] Braun (1877–8).   [5] Mras (1936).

but that used derisively by others (the derision is signified by 5 *naso suspendis adunco* and 46 *rodunt*). The phrase is only once repeated elsewhere, in the σφραγίς that closes *Epistles* I, which the poet offers to the book/slave as advertising copy. Here the word-order is slightly altered to *me libertino natum patre*, but the phrase clearly recalls its earlier occurrences and deserves quotation-marks here too, as the context makes clear:

> cum tibi sol tepidus pluris admoverit auris,
> me libertino natum patre et in tenui re
> maiores pennas nido extendisse loqueris
> ut quantum generi demas virtutibus addas.
>
> (*Ep.* I. 20. 19–22)

When a gentler sun shall have collected a larger number of ears around you, you will be found announcing that I, 'born of a freedman father' and in straitened circumstances, spread wings too big for my nest, with the result that, to the extent that you detract from my family, you add to my virtues.

He means that a work on practical ethics will attract more customers the humbler the author's beginnings and the less his physical attractiveness (as he goes on to elaborate in his own case), because the greater then will be his own moral strength and authority. There is no hint of his father's servile status anywhere else. So what the evidence amounts to is that men who wished to deride the poet described him as born of a freedman father, and in both passages where this phrase is offered the poet had a special interest in representing himself as suffering from a major social disadvantage (the better to emphasize the value of his own moral qualities).

Those moral qualities, he acknowledges, he owes to his father; and in *Satires* I. 4 he uses his father's method of moral instruction as an explanation and justification of his own type of social satire (in which the poet claims to be a moral instructor like his father). His father brought him to Rome to school (I will come back to the implications of this later), and the poet gives a picture of his father walking down the streets of Rome with him, exemplifying the various types of behaviour to avoid by pointing out prominent Romans—of whose private life he shows a remarkable knowledge. Is this a former imported slave? How has he gained his information about upper-class Romans? How often has he come to Rome?

How could this—apparently deeply heartfelt—portrait be made plausible to Horace's readers? As if this were not difficult enough, note the very words that the poet puts into his father's mouth:

> sapiens vitatu quidque petitu
> sit melius causas reddet tibi; mi satis est si
> traditum ab antiquis morem servare [possum].
>
> (*Sat.* I. 4. 115-17)

A philosopher will give you the theory of what should be avoided and what aimed at; for me it is sufficient if I am able to maintain the moral code handed down by our ancestors.

If this is a former slave speaking, then it is most reminiscent of Plautine jokes in which slaves refer to their ancestors. But if it is to be understood seriously (as it certainly seems to be), then this is the portrait of a man who has a strong sense of tradition—and a very practical homespun sense of tradition that regards typically Greek theoretical debates on ethics as superfluous. Centuries of living in the same stable society, with lovingly preserved traditional values, are surely to be understood to lie behind such attitudes. Inheritance, and the preservation of it, is important to such a man, and Horace represents his father as saying:

> nonne vides Albi ut male vivat filius, utque
> Baius inops? magnum documentum ne patriam rem
> perdere quis velit.
>
> (*Sat.* I. 4. 109-11)

Don't you see how wretchedly Albius' son lives, how poverty-stricken is Baius?—a powerful lesson against anyone's dissipating his inheritance.

By the time Horace wrote this satire, he had not only acquired a theoretical training in ethical philosophy at Athens, but he had also lost his inheritance (*Ep.* 2. 2. 43-52). In *Satires* I. 6 he represents his father as a *coactor* (86-7), a type of banker who specialized in the financing of auction sales, and as a small farmer (line 71). That style of life—combining a profession with the running of a farm—strikes one as entirely typical of life immediately below the level of the upper class in Italian towns.[6] The provincial aristocracy might despise the profession, but it played a very significant role in the economy of Italian towns,[7] and its considerable

---

[6] See, e.g. D'Arms (1981) 50, 102, 157.   [7] See Rauh (1989).

profits (for all Horace says) could be invested in land.[8] Such, I suspect, was the lifestyle of Horace's grandparents, so that Horace's father had good reason to value the prudent management of inheritances.

III

It is hard to see Horace's father as a former imported oriental slave, haphazardly sold in Venusia, through which town the Via Appia conveniently meanders on its way north from the east-facing port of Brundisium. But it is equally hard to see the poet as the son of such a man, for he constantly gives expression to feelings of pride and joy in belonging to a particular region of Italy, and those feelings also appeal to a sense of long-established tradition. That love of place appears everywhere.[9] In *Sat.* 1. 5. 77–8, where the Via Appia begins to lift steeply south of Beneventum into the mountains of Apulia, the poet writes 'incipit ex illo montis Apulia notos | ostentare mihi quos torret Atabulus'; this detail is surrounded by verbs in the first-person plural, but this moment of joy is private to the poet (as is the local name for the Sirocco). It appears in the σφραγίς to *Odes* 1–3 in the pride of the poet that his fame will reach to his own native region (*Odes* 3. 30. 10–12; cf. *Odes* 4. 6. 27 *Dauniae defende decus Camenae*, referring to the *Carmen Saeculare*).[10] It appears in his account of the miracle that saved him in infancy on Mt Voltur, when he wandered away from his nurse Pullia, and which became the talk of the little towns around:

> mirum quod foret omnibus
> quicumque celsae nidum Acherontiae
> saltusque Bantinos et arvum
> pingue tenent humilis Forenti . . .
>
> (*Odes* 3. 4. 13–16)

so that it was a miracle for all who dwell in the nest of lofty Acherontia and the glades of Bantia and the rich loam of low-lying Forentum . . .

An intense pride and joy in the region are expressed in the economical and vivid descriptions of the three little towns,

[8] Mommsen (1877).
[9] For collections of passages see e.g. Canter (1930–1); Sirago (1958).
[10] See the analysis by Fraenkel (1957).

unknown otherwise to history. But I want to mention an example
where I can now correct a regrettable error of my own. It is *Odes*
3. 6. 33–44:[11]

> non his iuventus orta parentibus
> infecit aequor sanguine Punico,
> > Pyrrhumque et ingentem cecidit
> > > Antiochum Hannibalemque dirum,
>
> sed rusticorum mascula militum
> proles, Sabellis docta ligonibus
> > versare glebas et severae
> > > matris ad arbitrium recisos
>
> portare fustis, sol ubi montium
> mutaret umbras et iuga demeret
> > bobus fatigatis, amicum
> > > tempus agens abeunte curru.

Not from parents like that did the youth arise who stained the sea with
the blood of Carthage and slew Pyrrhus and great Antiochus and fearful
Hannibal, but a masculine race born of rustic warriors, trained to turn the
turfs with Sabellian spades and, at the bidding of an austere mother, to
bring home cut wood when the sun altered the shadows of the mountains
and took yokes off weary oxen, bringing the friendly time with his flying
chariot.

In 1969 I carelessly translated *Sabellis* as 'Sabine'. But the poet is
thinking of the contributions to Roman forces so often made by the
tribes of Samnium, and, in particular, he is thinking of the steadfast loyalty of Venusia when Hannibal attacked southern Italy and
most other towns went over to him. That military contribution is
signalled by the prominence of the high-principled mother (the
father being away at war).

Horace specifically represents himself as a Sabellian.[12] Hence the
terrifying prophecy given to him as a child that he suddenly
remembers when he cannot escape from the pushy social climber
(neither poison nor sword nor illness will be the end of him, only
a compulsive talker); this prophecy was given to him by an old
Sabellian woman (*Sat.* 1. 9. 29). In *Ep.* 1. 16. 49 the interlocutor
(*Sabellus*) is a transparent disguise for the poet himself. Of the
Sabellian tribes, his own, the Apulians, are especially selected for
mention: they are praised as *impigri* (*Odes* 3. 16. 26) and, when
the poet wants to epitomize the shame caused to Roman soldiers

----

[11] Williams (1969) ad loc.   [12] Sonnenschein (1898).

in Parthian captivity, he selects the Marsi and the Apuli (*Odes* 3.
5. 9)—cf. *militaris Daunias* (*Odes* 1. 22. 13). The admiration for and
identification with the people of the region around Venusia find
purest expression in the superb portrait of the farmer Ofellus, a
neighbour of Horace's family whom the poet has known since boyhood (*Sat.* 2. 2. 112) and whose property was confiscated in 42 BC
at the same time as Horace's—though Umbrenus, the soldier who
was the beneficiary, put Ofellus back on the property as a tenant
farmer paying rent in kind (perhaps the same happened to Horace's
estate; he never says). Ofellus is portrayed unsentimentally with
loving admiration as an ideal human being, like the poet's father,
a natural philosopher of sturdy homespun wit; and, to some
extent, this portrait can be read as fleshing out the portrait of his
father (who, if he was alive in 42 BC, suffered the same fate as
Ofellus).[13]

C,   During his consultation of Q. Trebatius Testa in *Satires* 2. 1, the
poet reflects on his own identity in a particularly interesting way:

> sequor hunc, Lucanus an Apulus anceps:
> nam Venusinus arat finem sub utrumque colonus,
> missus ad hoc, pulsis, vetus est ut fama, Sabellis,
> quo ne per vacuum Romano incurreret hostis,
> sive quod Apula gens seu quod Lucania bellum
> incuteret violenta.   (34-9)

I take him [Lucilius] as my model, uncertain whether to call myself a
Lucanian or an Apulian, since the Venusian settler ploughs right up to the
territories of both; he was sent there—and the Sabellians, as the old story
goes, driven out—to prevent an enemy invading through a territory
unguarded by Romans, whether the violence of the Apulian or of the
Lucanian tribe should threaten war.

The source of the uncertainty here is surely not, as Kiessling and
Heinze appear to have thought, because Horace's 'father, the slave,
belonged to those *quorum nemo queat patriam monstrare parentis*
(Juvenal 8. 45)', but because his father's property was in a part of
the territory of Venusia that could originally have belonged either
to the Apuli or to the Lucani. That is, when land was seized for
the original colony, it was taken from a region that lay partly in
Apulia and partly in Lucania, but in such a way that the original

---

[13] He was almost certainly dead, since Horace represents the loss of the estate as
being his own loss (*Ep.* 2. 2. 50-1).

boundary was now impossible to trace. This seems the most reasonable interpretation if no assumptions are made about the father's servile status. That is, the poet regards himself as belonging to one of the pre-Roman Sabellian tribes, who, of course, re-established themselves in Venusia under Roman occupation. In fact, Oscan culture remained strong in Venusia even after it became a Latin colony, and fresh Roman colonists had to be sent out to the town on a number of occasions.

But this passage arouses a further puzzling question. How is it relevant for Horace to treat so explicitly the problem of border territories and of tribal identities in the course of consulting the jurist about writing satire? The disquisition cannot just be designed to show that Horace was endowed with a pugnacious frontier spirit, suited to satire.[14] The question admits of a different explanation.

In 89 BC the rebel forces had great success in Apulia under a certain Trebatius (Appian, *BC* I. 228-9), until he was finally defeated by C. Cosconius. This Trebatius may well have been the grandfather of C. Trebatius Testa,[15] just as Herius Asinius, commander of the rebel forces of the Marrucini till he was killed in action, was the grandfather of C. Asinius Pollio.[16] Trebatius Testa, as Cicero's letters to him show, had estates and relatives in Velia in Lucania, where Cicero happened to have been visiting (*Fam.* 7. 19); but he was also the patron in Rome of the people of Ulubrae. If the rebel Trebatius was his grandfather, then the family, although they had extensive property elsewhere, may have been Venusian (which would explain the prominence of Trebatius as a Sabellian praetor). In that case, the special point of the legal consultation of C. Trebatius Testa in *Satires* 2. I was that the families of the poet and the jurist had been friends of long standing and shared in common the same puzzle over tribal identity, carefully posed here as a parody of proper judicial deliberation (and sharpened for Trebatius by the fact that he had important links to Lucania). Trebatius Testa was probably born about 85 BC, Asinius Pollio was born in 76 BC, and Horace in 65 BC. I should guess that these two important men were patrons to the poet (and to his father) when he first came to Rome, and that Pollio, who held the consulship in 40 BC, used his power as consul to appoint the poet to the prestigious post of *scriba* after his disastrous flirtation with

---

[14] Kiessling and Heinze (1914-30) ad loc.
[15] Salmon (1967) 357 n. 4.   [16] ibid. 356.

the Republican/senatorial cause at Philippi (from which, for all he says about his poverty, Horace returned sufficiently wealthy to be able to purchase the highly profitable post).[17] Trebatius was then rewarded with *Satires* 2. 1, and Pollio with the splendid ode 2. 1 (both highly conspicuous poems). Both men were supporters of Julius Caesar, the patron of both, though Trebatius, unlike Pollio, shifted his support to Octavian—which made him the right person to be represented as offering the poet the Lucilian advice to write epic in support of Octavian.

The question can now be asked: what did Horace's grandfather do in the Social War? But unfortunately it cannot be answered. It would be interesting to know if the grandfathers of Trebatius, Pollio, and Horace all had one conspicuous thing in common— service for the rebel cause in the Social War, a cause for which all three suffered and died.

When he talks of his father in *Satires* 1. 6, Horace says that his father refused to send him to the local school run by a teacher called Flavius:

> causa fuit pater his, qui macro pauper agello
> noluit in Flavi ludum me mittere, magni
> quo pueri magnis e centurionibus orti,
> laevo suspensi loculos tabulamque lacerto,
> ibant octonos referentes Idibus aeris.
> sed puerum est ausus Romam portare, docendum
> artis quas doceat quivis eques atque senator
> semet prognatos. vestem servosque sequentis,
> in magno ut populo, si qui vidisset, avita
> ex re praeberi sumptus mihi crederet illos.
> ipse mihi custos incorruptissimus omnes
> circum doctores aderat. quid multa? pudicum,
> qui primus virtutis honos, servavit ab omni
> non solum facto, verum opprobrio quoque turpi;
> nec timuit sibi ne vitio quis verteret olim
> si praeco parvas aut, ut fuit ipse, coactor
> mercedes sequerer; neque essem questus. at hoc nunc
> laus illi debetur et a me gratia maior.

(Sat. 1. 6. 71–88)

For this [my moral strength of character] my father was responsible; he, though of modest means with a meagre little farm, refused to send me to

[17] For details of the purchase and operation and profits of the apparitorial office of *scriba* see Badian (1989); Purcell (1983).

the school of Flavius—to which hulking boys born of hulking centurions used to go, hanging their satchels and writing-tablets over their left shoulders and paying their fee of eight asses in the middle of every month. Rather, he had the audacity to take his boy to Rome to be taught the same subjects that any equestrian or senator would teach those born of his own blood. If anyone should have noticed—seeing that the crowds were dense—my clothing and the slaves at my heel, he would have assumed that the expenditure lavished on me came from ancestral inheritance. He used to escort me himself in person around all my teachers, a guardian of most steadfast integrity. And so he kept me chaste (and that is the prime distinction of virtue) not only from any disgraceful act but even from rumour. And yet he did not act out of fear that someone at some time might blame him were I to pursue a modest income as an auctioneer or, as he was himself, as a banker—and I would not have reproached him. So, for this reason, I now owe him even greater praise and gratitude.

It was clearly a bold and surprising move for Horace's father to take his son to school at Rome, and it is usually assumed that he did this to provide the boy with the best education possible. But more analysis is worthwhile here. The emphasis on the size of the centurions and the size of their sons should remind us that Horace describes himself as *corporis exigui* 'of diminutive physique' (*Ep.* 1. 20. 24). (It is worth recalling in this context that about 1,500 Sabellian skeletons were found at Aufidena and that they belonged, almost without exception, to dolichocephalic individuals of medium height.[18]) Perhaps in a Sabellian town Romans—and especially Roman soldiers—were instantly distinguishable from natives by their height and bulk. Further, the schoolmaster's name, Flavius, seems Roman. So this may have been a school in Venusia especially designed for the practical needs of sons of Roman soldiers. But Horace's father had higher aspirations for his son. Also, if there was one single origin for the ugly phrase *libertino patre natum*, it may have been the mockery of the poet by sons of the Roman veterans (who would have had access to the background information).[19] The bullying of the diminutive Horace by such ruffians may have been another strong motive for his father to go to such extraordinary lengths to avoid the local school.[20]

---

[18] Salmon (1967) 57.　　　　　　　　　　　　[19] Fraenkel (1957) 3.
[20] For schoolboy mockery and bullying see the anecdote of Cassius and Faustus, son of Sulla (Val. Max. 3. 1. 3; Plut. *Brutus* 9), or schoolboys fighting as 'Pompeians' and 'Caesarians' (Cassius Dio 41. 39. 4).

Further speculation is possible. Horace elsewhere tells us the name of probably the most famous of his teachers, Orbilius (*Ep.* 2. 1. 71).[21] L. Orbilius Pupillus came from Beneventum. He was aged 50 when he went to Rome in 63 BC to set himself up as a teacher—previously he had held the post of local magistrate's clerk (*apparituram magistratibus fecit*), and he had then served very successfully in the Roman army. Unlike Venusia, Beneventum did not join the rebel cause in the Social War, though the two towns are only fifty or sixty miles apart. Since Beneventum lies on the Via Appia north of Venusia, I should speculate that Horace's father had come to know the slightly older Orbilius (perhaps on journeys to Rome) before he moved to the capital; and it was that acquaintance and his knowledge of the man's talent and moral strength (he had suffered the loss of both his parents, who had been murdered by enemies on the same day) that persuaded him to make his very bold and expensive move and take his son to Orbilius' school in Rome. Orbilius was a man of such distinction in his home town that, after his death at the age of one hundred, a statue was erected on the Capitol in Beneventum representing him seated, dressed in a *pallium*, with two book-boxes by his side. Incidentally, the fact that Horace's father did not hire a talented private tutor for his son suggests that he did not have the resources of a Cicero and that he probably took his profession as *coactor* and practised it in Rome, perhaps preceding his son in the *decuriae* of the *apparitores*, in addition to practising as *coactor argentarius* privately.[22] Just to be in Rome enabled father and son to meet and form useful relationships with important people, and, if I am right about Pollio and Trebatius, Horace's father possessed influential friends in Rome who could introduce him to others.

Another father who took his son to Rome to be educated was Cicero's. However, Marcus and Quintus received their education in the house of Crassus, and that type of education was beyond the reach of Horace's father. Cicero's own son Marcus, who was also privately educated at Rome, was the same age as Horace, and we next meet the two of them, together with various other young upper-class Romans, in Athens, seeking the higher education in philosophy and rhetoric that was normal for wealthy young aristo-

---

[21] Biography in Suet. *De gramm. et rhet.* 9.

[22] For the opportunities that opened up to a man who became an *apparitor* see Purcell (1983) 147–8.

crats. Among those young men was L. Bibulus, the nephew of
Brutus, whom Horace later mentions as being a friend and valued
reader of his poetry (*Sat.* 1. 10. 86). Horace was therefore not
excluded from this group by being 'of lower station' (Syme 1939:
198). Brutus joined them all in Athens and attended philosophical
lectures with them. He concealed his military preparations but
recruited many of them to his cause, including Marcus Cicero and
Horace. He made Horace a *tribunus militum*, as was his right as
commander. But that post normally went to young equestrians
or senators starting on a career. Why did Brutus do it?[23] In the
case of young Cicero there was some reason: he had already seen
military service as a cavalry commander with the forces of Pompey
(*De off.* 2. 45). I suspect that Horace likewise had had military
experience in similar circumstances before Brutus recruited him.
But Brutus' act shows that Horace's father was most unlikely to
have been an ex-slave—perhaps he was even by now *equestri censu.*

Where, then, did the well-remembered insults to Horace as
libertino patre natus originate? I suspect that the answer lies in what
happened at Venusia during the Social War.

IV

Venusia was the only Latin colony to join the rebels in the Social
War. It is recorded specifically by Appian (*BC* 1. 42), together with
'Canusia and many other towns', as attaching itself to Gaius
Vidacilius, the rebel commander in the region. He killed the chief
Roman citizens, but enrolled the ordinary people and slaves in his
army. The town is not mentioned again until late 89 BC, when
the Roman praetor Gaius Cosconius, after defeating Trebatius, the
rebel commander, overran the territories of Asculum (?Ausculum),
Larinum, and Venusia; but Venusia itself, which is in a very strong
position, clearly held out till 88 BC. In that year, Diodorus recounts,
'Metellus [i.e. Q. Caecilius Metellus Pius, probably proconsul in
88 BC—he had been praetor in 89] took by storm Venusia in
Apulia, a very important city that was held by many soldiers, and

---

[23] See Suolahti (1955) 57; he gives the explanation 'due to the necessity of
admitting to the service in times of war elements rather weak in social origin, one
typical example being the above mentioned son of a freedman, Q. Horatius Flaccus'
(117). But other cases are very hard to find; for one see Treggiari (1969) 64-5.

he took captive more than three thousand prisoners' (37. 2. 10).
My hypothesis is that Horace's grandfather and father were among
those prisoners. What happened to such captives?

In November of 89 BC the consul Gnaeus Pompeius Strabo took
Asculum. This town had been the scene of the slaughter of the
Roman praetor Servilius and of his legate Frontinus and then of all
Romans in the town (Appian, *BC* 1. 38). The only evidence for
what happened after its capture is a curt epitome by Orosius: 'After
Pompeius entered Asculum he beat with rods and beheaded the
prefects, the centurions, and all of the chief men, the slaves and
all the loot he sold by auction, the rest he ordered to leave, free
certainly but naked and needy' (5. 18. 26). The wholesale execu-
tions were clearly in reprisal for the slaughter of Roman citizens.
The auction of slaves and loot was routine—but were only slaves
auctioned, and all others sent away free? There are two cases that
strongly suggest otherwise.

M. Aurius Melinus, a prominent citizen of Larinum (itself a rebel
town), was captured at Asculum and bought by a senator Q.
Sergius and placed in his *ergastulum* in the Ager Gallicus. When his
presence there was finally discovered, he was then murdered by
scheming relatives to prevent his inheriting his mother's estate
(Cic. *Pro Cluentio* 21–25). Aurius had probably been serving with
the rebel army, been shut up in Asculum, and then captured when
the town fell.

Another very interesting case is that of P. Ventidius Bassus. He
was captured by Pompeius Strabo at Asculum and was carried in
chains by his mother in the triumph (A. Gellius 15. 4; Cassius Dio
43. 51. 5). His romantically successful later career, culminating in
the consulship, is told by Aulus Gellius. What about his father? He
could have been killed in the siege; but he may have been among
those executed. The son was enslaved, but later enrolled as a
Roman citizen.

That is what I suspect happened to the three thousand prisoners
taken after the capture of Venusia. Reprisals are sure to have been
exacted for the slaughter of Roman and prominent citizens (not
to speak of the stubborn resistance of the town). Horace never
mentions his grandfather: he may have been executed. The father
may have been spared, like Ventidius, because of his youth, but
sold into slavery. Even as late as 25 BC, under the authority of
Augustus, when the Salassi revolted, all males of military age were

sold into slavery.[24] But to Romans, in any case, *captivitas* was a form of *servitus*, and how were such prisoners subsequently enrolled as Roman citizens? In the case of the Italians after the Social War, there was a considerable delay in the granting of *civitas*, certainly to 86 BC and possibly to 84 BC. Since they were not yet citizens, they could not regain their status by exercise of *ius postliminii*. They may well have had to undergo manumission in order to gain *civitas*. But, of course, they would then have been registered as full Roman citizens. Therefore, to call Horace's father *libertinus* was a gross travesty of the facts; but that is the essence of insult. This would be enough in itself to explain the sneers of military men that Horace recalls in *Satires* I. 6.

V

What all this amounts to is that Suetonius relied only on a very literal interpretation of that satire for his statement that Horace's father was a freedman. He had no independent evidence for it. His reliance on literal interpretation is clear when he adds, after saying that Horace's father was a freedman and auction-banker: 'It has been believed that he was a salted-fish merchant, since someone in a quarrel once insulted him by saying: "How often have I seen your father wiping his nose with his arm."' This pretty story was clearly invented on the basis of Bion's famous reply when the king enquired about his origins;[25] and it was stimulated by Horace's own description of his satires (*Ep.* 2. 2. 60) 'ille Bioneis sermonibus et sale nigro', where *sale nigro* is a pun derived from Bion's *bon mot*. The likeliest motive for the invention lies in the ironic response of a disingenuously literal reader (that is, a reader who knew that Horace's father had not really been a slave) to the repeated *libertino patre natum* of *Satires* I. 6, repeated as a prized anecdote sufficiently often to come to Suetonius' attention (who was by nature a literal reader).

A more responsive interpretation of *Satires* I. 6 is needed. Horace represents himself in the *Satires* and in the σφραγίς to *Epistles* I as the homespun philosopher, with a disadvantaged background, who had learnt life's lessons the hard way, and whose words are therefore worth taking seriously. *Satires* I. 6 is central to this

---

[24] Strabo 4. 6, 7.   [25] Fraenkel (1957) 6–7.

self-portrait. He never says that *libertino patre natum* is true; the words are always in quotation-marks. He opens the satire by saying to Maecenas:

> . . . [non] naso suspendis adunco
> ignotos ut me libertino patre natum.   (5–6)

You do not turn up your nose at unknowns like me, born of a freedman father.

We are at first inclined, with Suetonius, to take that literally, but doubts are aroused by what immediately follows:

> cum referre negas quali sit quisque parente
> natus, dum ingenuus, persuades hoc tibi vere . . .   (7–8)

When you assert that it does not matter from what sort of father any man was born, provided he was free-born, you rightly persuade yourself of this . . .

Now we feel forced to take *dum ingenuus* as modifying *quisque*, since we apparently already know that Horace's father was not *ingenuus*. This seems universally accepted—except that Schütz wanted to take the word in its moral sense (which is impossible in view of 21 'ingenuo si non essem patre natus'). But Schütz properly recognized the awkwardness of having Horace allow Maecenas to dismiss his father with contempt. Also the run of the Latin here, where the emphasis is heavily on *quali . . . parente*, properly requires *dum ingenuus* to modify these words rather than *quisque*. Palmer cheerfully explains that Maecenas is here following the example of Augustus: 'Maecenas would not, for instance, have associated with Horace's father.' But if we read on, suspending judgement and recognizing that the reference of *dum ingenuus* is ambiguous, we soon come to this:

> censorque moveret
> Appius, ingenuo si non essem patre natus—
> vel merito quoniam in propria non pelle quiessem.   (20–2)

And [let us suppose] Appius as censor would have expelled me if I had not been born of a free-born father—perhaps rightly, because I had not been content to stay inside my own skin.

There is double irony here: Appius had notoriously admitted freedmen to the senate in 312 BC, while a descendant had carefully expelled them in 50 BC, and the possibility that Horace's father was not free-born is framed as an impossible condition. The truth—that the words *libertino patre natum* are spoken only by enemies who wish to injure (and whose words consequently have the status of what Demosthenes says about Aeschines' mother)—finally emerges at lines 45-6, where the poet reviews the circumstances of his friendship with Maecenas in preparation for describing at length what a wonderful father he had—such that, were he given his life to live over again, he would not choose any other.

One important rhetorical strategy of *Satires* 1. 6 is to display the poet as starting life with no advantages whatever, except for a father of strong moral character. But he burdens that father with a disability reminiscent of Bion's (and Bion was clearly in the poet's mind) that had a tenuous basis in a reality that went back to the Social War half a century earlier. We should not follow Suetonius in using the satire as evidence for the social status of Horace's father, any more than we should accept Horace's protestations of his father's or his own poverty. A combination of disadvantaged birth and poverty too perfectly suits the pretensions of a moral philosopher. Horace's father was, in fact, a proud native-born Sabellian whose family had suffered for supporting the rebel cause in 90 BC, though he had been able to lift the family's fortunes again in a short time, after he gained Roman citizenship.

This hypothesis removes any need for surprise that Horace, labouring under the social disadvantage of being a freedman's son, chose two such aggressive genres as *Epodes* and *Satires* for his earliest poetry. It also leaves us free to accept what Suetonius tells us about the mirrors in Horace's bedroom (since Sabellians were reputed to be especially prone to lechery!)[26]—a detail that Eduard Fraenkel asserted was 'filthy', 'a *locus communis*', and 'based on nothing but *rumores*'. Hostius Quadra will not have been the only wealthy Roman to indulge his special tastes in this way (Sen. *NQ* 1. 16).

Another of the delicate rhetorical strategies in *Satires* 1. 6 is designed to portray the poet's relationship to Maecenas in such a way that due deference and gratitude to the patron can be expressed, but only together with a strong sense of the client's—or rather, the friend's—self-sufficiency and independence (which are seen especially in the lengthy sketch of the poet's lifestyle that ends the poem). The topic of the relationship between inferior and

[26] Salmon (1967) 59 defends them against the charge.

superior dominates both books of *Satires* and the first book of *Epistles*. The trouble was that, just as the poet could be insulted by the envious or hostile as *libertino patre natus*, so could he also be represented as the *scurra* of Maecenas.[27] He deals defensively with the latter insult by making Damasippus and Davus come right out and say so: that is, the defence consists in creating a setting in which the charge must appear ridiculous—if only for the reason that the poet would not dream of giving it such publicity if there were the slightest truth in it. The use of the ugly phrase *libertino patre natum* should be viewed in the same light. Of course, expressed in such blunt terms, the phrase was indeed a mere insult that misrepresented Horace's birth. Nevertheless, there was a sufficiently significant grain of truth in it for Horace to feel injured by it and therefore compelled to deflect its sting by publishing it in a setting where its essential falsity would be immediately apparent. The extraordinary attack (*Epodes* 4) on the unnamed ex-slave who has (like Horace) become a *tribunus militum* is emphatically represented as a personal vendetta on the part of the poet (1–2 'lupis et agnis quanta sortito obtigit | tecum mihi discordia est'), as if he had a special personal interest in the case. This too can be read as a defensive gesture: if the poet selects such a man as a target, that fact in itself demonstrates that he can have nothing whatever in common with the man. Horace's father had not been a slave.

Eduard Fraenkel put two entries in the index to his *Horace* under the rubric 'Horace—never lies'; one concerns his interpretation of *Odes* 1. 38, the other 3. 25. The argument in this essay has not been to expose Horace as a liar, but to make the point that interpreters cannot accept what the poet seems to say as simple statements of historical fact.

NOTE. I have not said anything about the name 'Horatius', mainly because I am inclined to regard it as a Latinized form of an Oscan name. But it may be a Roman/Latin name, and the family may have been sent to Venusia as settlers. They will have had no connection with the patrician *gens Horatia* which died out earlier. But the fact that the new citizens of Venusia after the Social War were enrolled in the *tribus Horatiana* may suggest an influential family of Horatii in Venusia who thought that choice of tribe appropriate. If the family was indeed Roman, and if Horace's

---

[27] On this aspect of *Satires* 2 see Oliensis (forthcoming).

grandfather was therefore a Roman citizen (though this is a less likely hypothesis in view of the interpretation of *Sat.* 2. 1. 34–9 offered above), why would he join the rebel cause? He may have married a Sabellian woman and been caught by the provision of the *lex Minicia* (perhaps of 91 BC) which decreed that the children of marriages between a citizen and a non-citizen should take the lesser status.[28] That would have meant that Horace's father would suddenly have lost Roman citizenship.

[28] See Salmon (1967) 338 n. 4.

17

Towards a History of the Poetic Catalogue of Philosophical Themes

ANTONIO LA PENNA

I

IT is a small and involuntary paradox that this short discussion of poetic catalogues of philosophical themes should begin with a catalogue written in prose. I shall in fact start from a catalogue in Seneca's *De brevitate vitae* (19. 1). After trying to persuade his addressee Paulinus, very likely his father-in-law and the *praefectus annonae*, to leave his heavy political duties, Seneca urges him to take refuge in the study of philosophy:

recipe te ad haec tranquilliora, tutiora, maiora! Simile tu putas esse utrum cures ut incorruptum et a fraude advehentium et a neglegentia frumentum transfundatur in horrea, ne concepto umore vitietur et concalescat, ut ad mensuram pondusque respondeat, an ad haec sacra et sublimia accedas, sciturus quae materia sit dei, quae voluntas, quae condicio, quae forma; quis animum tuum casus expectet; ubi nos a corporibus dimissos natura componat; quid sit quod huius mundi gravissima quaeque in medio sustineat, supra levia suspendat, in summum ignem ferat, sidera vicibus suis excitet, cetera deinceps ingentibus plena miraculis?

The choice here is the well-known one between active and contemplative lives, a topic which probably goes back to Thales, and had already emerged, in any case, as the paramount ethical issue of Greek philosophy in the fourth century BC, especially in Aristotle. I shall deal first of all with the syntactical and stylistic aspects of this procedure. Seneca lists a series of issues, each one expressed in an indirect question: this is precisely the cliché which we shall find in all our examples. The order in which the issues are presented is Stoic in tone, and is obviously not casual: theology, the fate of the soul, cosmology, and physics. The catalogue of philosophical themes as a series of indirect questions is common in Seneca. Let me quote here just one other example, from the *Epistulae ad Lucilium* (65. 19–20), and refer to others in the notes:[1] 'interdicis mihi inspectionem rerum naturae, a toto abductum redigis in partem? Ego non quaeram quae sint initia universorum? quis rerum formator? quis omnia in uno mersa et materia inerti convoluta discreverit?' I shall stop here, but indirect questions go on for another ten lines. The topics are pretty much the same as the ones mentioned in *De brevitate vitae*: the gods, the formation of the world, natural phenomena, the fate of the soul. We can easily compare cases where the catalogue is made up of a series of nouns, as, for instance, at the end of *Consolatio ad Helviam matrem* (20. 1), where the topics are geography and meteorology, but also the eternity of the world and the soul: 'terras primum situmque earum [animus] quaerit, deinde condicionem circumfusi maris cursusque eius alternos et recursus; tunc quidquid inter caelum terrasque plenum formidinis interiacet perspicit . . .'

Let us go back to our starting-point, the passage from *De brevitate vitae*. After the catalogue of philosophical themes, Seneca goes on (19. 2): 'vis tu, relicto solo mente ad ista respicere? Nunc, dum calet sanguis, vigentibus ad meliora eundum est.' This exhortation obviously makes a polemical point: Seneca is here attacking those who believe that philosophical reflection should be put off until old age; on this crucial point, as in fact on other aspects of ethical behaviour, the Stoic thinker agrees with Epicurus, who in turn was close, as far as this issue was concerned, to Plato's dictum that 'both young and old must apply themselves to philosophy'.[2] Seneca does not waver on this point: at *De otio* 2. 1 he maintains that one can devote oneself entirely to the contemplation of truth *vel a prima aetate*.[3] Although this polemic is of a general nature, I believe that Seneca must have had in mind a more specific target. The opposite point of view, according to which youth is the age of poetry, love, and the pleasures of *convivia*, while old age should be reserved for philosophical reflection, had been defended by Propertius. In elegy 3. 5 Propertius sings of Eros as the

---

[1] Cf. *De otio* 4. 2 (with the topics *virtus*, cosmology, and theology); *NQ* 1 praef. 3 (the gods and fate). These passages are collected by Traina (1970). One can add *De otio* 5. 5 and 5. 6 (issues of cosmology and physics).

[2] Epic. *Ep. Men.* 122; for Plato cf. *Ap.* 33 A.

[3] Cf. the useful commentary of Dionigi (1983) ad loc.

god of peace and leaves to others the labours and glories of war.
From this well-known poem I shall quote the passage which is
relevant to my issue, lines 19 ff.:

> Me iuvat in prima coluisse Helicona iuventa
>   Musarumque choris implicuisse manus;   20
> me iuvet et multo mentem vincire Lyaeo
>   et caput in verna semper habere rosa.
> Atque ubi iam Venerem gravis interceperit aetas
>   sparserit et nigras alba senecta comas,
> tum mihi naturae libeat perdiscere mores,   25
>   quis deus hanc mundi temperet arte domum,
> qua venit exoriens, qua deficit, unde coactis
>   cornibus in plenum menstrua luna redit,
> unde salo superant venti, quid flamine captet
>   Eurus et in nubes unde perennis aqua . . .   30

The rest of the catalogue goes on for another eight couplets. Its
overall topic is *naturae mores*: except for the reference to the god
who governs the world, approximately two-thirds of the topics of
the catalogue are astronomical and meteorological. Later on
Propertius debates the issue whether there are punishments for
guilty men in the underworld or whether these are only a *ficta
fabula,* so that men should fear nothing after the funeral pyre. All
these issues could be part of an Epicurean treatment, but the
reference to world-governing deities could not coexist with a profession of Epicurean faith: the issue here is *which* god governs
the world, not *whether* one does so at all. The string of indirect
questions leaves the issue open, but it is still possible to say that
Epicureanism is an important point of reference here. Before the
catalogue the choice of youth is enthusiastically against philosophy. Textual problems make us wonder whether the text is here
simply stating this or actually exhorting it. Out of caution, more
than firm belief, I would preserve the reading of the most reliable
manuscript tradition: *me iuvat,* with the whole of the tradition, at
line 19, and *me iuvet,* with NFL, at line 21. The choice of poetry
is part of a calling which Propertius has followed since his youth.
His choice of the φιλήδονος βίος is either recent or new: the contrast between the perfect infinitives *coluisse* and *implicuisse* and
the present infinitives *vincire* and *semper habere* could easily be
explained if we keep the text in this form. Among recent editors
this is, for instance, Hanslik's solution. But I must confess that I

am strongly tempted to read *me iuvat* at line 21, as manuscripts P and Δ do. This is almost certainly a humanistic corruption due to the influence of line 19, but on the other hand poetry, love, and convivial pleasures are so closely bound together in ancient love poetry that it is not easy to separate them. The perfect infinitives could function here, as they do at other times in Augustan poetry, as present infinitives. We would thus have a clear contrast between the indicative *me iuvat* and the subjunctive at line 25, *libeat*, which is referred to the future, to the plan of devoting oneself to philosophy in old age. This solution was preferred in the OCT by Barber, whose *iudicium* I generally hold in high esteem. The weakest solution seems to me to emend the reading offered by the part of the manuscript tradition that carries the greatest authority in both line 19 and line 21, and write *me iuvet* in both cases.[4] Taken in isolation, neither the catalogue of philosophical themes nor the debate whether one should devote oneself to philosophy already in youth, rather than waiting for old age, must necessarily refer to Propertius, but their connection in the same line of argumentation makes me think of him. Obviously, this is only a hypothesis.

Against this hypothesis one might offer the fact that Propertius is not a poet familiar to Seneca, who never quotes him in his prose works.[5] In the tragedies, however, there are traces of Propertius, although the matter is very delicate. A list of *loci similes* points out lexical similarities and shared *iuncturae* which have little importance for literary history.[6] For some time now, the inflation of philological research on intertextual connections has reached daunting proportions. Yet I believe that some important traces remain even after these careful evaluations. I would like to mention, for instance, Sen. *HF* 702 *aeterno situ*, from Prop. 1. 7. 18; *Ag.* 392–3 *Tantalidos | funera* from Prop. 2. 31. 4 *funera Tantalidos*; *HO* 594 *orgia ferre* from Prop. 3. 1. 4. I have noticed that some of the less uncertain echoes refer precisely to Propertius' catalogue of philosophical themes: Prop. 3. 5. 35 *cur serus versare boves et plaustra Bootes* is echoed at *Med.* 314–15 *flectitque senex | Arctica tardus plaustra Bootes* and *Ag.* 70 *lucida versat plaustra Bootes*

---

[4] For discussion see Fedeli (1985) ad loc. Unfortunately Fedeli prefers the weakest solution.   [5] See Mazzoli (1970).

[6] Much relevant material can be found in the apparatus critici of editions of Propertius, e.g. that of Hanslik (1979); cf. also Enk (1946) 55; Shackleton Bailey (1952); Fletcher (1960; 1961). Fletcher and Hanslik are the most comprehensive collections.

(cf. also [Sen.] *Oct.* 233–4 *qua plaustra tardus noctis aeterna rite* |
regit Bootes); and perhaps Prop. 3. 5. 37 *curve suos finis altum non
exeat aequor* is echoed at *NQ.* 3. 30. 2 *non vides ut aestus fines suos
transeat?* I am aware that this last example is doubtful, but I would
be more confident about a line before the catalogue: the image of
3. 5. 22 *et caput in verna semper habere rosa* is found at *Thy.* 947
vernae capiti fluxere rosae, and both lines refer to a banquet. Overall,
I believe that this passage of Propertius must have been particularly present in Seneca's memory.[7]

In this Propertian passage a certain and important presence is
that of Virgil's *Georgics*:[8] in a famous passage, the final excursus of
book 2 (lines 475–540), Virgil deals with the issue of the choice of
life: the ἄριστος βίος is Lucretian, to sing in a poem the science of
nature. Lucretius is here recalled through clear allusions. But the
didactic poet's goal is to justify, together with this ideal, the peaceful and quiet life of the farmer, arguing that if it is not equal in
value, it is certainly no less worthy. Already in Virgil this goal is
expressed in a catalogue of philosophical themes, partly introduced
by indirect questions:

> Me vero primum dulces ante omnia Musae,   475
> quarum sacra fero ingenti percussus amore,
> accipiant caelique vias et sidera monstrent,
> defectus solis varios lunaeque labores;
> unde tremor terris, qua vi maria alta tumescant
> obicibus ruptis rursusque in se ipsa residant,   480
> quid tantum Oceano properent se tingere soles
> hiberni vel quae tardis mora noctibus obstet.

Astronomical themes are clearly privileged. One might say that
Propertius' not very exciting *aemulatio* is an attempt to surpass his
model in quantity. Horace could have warned him, as the young
Corinna had done with Pindar, that one should sow with the hand,
not with the sack. In any event, it would not have been easy to

---

[7] I list other *loci similes* which perhaps deserve some attention: *HF.* 177–8 ~
Prop. 2. 15. 25; *Med.* 640 ~ Prop. 3. 13. 21; *Ph.* 56–7 ~ Prop. 3. 17. 21; *Ph.* 318
~ Prop. 2. 19. 21; *Ph.* 774 ~ Prop. 1. 19. 25; *Oed.* 454 ~ Prop. 2. 20. 5–6; *Ag.*
864 ~ Prop. 1. 9. 1; *HO* 129 ~ Prop. 1. 16. 16; *HO* 1272–3 ~ Prop. 1. 16. 29–30;
HO 1293 ~ Prop. 2. 28b. 40; *HO* 1689 ~ Prop. 4. 11. 80 (but cf. Ov. *Tr.* 1. 1. 28,
5. 1. 58; *Her.* 11. 10); *HO* 1758–9 ~ Prop. 2. 9. 13–14; *HO* 1825 ~ Prop. 4. 11.
14; [Sen.] *Oct.* 831–2 ~ Prop. 2. 27. 19; *Rem. fort.* 12 ~ Prop. 2. 15. 12.

[8] Cf. La Penna (1951) 51 ff., referring to earlier work by Paratore, and Fedeli
(1985) 175.

stop Propertius in time in his catalogic exploits. From the *Georgics* passage it could be gleaned that Virgil put off indefinitely his poetic philosophical task, but as an admirer of Lucretius he would have never said that philosophy was a task to be left to the old.

In practice, however, Virgil did not achieve the task he cherished, and after his early youth, even before his literary production, he never gave philosophy pride of place among his activities. According to the biography assembled by Donatus on the basis of Suetonius, Virgil planned to devote himself to philosophy after completing and correcting the *Aeneid*: 'Anno aetatis quinquagesimo secundo impositurus Aeneidi summam manum statuit in Graeciam et in Asiam secedere triennioque continuo nihil amplius quam emendare ut reliqua vita tantum philosophiae vacaret' (Donat. *Vita Verg.* 35. 123-6, pp. 13-14 Hardie). According to some scholars, e.g. Diehl (1911) 17, this piece of information would have been inspired by the passage in *Georgics* 2; but the connection is not at all obvious, and I am inclined to think that the information is credible.

And Horace? Horace's philosophical reading goes back to his early youth, and within it Lucretius stands out. It has long been discussed, and still is, what use Horace makes of *placita*, of collections of philosophical abstracts and *gnomologia*. In any event he must have read at least one book entirely devoted to philosophy, and that was the *De rerum natura* of the Epicurean Lucretius. However, after the publication of the first collection of *Odes*, Horace feels the need of philosophy as if he had never experienced it before. He is not looking for a solution to cosmological and theological problems, nor is he attracted to the philosophy of nature. What he seeks is a philosophy for life, to give a coherent sense to his existence. His new need for *sapientia* cannot be put off, and he is therefore reminded of Epicurus' warning that both young and old must attend to philosophy. This is not the conversion to Stoicism that Courbaud saw in the first book of the *Epistles*, but it is a choice: *ludicra pono*, the time has come to devote oneself entirely to the search for wisdom which is necessary for life. But for Horace the turning-point is at the threshold of old age, an old age which he begins to feel prematurely.

On the whole, the Augustan poets had not followed Epicurus' warning, and had kept philosophy for their old age. Propertius had only been more self-aware and more determined in his choice. His anti-Epicurean stance is, I believe, intentionally polemical. If it is possible to detect a generic similarity between the hedonism of the erotic poets and Epicurean hedonism, still there was in fact a noticeable difference, and a strain of anti-Epicurean polemic can be perceived *vis-à-vis* other problems as well, chief among them the issue of erotic choice. As in his poetry, in love the elegiac poet chooses what is rarest and most difficult to attain. He is a Callimachean in both life and style. Only when he is desperate because of his *puella*'s *saevitia* does he resort to *puellae viles*. Thus, the Lucretian exhortation towards *Venus vulgivaga* is followed only under exceptional circumstances. This is the meaning of Propertius' 20-23, where I see also a polemic against the Epicurean sexual ethics hailed by Horace in one of his earliest satires, I. 2.

Leaving aside for the moment this complex web of connections between Callimacheanism and Epicureanism, I would like to maintain that Seneca's exhortation to young men to devote themselves to philosophy is in fact intentionally attacking Augustan poetry as a whole. By Seneca's time that poetry had already become classic, and it exerted a very strong influence on the ethical education of youth, both inside and outside the classroom.

II

In Virgil's poetic *iter* the poetic catalogue of philosophical themes that we read in the *Georgics* occupies a place between two other catalogues with similar themes and a similar syntactical and stylistic structure (we find again a series of nouns and a series of indirect questions). One is Silenus' song in the *Eclogues* (6. 31-40), the other is the catalogue Iopas sings in the *Aeneid* during the banquet which Dido offers to her Trojan guests (1. 742-6). It might be useful to analyse closely the differences between these passages, but that lies outside the scope of the present paper. Instead, I shall briefly focus on their clear points of contact. Silenus' song is essentially cosmogonic: the world is made up of atoms, and there are evident lexical allusions to Lucretius. However, in its present division into earth, sea, air, and fire, the world is the result of a process of separation which resembles Empedocles' theory of the four elements. From this the catalogue moves towards the origin of the sun, and of clouds, plants, and animals. In the *Georgics* catalogue we find astronomy, eclipses, earthquakes, tides, the cycle of seasons. The *Aeneid* catalogue is the shortest one, only five lines: one of them is a variation on a line in the *Georgics* catalogue, and two more are culled from the same passage. Of the two remaining lines, one (743 *unde hominum gens et pecudes, unde imber et ignes*) reiterates some themes in Silenus' catalogue, the other (744) expands on the astronomical themes with a reference to three constellations. This catalogue is an elegant condensation of the other two, without any new element.

I do not think that it is possible to detect an adaptation of the catalogue to its context. Let the credulous believe that *solis labores* in the *Aeneid*, a modification of the *lunae labores* in the *Georgics*, foreshadows Aeneas' and Dido's tragedy, even if in this case the credulous is a well-known German colleague. It would be just as useless to attempt to glean from the catalogues information on Virgil's own philosophy. Silenus' song is generically Epicurean, but it would be indelicate to demand strict orthodoxy; and it would be wrong to conjecture on its basis that Virgil, when he was writing the *Eclogues*, was a member of the Epicurean school. More striking is the fact that all three catalogues focus closely on the philosophy of nature, and do not make any statement concerning the gods or ethical issues. Perhaps, as we shall see shortly, this fact can be explained in the light of the Greek literary tradition, where this cliché had first been shaped.

As far as Iopas' song in the *Aeneid* is concerned, commentators rightly refer back to Orpheus' song in the first book of Apollonius Rhodius (496–511). This comparison explains why the song's topics are themes of natural philosophy, whereas the Homeric bard, Demodocus, had sung of epic deeds. Orpheus too sings during a banquet, that of the Argonauts, and thanks to his song he is able to assuage passions, namely the wrath of Idas and Idmon, who are about to confront each other in a dangerous fight. Orpheus sings first about the division of the elements, then astronomy and the first appearance of mountains, rivers, Nymphs, and animals. The cosmogonic themes taken from philosophy, chiefly that of Empedocles, who is recalled through a reference to the 'ominous strife' that separates the elements, are followed by themes similar to some found in Hesiod's *Theogony*, which in turn are enriched by elements taken from more recent cosmogonies such as that of Pherecydes of Syros. Reading the first part of Apollonius'

catalogue, one can see that Virgil—as has long been known—
found inspiration for Silenus' song in Apollonius' Orpheus. The
Roman poet gives less prominence to the Empedoclean source and
focuses instead on the atomic structure of nature, but he clearly
alludes to Apollonius and does nothing to hide this connection.
Apollonius' influence is detectable not only in the way the cosmogonic process is represented, but also in the decision to connect a
Hesiodic theogony to an Empedoclean cosmogony. Virgil's Silenus
follows the same path, but then he links to the Hesiodic theogony
a tale of ἐρωτικὰ παθήματα. According to a hypothesis I proposed a
long time ago, this path was suggested to him by ancient Hesiodic
editions in which the Ἠοῖαι were connected to the *Theogony* by
an editorial link of which the manuscript tradition preserves clear
traces.[9]

In the story I am trying to reconstruct, the importance of
Apollonius Rhodius has been sufficiently highlighted, while I
believe that not enough attention has been paid to the role played
by a text which in antiquity was much better known and widespread, Euripides' *Antiope*. Following the lead of distinguished
scholars,[10] I believe that the μακαρισμός of the man devoted to the
science of the cosmos (fr. 910N²) belongs precisely to this tragedy:

> ὄλβιος ὅστις τῆς ἱστορίας
> ἔσχε πάθησιν,
> μήτε πολιτῶν ἐπὶ πημοσύνας
> μήτ' εἰς ἀδίκους πράξεις ὁρμῶν,
> ἀλλ' ἀθανάτου καθορῶν φύσεως
> κόσμον ἀγήρω πῇ τε συνέστη
> χὦθεν χὦπως·
> τοῖς δὲ τοιούτοις οὐδέποτ' αἰσχρῶν
> ἔργων μελέτημα προσίζει.

In this song the chorus, probably after the famous ἀγών between
Zethus and Amphion, extols the philosopher's life, more precisely
the contemplative life, characterized by a unity of music, poetry,
and philosophy, also regarded as a life of moral purity. He who has
chosen this life can see 'by what process (πῇ), from what origins
(ὅθεν), in what way (ὅπως) the ever-young κόσμος of immortal
nature has been formed'. Here again we encounter a series of
indirect questions. We are clearly far from the catalogues I have

9 See La Penna (1960) 220 ff.
10 See Snell (1971) 96 ff.

mentioned so far, but it should be remembered that in this play the
cosmogony had been sung by Amphion in a lyric section, probably
before the ἀγών, of which is preserved but one hexameter, probably
the initial one:[11]

> Αἰθέρα καὶ Γαῖαν πάντων γενέτειραν ἀείδω.

I believe that if it were not for this song by Amphion, Orpheus'
song in Apollonius Rhodius would not have begun with a cosmogony. The Alexandrian epic poet has been inspired in this case by
the poet he loved most after Homer, Euripides. But the influence of
Antiope on Latin poetry is not only indirect: as we know, this
tragedy, both directly and indirectly—through Pacuvius' rewriting—played a part in Latin literature from the second century BC
to the Augustan age. It is hardly necessary to remember the
evidence we find in *Rhetorica ad Herennium* (2. 3. 5), Propertius
(3. 15. 11 ff.), and Horace (*Ep.* 1. 18. 43-4). Since the second
century BC the debate about active and contemplative lives, about
negotia and *otium*, had been prominent in Roman culture. I believe
that Virgil too, in his excursus at the end of *Georgics* 2, was alluding to the chorus in *Antiope*, which he knew was well known to
his readers: 490 'Felix qui potuit rerum cognoscere causas . . .'
adapts to Epicureanism Euripides' μακαρισμός: ὄλβιος ὅστις τῆς
ἱστορίας | ἔσχε μάθησιν . . . In another fragment from this tragedy
(fr. 198 N² = 16 Kambitsis), which in all probability belongs to a
speech by Amphion, a distinction is made between εὐτυχῶν and
εὐδαίμων on the one hand, and ὄλβιος on the other. This fragment
has been carefully interpreted by Bruno Snell in his excellent
study:[12]

> εἰ δ' εὐτυχῶν τις καὶ βίον κεκτημένος
> μηδὲν δόμοισι τῶν καλῶν θηράσεται,
> ἐγὼ μὲν αὐτὸν οὔποτ' ὄλβιον καλῶ,
> φύλακα δὲ μᾶλλον χρημάτων εὐδαίμονα

For Amphion the happiness of contemplative life is higher than
that afforded by prosperity and wealth. In his interpretation Snell
is probably right to emphasize the religious meaning of ὄλβιος.[13] If

---

[11] Fr. 1023N², connected to fr. 925, makes up fr. 182a of the *Supplementum*
added by Snell to the third edition of Nauck's *Tragicorum Graecorum Fragmenta*
(1964). The connection with fr. 925 guarantees that it belongs to *Antiope*. This is
fr. 6 in Kambitsis (1972), who also includes fr. 910.
[12] Snell (1971) 92 ff.
[13] ibid. 93, 99 ff.

I may supplement his analysis with a hypothesis, I would say that perhaps Euripides in making this distinction is alluding to and discussing a text which was familiar to ancient Greeks at all periods, the end of Hesiod's *Works and Days* (826–8), where εὐδαίμων and ὄλβιος are synonymous:

> τάων εὐδαίμων καὶ ὄλβιος ὃς τάδε πάντα
> εἰδὼς ἐργάζηται ἀναίτιος ἀθανατοῖσι,
> ὄρνιθας κρίνων καὶ ὑπερβασίας ἀλεείνων.

The analogous distinction between ὄλβιος and εὐτυχής must have been fairly common in Euripides' day. Herodotus, in fact, quotes a famous dictum which he attributes to Solon: πρὶν δ' ἂν τελευτήσῃ ἐπισχεῖν μηδὲ καλέειν κω ὄλβιον ἀλλ' εὐτυχέα (I. 32. 6).[14] Going back to Virgil, I wonder whether the distinction between ὄλβιος and εὐτυχῶν cannot be found also in the poet's distinction between *felix* referred to the philosopher and *fortunatus* used for the *agricola* (493 *fortunatus et ille, deos qui novit agrestes* . . .). I would not want to push the analogy too far: as I have said, Virgil wants to portray the life of the *agricola* as worthwhile, not to belittle it. But the final excursus of *Georgics* 2 is part of the long debate opened by Euripides' ἀγών between the two brothers. On the other hand, Amphion did not triumph: the contrast, as is now thought likely,[15] must have been resolved with a reconciliation or a compromise which accepted both βίοι and which Horace could interpret as Amphion's yielding. Perhaps the conclusion was the one indicated in a fragment of Pacuvius' *Antiope* (12–14R³): without the alternation between day and night Nature would be destroyed by heat or cold; similarly, human life would be impossible without the alternation of activity and contemplation. The relativistic ethics which were thus sketched were going to play an important role in Roman culture. The choice of a contemplative life and the choice of the *agricola*'s life are placed side by side as equally valid and legitimate, and are not set one against the other.

If Euripides' *Antiope* really stands at the origin of the tradition of the poetic catalogues of philosophical themes, we can explain a surprising characteristic of these catalogues, the clearly larger weight given to themes of natural philosophy—indeed, until Virgil, their exclusive presence: cosmogony, cosmology, astronomy,

---

[14] There are useful remarks on the use of these terms in Kambitsis (1972) 54.
[15] See Snell (1971) 96.

natural phenomena of obscure origin such as eclipses and tides, and meteorological phenomena. In antiquity Euripides was considered to be, like Pericles, a pupil of Anaxagoras. Anaxagoras' influence, it is hardly necessary to add, is interpreted in different ways by different critics, but many are ready to recognize Anaxagorean traces in *Antiope*, *Phaethon*, *Chrysippus*, and Μελανίππη ἡ σοφή.[16] Anaxagoras was mainly interested in the scientific explanation of natural phenomena: the flood of the Nile (A 42 DK = Hipp. *Refut.* I. 8. 4–5; A 91), eclipses (A 42 = Hipp. *Refut.* I. 8. 10; A 77), winds, thunder, lightning (A 42 = Hipp. *Refut.* I. 8. 11), other meteorological phenomena (A 84 ff.), comets (A 81; A 83), the rainbow (B 19). The famous fragment from *Chrysippus* on the Aither as father and the Earth as mother (fr. 839N²), from whose union all life is created and transforms itself, while nothing perishes, is certainly inspired by Anaxagoras. In the light of all these elements it is reasonable to think that Amphion's hymn in the *Antiope* dealt with this type of issue.

The fortune that this chorus from *Chrysippus* had in Latin poetry invites a brief digression on the formation of a sublime style in Latin philosophical poetry. It is thought likely that Pacuvius found inspiration for the philosophical piece in the *Chryses* precisely in Euripides' *Chrysippus*. A very beautiful adaptation was written by Lucretius (1. 250–64; cf. also 2. 992–8),[17] and Lucretius in turn inspired Virgil's *Georgics* (2. 325–35). Each one of these passages displays individual characteristics, but it will suffice to notice that the style is always kept at a sublime level. This instance can remind us of the fact that the sublime style in Latin philosophical poetry is based not only on Empedocles, Homer, and Ennius' epic poetry, but also on Greek tragedy (especially Euripides) and archaic Latin tragedy. Naturally, the poets of the early Augustan age found an important model in Lucretius, as far as both the choice of topics and the stylistic level were concerned. Lucretius' presence, which is sometimes openly declared, sometimes dissimulated—as, for instance, in the *Aeneid* catalogue—is still important.

---

[16] On this problem see Di Benedetto (1971) 307, brief but in the right direction (he also offers a rich bibliography). Among earlier studies Parmentier (1892) is worth mentioning; references can of course also be found in Diels–Kranz. For the *Antiope* Kambitsis (1972) is useful.

[17] Cf. Nauck's apparatus and Bailey's note on Lucr. 1. 251.

III

All the early Augustan poets we know pay tribute to this famous topos. Sometimes they do so only by way of refusing it as a subject for their poetry, as Tibullus does very briefly at 2. 3. 18 ff.:

> nec refero Solisque vias et qualis, ubi orbem
> complerit, versis Luna recurrit equis . . .

or, in a more extended if less elegant way, like the unknown author of the *Panegyricus Messallae* (18 ff.):

> alter dicat opus magni mirabile mundi,
> qualis in immenso desederit aere tellus,
> qualis et in curvum pontus confluxerit orbem . . .

and so on. Ovid too was faithful to the tradition of Euripides, Apollonius Rhodius, and Virgil, for he chose as an introduction to a speech on Pythagorean philosophy pretty much the same topics: cosmogony, cosmology, meteorology (*Met.* 15. 67–72).

Before concluding I shall focus on the catalogues by Horace, as we are honouring one of Horace's greatest critics, Professor Nisbet. Horace recalled only late, in the first book of the *Epistles*, this common topic, and then only in order to produce a witty parody of it (1. 12. 15–20). From the ode Horace writes to him a few years earlier (*Odes* 1. 29), we already know that Iccius is an amateur philosopher;[18] his favourite authors seem to be Panaetius and Socrates' followers: Plato, perhaps Xenophon, the Cyrenaics, the Cynics. His interest, in any event, seems to be mainly in ethics. (This item of information is useful for assessing the importance of Panaetius, who, after the Augustan age, will be overshadowed by earlier Stoic philosophers, especially Chrysippus, and more recent ones such as Posidonius.) Do we have to think that his interests have now moved towards the philosophy of nature? I do not think that these details should be taken too seriously. When he wanted to mention philosophical studies, Horace used a cliché which had by now become a classic. The topics we find here are the usual ones—tides, seasons, the movement of celestial bodies, the phases of the moon, the fundamental principles of the universe (chance or divine providence, harmony or strife). Both in the ode and in the

---

[18] See (of course) Nisbet and Hubbard (1970) on that poem.

epistle the irony is aimed not only at the character, an amateur who does not worry too much about leading his life according to high moral principles, but also at the conventional cliché. At the end of the catalogue irony becomes more evident: 20 *Empedocles an Stertinium deliret acumen.* This resembles an epigrammatic ending. Both men are delirious; old Empedocles, who at the end of the *Ars poetica* will be remembered as the poet who throws himself into Etna in a frenzy, and the more recent Stertinius, who, like certain Stoics, mixes a fanatic pursuit of virtue with ridiculous subtleties of logic, probably similar to the ones ridiculed by Seneca. Perhaps more authentic concerns on Iccius' part are reflected, outside the cliché, in the reference to the avoidance of meat and certain vegetables which comes after the catalogue (21 *seu piscis seu porrum et caepe trucidas*). Horace doubts whether Iccius actually avoids these foods, but we do know that these strange Pythagorean and Empedoclean habits enjoyed a certain degree of popularity in the age of Nigidius Figulus and the Sextii.[19]

However, this traditional catalogue in the letter to Iccius is not the only one, nor the most interesting, in the first book of *Epistles*. In the second letter to Lollius Maximus, *Epistles* 1. 18, a short collection of advice on how the *cliens* should behave towards his *dives amicus*,[20] Horace ends up with an exhortation to read philosophy (96-103) as a remedy against the nuisances and the ugliness of the *cliens'* life:

> inter cuncta leges et percontabere doctos
> qua ratione queas traducere leniter aevum
> num te semper inops agitet vexetque cupido . . .

The catalogue is relatively long by Horatian standards, even if it is only about a third the length of Propertius' own catalogue. As the syntactical and stylistic structure—the series of indirect questions—shows, Horace is here following the usual cliché. On a first reading it is striking that no mention is made of problems pertaining to the science of nature; all the topics are ethical and the tone is Epicurean, since at the end (102-3) there is a clear reference to λάθε βιώσας:

> quid pure tranquillet, honos an dulce lucellum,
> an secretum iter et fallentis semita vitae.

---

[19] See Ferrero (1955) 378 ff.   [20] See La Penna (1992).

Certainly the contrast with the usual cliché is intentional. According to Epicurus and Lucretius, the science of nature is indispensable in order to free oneself from fear and false hopes and attain ἀταραξία. Horace never felt the same way, and is certainly not feeling that way in the *Epistles*: what one needs is a small reservoir of moral precepts which can assist in everyday life. Whatever is not necessary to conquer peace of mind in everyday life is useless, and in the vast mass of useless things Horace puts *naturales quaestiones* as well.

Perusing the poetic catalogues of philosophical themes, one is left with the impression that they form a rather fixed and unchangeable tradition. However, if one situates each catalogue in its cultural context, establishes what issues lie in its background, above all the choice of the ἄριστος βίος, and connects it to the personality of its author, it is possible to see that on each occasion the catalogues arise from different concerns. I hope this is already clear from my rapid survey, but I am convinced that a more careful and painstaking analysis could reveal much more.

18

Reading Horace in the Quattrocento:
The *Hymn to Mars* of Michael Marullus

M. J. MCGANN

IN 1482, about a decade after the appearance of the *editio princeps*, Cristoforo Landino's edition of Horace was published in Florence. It was prefaced by a poem in asclepiads composed by Politian, in which he welcomed the liberation of Horace from the barbarian fetter, the removal of the cloud from his brow, and his restoration, rejuvenated and all nicely scrubbed, to the band of nimble dancers:

> Quis te a barbarica compede vindicat?
> Quis frontis nebulam dispulit, & situ
> Deterso levibus restituit choris
> Cur⟨a⟩ta iuvenem cute?[1]   (9–12)

This was not Politian's first essay in a Horatian form. An ode to the bishop of Arezzo arises from the Pazzi conspiracy of 1478 against the Medici.[2] In 1480, during his absence from Florence after a disagreement with Clarice Orsini, the wife of his employer Lorenzo il Magnifico, he had composed his *Orfeo* in Italian at Mantua, inserting in it as Orpheus' opening words an aria in Latin sapphics (the only Latin in the play) in honour of Cardinal Francesco Gonzaga.[3] Another ode celebrates the accession of Innocent VIII to the throne of Peter in 1484,[4] when Politian was part of the Florentine embassy which went to Rome on that occasion to congratulate the new pope. The ode *Ad iuventutem* greets the beginning of the academic year in 1487 as the poet assures the *docilis turba* that he comes to them in whichever guise

---

[1] The text is given, with some modification of orthography and punctuation but with original layout, as it appears in Landino (1482). The poem was printed by del Lungo (1867) 261–2.

[2] Del Lungo (1867) 259–60.   [3] ibid. 257–8.   [4] ibid. 262–4.

they prefer, *comes* or *dux*.[5] Politian's Latin lyrics, however, are few
in number compared with his epigrams. In general his taste ran
rather in the direction of post-classical literature, and while he has
read Horace carefully (his sapphics, for example, conform to the
metrical practice of Horace rather than Catullus), his reading seems
never to have led him to a serious engagement with the poet.
No anxiety of influence there. But with his younger contemporary
and enemy, Michael Marullus, the situation is different. Here it is
possible to observe an increasing involvement with Horace's lyrics
(perhaps, indeed, to connect Politian with that development), and
the involvement is a serious one, with Marullus applying and
adapting Augustan themes to his own world.

As well as being a poet, Marullus was by birth a Greek, two facts
classicists may be in danger of forgetting as they recall his name
occurring again and again in the apparatus criticus of their texts
of Lucretius. Called *Spartanus* by one of his Italian contemporaries,[6]
he was born in the Morea *c.* 1461, around the time of its subjugation by the Turks, the son of a man variously known as Manoli
Marulo, Emanuel Marulla, and, in one of his son's poems and the
titulus of another as well as in his own epitaph, Manilius Marullus.[7]
The various forms of his surname appear to represent a Byzantine
name, derived from μαροῦλι 'lettuce', which is itself attested in
several forms, Μαρουλᾶς, Μαρούλας, Μαροῦλας, Μαρούλλης, and
Μαρούλης.[8] It is not unlikely that it was Michael himself (or one of
his teachers) who Latinized the family name and happily produced
in 'Marullus' a genuinely ancient Latin name with supposedly
imperial connections.[9] (The form Μάρουλλος, which occurs in a
letter written by Janus Lascaris,[10] is a learned back-formation, with
its proparoxytone accent, which is never found in Byzantine
forms of the name, imitating renderings into ancient Greek of the
Latin name 'Marullus').[11] The poet's mother was Euphrosyne
Tarchaniotissa, bearer of a more distinguished family name than

---

[5] Del Lungo (1867) 265-6.

[6] Sannazaro, *El.* 2. 2. 25 (1728: 200). For further discussion of his origins see
below, nn. 30 and 32.

[7] The account of Marullus's family and early life given here is based largely on
unpublished research. See, however, McGann (1980; 1981; 1986; 1991).

[8] Moritz (1897-8) 18; *Prosopographisches Lexikon der Palaiologenzeit*, s. vv.

[9] McGann (1980).

[10] Legrand (1885) 324.

[11] See Jos. *AJ* 18. 237; Plut, *Caes.* 61. 8. In both passages the simple vowel u
and not the diphthong ou is used.

her husband's and friend of Francesca Marzano, niece of Ferrante I, king of Naples, and second wife of Leonardo III Tocco, despot of Arta. By 1465 the family had taken refuge in Ragusa, where Manoli practised medicine under contract to the city and Michael, as he tells us in one of his poems (*De laudibus Rhacusae*: *Ep.* 4. 17), spent his earliest years. Michael was to make his home in Italy, but it is unclear when he settled there. The family appears in some degree to have straddled the Adriatic. In 1470 Manoli was in Rome obtaining an indulgence on behalf of the city of Ragusa. There is no record of his being employed by Ragusa between 1477 and 1480, and it may have been during that period that he joined his wife in Calabria, subsequently moving on to Naples. But in 1481 he is once again attested as being in the employment of Ragusa.

Michael's poetry suggests that he received a good, basically Latin, education. This was probably acquired in the kingdom of Naples rather than in Ragusa. (The poem on Ragusa makes no mention of an educational debt to the city.) The only contemporary reference to his education, made by his friend and fellow Greek Manilius Rhallus, describes him as a pupil of the Neapolitan humanist Pontano, and both of them as men *secretioris doctrinae*.[12] It is unclear whether Rhallus's description of Marullus as Pontano's pupil should be taken to imply the existence of a real teacher–pupil relationship or is rather a reflection of the friendship and intellectual links, attested in the poetry of both, between a distinguished man who presided over the academy which bore his name and his younger contemporary. In any case Pontano is unlikely to have played any part in the poet's earliest education.[13] Marullus subsequently lived in Rome, having left Naples perhaps because of the cruel suppression of the Barons' Revolt of 1485, in which several of his friends perished. Another, Antonello Sanseverino, prince of Salerno, took refuge in France, where he intrigued against the king of Naples and worked to further a French invasion of the Kingdom. Two books of *Epigrams*, many of them reflecting Marullus's life in Naples, were published in 1488 or 1489, probably in Rome. In 1489 he moved to Florence, where he was closely associated with the Francophile sons of Pierfrancesco de' Medici. The intrigues

[12] Rallus (1520) iii. For a sketch of at least part of what may lie behind the application of this description to Marullus see the discussion of Orphic song at the end of this paper.

[13] A younger contemporary of Marullus, Lilius Gyraldus (1580: 384), makes both him and Rhallus products of the Accademia Pontaniana.

of his friend the prince of Salerno came to fruition in 1494, when Charles VIII of France moved against the Kingdom. Marullus participated in the campaign. His knowledge of Greek proved useful in the course of the king's propaganda offensive against Pope Alexander VI, when, described as the prince of Salerno's secretary, he assisted in the translation of intercepted dispatches sent from Istanbul to the pope. Two further books of *Epigrams* were added to the two already published, and these together with four books of *Hymni naturales* were published in Florence in 1497. Marullus assisted Caterina Sforza, widow of his Florentine friend Giovanni di Pierfrancesco de' Medici, in the defence of Forlì against Cesare Borgia during December 1499 and January 1500. He died a few months later, accidentally drowned. Some poems, principally a collection of *Neniae* and an unfinished poem on the education of a prince, *Institutio principalis*, were published posthumously.

Marullus's only mention of Horace by name, in an early poem entitled *De poetis Latinis* (*Ep.* I. 16), occurs in a survey by genre of outstanding Latin poets, where he is placed in the company of Tibullus, Virgil, Terence, and Catullus. (Interestingly, and surprisingly in view of Marullus's reputation as a student of the poet, Lucretius receives no mention in the printing of the poem.)

> Amor Tibullo, Mars tibi, Maro, debet,
> Terentio soccus levis,
> Coturnus olim nemini satis multum,
> Horatio satyra & chelys,
> Epigramma cultum, teste Rhallo, adhuc nulli,
> Docto Catullo syllabae.
> Hos si quis inter ceteros locat vates,
> onerat quam honorat verius.[14]

In spite of this acknowledgement of Horace's pre-eminence in *carmina*, Marullus's practice in books 1 and 2 of the *Epigrams* shows that *Orazio lirico* did not bulk large at that time. Only one poem (*Ep.* I. 63) is in Horatian metre (sapphics—though his metrical practice, unlike Politian's, of admitting a light fourth syllable and tolerating the absence of the usual caesura is Catullan rather than Horatian), but it is an important poem, the last in book 1, addressed to his fellow Greek Manilius Rhallus.

[14] This and other quotations from Marullus are taken, with some modification of punctuation and capitalization, from the Florentine edition of 1497. The two lines on Lucretius have been omitted in order to reflect the earlier version of the poem. For details of variants in the text of Marullus here and elsewhere see Perosa (1951).

Non vides verno variata flore
Tecta? Non postes viola revinctos?
Stat coronatis viridis iuventus
    Mixta puellis.

Concinunt Maias pueri Kalendas,   5
Concinunt senes bene feriati,
Omnis exultat locus, omnis aetas
    Laeta renidet.

Ipse reiectis humero capillis
Candet in palla crocea Cupido,   10
Acer & plena iaculis pharetra,
    Acer et arcu.

Et modo huc circumvolitans & illuc
Nectit optatas iuvenum choreas,
Artibus notis alimenta primo   15
    Dum parat igni.

Nunc puellaris medius catervae
Illius flavum caput illiusque
Comit & vultus, oculisque laetum
    Addit honorem.   20

'Mitte vaesanos, bone Rhalle, questus:
Iam sat indultum patriae ruinae est.
Nunc vocat lusus positisque curis
    Blanda voluptas.

Quid dies omnis miseri querendo   25
Perdimus dati breve tempus aevi?
Sat mala laeti quoque sorte, caelum hoc
    Hausimus olim.

Profer huc cadum, puer Hylle, trimum;
Cedat & maeror procul & dolores   30
Tota nimirum Genio mihique
    Fulxerit haec lux.

The theme is Horatian: a call to dismiss *vaesanos questus* (21) when all around there is joy (cf. *Odes* 3. 8, 29; 2. 11). When Horace addresses a friend in terms like these, it is the prospect of war on the frontier or worry about constitutional questions which threatens the happiness of the moment. For Marullus, however, it is not the present or future but the past that impinges on present joy. Rhallus as a Greek has experienced the pain of his country's subjugation, and this is the source of his complaints. But the speaker of the poem, who being a Greek also has known the same sorrow, has come to see that there has been enough grieving— *Iam sat indultum patriae ruinae est* (22)—and he reminds Rhallus that once they were happy enough even in their misfortune as they breathed the air of exile (27-8). The poem is a neat recasting of a Horatian theme to fit the situation of two exiles.

Books 3 and 4 of the *Epigrams* belong to Marullus's life in Florence. There is now a marked increase in the number of poems in Horatian lyric metres. There are three alcaics, two sapphics, and one asclepiad. As well as these stanzaic poems, there are also five in couplets consisting of glyconics followed by asclepiads, which is the reversal of a Horatian system. Another lyric poem (*Ep.* 3.10) is composed in the 5-line stanza of Catullus 61. Marullus's greatest achievement, the *Hymni naturales*, belongs mainly if not entirely to his years in Florence. Here too Horatian lyric metres are prominent: out of twenty-one hymns, four are alcaics, three sapphics, and the couplet consisting of glyconic followed by asclepiad is again used, in three hymns. The hymn to Juppiter (*Ep.* 2.5) is in the metre of Catullus' hymn to Diana (34).

A full answer to the question why Marullus turned so markedly at this time to stanzaic and above all Horatian lyric forms cannot of course be given, but some consideration of his position in Florence may throw some light on it. Though Florence was a city where he might hope to advance himself, he was not ideally placed to take advantage of the opportunities which it offered. He had arrived there with some reputation as a poet, based on the two books of *Epigrams* published just before, but he now faced the rivalry of Politian. He had already established friendly relations with the wealthy sons of Pierfrancesco de' Medici, but they were often at odds with the most powerful member of the family, their second cousin Lorenzo il Magnifico, with whom Marullus's relations were more distant. (Lorenzo was Politian's patron too.) Marullus was a friend of the philosopher Giovanni Pico della Mirandola, count of Concordia, whom he had known in Rome. Pico had taken refuge in Florence after fleeing from Rome and spending some time in a French prison. Marullus was not in a position to call on the patronage of an 'establishment'. Contemporary letters indeed paint a rather sad picture of Marullus after his arrival in Florence. Referred to as a *domesticus*, a dependant in a great house, he is described as suffering the last straw when a thief makes off with some of his clothes.[15] And within days of his arrival Politian was spreading reports calculated to cause a breach between Marullus and two friends in the Roman curia, the brothers Alessandro and Paolo Cortesi.[16] He had a name to make and a place to secure in Florentine society. He married Alessandra Scala, daughter of the chancellor, Bartolomeo Scala. Unwisely, he challenged Politian in verse on a number of points of scholarship, and the enmity of the two, fuelled possibly by rivalry over Alessandra and certainly by Politian's disdain for *Graeculi*, was notorious.[17] But there is more to verse than polemic, and Marullus perhaps felt that in the area of Horatian lyric Politian had left him space in which to excel. Politian had only dabbled there, and it should not prove too difficult to surpass him.

And the great project of the *Hymni naturales* raised the question of choice of metre. Looking back to the Homeric hymns, the *Hymn to Zeus* of Cleanthes, the Orphic hymns and those of Proclus, and to the hymns recently included in his *Laws* by Gemistos Plethon as well as to the tradition of didactic poetry represented by Parmenides, Empedocles, and Lucretius, he might have decided to write all of them in hexameters. In fact he chose metrical ποικιλία. He placed in strategic positions four substantial hexameter pieces, which stand closer to Cleanthes and Lucretius than to Proclus: the first and last in the collection, *Iovi optimo maximo* and *Terrae* (1. 1 and 4. 5); the massive hymn *Soli*, which opens, and accounts for almost the whole of, book 3 (3. 1), and what was originally the last hymn of book 1, *Aeternitati*.[18] Rejecting the jejuneness of the hexameter hymns of Proclus, the Orphic collection, and Plethon, he composed the rest in epodic (1. 2, 4; 2. 2; 3. 2; 4. 4) and lyric (1. 3, 6; 2. 1, 3-8; 4. 1-3) forms, in which the presence of Horace is manifest.

The hymns are arranged in an order which mirrors a familiar hierarchical view of the universe, beginning in the first book with the realm, unchanging and timeless, of hypercosmic deities, passing in the second by way of Pan as demiurge, Coelus, and Stellae

---

[15] Acciaoli (1489).　　　　　　　　　　[16] Tosto (1979) 568-9.

[17] Paolo Cortesi (1510), lib. I, f. II^r (from the section entitled *memoria*) gives as an example of the stimulation of memory *ex contrario genere* the fact that because of the long literary quarrel between the two someone wishing to recall Marullus could do so by bringing Politian to mind!

[18] Subsequently *Baccho*, which had been in penultimate position, was put in final position as 1. 6, and *Aeternitati* became 1. 5.

(the fixed stars) to the five planetary deities, then in the third book
to the divinities of Sun and Moon, and lastly in the fourth by way
of Aether to the four elemental deities, Jupiter Fulgerator (fire),
Juno (air), Oceanus, and Terra. None of these gods is strictly speaking an Olympian, but Marullus draws freely on the mythological
traditions associated with the Olympian homonyms of his hypercosmic, cosmic, and elemental gods.

The hymn which displays the most vigorous interaction with a
number of Horatian texts is 2. 6, *Marti*.

> Antiqua Codri progenies, licet
> Hinc arva bubus mille teras tuis,
>   Hinc dite seponas in arca
>   Quicquid Arabs vehit aestuosus,
>
> Frustra clientum dinumeres greges   5
> Et consularis praemia purpurae,
>   Frustra renidentes curules
>   Et veterum decora alta patrum
>
> Ni cuncta prudens diis referas bonis.
> Hos nocte, castis hos precibus die   10
>   Supplex adores, hos in omne
>   Tempus opem veniamque poscas.
>
> Nec vero siquid durius accidit
> (Quae multa vitae fert varius tenor)
>   Spem praeter, iccirco labare   15
>   Religio pietasque debet.
>
> Nam nec perenni terra viret coma,
> Et saepe sudo nunc capimur brevi
>   Nunc frustra inundantes procellae
>   Terrificant redeunte sole.   20
>
> Quare, tot olim quanquam opibus patrum
> Excussi Ethrusco carpimur otio,
>   Dic, sancta, dic, Clio, parentum
>   Laude patrem solita Gradivum,
>
> Heu, tot suorum quem miserae iuvant   25
> Clades, repulso Strimone Thracio
>   Tectisque Byzanti superbis,
>   Tristia dum fovet arma Turcae.
>
> Sed quid benignae non faciunt preces?
> Forsan minarum desinet hic quoque   30
>   Iam tandem & oblitus peracti
>   Respiciet propior nepotes.

Tunc me nec Orpheus carminibus pater
Aequet canentem nec pecorum deo
    Laudatus aestiva sub umbra   35
       Multiloquae fidicen Camenae,

Quanquam sonoris hic fidibus rudes
Duxisset ornos & vaga flumina
    Frenasset, hunc dignatus ipse
       Vltro epulis decimaque Phoebus;   40

Sed plena solvens pectora numine,
Dicam arma, plectro dicam adamantino
    Currus & adversa iacentem
       Cuspide terrigenam cohortem

Cum saeva cunctis bella timentibus   45
Superque moles molibus additas
    (Sic prima nil virtus perhorret)
       Mars cuperet tamen arma solus,

Mars tunc Olympo primum oculis patris
Admissus, alta sub Rhodope puer   50
    Haemoque adhuc suetus leones
       Cominus exagitare aprosque.

Vt vero cunctos ancipitis mali
Concussit horror Terraque partubus
    Superba crescebat sereno   55
       Iam propior propiorque caelo,

'Quid, o quid, annos digeritis rudes?
An sic creari nil' ait 'ab Iove est,'
    Pean, 'o aeternum carentes
       Morte dei & bone rex deorum?'   60

Simulque & ensem dat puero & galeam
Aeratam & hamis undique nexilem
    Auroque loricam trilicem,
       Aeolii Steropis laborem.

Excepit omnis regia plausibus,   65
Primusque nutu Iuppiter annuens
    Terrasque concussitque caelum,
       Cynthe, tua domina invidente.

Et iam prophanae versae acies retro,
Iam Terra monstris ipsa suis gravis,   70
    Aeterna quid distent caducis
       Senserat & manibus Tonantis

Contorta Rhethi fulmina fraxinis,
Iam laeta signo sancta deum cohors
    Redibat audito receptu   75
      Arma Iovis pariter canentes.

At non receptus ille nec imperi
Audit verendi signa, sed improba
    In caede perstabat ferocum
      Impatiens animorum et irae   80

Ni iam tum & annos & pueri Venus
Mirata dextram nec faciem minus,
    Complexa germanum benignis
      Aurea continuisset ulnis.

Salve, & virorum Mars pater & pater   85
Armorum, & olim (si merui modo)
    Da, quaeso, da, Gradive, pulchraque
      Ob patriam atque inopina fata.

Most of Marullus's hymns begin with an invocation to the relevant deity or to the Muses. The address here to *Antiqua Codri progenies* is without parallel. At the outset it strikes a Horatian note, echoing not only the opening of *Odes* 3. 29, *Tyrrhena regum progenies*, also in alcaics, but the mention as well of Codrus at *Odes* 3. 19. 1–2 'quantum distet ab Inacho | Codrus pro patria non timidus mori'. In *Odes* 3. 29 the identity of the *Tyrrhena progenies* is revealed two lines later. It is one specific descendant of Etruscan kings, Maecenas. The vocative is best compared with *Romane* in the sixth Roman ode (*Odes* 3. 6. 2), a generalizing address to a category of persons. But who is this 'ancient progeny of Codrus'? Firstly they are contemporaries: it is not they but their lineage which is ancient. (This view is confirmed by line 8, *veterum decora alta patrum*.) The reference to Codrus, last of the kings of Athens, connotes ancient roots in Attica or more generally in Greece, and also heroic patriotism: in Horace's words, he was not afraid to die for his country. We are dealing, then, with Greek contemporaries of the poet, who are addressed in terms reminding them of the antiquity of their race and its traditions of self-sacrifice. While there are two other passages in the *Hymni naturales* which speak of Greeks in exile and of the preservation in Italy of the records of Greece and its language (2. 8. 1–20; 3. 1. 267–87), Marullus nowhere addresses Greeks who are subject to the Turk.[19] The 'progeny of Codrus' may be safely identified as Greeks of the contemporary diaspora, above all those living in Italy.

A further word on Codrus may be added. The opening address relates not only to Horace's description of him as 'not afraid to die for his country', but also to a mention of Codrus in a text much closer in time to Marullus. In his fourteenth *Bucolicum carmen* Boccaccio makes an interesting attempt to deal with Christian themes in pagan terms. The poem is an allegory in which Boccaccio, who has suffered the loss of a daughter, presents himself as Silvius, a pagan shepherd whose daughter Olympia has died and, having gone to heaven (surprisingly, since in terms of the pagan setting of the poem there is no reason to believe that she has been baptized), has had revealed to her the truths of religion. She appears to her father at his sheepfold and in terms that at times owe a great deal to Dante's *Paradiso* she tells what she has seen. But first she speaks of man's redemption. She does so pastorally, telling how the saviour left high Olympus for the womb of a *parthenos*, thereby restoring the golden age; how he suffered the abuse of shepherds, was nailed to a cedar, and with his glorious blood washed away the filth, diseases, and ancient *scabies* of the sick flock; how he burst open the sheepfold of Plutarcus and brought into the sunlight the flocks and herds of 'our fathers':

> Vivimus eternum meritis et numine Codri.
>
> Aurea qui nuper, celso dimissus Olympo
> Parthenu in gremium, revocavit secula terris;
> turpia pastorum passus convitia, cedro
> affixus, leto concessit sponte triumphum.   95
> Vivimus eternum meritis et numine Codri.
>
> Sic priscas sordes, morbos scabiemque vetustam
> infecti pecoris preclaro sanguine lavit:
> hincque petens valles Plutarci septa refrinxit,
> in solem retrahens pecudes armentaque patrum.   100
> Vivimus eternum meritis et numine Codri.
>
> Morte hinc prostrata, campos reseravit odoros
> Elysii, sacrumque gregem deduxit in ortos
> mellifluos victor lauro quercuque refulgens,
> optandasque dedit nobis per secula sedes.   105
> Vivimus eternum meritis et numine Codri.

[19] He does, however, speak with sympathy of Greek and Oriental Christians who are subjects of the Turk in *Ep.* 4. 32. 6–12.

Exuvias in fine sibi pecus omne resummet;
ipse, iterum veniens, capros distinguet ab agnis,
hosque feris linquet, componet sedibus illos
perpetuis celoque novo post tempora claudet.   110
Vivimus eternum meritis et numine Codri.[20]

Plutarcus is Pluto, and the reference is to the harrowing of hell.
Elsewhere in the poem (line 201) God the Father is referred to as
Archesilas, but most remarkable of all is the name given to Christ
in the refrain which runs through this speech: *Vivimus eternum
meritis et numine Codri.* The self-sacrificing pagan king of Athens
has become Christ the saviour. Something of that Christian reinterpretation of the name and death of Codrus can be read in
Marullus's address to his Greek contemporaries. Calling them *Codri
progenies* is a subtle acknowledgement that in spite of the pagan
dress in which the hymn is clothed, those whom it addresses are
Christians.

After this opening vocative phrase, the first sentence (1-9) falls
into three parts: a concessive clause which refers to great wealth
(1-4), an apodosis (5-8) which speaks of marks of socio-political
distinction, and a protasis (9) which calls for an acknowledgement
that all blessings are owed to the gods. Of the four categories of
distinction which are enumerated in the second stanza, the last, as
we have seen, is part of the heritage of contemporary Greeks:
veterum decora alta patrum. Bearing in mind the generally humble
position held by the exiles (Janus Lascaris's achievement of
ambassadorial status in the service of France was exceptional),
we may count the clients, consulships, and curule offices of the
second stanza as also belonging to family history. (Elsewhere, in a
poem about exile, *Ep.* 3. 37. 15-22, Marullus speaks bitterly of
being a laughing-stock in foreign places, where neither nobility
nor distinguished ancestry nor a house supported by ancient titles
counts for anything.) That these past honours in lines 5-8 have a
distinctly Roman appearance need not surprise us. The Byzantines
after all called themselves Ῥωμαῖοι, and the poet himself, relying
on the Latinization of his not very distinguished Byzantine name,
elsewhere lays claim to an ancestry which he says included Roman
duces (*Ep.* 2. 32. 135-6). (These *duces* are revealed in the epitaph

---

[20] Boccaccio (1928 edn.) 69, with some changes in punctuation and setting out
of lines.

of the poet's father to have been the Gordian emperors.[21]) The concessive clause, on the other hand, speaks of present wealth, though this may be more hypothetical than real. The warning conveyed in *Frustra . . . dinumeres* (5) is vague, but it is clear that the gods must be recognized as the source of all good, present as well as past (9). Constant prayer is required, and the gods' help and favour must be sought. Unexpected misfortune must not lead to an irreligious attitude, for change is characteristic of life itself and brings with it many troubles. With this moralizing observation the worshipper strikes a characteristically Horatian note. The *non semper* topos of *Odes* 2. 9 and 11 appears at line 17 with reference to the seasons and the weather, with *redeunte sole* (20) ending the stanza and the whole introduction on an encouraging note.

Having thus emphasized the importance of prayer, the worshipper invokes the Muse of history (23), asking her to tell *laude solita* of Gradivus, *parentum patrem*. This is the only occurrence in Marullus of Clio's name, which is connected with κλέος 'glory'. In Horace too she is named just once, at *Odes* 1. 12. 2, where also she is invoked in a context of praise, being asked which man, hero, or god she is proposing to celebrate. The phrase *parentum patrem* (23-4) again recalls the Ῥωμαιοσύνη of the Byzantines. Juxtaposed with the invocation to Clio is a concessive clause: the worshipper calls for praise of the god of war, although he and his fellow exiles have lost their ancestral possessions through defeat in war so that they are now leading lives of wasteful inactivity in Tuscany (21-4). The worshipper and his addressees are in exile because Mars has turned against his own people (25-8), rejoicing in the disasters which have overwhelmed them, spurning the River Strymon (26 *repulso Strimone*, or in an earlier version of the hymn *neglecto Strimone*), spurning also the proud buildings of Byzantium (or in the earlier version 'of the Greeks') while giving comfort to Ottoman arms.

Marullus has treated the theme of the god who turns against his own people in terms of the account of the wrathful Tiber and to a lesser extent of Mars himself in Horace, *Odes* 1. 2. Already at line 22 in Marullus the juxtaposition of *excussi* and *Ethrusco*, though they are not syntactically connected and *Ethrusco* has a somewhat different meaning, may bring to mind *retortis litore Etrusco* in the

---

[21] For Maecius Marullus, supposedly father of Gordian I, see *SHA Gordiani tres* 2. See in general McGann (1980).

ode (13-14). The riverine origin of the passage in Marullus may account for the presence there of the Thracian Strymon. This is at a considerable distance from Byzantium, but the second Rome does not possess a river of its own comparable with the Tiber. (Marullus's earlier thoughts on this passage, as we have seen, had *neglecto* rather than *repulso*. *Neglecto* may derive from Horace's *neglectum genus*, which occurs at line 35 of the ode, in the passage addressing Mars himself.) The reference to the weapons of the Turk at line 28 (*tristia . . . arma Turcae*) may remind us that Marullus found the name of an enemy of Rome at line 39 in his text of Horace, reading *Mauri* rather than our *Marsi*, a correction which would not be made for another two centuries. From the same stanza in Horace come Marullus's *quem . . . iuvant* (25) and perhaps *Iam tandem* (31), suggested by Horace's *nimis longo* (37). Marullus uses almost the same words as Horace for the hoped-for change in the attitude of Mars: *Respiciet propior nepotes* at line 32 of Marullus and *nepotes respicis auctor* at lines 35-6 of Horace. In the event of such a change, the worshipper is confident that as a singer he would equal both Orpheus and Pindar (33-40). Pindar is not named, but described in terms of stories about his close links with Pan and Apollo, stories which Marullus could have read in the Pindar scholia, Plutarch, or Pausanias.[22] Inspired by Mars' hypothetical change of heart, the worshipper would sing of the battle of gods and Giants.

What we have here is a kind of variation on the *recusatio*: instead of saying 'If I were able to, I should heed your request and write sublimely about . . .' and then giving a sample of the kind of writing which he claims to be unable to produce, he declares that if Mars were to show favour to his Roman/Byzantine descendants, the poet-worshipper would open himself to divine power (*plena solvens pectora numine*), which would inspire him to write . . . as follows. And he proceeds at greater length (42-84) than might be expected in a *recusatio* to sing of the battle of gods and Giants, in which Mars, only recently admitted to Olympus after a boyhood spent hunting lions and boars around Rhodope and Haemus, distinguishes himself by his pugnacity and courage. Although the Gigantomachy has, in both text and image, a long history in ancient times,[23] Mars (or Ares) appears to be a stranger to its

[22] Perosa (1951) 238 (Index nominum s.v. *Camaena*).

[23] Hardie (1986) 85-90; the connection between *recusatio* and Gigantomachy is noted at 87. See also Nisbet and Hubbard (1978) on *Odes* 2. 12. 7.

traditions. Marullus's treatment of the theme, however, is far from isolated as it exhibits close links with the Gigantomachy in the longest and grandest of Horace's odes, 3. 4.

Two themes common to both poems are the building of a land bridge between earth and heaven (Horace 51-52; Marullus 46, 54-6) and the fear inspired by the Giants (Horace 49-52; Marullus 45-46, 53-4). Marullus makes more of the gods' fear—understandably since he is concerned to glorify one of them above the rest. More striking than these is the role of Terra in the two poems. In Horace there is the pathos of her being used to smother her own monstrous offspring (73-5); in the hymn her rise towards heaven (55-6) is followed by a pathetic fall as she weighs down upon her children (70). There is a verbal link here: *iniecta monstris Terra dolet suis* in Horace (73) and *Terra monstris ipsa suis gravis* in Marullus (70). In the ode Jupiter destroys his enemies *fulmine . . . caduco* 'with falling thunderbolt' (44); the same adjective is used substantivally in the hymn, but in the sense of 'perishable things', contrasting with *aeterna*, 'eternal things' (71); Jupiter's *fulmina* appear a little later in the hymn (73), contrasted with the ash-trees (*fraxinis*) of Rhoetus, whose name occurs in the ode also, where it is juxtaposed with, but syntactically separate from, a mention of the tree-trunks which are the attributes of another attacker, Enceladus (55 *Rhoetus evolsisque truncis*). The ode ends with a gently erotic diminuendo,[24] naming two enemies of the gods whose offences are sexual: Tityos, would-be rapist of Diana, and Pirithous the lover, who would have carried Proserpine from Hades. (Would that have been more a rescue than an abduction?) In Marullus's hymn the violence of Mars's battle-fury gives way before the power of golden Venus as she admires his youth, prowess, and beauty, enfolding him, her boyish brother, in her loving arms (81-4). Already the stage is being prepared for the love-scene between Mars and Venus which teasingly concludes the next hymn, to Venus.

All this appears to be rather a long way from the divine workings of the cosmos, which is the theme of the *Hymni naturales*. Yet love and strife are cosmological forces, and one possible reading would in the light of the poet's Greek background recall the fact that Byzantine commentators explained Hesiod's Gigantomachies

[24] Fraenkel (1957) 285.

by reference to cosmic events,[25] and would thus view the poem as
a cosmological allegory. But allegory is figurative, and figure—in
particular the undecidable possibility that figure *may* be present—
involves indeterminacy. Our reading of lines 41–84 of the hymn
cannot avoid being indeterminate. We cannot answer the question
whether the narrative is allegorical or simply laudatory and non-
figurative; and if it is allegorical, of what is it an allegory: cosmological conflict or national struggle? Here a quotation from Terence
Cave may be relevant. Discussing the Gigantomachy in Ronsard's
Hymne d'hyver, he writes:

What is striking about the Gigantomachy of *Hyver* is its relative indeterminacy. It may function as a historico-political *topos* (if a given range of
contemporary texts is placed alongside it), but it may also carry a psychological layer of reference (in the tradition of the 'Psychomachia'), or more
generally the outline of a dialectic between order and disorder: Winter is
tolerated (like the Huguenots) provided it is contained within a prescribed
space, which clarifies in turn the space of the other seasons.[26]

Discussion of the last stanza and final address must focus on
patriam (88). In the setting of the *Hymni naturales* it is tempting to
understand the word as denoting the soul's heavenly homeland, a
Platonic recognition of the pre-existence of the soul.[27] Here Mars is
asked to grant *Ob patriam* at some time a destiny that is lovely and
unexpected. *Patria*, it would appear, denotes something which
gives the worshipper a claim to the god's favour, something in a
fashion shared by the worshipper with his god. This inference
appears to go against the interpretation which would see in *patria*
a reference to the heavenly homeland of Platonism, for it is difficult
to see how an encosmic deity like Mars can share such a *patria*
with the human soul, which is possessed of a capacity for union
with the supreme godhead.[28] On the other hand, many gods have
an earthly *patria*, and few more emphatically than Mars in this
hymn, whose translation from his earthly home is attested in lines
49–52. His earthly *patria* is Thrace, and Thracian elements are
prominent in the hymn: there is the Strymon (26), Thracian
Orpheus (33–4, 37–9), and Rhodope and Haemus (50–2). Is

---

[25] For the Byzantine connection see Hardie (1986) 95–6, 140. See in general
Innes (1979), who, however, draws a sharp contrast between the themes of
Gigantomachy and cosmology.   [26] Cave (1979) 54–5.

[27] Cf. *Hymni naturales* 1. 105 and the use of *domus* at 2. 3. 50. The lost *patria* of
the Greek exile may also be involved.

[28] ibid. 1. 5. 36 'cognatoque adiice [sc. nos] caelo' (Aeternitas is being addressed).

Thrace the link which joins god and worshipper? Is the voice of the worshipper to which we have been listening in some sense a Thracian voice? Can the poet himself be described as Thracian?

An older contemporary of his, Demetrios Raoul Kabakes, who was the father of his friend Manilius Rhallus, on occasion signed himself 'Hellene and Thracian' and 'Spartan and Byzantine', thereby laying claim to two πατρίδες, Sparta and Byzantium.[29] Marullus's situation was hardly different. He also had two πατρίδες, his birthplace in the Morea and Constantinople, to which the title-pages of the two editions of his poems which were published in his lifetime assign him, describing him as *Constantinopolitanus*.[30] Constantinople was, after all, a city of Thrace,[31] and the voice of a *poeta Constantinopolitanus* is in that sense Thracian. Besides and more specifically, there is his maternal lineage, of which he was sufficiently proud to call himself 'Michaelis Tarchaniotae Marulli', on the title-page of the Florentine edition of his *Hymni et Epigrammata*. The precise origins of the Ταρχανειῶται are uncertain, but it seems very probable that the family was Thracian.[32]

Thus there are elements in what is known about the background of the man Marullus which make understandable the worshipper's concluding appeal to Mars on the basis of *patria*. But it is possible also in another, less material, sense to discern a Thracian strain in the words of the hymn. At the beginning of the *Hymn to Mercury* (*Hymni naturales* 2. 8) the poet-worshipper strikes a rueful personal note:

> Ergo restabat mihi, proh deorum
> Rex bone, hoc fatis etiam malignis,
> Patria ut Graecus sacra non Pelasga
> Voce referrem,
>
> Quique tot saeclis tripodas silentes   5
> Primus Orpheo pede rite movi
> Exul Ethrusci streperem sonanda
> Vallibus Arni.

[29] Legrand (1885) 262 n. 1; Chatzes (1909) 41–8; Fassoulakis (1973) 83–5. For the comparable case of Michael Trivolis see Denisoff (1943) 91, 137–8, 404–5.

[30] The family may have had Constantinopolitan roots (Manilius's epitaph also calls him *Constantinopolitanus*.) In any case the City is the 'common fatherland' of all 'Byzantines'; See Magdalino (1989) 184.   [31] Lib. *Or.* 1. 279.

[32] Amantos (1929) believed that the name derives from the village of Tarchanion near Kypsella in Thrace; cf. Lemerle (1946) 125; Polemis (1968) 183 nn. 3 and 4; Kazhdan (1991) 2011 speaks of a Bulgarian origin and describes the family as belonging to the nobility of Adrianople.

Is the Thracian voice in the *Hymn to Mars* that of an Orphic singer in Tuscany? Among the many threads of discourse to which the *Hymni naturales* relate is the corpus of Orphic hymns, which at that time did not exist merely as Greek texts or in Latin translation (there are links between one of those translations[33] and Marullus, *Hymni naturales* 2. 2); they enjoyed another mode of existence, for the Orphic hymns were also realized among Florentine Platonists as liturgical song. Perhaps the voice embodied in this text and maybe in all Marullus's hymns is a written echo of occasions when Orphic text was transmuted by the voice of Marsilio Ficino into Orphic song.[34] It seems very appropriate that in the sixteenth-century library of Fulvio Orsini his copy of the 1497 edition of Marullus's *Epigrammata et Hymni naturales* was bound in one volume with a text which, like the writings attributed to Orpheus, was a representative of the *prisca theologia*, Ficino's edition of *Poimandres*.[35]

Marullus's *Hymn to Mars* has in the end brought us to a world very different from that of Horace. And yet the relationship between the hymn and *Odes*. 1. 2 and 3. 4 goes beyond matters of topoi and verbal echoes. Whatever the truth about the allegorical or non-allegorical status of the Gigantomachy, it is clear that in the hymn Marullus is raising the question of what a later age would call ἡ μεγάλη ἰδέα, the recovery of Constantinople from the Turk. In *Ep*. 4. 32 he discussed the reconquest of the east in terms of a crusade, with Charles VIII of France as crusader king.[36] In the *Hymn to Mars*, however, the liberation of his country will be simply the result of divine intervention, and there is no role for crusaders, nor even for the Greeks themselves. In *Odes* 1. 2 Horace had dealt with a political matter in religious terms, in a way which offended 'against the Horatian qualities of moderation and rationality'.[37] And in *Odes* 3. 4 the poet is unsure enough of

---

[33] Kristeller (1937) 97-8.
[34] Kristeller (1944) 271-3 n. 86; Walker (1953) 101-3; (1954); (1958) 22-4; (1972) 24-5. See Klutstein (1987) for the view, reported in *Bibliography of Philosophy*, 36 (1989) 205, that Latin translations of texts of the *prisca theologia*, including Orphic hymns, contained in Laur. XXXVI, 35 and Ottob. Lat. 2966 and for long attributed to Ficino (cf. Kristeller 1944: 272 n. 85a) proceed in fact from an independent philosophical tradition, to which Plethon and Greeks living in Italy contributed.
[35] De Nolhac (1887) 159. The edition was published at Venice in 1491 as *Mercurii Trismegisti liber de potestate et sapientia Dei*.
[36] McGann (1991) *passim*.   [37] Nisbet and Hubbard (1970) 20.

his own sanity to raise the question whether he may not be the deluded victim of an *amabilis insania* (5-6). In both odes Horace comes close to transgressing the limits of rationality within which he normally operated. Marullus showed himself to be a sensitive and sympathetic reader of Horace by choosing to work precisely through these poems when he undertook by celebrating Thracian Mars in the measures of Thracian Orpheus (*Orpheo pede*) to offer like Horace a revelation in terms of pagan piety of *pulchraque . . . atque inopina fata* (87-8), that lovely destiny for his country to which rationally he could not look forward.

Bibliography

ABLEITINGER-GRÜNBERGER, D. (1971), *Der junge Horaz und die Politik: Studien zur 7. und 16. Epode* (Heidelberg).

ACCAIOLI, Z. (1489), letter dated 20 Sept. 1489 to Amerigo Vespucci, in *Rivista delle biblioteche e degli archivi*, 13 (1902): 187.

ADAMS, J. N. (1981), 'Ausonius *Cento Nuptialis* 101–31', *SIFC* 53: 199–215.

AHERN, C. F., jun. (1991), 'Horace's Rewriting of Homer in Carmen I. 6', *CP* 86: 301–14.

ALFÖLDI, A. (1970), *Die monarchische Repräsentation im römischen Kaiserreiche* (Darmstadt).

—— (1971), *Der Vater des Vaterlands im römischen Denken* (Darmstadt).

ALLEN, P. S., and ALLEN, H. M. (1906–58), *The Letters of Erasmus* (12 vols.; Oxford).

AMANTOS, K. (1929), 'Πόθεν τὸ ὄνομα Ταρχανειώτης;', Ἑλληνικά, 2: 435–6.

ANDERSON, A. R. (1928), 'Herakles and his Successors', *HSCP* 39: 422–36.

ANDERSON, W. S. (1982), *Essays on Roman Satire* (Princeton).

—— (1984), 'Ironic Preambles and Satiric Self-definition in Horace *Satire* 2. 1', *PCP* 19: 35–4.

APPEL, G. (1909), *De Romanorum Precationibus* (Giessen).

ARMSTRONG, D. H. (1986), 'Horatius Eques et Scriba: Satires 1. 6 and 2. 7', *TAPA* 116: 155–88.

—— (1989), *Horace* (New Haven and London).

ARNALDI, F. (1963), *Orazio: Odi ed epodi*, 5th edn. (Milan and Messina).

ASTLEY, N., ed. (1991), *Bloodaxe Critical Anthologies, i. Tony Harrison* (Newcastle).

AXELSON, B. (1945), *Unpoetische Wörter* (Lund).

BABCOCK, C. L. (1966), 'Si Certus Intrarit Dolor: A Reconsideration of Horace's Fifteenth Epode', *AJP* 87: 400–19.

—— (1981), 'Critical Approaches to the Odes of Horace', *ANRW* II. 31.3: 1560–611.

BADIAN, E. (1985), review of Gold (1982), in *CP* 80: 341–57.

—— (1989), 'The *Scribae* of the Roman Republic', *Klio*, 71: 582–603.

BALBO, E. (1937), *Augusto e Mussolini* (Rome).

BARKER, A. (1984), *Greek Musical Writing, i. The Musician and his Art* (Cambridge).

BARNES, T. D. (1974), 'The Victories of Augustus', *JRS* 64: 21–6.

BARTOL, K. (1992), 'Where was Iambic Poetry Performed? Some Evidence from the Fourth Century?', *CQ* 42: 65–71.

BAUMAN, R. A. (1967), *The Crimen Maiestatis in the Roman Republic and the Augustan Principate* (Johannesburg).

—— (1985), *Lawyers in Roman Transitional Politics* (Munich).

BEARD, M., and North, J. A., eds. (1990), *Pagan Priests* (London).

BECKER, C. (1963), *Das Spätwerk des Horaz* (Heidelberg).

BELLINGER, A. R. (1957), 'The Immortality of Alexander and Augustus', *YCS* 15: 103–12.

BENARIO, J. M. (1960), 'Book 4 of Horace's *Odes*: Augustan Propaganda', *TAPA* 91: 339–52.

BENJAMIN, W. (1968), 'The Work of Art in the Age of Mechanical Reproduction', in *Illuminations*, ed. H. Arendt (London), 219–53.

BENTLEY, R. (1869), *Q. Horatius Flaccus*, 3rd edn. (2 vols.; Berlin).

BÉRANGER, J. (1953), *Recherches sur l'aspect idéologique du principat* (Basle).

BERGSON, L. (1970), 'Zu Horaz, Carm. IV. 5', *RM* 113: 358–63.

BERRES, T. (1992), ' "Erlebnis und Kunstgestalt" im 7. Brief des Horaz', *Hermes*, 120: 216–37.

BERVE, H. (1967), *Die Tyrannis bei den Griechen* (Munich).

BICKERMAN, E. J. (1980), *Chronology of the Ancient World* (London).

BILLOWS, R. (1993), 'The Religious Procession of the *Ara Pacis Augustae*: Augustus' *Supplicatio* in 13 BC.', *JRA* 6: 80–92.

BINDER, G. (1971), *Aeneas und Augustus: Interpretationen zum 8. Buch der Aeneis* (Meisenheim).

BING, P. (1990), 'A Pun on Aratus' Name in Verse 2 of the *Phainomena?*', *HSCP* 93: 281–5.

BLÄNSDORF, J. (1974), 'Komödie in der späten Republik', in *Musa iocosa* [Festschrift A. Thierfelder] (Hildesheim and New York).

Bo, D. (1957–9), *Q. Horati Flacci Opera* (2 vols.; Turin) [vol. i is a revision of De Gubernatis (1945)].

—— (1965–6), *Lexicon Horatianum* (2 vols.; Hildesheim).

BOCCACCIO, G. (1928 edn.), *Opere latine minori*, ed. A. F. Massèra (Bari).

BOHNENKAMP, K. E. (1972), *Die Horazische Strophe: Studien zur Lex Meinekiana* (Hildesheim).

BÖMER, F., ed. (1958), *P. Ovidius Naso: Die Fasten* (2 vols.; Heidelberg).

—— ed. (1969–86), *P. Ovidius Naso: Metamorphosen* (6 vols.; Heidelberg).

BONNANO, M. G. (1980), 'Nomi e soprannomi archilochei', *MH* 37: 65–88.

BOOTH, J., ed. (1991), *Ovid: The Second Book of Amores* (Warminster).

BORZSÁK, St. (1984), *Q. Horati Flacci Opera* (Leipzig).

BOUCHÉ-LECLERQ, A. (1899), *L'Astrologie grecque* (Paris).

BOVIE, SMITH PALMER (1959), *The Satires and Epistles of Horace* (Chicago).

BOWERSOCK, G. W. (1971), 'A Date in the Eighth *Eclogue*', *HSCP* 75: 73–80.

BOWERSOCK, G. W. (1990), 'The Pontificate of Augustus', in Raaflaub and Toher (1990), 380–94.

BOWRA, C. M. (1961), *Greek Lyric Poetry*, 2nd edn. (Oxford).

—— (1964), *Pindar* (Oxford).

BRADSHAW, A. (1978), 'Horace and the Therapeutic Myth: *Odes* 3,7, 3,11 and 3,27', *Hermes*, 106: 156–76.

BRAMBLE, J. C. (1974), *Persius and the Programmatic Satire* (Cambridge).

BRAUN, G (1877–8), 'La originaria nazionalità di Orazio', *Archeografo triestino*, 5: 247–82.

BRAUND, S. H., ed. (1989), *Satire and Society in Ancient Rome* (Exeter).

BRECHT, F. J. (1930), *Motiv und Typengeschichte des griechischen Spottepigram* (*Philologus* supp. 22.2; Leipzig).

BREMER, D. (1976), *Licht und Dunkel in der frühgriechischen Dichtung* (Archiv für Begriffsgeschichte, supp. 1; Bonn).

BREMER, J. M. (1990), 'Pindar's Paradoxical ἐγώ and a Recent Controversy about the Performance of his Epinikia', in Slings (1990), 41–58.

—— VAN ERP TALMAN KIP, A., and SLINGS, S. R. (1987), *Some Recently Found Greek Poems* (*Mnemosyne* supp. 99; Leiden).

BRIND'AMOUR, P. (1983), *Le Calendrier romain* (Ottawa).

BRINK, C. O. (1963a), 'Horace and Varro', in *Varron* (Entretiens Hardt, 9; Geneva), 173–200.

—— (1963b), *Horace on Poetry, i. Prolegomena to the Literary Epistles* (Cambridge).

—— (1965), *On Reading a Horatian Satire: An Interpretation of* Sermones II. 6 (Sydney)

—— (1971), *Horace on Poetry, ii. The 'Ars Poetica'* (Cambridge).

—— (1982), *Horace on Poetry, iii. Epistles Book II* (Cambridge).

—— (1987), 'Horatian Notes IV: Despised Readings in the Manuscripts of Horace's *Satires*', *PCPS*, NS 33: 16–37.

BROWN, C. (1984), 'Ruined by Lust: Anacreon, Fr. 44 Gentili (432 *PMG*)', *CQ* 34: 37–42.

BROWN, P. G. McC. (1992), 'Menander, Fragments 745 and 746 K-T: Menander's *Kolax* and Parasites and Flatterers in Greek Comedy', *ZPE* 92: 91–107.

BROWN, P. M. (1993), *Horace: Satires I* (Warminster).

BRUNT, P. A. (1971), *Italian Manpower 225 B.C.-A.D. 14* (Oxford).

—— (1984), 'The Role of the Senate in the Augustan Regime', *CQ* 34: 423–44.

—— (1988), *The Fall of the Roman Republic* (Oxford).

—— and MOORE, J. M. (1967), *Res Gestae Divi Augusti* (Oxford).

BÜCHELER, F. (1889), 'Zu Horaz Od. IV 2', *RM* 44: 161–3.

—— (1930), *Kleine Schriften, iii* (Leipzig).

BUCHHEIT, V. (1962), *Studien zum Corpus Priapeum* (Munich).

BUCHNER, E. (1982), *Die Sonnenuhr des Augustus* (Mainz).
—— (1988), 'Horologium Solarium Augusti', in Heilmeyer (1988), 240–5.
BÜCHNER, K. (1962*a*), 'Die Epoden des Horaz', in Büchner (1970).
—— (1962*b*), *Studien zur römischen Literatur, iii. Horaz* (Wiesbaden).
—— (1970), *Studien zur römischen Literatur, viii: Werkanalysen* (Wiesbaden).
BULLE, H. (1928), *Untersuchungen an griechischen Theatern* (ABAW 33; Munich).
BURNETT, A. P. (1983), *Three Archaic Poets* (London).
—— (1989), 'Performing Pindar's Odes', *CP* 84: 283–93.
CAIRNS, F. (1971*a*), 'Horace *Odes* 1. 2', *Eranos*, 69: 68–88.
—— (1971*b*), 'Five "Religious" Odes of Horace', *AJP* 92: 433–52.
—— (1972), *Generic Composition in Greek and Roman Poetry* (Edinburgh).
—— (1977), 'Horace on Other People's Love Affairs (*Odes* I 27; II 4; I 8; III 12)', *QUCC* 24: 121–47.
—— (1979), *Tibullus: A Hellenistic Poet at Rome* (Cambridge).
—— (1984*a*), 'The Etymology of *Militia* in Roman Elegy', *Estudios clásicos*, 26/2 = Gil and Aguilar (1984), ii. 211–22.
—— (1984*b*), 'Propertius and the Battle of Actium (4. 6)', in Woodman and West (1984), 129–68, 229–36.
—— (1989), *Virgil's Augustan Epic* (Cambridge).
—— (1992), 'Theocritus *Idyll* 26', *PCPS* 38: 1–38.
CAMPBELL, A. Y. (1924), *Horace* (London).
—— (1945), *Q. Horati Flacci Carmina cum Epodis* (London).
—— (1953), *Horace, Odes and Epodes* (Liverpool).
CANTER, H. V. (1930–1), 'Venusia and the Native Country of Horace', *CJ* 26: 439–56.
CAPASSO, M., ed. (1992), *Papiri letterari greci e latini* (Lecce).
CAREY, C. (1986), 'Archilochus and Lycambes', *CQ* 36: 60–7.
—— (1989), 'The Performance of the Victory Ode', *AJP* 110: 545–65.
—— (1991), 'The Victory Ode in Performance: The Case for the Chorus', *CP* 86: 192–200.
CARRUBBA, R. W. (1969), *The Epodes of Horace: A Study in Poetic Arrangement* (The Hague and Paris).
CARTER, J. M. (1982), *Suetonius: Divus Augustus* (Bristol).
CASSON, L. (1971), *Ships and Seamanship in the Ancient World* (Princeton).
CAVARZERE, A. (1992), *Orazio: Il libro degli epodi* (Venice).
CAVE, T. (1979), *The Cornucopian Text: Problems of Writing in the French Renaissance* (Oxford).
CHASTAGNOL, A. (1992), *Le Sénat romain à l'époque impériale* (Paris).
CHATZES, A. C. (1909), Οἱ Ῥαούλ, Ῥάλ, Ῥάλαι (1080–1800): Ἱστορικὴ μονογραφία (Kirchlain).

CHRIST, K. (1977), 'Zur Augusteischen Germanienpolitik', *Chiron*, 7: 149–205.

CHRISTES, J. (1971), *Der frühe Lucilius* (Heidelberg).

CLAUSS, J. J. (1985), 'Allusion and Structure in Horace *Satires* 2. 1: The Callimachean Response', *TAPA* 115: 197–206.

—— (1988), 'Vergil and the Euphrates', *AJP* 109: 309–20.

CLAYMAN, D. L. (1980), *Callimachus' Iambi* (Leiden).

CLOUD, J. D. (1989), 'Satirists and the Law', in Braund (1989), 49–68.

COFFEY, M. (1989), *Roman Satire*, 2nd edn. (Bristol).

COLIE, R. L. (1973), *The Resources of Kind: Genre-theory in the Renaissance* (Berkeley).

COLLINGE, N. E. (1961), *The Structure of Horace's Odes* (London).

COMMAGER, H. S. (1962), *The Odes of Horace* (New Haven and London).

CONNOR, P. J. (1987), *Horace's Lyric Poetry: The Force of Humour* (Berwick, Vic.).

COOPER, L. (1916), *A Concordance to Horace* (Washington).

COPLEY, F. O. (1956), *Exclusus Amator: A Study in Latin Love Poetry* (Baltimore).

CORTESI, P. (1510), *De Cardinalatu* (Castel Cortesiano).

COSTA, C. D. N., ed. (1973), *Horace* (London).

COURBAUD, E. (1914), *Horace, sa vie et sa pensée à l'époque des Épîtres* (Paris).

COURTNEY, E. (1993), *The Fragmentary Latin Poets* (Oxford).

CRACA, C. (1989), 'Gli epodi 8 e 12: Una rassegna', in Fedeli (1989), 129–55.

CREMONA, V. (1982), *La poesia civile di Orazio* (Milan).

—— (1993), 'Orazio, poeta civile', in Ludwig (1993), 95–123.

CROOK, J. A. (1967), *Law and Life of Rome* (London).

CUNTZ, O. (1923), *Die Geographie des Ptolemaeus* (Leipzig).

CUPAIUOLO, F. (1976), *Lettura di Orazio lirico: Struttura dell'ode oraziana*, 2nd edn. (Naples).

CURCIO, G. (1907), 'Commenti medioevali ad Orazio', *RFIC* 35: 43–64.

—— (1913), *Orazio Flacco studiato in Italia dal secolo XIII al XVIII* (Catania).

CURRAN, L. C. (1970), 'Nature, Convention, and Obscenity in Horace, *Satires* 1. 2', *Arion* 9: 220–45.

DACIER, A. (1709), *Œuvres d'Horace* (Paris).

DAHLMANN, H. (1953), *Varros Schrift 'De poematis' und die hellenistisch-römische Poetik* (Wiesbaden).

—— (1958), 'Die letzte Ode des Horaz', *Gymnasium*, 65: 340–55.

—— (1962), *Studien zu Varro 'De poetis'* (Wiesbaden).

D'ALTON, J. H. (1917), *Horace and his Age* (London).

DAMON, C. (1992), 'Sex. Cloelius, *Scriba*', *HSCP* 94: 227–50.

DANIELS, G. (1940), *Die Strophengruppen in den Horazoden* (diss. Königsberg).

D'ARMS, J. H. (1981), *Commerce and Social Standing in Ancient Rome* (Cambridge, Ma.).

DAUBE, D. (1951), ' "Ne quid infamandi causa fiat": The Roman Law of Defamation', in *Atti del congresso internazionale di diritto romano e storia del diritto, 1948*, iii (Milan), 411–50.

DAVIES, M. (1980), 'The Eyes of Love and the Hunting-net in Ibycus 287 P.', *Maia*, 32: 255–7.

—— (1988), 'Monody, Choral lyric and the Tyranny of the Handbook', *CQ* 38: 52–64.

—— (1991), *Poetarum Melicorum Graecorum Fragmenta*, i (Oxford).

DAVIS, G. (1987), 'Quis . . . digne scripserit? The *Topos* of *Alter Homerus* in Horace *C*. 1. 6', *Phoenix*, 41: 292–5.

—— (1991), *Polyhymnia: The Rhetoric of Horatian Lyric Discourse* (Berkeley).

DEGANI, E. (1983), *Hipponax: Testimonia et Fragmenta* (Leipzig).

DEGRASSI, A. (1963), *Fasti Anni Numani et Iuliani* [*Inscriptiones Italiae 13.2*] (Rome).

DE GRUMMOND, N. T. (1990), 'Pax Augusta and the Horae on the Ara Pacis Augustae', *AJA* 94: 663–77.

DE GUBERNATIS, M. (1945), *Q. Horati Flacci Opera*, i (Turin).

DELATTE, L. (1942), *Les Traités de la royauté d'Ecphante, Diotogène et Sthenidas* (Liège).

DEL LUNGO, I. (1867), *Prose volgari inedite e poesie latine e greche di Angelo Ambrogini Poliziano* (Florence).

DELZ, J. (1988), review of Shackleton Bailey (1985a), in *Gnomon*, 60: 495–501.

DEN BOER, W., ed. (1973), *La Culte des souverains dans l'empire romain* (Entretiens Hardt, 19; Geneva).

DENISOFF, E. (1943), *Maxime le Grec et l'Occident* (Université de Louvain: Recueil de travaux d'histoire et de philologie, ser. 3/14; Paris).

DE NOLHAC, P. (1887), *La Bibliothèque de Fulvio Orsini* (Paris).

DEROUX, C., ed. (1980), *Studies in Latin Literature and Roman History*, ii (Brussels).

—— ed. (1986), *Studies in Latin Literature and Roman History*, iv (Brussels).

DES BOUVRIE, S. (1984), 'Augustus' Legislation on Morals: Which Morals and What Aims?', *SO* 59: 93–113.

DESPREZ, L. (1691), *Quinti Horati Flacci Opera* (2 vols.; Paris).

DI BENEDETTO, A. (1962), 'Echi terenziani in Orazio', *Rend. della Acc. di Arch., lett. e Belle Arti di Napoli*, NS 37: 35–57.

DI BENEDETTO, V. (1971), *Euripide: Teatro e società* (Turin).

DICKIE, M. W. (1981), 'The Disavowal of *Invidia* in Roman Iamb and Satire', *PLLS* 3: 183–208.

DIEHL, E. (1911), *Die Vitae Vergilianae und ihre antiken Quellen* (Bonn).

DIETZE, K. (1900), 'Anspielungen auf die Komödie bei Horaz', in *Berichte des Freien deutschen Hochstiftes zu Frankfurt a. M., 1900* (Frankfurt).

DIGGLE, J., HALL, J. B., and JOCELYN, H. D., eds. (1989), *Studies in Latin Literature and its Tradition in Honour of C. O. Brink* (Cambridge).

DILKE, O. A. W. (1961), *Horace, Epistles, Book 1*, rev. 2nd edn. (London) [1st edn. 1954].

—— (1981), 'The Interpretation of Horace's Epistles', *ANRW* II. 31.3: 1837-65.

DIONIGI, I. (1983), *Seneca: De Otio* (Brescia).

DOBLHOFER, E. (1966), *Die Augustuspanegyrik des Horaz in formalhistorischer Sicht* (Heidelberg).

—— (1981), 'Horaz und Augustus', *ANRW* II. 31. 3. 1922-86.

—— (1992), *Horaz in der Forschung nach 1957* (Darmstadt)

DOVER, K. J. (1963), 'The Poetry of Archilochus', in *Archiloque* (Entretiens Hardt, 10; Geneva), 183-222.

—— (1978), *Greek Homosexuality* (London).

DRACHMANN, A. B. (1903), *Scholia Vetera in Pindari Carmina* (Leipzig).

DUNN, F. (1989), 'Horace's Sacred Spring', *Latomus*, 48: 97-109.

—— (forthcoming), 'Ends and Means in Euripides' *Herakles*', in Dunn, Fowler, and Roberts (forthcoming).

——, FOWLER, D. P. and ROBERTS, D., eds., (forthcoming), *Ancient Closure* (Princeton)

DU QUESNAY, I. M. LE M. (1981), 'Vergil's First Eclogue', *PLLS* 3: 29-182.

—— (1984), 'Horace and Maecenas: The Propaganda Value of *Sermones* 1', in Woodman and West (1984), 19-58.

DYSON, M. (1990), 'Horace *Carmina* 4. 5. 36-37', *CP* 85: 126-9.

EDEL, L. (1987), *Henry James: A Life* (London).

EDMUNDS, L. (1992), *From a Sabine Jar: Reading Horace Odes 1. 9* (Chapel Hill).

EHRENBERG, V. and JONES, A. H. M. (1976), *Documents Illustrating the Reigns of Augustus and Tiberius*, 2nd edn. (Oxford).

EISENHUT, W., ed. (1970), *Antike Lyrik* (Darmstadt).

ELLIOTT, R. C. (1960), *The Power of Satire: Magic, Ritual, Art* (Princeton).

Enciclopedia oraziana (1992) (Rome).

ENK, P. J. (1946), *Sex. Propertii Elegiarum Liber Primus* (Leiden).

—— (1962), *Sex. Propertii Elegiarum Liber Secundus* (2 vols.; Leiden).

ERKELL, H. (1952), *Augustus, Felicitas, Fortuna: Lateinische Wortstudien* (Göteborg).

ESSER, D. (1976), *Untersuchungen zu den Odenschlüssen des Horaz* (Meisenheim).

ESTIENNE, H. (1587). *De Criticis Veteribus Graecis et Latinis Eorumque Variis apud Poetas Potissimum Reprehensionibus Dissertatio* (Paris).

EVANS, J. D. (1992). *The Art of Persuasion* (Ann Arbor).

FASSOULAKIS, S. (1973), *The Byzantine Family of Raoul-Ral(l)es* (Athens).

FATOUROS, G. (1966), *Index Verborum zur frühgriechischen Lyrik* (Heidelberg).

FEARS, J. R. (1981*a*), 'The Cult of Virtues and Roman Imperial Ideology', *ANRW* II. 17.2: 827–948.

—— (1981*b*), 'The Theology of Victory at Rome: Approaches and Problems', *ANRW* II. 17.2: 736–826.

FEDELI, P. (1980), *Sesto Properzio: Il primo libro delle elegie* (Florence).

—— (1985), *Sesto Properzio: Il libro terzo delle elegie* (Bari).

—— (1989), *Orazio in colloquio* (Venosa).

FEENEY, D. C. (1991), *The Gods in Epic* (Oxford).

—— (1992), 'Si licet et fas est: Ovid's *Fasti* and the Problem of Free Speech under the Principate', in Powell (1992), 1–25.

—— (1993), 'Horace and the Greek Lyric Poets', in Rudd (1993), 41–63.

FENSTERBUSCH, C. (1936), 'Zu Vitruv v 6, 8–9', *Philologus*, 91: 117–20.

—— (1976), *Vitruvii de Architectura Libri X* (Darmstadt).

FERRERO, L. (1955), *Storia del pitagorismo nel mondo romano* (Cuneo).

FERRI, R. (1993), *Il dispiacere di un epicureo* (Pisa).

FESTA, N. (1940), 'Asterie', *Atti della Reale Accademia d'Italia: Rendiconti della classe di scienze morali e storiche*, 7/1: 65–9.

FIECHTER, E. H. (1914), *Baugeschichtliche Entwicklung des antiken Theaters* (Munich).

FISHWICK, D. (1987), *The Imperial Cult in the Latin West*, i/1–2 (Leiden).

—— (1991), *The Imperial Cult in the Latin West*, ii/1 (Leiden).

FISKE, G. C. (1920), *Lucilius and Horace* (Madison, Wis.).

FITZGERALD, W. (1988), 'Power and Impotence in Horace's *Epodes*', *Ramus*, 17: 176–91.

FLETCHER, G. B. A. (1960), 'Propertiana', *Latomus*, 19: 736–48.

—— (1961), 'Propertiana', *Latomus*, 20: 85–92.

FORTENBAUGH, W. W. (1989), 'The Rhetorical Treatises of Aristotle and Theophrastus', in W. W. Fortenbaugh and P. Steinmetz (eds.), *Cicero's Knowledge of the Peripatos* (New Brunswick and London), 39–60.

FOWLER, A. (1982), *Kinds of Literature: An Introduction to the Theory of Genres and Modes* (Oxford).

FOWLER, D. P. (1989*a*), 'First Thoughts on Closure: Problems and Prospects', *MD* 22: 75–122.

—— (1989*b*), 'Lucretius and Politics', in Griffin and Barnes (1989), 120–50.

—— (forthcoming), 'Laocoon's Point of View', in Habinek and Schiesaro (forthcoming).

FRAENKEL, E. (1925), 'Anzeige von Beckmann, *Zauberei und Recht in Roms Frühzeit*', *Gnomon*, 1: 185–200 = *Kleine Beiträge* (Rome, 1964), 2: 397–415.

FRAENKEL, E. (1932–3), *Das Pindargedicht des Horaz* (SB Heid. Ak. Wiss. 23/2, Heidelberg).

—— (1957), *Horace* (Oxford).

FRASER JENKINS, A. D. (1970), 'Cosimo de' Medici's Patronage of Architecture and the Theory of Magnificence', *Journal of the Warburg and Courtauld Institutes*, 33: 162–70.

FREADMAN, A., and MACDONALD, A. (1992), *What is this Thing called 'Genre'?* (Mt Nebo, Qld).

FREIS, R. (1983), 'The Catalogue of Pindaric Genres in Horace *Odes* 4. 2', *CA* 2: 27–36.

FREUDENBURG, K. (1990), 'Horace's Satiric Program and the Language of Contemporary Theory in *Satires* 2. 1', *AJP* 111: 187–203.

—— (1993), *The Walking Muse: Horace on the Theory of Satire* (Princeton).

FREYBURGER, G. (1978). 'La supplication d'action de grâces', *ANRW* II. 16. 2: 1418–39.

FRIER, B. W. (1985), *The Rise of the Roman Jurists* (Princeton).

FROUDE, J. C. (1894), *The Life and Letters of Erasmus* (London).

FUCHS, H. (1926), *Augustin und der antike Friedensgedanke* (Berlin).

GALINSKY, K. (1981), 'Augustus' Legislation on Morals and Marriage', *Philologus*, 125: 126–44.

GALL, D. (1981), *Die Bilder der horazischen Lyrik* (Königstein).

GARNSEY, P. (1988), *Famine and Food Supply in the Roman World* (Cambridge).

GARROD, H. W. (1912), *Horati Opera* (Oxford) [revision of Wickham (1900)].

GAUTIER, P. (1975), *Nicéphore Bryennios: Histoire* (*Nicephori Bryenii; Historiarium Libri Quattuor*) (Corpus Fontium Historiae Byzantinae, 9; Brussels).

GELLER, H. (1966), *Varros Menippea 'Parmeno'* (diss. Cologne).

GERBER, D. E. (1973), 'Eels in Archilochus', *QUCC* 16: 105–9.

—— (1989), 'Archilochus fr. 34 West', *AC* 32: 99–103.

GEYMONAT, M. (1978–9), 'Verg. Buc. II 24', *Museum Criticum*, 13–14: 371–6.

GIANGRANDE, G. (1971), 'Theocritus' Twelfth and Fourth Idylls: A Study in Hellenistic Irony', *QUCC* 12: 95–113.

GIL, L., and AGUILAR, R. M., eds. (1984), *Apophoreta Philologica Emmanueli Fernández-Galiano a Sodalibus Oblata* (2 vols.; Madrid).

GOLD, B. K., ed. (1982), *Literary and Artistic Patronage in Ancient Rome* (Austin).

—— (1992), 'Openings in Horace's *Satires* and *Odes*: Poet, Patron, and Audience', *YCS* 29: 161–85.

GOLDEN, M. (1990), *Children and Childhood in Classical Athens* (Baltimore).

GOW, A. S. F., and PAGE, D. L., eds. (1965), *The Greek Anthology*, i. *Hellenistic Epigrams* (2 vols.; Cambridge).

Gow, J. (1896), *Q. Horati Flacci Carmina: Liber Epodon* (Cambridge).

Gowers, E. (1993), *The Loaded Table: Representations of Food in Roman Literature* (Oxford).

Grafton, A. T. and Swerdlow, N. M. (1985), 'Technical Chronology and Astrological History in Varro, Censorinus and Others', *CQ* 35: 454–65.

Graham, A. J. (1983), 'The Foundation of Thasos', *ABSA* 73: 61–98.

Grassmann, V. (1966), *Die erotischen Epoden des Horaz* (Munich).

Grasso, G. (1893–6), *Studi di storia antica e di topografia* (2 vols.; Ariano).

Green, L. (1990), 'Galvano Fiamma, Azzone Visconti and the Revival of the Classical Theory of Magnificence', *Journal of the Warburg and Courtauld Institutes*, 53: 98–113.

Griffin, J. (1985), *Latin Poets and Roman Life* (London).

Griffin, M. T., and Barnes J., eds. (1989), *Philosophia Togata* (Oxford).

Griffith, J. G. (1970), 'The Ending of Juvenal's First Satire and Lucilius, Book XXX', *Hermes*, 98: 56–72.

Grimal, P. (1958), *Horace* (Paris).

Groag, E. (1927), 'Lollius', *RE* xiii. 1387. 30–42.

Groselji, M. (1953), 'Dvě Horacovi pesmi', *Živa Antika* 3: 74–8.

Gruner, A. (1920), *De Carminum Horatianorum Personis Quaestiones Selectae* (diss. Halle).

Gyraldus, L. G. (1580), *L. G. Gyraldi Operum Quae Extant Omnium Tomi Duo* (Basle).

Habicht, C. (1973), 'Die Augusteische Zeit und das erste Jahrhundert nach Christi Geburt', in den Boer (1973), 41–8.

Habinek, T. and Schiesaro, A., eds. (forthcoming), *The Roman Cultural Revolution* (Princeton).

Halfmann, H. (1986), *Itinera Principum* (Stuttgart).

Halkin, L. (1935), 'Le père d'Horace: a-t-il été esclave public?', *AC* 4: 125–40.

Halperin, D. (1990), *One Hundred Years of Homosexuality* (London and New York).

Händel, P., and Meid, W., eds. (1983), *Festschrift R. Muth* (Innsbruck).

Hanslik, R. (1979), *Propertius* (Leipzig).

Hardie, A. (1990), 'Juvenal and the Condition of Letters: The Seventh Satire' *PLLS* 6: 145–209.

Hardie, P. R. (1986), *Virgil's Aeneid: Cosmos and Imperium* (Oxford).

Harrison, G. (1987), 'The Confessions of Lucilius (Horace *Sat.* 2. 1. 30–34): A Defense of Autobiographical Satire?', *CA* 6: 38–52.

Harrison, S. J. (1988), 'Horace, *Odes* 3. 7: An Erotic *Odyssey*?', *CQ* 38: 186–92.

—— (1990), 'The Praise Singer: Horace, Censorinus and *Odes* 4. 8', *JRS* 80: 31–43.

HARRISON, S. J. (1993), 'The Literary Form of Horace's *Odes*', in Ludwig (1993), 131–62.

HÄUSSLER, R., ed. (1968), *Nachträge zu A. Otto: Sprichwörter und sprichwörtliche Redensarten der Römer* (Darmstadt).

HEATH, M. (1988), 'Receiving the κῶμος: The Context and Performance of Epinician', *AJP* 109: 180–95.

—— and LEFKOWITZ, M. (1991), 'Epinician Performance', *CP* 86: 173–91.

HEILMEYER, W.-D., ed. (1988), *Kaiser Augustus und die verlorene Republik* (Berlin).

HEINIMANN, F. (1952), 'Die Einheit der Horazischen Ode', *MH* 9: 193–203.

HEINZE, R. (1914–30), *Horaz* (3 vols.; Leipzig) [revision of Kiessling (1884–9)].

—— (1918), *Die lyrischen Verse des Horaz* (Leipzig); repr. in Heinze (1972), 227–94.

—— (1919), 'Horazens Buch der Briefe', *NJ* 43: 305–16; repr. in Heinze (1972), 295–307.

—— (1923), 'Die Horazische Ode', *NJ* 51: 153–68; repr. in Heinze (1972), 172–89.

—— (1972), *Vom Geist des Römertums*, 4th edn. (Darmstadt).

HELD, D. T. D. (1993), '*Megalopsuchia* in Nicomachean Ethics iv', *Ancient Philosophy*, 13: 95–110.

HELLEGOUARC'H, J. (1972), *Le Vocabulaire latin des relations et des partis politiques sous la République* (Paris).

HENDERSON, J. (1975), *The Maculate Muse* (New Haven, Conn.).

—— (1987), 'Older Women in Attic Old Comedy', *TAPA* 117: 105–29.

HENDERSON, J. G. W. (1989), 'Not "Women in Roman Satire" but "When Satire writes 'Woman' " ', in Braund (1989), 89–125.

HERTER, H. (1957), 'Dirne', *RAC* 3: 1149–213.

—— (1960), 'Die Soziologie der antiken Prostitution', *JbAC* 3: 70–111.

—— (1961), 'Das unschuldige Kind', *JbAC* 4: 146–62; repr. in Herter (1975), 598–619.

—— (1975), *Kleine Schriften* (Munich).

HIGHBARGER, E. L. (1935), 'The Pindaric Style of Horace', *TAPA* 66: 222–35.

HIGHET, G. (1973), 'Libertino Patre Natus', *AJP* 94: 268–81.

HITLER, A. (1937), *My Struggle* [trans.] (London).

HOELZER, V. (1899), *De Poesi Amatoria a Comicis Atticis Exculta, ab Elegiacis Imitatione Expressa*, pt. 1 (diss. Marburg).

HOFMANN, J. B., and SZANTYR, A. (1965), *Lateinische Syntax und Stilistik* (Munich).

HOLLIS, A. S. (1976), 'Some Allusions to Earlier Hellenistic Poetry in Nonnus', *CQ*, NS 26: 142–51.

HORSFALL, N. M. (1981), 'Poet and Patron', *Publ. of the Macquarie Ancient History Association*, 3: 1–24.

—— (1993), *La villa sabina di Orazio: Il galateo della gratitudine* (Venosa).

HOUSMAN, A. E., ed. (1912), *M. Manilii Astronomicorum Liber Secundus* (London).

HOWIE, J. G. (1977), 'Sappho Fr. 16 (LP): Self-consolation and Encomium', *PLLS* 1: 207–35.

HUBBARD, T. K. (1985), *The Pindaric Mind: A Study of Logical Structure in Early Greek Poetry* (*Mnemosyne* Supp. 85; Leiden).

HUBY, P. M. (1989), 'Cicero's *Topics* and its Peripatetic Sources', in W. W. Fortenbaugh and P. Steinmetz (eds.), *Cicero's Knowledge of the Peripatos* (New Brunswick and London), 61–76.

INGALLINA, S. S. (1974), *Orazio e la magia* (Palermo).

INNES, D. C. (1979), 'Gigantomachy and Natural Philosophy', *CQ* NS 29: 165–71.

ISO ECHEGOYEN, J.-J. (1990), *Concordantia Horatiana* (Hildesheim).

JACOBSON, H. (1976), 'Structure and Meaning in Propertius Book 3', *ICS* 1: 160–73.

JACOBY, F., (1926), *Die Fragmente der griechischen Historiker*, pt. 2 (Berlin).

JOCELYN, H. D. (1980), 'Horace, *Odes* 2. 5', *LCM* 5/9: 197–200.

—— (1991), 'Aeneas Silvius Piccolomini's *Chrysis* and the Comedies of Plautus', *RP Litt.* 14: 101–14.

—— (1992), 'Le théâtre et l'histoire du texte des comédies de Plaute', *Pallas* 38: 337–44.

—— (1993), review of Zwierlein (1990), in *Gnomon*, 65: 122–37.

JOLIVET, V. (1989), 'Les cendres d'Auguste: Note sur la topographie monumentale du Champ de Mars septentrionale', *Archeologia laziale*, 9: 90–6.

JONES, A. H. M. (1960), *Studies in Roman Government and Law* (Oxford).

JONES, C. P. (1971), '*Tange Chloen semel arrogantem*', *HSCP* 75: 81–3.

JONES, F. (1986), 'Horace, *Odes* 1, 33; 1, 22; 2, 9', in Deroux (1986), 366–82.

—— (1993), 'The Role of the Addressee in Horace, *Epistles*', *LCM* 18/1:7–11.

KAJANTO, I. (1965), *The Latin* Cognomina (Helsinki).

KAMBITSIS, J. (1972), *L'Antiope d'Euripide* (Athens).

KAY, N. M. (1985), *Martial Book 11: A Commentary* (London).

KAZHDAN, A. P. (1991), 'Tarchaneiotes', in *The Oxford Dictionary of Byzantium* (New York).

KELLER, O., and Holder, A. (1899–1925), *Horati Opera*, 3rd edn. (2 vols.; Leipzig).

KELLY, J. M. (1976), *Studies in the Civil Judicature of the Roman Republic* (Oxford).

KEPPIE, L. J. F. (1983), *Colonization and Veteran Settlement in Italy 47-14 BC* (London).

KIENAST, D. (1969), 'Augustus und Alexander', *Gymnasium*, 76: 430-56.

—— (1982), *Augustus: Prinzeps und Monarch* (Darmstadt).

KIESSLING, A. (1884-9), *Horaz* (3 vols.; Leipzig); *see* Heinze (1914-30).

KILPATRICK, R. S. (1986), *The Poetry of Friendship: Horace Epistles I* (Edmonton).

—— (1990), *The Poetry of Criticism: Horace Epistles II and Ars Poetica* (Edmonton).

KISSEL, W. (1981), 'Horaz 1936-1975', *ANRW* II. 31. 3: 1403-558.

KLEVE, K., and LONGO AURICCHIO, F. (1992), 'Honey from the Garden', in Capasso (1992), 213-26.

KLINGNER, F. (1953), *Römische Geisteswelt*, 2nd edn. (Wiesbaden).

—— (1959), *Q. Horati Flacci Opera*, 3rd edn. (Leipzig).

—— (1964), *Studien zur griechischen und römischen Literatur* (Zurich).

—— (1965), *Römische Geisteswelt*, 5th edn. (Munich).

KLUTSTEIN, I. (1987), *Marsilio Ficino et la théologie ancienne: Oracles chaldaïques, Hymnes orphiques, Hymnes de Proclus* (Florence).

KOST, K. (1971), *Musaios: Hero und Leander* (Bonn).

KRAFT, K. (1967), 'Der Sinn des Mausoleums des Augustus', *Historia*, 16: 189-206.

—— (1978), *Gesammelte Aufsätze zur antiken Geldgeschichte und Numismatik*, i (Darmstadt).

KRAGGERUD, E. (1984), *Horaz und Actium: Studien zu den politischen Epoden* (Oslo).

KRISTELLER, P. O. (1937), *Supplementum Ficinianum*, ii (Florence).

—— (1944), 'The Scholastic Background of Marsilio Ficino', *Traditio*, 2: 257-318; repr. in Kristeller (1956), 35-97.

—— (1956), *Studies in Renaissance Thought and Letters* (Rome).

KUMANIECKI, C. F. (1935), 'De Epodis Quibusdam Horatianis', in *Commentationes Horatianae* (Cracow), 139-57.

LACHMANN, K. (1845), 'Verbesserungen zu Horazens Oden', *RM* 3: 615-17.

—— (1876), *Kleinere Schriften zur klassischen Philologie*, ii (Berlin).

LAFLEUR, R. A. (1981), 'Horace and *Onomasti Komodein*: The Law of Satire', *ANRW* II. 31.3: 1790-826.

LAMBIN, D. (1561), *Q. Horatius Flaccus* (Lyons).

LANDINO (1482), untitled edition of Horace (Florence).

LA PENNA, A. (1951), 'Properzio e i poeti latini dell'età aurea', *Maia*, 4: 51-69.

—— (1960), 'Esiodo nella cultura e nella poesia di Virgilio', in *Hésiode et son influence* (Entretiens Hardt, 9; Geneva), 213-52.

—— (1963), *Orazio e l'ideologia del principato* (Turin).

LA PENNA, A. (1969), *Orazio e la morale mondana europea* (Florence).

—— (1992), 'I poeti e i principi: Lettura di Orazio, *Epistole* I 18', in M. G. Vacchina (ed.), *Attualità dell'antico* (Aosta), 337-60.

—— (1993), *Saggi e studi su Orazio* (Florence).

LATTE, K. (1929), 'Hipponacteum', *Hermes*, 64: 385-8.

LEEMAN, A. D. (1982), 'Rhetorical Status in Horace, *Serm.* 2. 1', in Vickers (1982), 159-63.

—— (1983), 'Die Konsultierung des Trebatius: Statuslehre in Horaz, *Serm.* 2. 1', in Händel and Meid (1983), 209-15.

LEFÈVRE, E., ed. (1975), *Monumentum Chiloniense: Studien zur augusteischen Zeit* (Amsterdam).

LEFKOWITZ, M. (1981), *The Lives of the Greek Poets* (London).

—— (1985), 'The Scholia to Pindar', *AJP* 106: 269-82.

—— (1988), 'Who Sang Pindar's Victory Odes?', *AJP* 109: 1-11.

LEGRAND, P. (1885), *Bibliographique hellénique, ou description raisonée des ouvrages publiés en grec par les Grecs aux xvᵉ et xvᵉ siècles*, ii (Paris).

LEJAY, P. (1911), *Les Satires d'Horace* (Paris).

LEMERLE, P. (1946), *Actes de Kutlumus: Texte* (Archives de l'Athos, 2; Paris).

LEO, F. (1913), *Geschichte der römischen Literatur, i, Die archäische Literatur* (Berlin).

LEUTSCH, E. L., and SCHNEIDEWIN, F. G., eds. (1839), *Paroemiographi Graeci* (2 vols.; Göttingen).

LIEBESCHUETZ, J. H. W. G. (1979), *Continuity and Change in Roman Religion* (Oxford).

LOWE, J. C. B. (1989), 'Plautus' Parasites and the Atellana', in Vogt-Spira (1989).

LUCK, G. (1959), 'Kids and Wolves', *CQ*, NS 9: 34-7.

LUDWIG, W. (1963), review of Collinge (1961), in *Gnomon*, 35: 171-7.

—— ed. (1993), *Horace* (Entretiens Hardt, 39; Geneva).

LYNE, R. O. A. M. (1980), *The Latin Love Poets* (Oxford).

McCARTHY, J. H. (1931), 'Octavianus Puer', *CP* 26: 362-73.

MacCORMACK, S. G. (1972), 'Change and Continuity in Late Antiquity: The Ceremony of Adventus', *Historia*, 21: 721-52.

—— (1981) *Art and Ceremony in Late Antiquity* (Berkeley).

McGANN, M. J. (1969), *Studies in Horace's First Book of Epistles* (Brussels).

—— (1980), 'The Ancona Epitaph of Manilius Marullus', *Bulletin d'humanisme et renaissance*, 42: 401-4.

—— (1981), 'Medieval or Renaissance? Some Distinctive Features in the Ancona Epitaph of Manilius Marullus', *Bulletin d'humanisme et renaissance*, 43: 341-3.

—— (1986), '1453 and All That; The End of the Byzantine Empire in the Poetry of Michael Marullus', in I. D. McFarlane (ed.), *Acta conventus neo-*

latini Sanctandreani. Proceedings of the 5th International Congress of Neo-Latin Studies (Binghampton, NY), 145-51.

—— (1991), 'A Call to Arms: Michael Marullus to Charles VIII', *Byzantinische Forschungen* 16: 341-9.

MCKEOWN, J. C. (1987), *Ovid:* Amores: I (Liverpool).

MACLEOD, C. W. (1983), *Collected Essays* (Oxford).

—— (1986), *Horace: The Epistles* (Rome).

MAGDALINO, P. (1989), 'Honour among Romaioi: The Framework of Social Values in the World of Digenes Akrites and Kekaumenos', *Byzantine and Modern Greek Studies*, 13: 183-218; repr. in Magdalino (1991) ch. 3.

—— (1991), *Tradition and Transformation in Medieval Byzantium* (Aldershot).

MALTBY, R. (1991), *A Lexicon of Ancient Latin Etymologies* (Leeds).

MANFREDINI, A.-D. (1979), *La diffamazione verbale nel diritto romano, i. età repubblicana* (Milan).

MARTIN, R. (1928), *Lehrbuch der Anthropologie* (Jena).

MARTIN, T. (1869), *Horace* (Edinburgh and London).

MARTINDALE, C. A. (1993a), 'Introduction', in Martindale and Hopkins (1993), 1-26.

—— (1993b), *Redeeming the Text* (Cambridge).

—— and HOPKINS, D., eds. (1993), *Horace Made New* (Cambridge).

MARULLUS, M. T. (1488-89), *Epigrammata* (?Rome).

—— (1497), *Hymni et Epigrammata* (Florence).

MARX, F. (1904), *C. Lucilii Carminum Reliquiae* (Leipzig).

—— (1932), 'De Horati Poetae Praenomine', *RM* 81: 304.

MAZZOLI, G. (1970), *Seneca e la poesia* (Milan).

METTE, H. J. (1961a), '*Genus tenue* und *mensa tenuis* bei Horaz', *MH* 18: 136-9; repr. in Mette (1988), 188-91.

—— (1961b), 'Der "große Mensch" ', *Hermes*, 89: 332-44.

—— (1988), *Kleine Schriften* (Frankfurt).

METTE-DITTMANN, A. (1991), *Die Ehegesetze des Augustus* (Historia Einzelschriften, 67: Stuttgart).

MILLAR, F. (1964), *A Study of Cassius Dio* (Oxford).

—— (1977), *The Emperor in the Roman World* (London).

—— and SEGAL, E. (1984), *Caesar Augustus: Seven Aspects* (Oxford).

MIRALLES, C., and PÒRTULAS, J. (1983), *Archilochus and the Iambic Poetry* (Rome).

—— (1988), *The Poetry of Hipponax* (Rome).

MOLES, J. (1985), 'Cynicism in Horace *Epistles* 1', *PLLS* 5: 33-60.

MOMMSEN, Th. (1877), 'Die pompeianischen Quittungstafeln des L. Caecilius Jucundus', *Hermes*, 12: 88-141.

MONTEVERDI, A. (1936), 'Orazio nel Medio Evo', *Stud. Med.*, NS 9: 162-80.

MORETTI, L. (1984), 'Frammenti vecchi e nuovi del Commentario dei Ludi Secolari', *Rend. Pont. Acc.* 55-6: 361-79.

MORGAN, J. D. (1988), 'Horace, *Epod.* 6. 16', *CQ*, NS 38: 565-6.

MORITZ, H. (1897-8), *Die Zunamen bei den byzantinischen Historikern und Chronisten*, ii (Landshut).

MORITZ, L. A. (1968), 'Some "Central" Thoughts on Horace's Odes', *CQ*, NS 18: 116-31.

MRAS, KARL (1936), 'Horaz als Mensch und als Dichter', *WS* 54: 70-85.

MUECKE, F. (1993), *Horace: Satires II* (Warminster)

MÜLLER, L. (1891-1900), *Die Satiren und Episteln des Horaz* (Vienna).

MÜLLER, R. (1952), *Motivkatalog der römischen Elegie: Eine Untersuchung zur Poetik der Römer* (diss. Zurich).

MUNK OLSEN, B. (1982), *L'Étude des auteurs classiques latin aux* XIᵉ *et* XIIᵉ *siècles, i. Catalogue des manuscrits classiques latins copiés du* XIᵉ *au* XIIᵉ *siècle* (Paris).

MURRAY, O. (1968), review of F. Dvornik, *Early Christian and Byzantine Political Philosophy*, in *JTS* 19: 673-8.

—— (1985; 1993), 'Symposium and Genre in the Poetry of Horace', *JRS* 75: 39-50, rev. repr. in Rudd (1993), 89-105.

—— ed. (1990), *Sympotica: A Symposium on the Symposium* (Oxford).

MUTSCHLER, F.-H. (1978), 'Kaufmannsliebe: Eine Interpretation der Horazode "Quid fles Asterie" (c. 3,7)', *SO* 53: 111-31.

—— (1988), 'Horaz und Augustus', *WJ* 16: 117-36.

NADEAU, Y. (1980), 'Speaking Structures: Horace *Odes* 2. 1 to 2. 19', in Deroux (1980), 177-222.

—— (1983), 'Speaking Structures, 2: Horace *Odes* 3. 1-3. 6', *Latomus*, 42: 303-31.

—— (1986), 'Speaking Structures, 3: Horace *Odes* 3. 7-3. 12', *Latomus*, 45: 522-40.

—— (1989), 'Speaking Structures, 4: Horace *Odes* 3. 13-17', *QUCC* 36: 85-104.

NAGY, G. (1979), *The Best of the Achaeans* (Baltimore and London).

—— (1994), 'Copies and Models in Horace *Odes* 4. 1 and 4. 2', *CW* 87: 413-26.

NEDERGAARD, E. (1988), 'Zur Problematik der Augustusbögen auf dem Forum Romanum', in Heilmeyer (1988), 224-39.

NESSELRATH, H.-G. (1985), *Lukians Parasitendialog: Untersuchungen und Kommentar* (Berlin and New York).

—— (1990), *Die attische Mittlere Komödie: Ihre Stellung in der antiken Literaturkritik und Literaturgeschichte* (Berlin and New York).

NETHERCUT, W. (1971), 'Propertius 3. 11', *TAPA* 102: 411-43.

NEUE, F. (1902), *Formenlehre der lateinischen Sprache*, i, 3rd edn., rev. C. WAGENER (Leipzig)

NEUKIRCH, J. H. (1833), *De Fabula Togata Romanorum* (diss. Leipzig).

NEWMAN, J. K. (1990), *Roman Catullus* (Hildesheim).

NICOLET, C. (1976), 'Le cens sénatorial sous la République et sous Auguste', *JRS* 66: 20-38.

—— (1984), 'Augustus, Government and the Propertied Classes', in Millar and Segal (1984), 89-128.

NIEBLING, G. (1956), '*Laribus Augustis Magistri Primi*: Der Beginn des Compitalkultes der Lares und des Genius Augusti', *Historia*, 5: 303-31.

NIEBUHR, B. G. (1848), *Vorträge über römische Geschichte* (Berlin).

NILSSON, N.-O. (1952), *Metrische Stildifferenzen in den Satiren des Horaz* (Uppsala).

NISBET, R. G. M. (1962), '*Romanae fidicen lyrae*: The *Odes* of Horace', in Sullivan (1962), 181-218.

—— (1969), review of Doblhofer (1966), in *CR* 19: 173-5.

—— (1983), 'Some Problems of Text and Interpretation in Horace *Odes* 3. 14 (Herculis ritu)', *PLLS* 4: 105-19.

—— (1984), 'Horace's *Epodes* and History', in Woodman and West (1984), 1-18.

—— (1986), review of Shackleton Bailey (1985*a*), in *CR* 36: 227-33.

—— (1987), review of Griffin (1985), in *JRS* 77: 184-90.

—— (1989), 'Footnotes on Horace', in Diggle, Hall, and Jocelyn (1989), 87-96.

—— (1992), review of Iso Echegoyen (1990), in *CR* 42: 192-3.

—— and HUBBARD, M. (1970), *A Commentary on Horace: Odes: Book 1* (Oxford).

—— (1978), *A Commentary on Horace: Odes: Book 2* (Oxford).

NOIRFALISE, A. (1952), 'L'art de réussir auprès des grands, d'après les *Épîtres* d'Horace', *LEC* 20: 358-63.

NORDEN, E. (1927), *P. Vergilius Maro: Aeneis Buch VI*, 3rd edn. (Stuttgart).

OLIENSIS, E. (1991), 'Canidia, Canicula, and the Decorum of Horace's Epodes', *Arethusa* 24: 107-38.

—— (forthcoming), '*Ut arte emendaturus fortunam*: Horace, Nasidienus, and the Art of Satire', in Habinek and Schiesaro (forthcoming).

OPPERMANN, H., ed. (1972), *Wege zu Horaz* (Darmstadt).

ORAZIO (1936) = *Orazio nella letteratura mondiale* (Rome).

ORELLI, J. C. (1886, 1892), *Horatius*, 4th edn., rev. J. G. Baiter and W. Hirschfelder (2 vols.; Berlin).

ORR, D. G. (1978), 'Roman Domestic Religion: The Evidence of the Household Shrines', *ANRW* II. 16.2: 1557-91.

OTT, W. (1970), *Metrische Analysen zur Ars Poetica des Horaz* (Göppingen).

OTTO, A. (1890), *Die Sprichwörter und sprichwörtlichen Redensarten der Römer* (Leipzig).

OWENS, W. M. (1992), 'Nuntius Vafer et Fallax: An Alternative Reading of Horace, C. 3. 7', *CW* 85: 161-71.

PAGE, D. L. (1955), *Sappho and Alcaeus* (Oxford).

PAGE, T. E. (1896), *Q. Horati Flacci Carminum Libri IV* (London).

PALMER, A. S. (1885), *The Satires of Horace*, 2nd edn. (London).

PARMENTIER, L. (1892), *Euripide et Anaxagore* (Paris).

PASQUALI, G. (1920; 2nd edn. 1966), *Orazio lirico* (Florence); 2nd edn. rev. A. La Penna (Florence).

PATTERSON, J. R. (1992), 'The City of Rome: From Republic to Empire', *JRS* 82: 186–215.

PEARCE, T. E. V. (1970), 'Notes on Cicero *In Pisonem*', *CQ*, NS 20: 311–21.

PEARSON, A. C. (1917), *The Fragments of Sophocles*, ii (Cambridge).

PEROSA, A. (1951), *Michaelis Marulli Carmina* (Zurich).

PERRET, J. (1959), *Horace* (Paris); Eng. trans. New York, 1964.

PETERSON, E. (1926), *Εἷς θεός: Epigraphische formgeschichtliche und religions-geschichtliche Untersuchungen* (Göttingen).

—— (1930), 'Die Einholung Des Kyrios', *Zeitschrifte für systematische Theologie*, 7: 682–702.

PFEIFFER, R. (1949–53), *Callimachus* (2 vols.; Oxford).

PICHON, R. (1902), *De Sermone Amatorio apud Latinos Elegiarum Scriptores* (Paris).

POLEMIS, D. I. (1968), *The Doukai: A Contribution to Byzantine Prosopography* (London).

POLLINI, J. (1990), 'Man or God: Divine Assimilation and Imitation in the Late Republic and Early Principate', in Raaflaub and Toher (1990), 334–57.

PORTE, D. (1981), 'Romulus-Quirinus, prince et dieu, dieu des princes', *ANRW* II. 17.1: 5. 300–42.

PORTER, D. H. (1987), *Horace's Poetic Journey: A Reading of Odes 1–3* (Princeton).

PÖSCHL, V. (1956; 2nd edn. 1963), *Horaz und die Politik* (SHAW 1956/4; Heidelberg).

—— (1970), *Horazische Lyrik: Interpretationen* (Heidelberg).

—— (1991), *Horazische Lyrik: Interpretationen*, 2nd edn. (Heidelberg).

PÖTSCHER, W. (1978), '"Numen" und '"Numen Augusti"', *ANRW* II. 16. 1: 355–92.

POWELL, A., ed. (1992), *Roman Poetry and Propaganda in the Age of Augustus* (London).

PRÉAUX, J. (1968), *Q. Horatius Flaccus: Epistulae: Liber Primus* (Paris).

PRICE, S. R. F. (1980), 'Between Man and God: Sacrifice in the Roman Imperial Cult', *JRS* 70: 28–43.

—— (1983), *Rituals and Power: The Roman Imperial Cults in Asia Minor* (Cambridge).

Prosopographisches Lexikon der Palaiologenzeit (1976–8), ed. E. Trapp.

PURCELL, N. (1983), 'The *Apparitores*: A Study in Social Mobility', *PBSR* 51: 125–73.

PUTNAM, M. C. J. (1976), 'Propertius 1. 22: A Poet's Self-definition', *QUCC* 23: 93–123; repr. in Putnam (1982), 177–207.

—— (1982), *Essays on Latin Lyric, Elegy, and Epic* (Princeton).

—— (1986), *Artifices of Eternity: A Commentary on Horace's Fourth Book of Odes* (Ithaca, NY).

QUINN, K. F. (1962), review of Collinge (1961), in *AUMLA* 18: 215–17.

—— (1970), *Catullus: The Poems* (London).

—— (1980), *Horace: The Odes* (London).

QUINT, M.-B. (1988), *Untersuchungen zur mittelalterlichen Horaz-Rezeption* (Frankfurt, Berne, New York, and Paris).

RAAFLAUB, K. A., and SAMONS, L. J. II (1990), 'Opposition to Augustus', in Raaflaub and Toher (1990), 417–54.

—— and TOHER, M., eds. (1990), *Between Republic and Empire* (Berkeley).

RACE, W. J. (1985), 'Pindar's Heroic Ideal at *Pythian* 4. 186–87', *AJP* 106: 355 ff.

RADKE, G. (1959), 'Fachberichte', *Gymnasium*, 66: 336.

—— (1964*a*), 'Aequum Tuticum', in *Der kleine Pauly*, i (1964) 98.

—— (1964*b*), 'Die Erschließung Italiens durch die römischen Straßen', *Gymnasium*, 71: 204–35.

—— (1964*c*), 'Dux bonus (Horat. C. 4. 5)', in *Interpretationen* (Gymnasium Beiheft 4; Heidelberg), 57–76.

—— (1967), 'Herdoniae', in *Der Kleine Pauly*, ii. 1058.

—— (1989), 'Topographische Betrachtungen zum Iter Brundisianum des Horaz', *RM* 132: 54–72.

RAKOB, F. (1987), 'Die Urbanisierung des nördlichen Marsfeldes', in *L'Urbs: Espace urbain et histore* (CEFR 98; Rome), 687–711.

RALLUS, M. C. (1520), *Manilii Cabacii Ralli Juveniles Ingenii Lusus* (Naples).

RAMAGE, E. S. (1985), 'Augustus' Treatment of Julius Caesar', *Historia*, 34: 223–45.

RANDALL, J. G. (1979), 'Mistresses' Pseudonyms in Latin Elegy', *LCM* 4: 27–35.

RANKIN, H. D. (1977), *Archilochus of Paros* (Park Ridge).

RAUH, N. K. (1989), 'Auctioneers and the Roman Economy', *Historia*, 38: 451–71.

RAWSON, E. (1985*a*), *Intellectual Life in the Late Roman Republic* (London).

—— (1985*b*), 'Theatrical Life in Republican Rome and Italy', *PBSR* 53: 97–113; repr. in her *Roman Culture and Society: Collected Papers* (Oxford, 1991) 468–87.

REIFFERSCHEID, A. (1860), *C. Suetonii Tranquilli Praeter Caesarum Libros Reliquiae* (Leipzig).

REINCKE, A. (1929), *De Tripartita Carminum Horatianorum Structura* (diss. Berlin).

REINHOLD, M. (1988), *From Republic to Principate: An Historical*

Commentary on Cassius Dio's Roman History, *Books* 49-52 (36-29 B.C.) (Atlanta).

REITZENSTEIN, R. (1963), *Aufsätze zu Horaz* (Darmstadt).

REYNOLDS, L. D., ed. (1983), *Texts and Transmission* (Oxford).

RICH, J. W. (1990), *Cassius Dio: The Augustan Settlement* (Warminster).

RICHARDSON, L. (1992), *A New Topographical Dictionary of Ancient Rome* (Baltimore).

RICHLIN, A. (1978), 'Sexual Terms and Themes in Roman Satire and Related Genres' (diss. Yale).

—— (1981), 'The Meaning of *Irrumare* in Catullus and Martial', *CP* 76: 40-6.

—— (1992), *The Garden of Priapus*, 2nd edn. (Oxford).

RITSCHL, F. W. (1860), ed. Suetonius, *Vita Terenti*, in Reifferscheid (1860), 26-35, 481-538; repr. in Ritschl (1877), 204-80.

—— (1876), 'Philologische Unverständlichkeiten, II. Die Plautinische Sprache und Herr N. Madvig', *RM* 31: 539-57; repr. in Ritschl (1877), 155-75.

—— (1877), *Opuscula Philologica* iii (Leipzig).

RONCONI, A. (1970), 'Sulla fortuna di Plauto e di Terenzio nel mondo romano', *Maia*, 22: 19-37.

—— (1972), *Interpretazioni letterarie nei classici* (Florence).

—— (1979), 'Orazio e i poeti latini arcaici', in *Studi di poesia latina in onore di Antonio Traglia* (Rome) ii. 501-24.

ROSE, C. B. (1990), ' "Princes" and Barbarians on the Ara Pacis', *AJA* 94: 453-67.

ROSE, V. (1867; 2nd edn. 1899), *Vitruvii De Architectura Libri X* (Leipzig).

ROSEN, R. (1988), 'Hipponax, Boupalos, and the Conventions of the Psogos', *TAPA* 118: 29-41.

ROSENSTEIN, N. S. (1990), *Imperatores Victi* (Berkeley).

RÖSLER, W. (1976), 'Die Dichtung des Archilochos und die neue Kölner Epode', *RM* 119: 289-310.

ROSS, D. O., jun. (1975), *Backgrounds to Augustan Poetry: Gallus, Elegy and Rome* (Cambridge, Mass.).

ROSSI, L. E. (1971), 'I generi letterari e le loro leggi scritte e non scritte nelle letterature classiche', *BICS* 18: 69-94.

ROUECHÉ, C. (1984), 'Acclamations in the Later Roman Empire: New Evidence from Aphrodisias', *JRS* 74: 181-99.

RUDD, N. (1966), *The Satires of Horace* (Cambridge; 2nd edn. Bristol, 1982).

—— (1986), *Themes in Roman Satire* (London).

—— (1989), *Epistles Book II and the Epistle to the Pisones* (Cambridge).

—— ed. (1993), *Horace 2000: A Celebration* (London).

SALLER, R. P. (1982), *Personal Patronage under the Early Empire* (Cambridge).

SALLER, R. P. (1989), 'Patronage and Friendship in Early Imperial Rome', in Wallace-Hadrill (1989*a*), 49-62.

SALMON, E. T. (1958), 'Notes on the Social War', *TAPA* 89: 159-84.

—— (1967), *Samnium and the Samnites* (Cambridge).

SANNAZARO, J. (1728), *Actii Sinceri Sannazarii ... Opera Latine Scripta*, ed. J. Broukhuis (Amsterdam).

SANTIROCCO, M. (1985), 'The Two Voices of Horace: *Odes* 3. 1-15', in Winkes (1985), 9-28.

—— (1986), *Unity and Design in Horace's* Odes (Chapel Hill).

SBORDONE, F. (1981), 'La poetica oraziana alla luce degli studi più recenti', *ANRW* II. 31.3: 1866-920.

SCHEID, J. (1990), *Romulus et ses frères: Le collège des frères arvales* (Rome).

SCHIESARO, A. (forthcoming), 'The Boundaries of Knowledge in Vergil's *Georgics*', in Habinek and Schiesaro (forthcoming).

SCHLUNK, R. R. (1984), 'The Wrath of Aeneas: Two Myths in *Aeneid* X', in D. F. Bright and E. S. Ramage (eds.), *Classical Texts and their Traditions: Studies in Honor of C. R. Trahman* (Chico, Calif.), 223-9.

SCHMIDT, E. A. (1977), '*Amica Vis Pastoribus*: Der Iambiker Horaz in seinem Epodenbuch', *Gymnasium*, 84: 401-23.

SCHNETZ, J., ed. (1940), *Itineraria Romana*, ii (Leipzig; repr. Stuttgart, 1990).

SCHRIJVERS, P. H. (1973), 'Comment terminer une ode?', *Mnemosyne*, 26: 140-59.

SCHUBERTH, D. (1968), *Kaiserliche Liturgie* (Göttingen).

SCHULZE, W. (1904), *Zur Geschichte lateinischer Eigennamen* (Berlin).

SCHÜTZ, H. (1881), *Q. Horatius Flaccus, Satiren* (Berlin).

SCHÜTZ, M. (1990), 'Zur Sonnenuhr des Augustus auf dem Marsfeld', *Gymnasium*, 97: 432-57.

SCHWARTZ, J. (1960), *Pseudo-Hesiodeia: Recherches sur la composition, la diffusion, et la disparition ancienne d'œuvres attribuées à Hesiode* (Leiden).

SCOTT, K. (1925), 'The Identification of Augustus with Romulus-Quirinus', *TAPA* 56: 82-105.

SEDGWICK, H. D. (1947), *Horace: A Biography* (Cambridge, Mass.).

SEECK, OTTO (1902), *Kaisar Augustus* (Bielefeld and Leipzig).

SEEL, O. (1970), '*Maiore poeta plectro*', in Eisenhut (1970), 143-81.

SEIDENSTICKER, B. (1978), 'Archilochus and Odysseus', *GRBS* 19: 5-22.

SELLAR, W. Y. (1892), *Horace and the Elegiac Poets* (Oxford).

SETAIOLI, A. (1981), 'Gli Epodi di Orazio nella critica dal 1937 al 1972 (con un appendice fino al 1978)', *ANRW*, II. 31.3: 1674-788.

SETTIS, S. (1988), 'Die Ara Pacis', in Heilmeyer (1988), 400-26.

SHACKLETON BAILEY, D. R. (1952), 'Echoes of Propertius', *Mnemosyne* (4th ser.) 5: 307-33.

—— (1971), *Cicero* (London).

SHACKLETON BAILEY, D. R. (1980), *Cicero: Epistulae ad Quintum fratrem et M. Brutum* (Cambridge).

—— (1982), *A Profile of Horace* (London).

—— (1985*a*), *Horatius: Opera* (Stuttgart).

—— (1985*b*), 'Vindiciae Horatianae', *HSCP* 89: 153–70.

SHARROCK, A. (forthcoming), 'Ovid and the Politics of Reading', forthcoming in *MD*.

SHOWERMAN, G. (1922), *Horace and his Influence* (London).

SIMON, E. (1957), 'Zur Augustusstatue von Prima Porta', *MDAI(R)* 64: 46–68.

—— (1975), *Pergamon und Hesiod* (Mainz).

—— (1986), *Augustus* (Munich).

SIRAGO, V. A. (1958), 'Lucanus an Apulus?', *AC* 27: 13–30.

SKUTSCH, F. (1897), 'Caecilius', *RE* iii/1. 1189–92.

SKUTSCH, O. (1972), 'Readings in Early Latin', *HSCP* 76: 169–71.

—— (1985), *The Annales of Quintus Ennius* (Oxford).

SLINGS, S. R., ed. (1990), *The Poet's 'I' in Archaic Greek Lyric* (Amsterdam).

SMITH, K. F., ed. (1913), *The Elegies of Albius Tibullus* (New York).

SMITH, R. E. (1951), 'The Law of Libel at Rome', *CQ* NS 1: 169–79.

SNELL, B. (1971), *Szenen aus griechischen Dramen* (Berlin).

SONNENSCHEIN, E. A. (1898), 'The Nationality of Horace', *CR* 12: 305.

SPAETH, B. S. (1994), 'The Goddess Ceres in the Ara Pacis Augustae and the Carthage Relief', *AJA* 98: 65–100.

SPELMAN, E. V. (1982), 'Woman as Body: Ancient and Contemporary Views', *Feminist Studies*, 8: 109–3.

SPRANGER, P. R. (1958), 'Der Große: Untersuchungen zur Entstehung des historischen Beinamens in der Antike', *Saeculum*, 9: 22–58.

STAEDLER, E., and MÜLLER, R. (1962), *Thesaurus Horatianus* (Berlin).

STEINER, D. (1986), *The Crown of Song: Metaphor in Pindar* (London).

STEINMETZ, P. (1964): 'Horaz und Pindar: Hor. carm. IV. 2', *Gymnasium*, 71: 1–17.

STEMPLINGER, E. (1906), *Das Fortleben der Horazischen Lyrik seit der Renaissance* (Leipzig).

—— (1921), *Horaz im Urteil der Jahrhunderte* (Leipzig).

STEVENSON, T. R. (1992), 'The Ideal Benefactor and the Father Analogy in Greek and Roman Thought', *CQ* NS 42: 421–36.

STEWART, J. A. (1892), *Notes on the Nicomachean Ethics of Aristotle* (Oxford).

STROH, W. (1991), 'De Amore Senili Quid Veteres Poetae Senserint', *Gymnasium*, 98: 264–76.

SULLIVAN, J. P., ed. (1962), *Critical Essays on Roman Literature: Elegy and Lyric* (London).

SUOLAHTI, J. (1955), *The Junior Officers of the Roman Army in the Republican Period: A Study on Social Structure* (Helsinki).

SUTHERLAND, C. H. V. (1984), *The Roman Imperial Coinage*, i: 31 BC–AD 69 (London).

SYME, R. (1933), 'Notes on Some Legions under Augustus', *JRS* 23: 14–33.

—— (1939), *The Roman Revolution* (Oxford).

—— (1958), *Tacitus* (2 vols.; Oxford).

SYME, R. (1978), *History in Ovid* (Oxford).

—— (1979), *Roman Papers*, i (Oxford).

—— (1986), *The Augustan Aristocracy* (Oxford).

—— (1989), 'Janus and Parthia in Horace', in Diggle, Hall, and Jocelyn (1989), 113–24.

SYNDIKUS, H. P. (1972–3), *Die Lyrik des Horaz* (2 vols.; Darmstadt).

TALBERT, R. J. A. (1984a), *The Senate of Imperial Rome* (Princeton).

—— (1984b), 'Augustus and the Senate', *G&R* 31: 55–63.

TARDITI, J. (1968), *Archilochus* (Rome).

TARRANT, R. J. (1978), 'The Addressee of Virgil's Eighth *Eclogue*', *HSCP* 82: 197–9.

—— (1983), 'Horace', in Reynolds (1983), 183–6.

TAYLOR, L. R. (1920), 'The Worship of Augustus in Italy during his Lifetime', *TAPA* 51: 116–33.

—— (1925), 'Horace's Equestrian Career', *AJP* 46: 161–70.

—— (1968), 'Republican and Augustan Writers Enrolled in the Equestrian Centuries', *TAPA* 99: 469–86.

TESCARI, O. (1936; 3rd edn. 1948), *Quinto Orazio Flacco: I carmi e gli epodi* (Turin).

THESLEFF, H. (1961), *An Introduction to the Pythagorean Writings of the Hellenistic Period* (Abo).

—— (1965), *The Pythagorean Texts of the Hellenistic Period* (Abo).

THILL, A. (1979), *Alter ab Illo: Recherches sur l'imitation dans la poésie personnelle à l'époque Augustéenne* (Paris).

THOMAS, R. F., and SCODEL, R. (1984), 'Vergil and the Euphrates', *AJP* 105: 339.

THOMPSON, S. (1958), *Motif-index of Folk-Literature* (Bloomington, Ind.).

TIMPE, D. (1975), 'Zur Geschichte der Rheingrenze zwischen Caesar und Drusus', in Lefèvre (1975), 124–47.

TORELLI, M. (1982), *Typology and Structure of Roman Historical Reliefs* (Ann Arbor).

TORRENTIUS, L. (1608), *Q. Horatius Flaccus cum Erudito . . . Commentario* (Antwerp).

TOSTO, R. (1979), 'Per la biografia di Michele Marullo Tarcaniota', in *Medioevo e Rinascimento veneto con altri studi in onore di Lino Lazzarini*, i. *Dal duecento al quattrocento* (Medioevo e Umanesimo, 34; Padua), 557–70.

TRAINA, A. (1970), *Seneca: De Brevitate Vitae* (Turin).

TRÄNKLE, H. (1993), 'Prinzipien und Probleme der Horaz-Edition', in Ludwig, (1993), 1–29.

TREGGIARI, S. (1969), *Roman Freedmen during the Late Republic* (Oxford).

—— (1991), *Roman Marriage* (Oxford).

TRILLMICH, W. (1988), 'Munzpropaganda', in Heilmeyer (1988), 474–528.

TSCHERNJAJEW, P. (1900), *Terentiana: Des traces de Térence dans Ovide, Horace et Tite-Live* (Kazan).

TYRRELL, R. Y. (1895), *Latin Poetry* (Boston).

VAN ROOY, C. A. (1966), *Studies in Classical Satire and Related Literary Theory* (Leiden).

VERSNEL, H. S. (1970) *Triumphus* (Leiden).

—— (1980), 'Destruction, *Devotio* and Despair in a Situation of Anomy: The mourning for Germanicus in Triple Perspective', in *Perennitas: Studi in onore di Angelo Brelich* (Rome), 541–618.

VEYNE, P. (1990), *Bread and Circuses*, trans. B. Pearce (London).

VIAN, F., ed. (1976), *Nonnos de Panopolis: Les Dionysiaques I* (Paris).

VIARRE, S. (1986), 'L'inclusion épique dans la poésie élégiaque augustéenne', in F. Decrens and C. Deroux (eds.), *Hommages à Jozef Veremans* (Brussels), 364–72.

VICKERS, B., ed. (1982), *Rhetoric Revalued* (Binghamton, NY).

VILLA, C. (1992), 'I manoscritti di Orazio, I', *Aevum*, 66: 95–135.

VILLENEUVE, F. (1927–34), *Horace* (2 vols.; Paris).

VOGEL, F. (1918), 'Redende Namen bei Horaz', *BPW* 38: 404–6.

VOGT-SPIRA, J., ed. (1989), *Studien zur vorliterarischen Periode im frühen Rom* (Tübingen).

VOLLMER, F. (1912) *Horati Opera*, 2nd edn. (Leipzig).

VON HESBERG, H. (1988), 'Das Mausoleum des Augustus', in Heilmeyer (1988), 245–51.

WALKER, D. P. (1953), 'Orpheus the Theologian and Renaissance Platonists', *Journal of the Warburg and Courtauld Institutes*, 16: 100–20.

—— (1954), 'Le chant orphique de Marsile Ficin', in *Musique et poésie au XVème siècle* (Colloques internationales du CNRS: Sciences Humaines, 5; Paris) 17–28; repr. in Walker (1985).

—— (1958), *Spiritual and Demonic Magic from Ficino to Campanella* (London).

—— (1972), *The Ancient Theology: Studies in Christian Platonism from the Fifteenth to the Eighteenth Century* (London).

—— (1985), *Music, Spirit and Language in the Renaissance* (London).

WALLACE-HADRILL, A. (1981), 'The Emperor and his Virtues', *Historia*, 30: 298–323.

—— (1982), '*Civilis Princeps*: Between Citizen and King', *JRS* 72: 32–48.

WALLACE-HADRILL, A. (1986), 'Image and Authority in the Coinage of Augustus', *JRS* 76: 66–87.

—— ed. (1989*a*), *Patronage in Ancient Society* (London).

—— (1989*b*), 'Rome's Cultural Revolution' [review of Zanker (1988) and Heilmeyer (1988)], *JRS* 79: 157–64.

WASZINK, J. H. (1972), 'Der dichterische Ausdruck in den Oden des Horaz', in Oppermann (1972), 271–301.

WASZINK, J. H. (1974), *Biene und Honig als Symbol des Dichters und Dichtung in der griechischen-römischen Antike* (SB Rhein. Westphal. Akad. Wiss.; Münster).

WATSON, A. (1974), *Law Making in the Later Roman Republic* (Oxford).

WATSON, L. C. (1983), 'Two Problems in Horace *Epode* 3', *Philologus*, 127: 80–6.

—— (1987), '*Epode* 9, or the Art of Falsehood' in Whitby, Hardie, and Whitby (1987), 119–29.

—— (1991), *Arae: The Curse Poetry of Antiquity* (Leeds).

WEHRLI, F. (1945), 'Horaz und Kallimachos', *MH* 1: 69–76.

WEINSTOCK, S. (1960), 'Pax and the Ara Pacis', *JRS* 50: 44–58.

—— (1971), *Divus Julius* (Oxford).

WELIN, E. (1939), 'Die beiden Festtage der Ara Pacis Augustae', in *Dragma M. P. Nilsson Dedicatum* (Lund), 500–13.

WESEL, U. (1967), *Rhetorische Statuslehre und Gesetze-Auslegung der römischen Juristen* (Munich).

WEST, DAVID (1967), *Reading Horace* (Edinburgh).

—— (1973), 'Horace's Poetic Technique in the Odes', in Costa (1973), 29–58.

WEST, M. L. (1966), *Hesiod:* Theogony (Oxford).

—— (1971–2), *Iambi et Elegi Graeci* (2 vols.; Oxford).

—— (1974), *Studies in Greek Elegy and Iambus* (Berlin and New York).

WHITBY, L. M., HARDIE, P. R., and WHITBY, M., eds. (1987), *Homo Viator: Classical Essays for John Bramble* (Bristol).

WHITE, P. (1978), '*Amicitia* and the Profession of Poetry in Early Imperial Rome', *JRS* 68: 74–92.

—— (1988), 'Julius Caesar in Augustan Rome', *Phoenix*, 42: 334–56.

—— (1991), 'Maecenas' Retirement', *CP* 86: 130–8.

—— (1993), *Promised Verse: Poets in the Society of Augustan Rome* (Cambridge, Mass.).

WICKERT, L. (1953), 'Princeps', *RE* xxii. 1998–2296.

WICKHAM, E. C. (1874–91), *The Works of Horace* (2 vols.; Oxford).

—— (1900), *Horati Opera* (Oxford).

WIELAND, W. (1801), *Horazens Briefe*, ed. M. Fuhrmann (Frankfurt, 1986).

WILAMOWITZ-MOELLENDORF, V. von (1913), *Sappho und Simonides* (Berlin).

WILI, W. (1948), *Horaz* (Basle).

WILKINS, A. S. (1886), *The* Epistles *of Horace* (London).

WILKINSON, L. P. (1945), *Horace and his Lyric Poetry* (Cambridge).

—— (1959), 'The Language of Virgil and Horace', *CQ* NS 9: 181–92.

—— (1963), *Golden Latin Artistry* (Cambridge).

WILLE, G. (1967), *Musica Romana* (Amsterdam).

—— (1977), *Einführung in das römische Musikleben* (Darmstadt).

WILLIAMS, G. W. (1964), review of Brink (1963*b*), in *JRS* 54: 186–96.

WILLIAMS, G. W. (1968), *Tradition and Originality in Roman Poetry* (Oxford).

—— (1969), *The Third Book of Horace's Odes* (Oxford).

—— (1972), *Horace* (Oxford).

—— (1974), review of Brink (1971), in *CR* NS 24: 52–7.

—— (1990), 'Did Maecenas Fall from Favour? Augustan Literary Patronage', in Raaflaub and Toher (1990), 258–75.

WIMMEL, W. (1960), *Kallimachos in Rom* (Hermes Einzelschriften, 16; Wiesbaden).

—— (1965): '*Recusatio*-Form und Pindarode', *Philologus*, 109: 83–103.

—— (1983), 'Der Augusteer Lucius Varius Rufus', *ANRW* II. 30.3: 1562–621.

WINKES, R., ed. (1985), *The Age of Augustus* (Providence and Louvain-la-neuve).

WINNICZUK, L. (1935), 'De Horatii Studiis Terentianis Observationes Aliquot', in *Commentationes Horatianae* (Cracow), 116–29.

WISEMAN, T. P. (1971), *New Men in the Roman Senate 139 B.C.–A.D. 14* (Oxford).

—— (1985), *Catullus and his World* (Cambridge).

—— (1988), 'Satyrs in Rome? The Background to Horace's *Ars Poetica*', *JRS* 78: 1–13.

—— (1989), 'Roman Legend and Oral Tradition', *JRS* 79: 129–37.

WISSOWA, G. (1912), *Religion und Kultus der Römer* (Munich).

WISTRAND, E. (1958), *Horace's Ninth Epode and its Historical Background* (Gøteborg).

WÖLFFLIN, E. (1893), 'Die Etymologien der lateinischen Grammatiker', *Archiv für lateinische Lexikographie und Grammatik*, 8: 421–40, 563–85.

—— and MELBER, E. (1886), *Polyaenus: Strategemata* (Leipzig).

WOODMAN, A. J. (1977), *Velleius Paterculus: The Tiberian Narrative (2. 94–131)* (Cambridge).

—— (1983), *Velleius Paterculus: The Caesarian and Augustan Narrative (2. 41–93)* (Cambridge).

—— (1984), 'Horace's First Roman Ode', in Woodman and West (1984), 183–214.

—— and POWELL, J. G. F., eds. (1992), *Author and Audience in Latin Literature* (Cambridge).

WOODMAN, A. J. and WEST, D. A., eds. (1984), *Poetry and Politics in the Age of Augustus* (Cambridge).

YOUNG, D. C. (1968), *Three Odes of Pindar: A Literary Study of Pythian 11, Pythian 3, and Olympian 7* (*Mnemosyne* supp. 9; Leiden).

ZANKER, P. (1972) *Forum Romanum* (Tübingen).

—— (1987), *Augustus und die Macht der Bilder* (Munich); trans. as Zanker (1988).

—— (1988), *The Power of Images in the Age of Augustus* (Ann Arbor).

ZETZEL, J. E. G. (1980), 'Horace's *Liber Sermonum*: The Structure of Ambiguity', *Arethusa*, 13: 59–77.

—— (1982), 'The Poetics of Patronage in the Late First Century BC', in Gold (1982), 87–102.

ZORZETTI, N. (1990), 'The *Carmina Convivalia*', in Murray (1990), 289–307.

ZWIERLEIN, O. (1990), *Zur Kritik und Exegese des Plautus*, i. Poenulus und Curculio (Stuttgart).

—— (1991a), *Zur Kritik und Exegese des Plautus*, ii. Miles Gloriosus (Stuttgart).

—— (1991b), *Zur Kritik und Exegese des Plautus*, iii. Pseudolus (Stuttgart).

—— (1992), *Zur Kritik und Exegese des Plautus*, iv. Bacchides (Stuttgart).

Index Nominum, Rerum, et Verborum

Index Locorum

figures in square brackets refer to line numbers within poems.